Industrial Applications of Machine Learning

Chapman & Hall/CRC
Data Mining and Knowledge Series

Series Editor: Vipin Kumar

Data Classification
Algorithms and Applications
Charu C. Aggarwal

Healthcare Data Analytics
Chandan K. Reddy and Charu C. Aggarwal

Accelerating Discovery
Mining Unstructured Information for Hypothesis Generation
Scott Spangler

Event Mining
Algorithms and Applications
Tao Li

Text Mining and Visualization
Case Studies Using Open-Source Tools
Markus Hofmann and Andrew Chisholm

Graph-Based Social Media Analysis
Ioannis Pitas

Data Mining
A Tutorial-Based Primer, Second Edition
Richard J. Roiger

Data Mining with R
Learning with Case Studies, Second Edition
Luís Torgo

Social Networks with Rich Edge Semantics
Quan Zheng and David Skillicorn

Large-Scale Machine Learning in the Earth Sciences
Ashok N. Srivastava, Ramakrishna Nemani, and Karsten Steinhaeuser

Data Science and Analytics with Python
Jesus Rogel-Salazar

Feature Engineering for Machine Learning and Data Analytics
Guozhu Dong and Huan Liu

Exploratory Data Analysis Using R
Ronald K. Pearson

Human Capital Systems, Analytics, and Data Mining
Robert C. Hughes

Industrial Applications of Machine Learning
Pedro Larrañaga et al

For more information about this series please visit:
https://www.crcpress.com/Chapman--HallCRC-Data-
Mining-and-Knowledge-Discovery-Series/book-series/
CHDAMINODIS

Industrial Applications of Machine Learning

Pedro Larrañaga
David Atienza
Javier Diaz-Rozo
Alberto Ogbechie
Carlos Puerto-Santana
Concha Bielza

CRC Press
Taylor & Francis Group
Boca Raton London New York

CRC Press is an imprint of the
Taylor & Francis Group, an **informa** business

A CHAPMAN & HALL BOOK

CRC Press
Taylor & Francis Group
6000 Broken Sound Parkway NW, Suite 300
Boca Raton, FL 33487-2742

First issued in paperback 2020

© 2019 by Taylor & Francis Group, LLC
CRC Press is an imprint of Taylor & Francis Group, an Informa business

No claim to original U.S. Government works

Version Date: 20181003

ISBN 13: 978-0-367-65687-4 (pbk)
ISBN 13: 978-0-8153-5622-6 (hbk)

Visit the Taylor & Francis Web site at
http://www.taylorandfrancis.com

and the CRC Press Web site at
http://www.crcpress.com

Contents

Preface

The fourth Industrial Revolution, known as Industry 4.0 or Industrial Internet of Things, is now in full swing and having a major impact on industrial companies of different sectors, such as automation, automotive branch, chemistry, construction, consumer services, energy, finance, healthcare, information technologies and telecommunications. The amount of industrial data generated by machine controllers, sensors, manufacturing systems, etc. is growing exponentially, and intelligent systems able to transform this huge quantity of data into knowledge, as represented by mathematical and statistical models, are more than necessary. Machine learning is a part of artificial intelligence that allows to build those models. Machine learning comprises several methods enabling this transformation in such a way that the resulting software systems can provide actionable insights towards optimal decisions. These decisions are present in different industrial sectors in problems such as diagnosis, predictive maintenance, conditioning monitoring, assets health management, etc.

This book aims to show how machine learning methods can be applied to address real-world industrial problems enabling the fourth industrial revolution and providing the required knowledge and tools to empower readers to build their own solutions founded upon a solid theoretical and practical groundwork. The book is organized into seven chapters. Chapter 1 introduces the reader to the fourth industrial revolution discussing the current situation, opportunities, trends, issues and challenges. Chapter 2 focuses on machine learning fundamentals and covers the most commonly used techniques and algorithms in an understandable way for any reader with a minimum mathematical training. Clustering, supervised classification, Bayesian networks and the modeling of dynamic scenarios are the discussed topics. Chapter 3 summarizes successful applications of machine learning in several industrial sectors organized according to the Industry Classification Benchmark of FTSE Russell. The next four chapters present four detailed case studies of our own organized hierarchically into four levels of abstraction in industry smartization: at the component level, the machine level, the production level, and finally at the distribution level. Chapter 4 discusses the use of hidden Markov models for estimating degradation in a real ball bearing remaining useful life problem. The dataset was borrowed from the IEEE Prognosis and Health Management 2012 Data Challenge. Chapter 5 deals with machine tool axis servomotors. The analyzed dataset has been presented by Aingura-IIoT and Xilinx, Inc. as a testbed in the Industrial Internet Consortium. The behavior of several clustering algorithms, such as agglomerative hierarchical clustering, k-means, spectral clustering, affinity propagation and Gaussian mixture model-based clustering, is compared in order to find servomotor type fingerprints. Chapter 6 showcases the application of dynamic Bayesian networks to build an automated visual inspection system capable of analyzing images from a laser surface heat treatment process. The dataset was gathered during a real experiment carried out by Ikergune A.I.E., the research and development department of Etxe-Tar S.A., a Spanish manufacturing company. Chapter 7 illustrates how machine learning can be used in the distribution industry. The real data were recorded by the Cargo iQ group, and contains different shipments possibly composed of several transport lines that need to be synchronized. Some supervised classification models $-k$-nearest neighbors, classification trees, rule induction, artificial neural networks, support vector machine, logistic regression, Bayesian network classifiers, and metaclassifiers– have been applied to address this problem.

The book's dedicated website at http://cig.fi.upm.es/book/ia-of-ml/ makes the four datasets accessible. As a book of this scope will inevitably contain small errors, the website also has a form for letting us know of any errors the readers may find.

The book primarily targets professionals, researchers and postgraduate students of both industrial engineering and machine learning who are interested in the state of the art, opportunities, challenges and trends of machine learning in the fourth industrial revolution and are eager to apply the latest techniques and algorithms to real-world problems. The book's secondary target is senior managers, government agencies and members of scientific societies interested in knowing how the fourth industrial revolution will influence businesses, jobs or people's lives and what machine learning is and how it can help accomplish key demands of a new emerging world.

We have been very fortunate to receive help and encouragement from many colleagues and friends when working on this book. Our lab mates at the Computational Intelligent Group (specially Mario Michiels) at the Universidad Politécnica de Madrid, and at the Aingura IIoT and Ikergune A.I.E., both part of Etxe-Tar Group, have been able to create a very exciting scientific atmosphere that we appreciate very much. The constant enthusiasm of Patxi Samaniego at Ikergune A.I.E. during the whole process has meant fresh air in some difficult situations. Enriching discussions on the nature of industrial data with José Juan Gabilondo at Etxe-Tar S.A. and Dan Isaacs at Xilinx, Inc. have helped us to understand the fourth industrial revolution and machine learning synergies. This work has been partially supported by funding agencies such as the Spanish Ministry of Economy and Competitiveness through the TIN2016-79684-P project, the Spanish Ministry of Education, Culture and Sport through the FPU16/00921 grant, and the Regional Government of Madrid through the S2013/ICE-2845-CASI-CAM-CM project, and by the private Fundación BBVA grant to Scientific Research Teams in Big Data 2016.

Pedro Larrañaga, *Universidad Politécnica de Madrid*
David Atienza, *Universidad Politécnica de Madrid*
Javier Diaz-Rozo, *Aingura IIoT* and *Universidad Politécnica de Madrid*
Alberto Ogbechie, *Universidad Politécnica de Madrid*
Carlos Puerto-Santana, *Universidad Politécnica de Madrid*
Concha Bielza, *Universidad Politécnica de Madrid*

Madrid, Spain
September 2018

1

The Fourth Industrial Revolution

1.1 Introduction

Nowadays, global economies are undergoing a technology shift with all its positive and negative connotations. As we have learned from history, technology changes enrich society in terms of education, cohesion and employment. However, the movements that have happened in recent history have taken time to build structures capable of setting off the desired leap in industrial development.

Technology shifts, shown in Figure 1.1, are commonly called industrial revolutions because they are closely related to productivity and have caused disruptive change in manufacturing processes since the 18th century. As a result, specific fields of technology were improved. The first industrial revolution used water and steam power to mechanize production. During the second industrial revolution, water and steam power were replaced by electricity, which boosted productivity even further. In the third industrial revolution, electronic systems and **information technologies (IT)** were used to increase factory automation[1].

Today's technology shift is called the **fourth industrial revolution (4IR)**. It is a blurry mixture of the digital and physical worlds, leveraging emerging digital technologies that are able to gather and analyze data across production machines, lines and sites. It merges the third industrial revolution's IT, such as computer integrated manufacturing (Bennett, 1985), machine learning (Samuel, 1959), the Internet (Kleinrock, 1961) and many other technologies, with **operational technologies (OT)** to create the disruptive technologies that are the backbone of the 4IR. A technical report published by PricewaterhouseCoopers (2017) listed the top ten technologies as being:

1. **Advanced materials** with improved functionality, mechanical and chemical properties, e.g., nanomaterials.

2. **Cloud technology** capable of delivering computational capabilities over the Internet without the need for local and expensive machines.

---

[1]The fourth industrial revolution: what it means and how to respond. https://www.weforum.org/agenda/2016/01/the-fourth-industrial-revolution-what-it-means-and-how-to-respond/

FIGURE 1.1
Industrial technology shifts.

3. **Autonomous vehicles** that are able to navigate with little or no human intervention, e.g., drones.

4. **Synthetic biology** that uses engineering principles to develop biological systems, also called biotechnology.

5. **Virtual (VR) or augmented reality (AR)** generated by a computer to simulate an overlay over the physical world or a whole environment.

6. **Artificial intelligence** that uses algorithms to perform specific tasks emulating human intelligence, e.g., machine learning.

7. **Robotics** that uses robots to automate, augment or assist human activities according to a set of instructions or autonomously.

8. **Blockchain** that uses software algorithms and distributed computing to record and confirm transactions in an electronic ledger.

9. **Additive manufacturing** that builds functional or non-functional three-dimensional objects by printing layer upon layer of materials.

10. **Internet of Things** (IoT) that networks different objects embedded with acquisition, preprocessing, processing and communication capabilities over the Internet to enable smart applications.

All these technologies can be used across the entire 4IR landscape: biological, digital and physical worlds. However, this book focuses exclusively on the manufacturing industry, where the digital and physical worlds take the shape of IT and advanced manufacturing systems available across different industrial sectors. Thanks mainly to new knowledge extracted from data analytics, this combination of the digital and physical worlds has the potential to boost the productivity, efficiency and flexibility of production systems, increasing industrial competitiveness.

Between both the digital and physical worlds, data could be addressed as the raw material to be converted into useful knowledge to realize the expected added value from the 4IR. As raw material, data have to be extracted, transported, stored, transformed and delivered to the end user as information with added

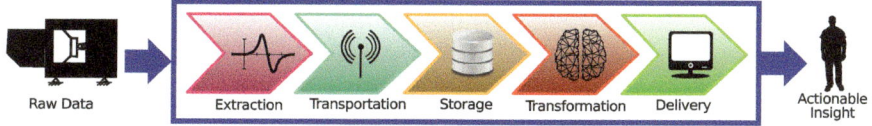

Raw Data — Extraction — Transportation — Storage — Transformation — Delivery — Actionable Insight

FIGURE 1.2
Giving added value to data from raw to actionable insights during the 4IR.

value defined as an **actionable insight** (Figure 1.2). Each data life cycle step is described below:

- **Extraction**: Connected devices generate 2.5 quintillion bytes of data every day[2]. In the industrial sector, data are generated by machines: machine control system, sensors and actuators. Therefore, ideally the only requirement needed to extract data is a handshake connection with the devices. However, data acquisition is by no means straightforward because data of guaranteed quality have to be collected at a required sampling rate from different desynchronized domains and data sources. For this reason, data acquisition systems need special characteristics, such as advanced communication technologies, filtering strategies or sensor fusion, to be able to efficiently capture and send data in a deterministic manner. Therefore, 4IR-enabled technologies, such as the IoT, are able to provide higher-level preprocessing and connectivity capabilities that increase data acquisition system efficiency. For example, wireless sensor networks (WSN) have processing, sensing and peer-to-peer communication capabilities where data can be shared between nodes without the need for a reader. In this case, the data could be acquired indirectly using sense perception (Akyildiz et al., 2002) for noise filtering. Additionally, Li et al. (2013) explain how the awareness of WSN could be used to guarantee determinism during extraction.

- **Transportation**: Extracted data have to be moved from the acquisition system to the next stage as efficiently as possible. Communication protocols play an important role in enabling fast, traceable, flexible and secure communication. The 4IR is pushing for new protocols, such as OPC-UA[3], RTI DDS-Secure[4] or MQTT[5], that can meet these requirements, enabling interoperability between different devices, real-time communication and a seamless flow.

- **Storage**: If 2.5 quintillion bytes of data are generated everyday, there is a need for an appropriate storage and management system, providing for efficient queries to support the transformation of data into usable information.

---

[2]https://www.ibm.com/blogs/insights-on-business/consumer-products/2-5-quintillion-bytes-of-data-created-every-day-how-does-cpg-retail-manage-it/
[3]OPC-UA. https://opcfoundation.org/about/opc-technologies/opc-ua/
[4]RTI DDS-Secure. https://www.rti.com/products/secure
[5]MQTT. http://mqtt.org/

Data production is ever increasing, requiring a high performance, scalable and usable storage system. Therefore, 4IR has developed the concept of big data with larger and more complex datasets. Commonly used data storage technologies are unsuitable for big data. Therefore, Hadoop-based solutions[6], targeting the distributed and highly scalable storage of large datasets, such as Cloudera, Hortonworks, and MapReduce, have been developed (Strohbach et al., 2016).

In this case, storage could, depending on the needs of the transformation step, be long term or instantaneous. Long-term storage is when data analytics are applied to databases storing data on time periods and the results are not time sensitive. For example, Kezunovic et al. (2017) describe the usage of big data to predict the impact of weather on power systems, where large datasets are needed to correctly correlate the effects and increase the prediction capabilities of the algorithm. On the other hand, instantaneous storage refers to time-sensitive information. In this case, in-memory databases are used as a high-performance temporal buffer with a relatively small storage size. Such databases are usually used and destroyed.

- **Transformation**: This step is related to the transformation of data into actionable insights. Machine learning is one of the key techniques able to generate data-driven predictive models that can be used for decision making. Other techniques for data transformation are visual analytics. This book focuses primarily on the application of machine learning to industrial applications, and the following chapters set out the entire industrial data-based factory smartization process. If the transformation step requires real-time accomplishment, computational power is also needed. Technologies such as **field-programmable gate array (FPGA)** or their integration into systems-on-chips (SoCs) are the cutting edge solutions providing robustness, low energy consumption, acceleration and flexibility. SoC manufacturers, such as Xilinx, Inc.[7], are pushing forward towards transformation platforms such as Zynq® Ultrascale+™ MPSoC, where their programmable logic is large enough to provide acceleration to commonly used machine learning algorithms without the need of complex devices.

- **Delivery**: When the output actionable insight has to be delivered to the end user. The insight could be delivered to the machine operator, plant manager or maintenance engineer using a human-machine interface or directly to the machine as a feedback inside the control loop.

The above data life cycle is the 4IR backbone for merging digital and physical worlds. This data life cycle has been adopted around the world, albeit according to slightly different approaches, which are briefly described in the following sections.

---

[6]Apache Hadoop. http://hadoop.apache.org/
[7]https://www.xilinx.com/

1.1.1 Industrie 4.0

Industrie 4.0 (also called **Industry 4.0**) concept was defined by Kagermann et al. (2013) as an initiative to secure the future of the German manufacturing industry. It is a broad definition that takes into account eight different key areas:

- **Standardization and reference architecture.** This is the most active area. The Industry 4.0 platform understands that the best possible way to enable collaborative partnerships between companies is by sharing data and information. Sharing requires common standards and a reference architecture to provide for communication between partners and facilitate implementation.

- **Managing complex systems.** This area focuses on the development of technology designed to manage increasingly complex products and manufacturing systems. Next-generation industrial systems will be harder to manage because of novel features like their interconnectivity and adaptive behavior.

- **A comprehensive broadband infrastructure for industry.** The development of new generations of communication networks is important to be able to reliably share high-quality data between different companies. Data and information sharing has scalability issues that need to be solved and are directly associated with factory size.

- **Safety and security.** This is an important area of activity and development because data and information sharing has to be reliable enough to ensure that the products and production facilities are not a danger to either people or the environment. Additionally, data and information has to be protected against misuse and unauthorized usage. There is a need for new technologies that are capable of managing large amounts of critical data and information.

- **Work organization and design.** As the final goal of this approach is to set up interconnected smart factories sharing data and information to improve the productivity of manufacturing systems, future jobs need to be adapted to the workflow requirements. For example, repetitive or low-skills tasks will be replaced by better, added value activities that enhance employee personal development.

- **Training and continuing professional development.** Because of the above changes in employee skills requirements, training strategies need to be reformed to provide the tools that employees need to do their job in the new working environment created by the industrial revolution.

- **Regulatory framework.** The new collaborative partnerships launched by the Industry 4.0 approach are based on data and information sharing about which legislation has not yet been developed. A clear framework has to be designed to help with the definition of data and information ownership boundaries, where, depending on the deployment scenario, a clear distinction should be made between personal, corporate, product and process data.

- **Resource efficiency.** The industrial sector is the world's largest energy consumer, as it takes a great deal of energy to transform raw materials into products. Additionally, factory interconnection, and all the resulting data management, sometimes requires the use of advanced technology equipment with higher energy requirements. Therefore, there is a need to study the trade-off between any additional resources required and potential energy savings in order to improve energy usage.

To develop these key areas, concepts like **cyber-physical systems (CPS)** defined by Gill (2006) have been introduced to support the exploitation of the IoT into the manufacturing environment. Therefore, Kagermann et al. (2013) defines CPS as **smart machines**, storage systems and production facilities that are able to exchange information, trigger actions and control in an unattended manner. CPS have been reported to play a number of different roles. The most important, however, is that they constitute the nexus between the digital and physical worlds.

Therefore, substituting the above data life cycle into Kagermann et al.'s definition, a CPS should be capable of extraction, transportation, storage, transformation and delivery. To be able to enact this life cycle, a CPS will have to be endowed with artificial intelligence to behave without supervision thanks to **self-learning** capabilities. Machine learning is the specific artificial intelligence enabling technology for **self-learning** capabilities, especially in the transformation stage.

The definition of Industrie 4.0 does not include any explicit references to artificial intelligence. However, one of the authors of the definition of the term Industrie 4.0 is Prof. Wolfgang Wahlster, CEO of the German Research Center for Artificial Intelligence (DFKI GmbH). Wahlster considers artificial intelligence as the main driver of smart factories supported by CPS.

Although, Industrie 4.0 is a German initiative designed to boost the German manufacturing industry, the broad concept has been rapidly adopted by almost all European countries. Adoption has taken place at many levels, ranging from local government, in the shape of policies, to companies.

1.1.2   Industrial Internet of Things

The first steps towards the **Industrial Internet of Things (IIoT)** were described in 2012 within the framework of the United States President's Council of Advisors on Science and Technology[8]. In this scenario, some of the cross-cutting technologies selected for advanced manufacturing were as follows: advanced sensing, information technologies, digital manufacturing and visualization, terminology that is similar to the data life cycle described above.

By March 2012, the United States Steering Committee for Foundations for

---

[8]Report to the President on Capturing Domestic Competitive Advantage in Advanced Manufacturing.   https://energy.gov/eere/downloads/report-president-capturing-domestic-competitive-advantage-advanced-manufacturing/

Innovation in CPS, led by Vanderbilt University and Boeing, had submitted a report about the strategic opportunities for CPS in the 21st century (Sztipanovits et al., 2012). This report defined CPS as a tightly coupled cyber and physical systems that exhibit a level of smart integration. These systems have computational processes that interact with physical components. Therefore, a call for action was expected as the future applications of CPS were understood to be more disruptive than IT was during the third industrial revolution.

By the end of 2012, the digital branch of a United States company, General Electric (GE), coined the term Industrial Internet, bringing together smart machines, advanced analytics, and people at work. GE described this integration as a network of connected devices that can extract, transport, store, transform and supply valuable actionable insights that can leverage faster business decisions at industrial companies, increasing their competitiveness[9].

The IIoT is mainly oriented to the application of the IoT, machine-to-machine (M2M) communications, and industrial big data analytics to industry with a clear focus on using data to generate added value. In view of the need to share data and information, the IIoT approach moves the major IoT technologies, like smart sensing, real-time, deterministic and wireless communications, sensor fusion for data preprocessing, artificial intelligence for data processing and delivery of information, into industry. Additionally, the IIoT approach defines different layers of technology deployment. Briefly, these deployment layers are the following:

- **Edge**, where the elements are near the connected assets, which is useful for real-time analytics and control technologies.

- **Cloud**, where the data are sent out to computing services over the Internet, which is useful for complex analytics and data storage.

Against this backdrop, GE, together with IBM and SAP, founded, in March 2014, the Industrial Internet Consortium (IIC)[10], with the aim of bringing together the companies and technologies needed to speed up the development, adoption, and widespread sharing of data and information, smart analytics, and people at work. Although IIoT started out as a mainly American initiative, the IIC has now gone global with more than 200 member companies around the world.

1.1.3 Other International Strategies

As explained in Section 1.1.1 and Section 1.1.2, the concept of 4IR has been adopted around the world inspired by the original initiatives launched by

---

[9]Everything you need to know about the Industrial Internet of Things. https://www.ge.com/digital/blog/everything-you-need-know-about-industrial-internet-things/

[10]http://www.iiconsortium.org/

Germany and the USA. However, there are several country-specific variations. Some of these approaches are briefly described below.

In France, 4IR was adopted in April 2015 as the Industrie du Futur, which is oriented towards the digital transformation of French industry. It is primarily an implementation of the achievements of European Commission (EU) initiatives such as Factory of the Future. Industrie du Futur has borrowed five main notions from the EU initiatives: (1) Development of the technology supply for the factories of the future in areas where France can become a leader in the next three to five years by supporting large structural projects out of industry. The supply of technologies will be based on additive manufacturing, IoT, augmented reality, etc. (2) Financial support for companies. (3) Training for the next generation of employees in the knowledge and skills needed to apply new technologies in the factories of the future. (4) Support for European and international cooperation, fostering innovation strategies together with other European countries, especially Germany, and other international alliances. (5) Promotion of activities oriented to showcase 4IR-related French developments and technology know-how.

In Spain, 4IR adoption is driven by Industria Conectada supported by the Ministry of Economy, Industry and Competitiveness. In this case, the initiative is designed to provide financial support and assistance to promote the digital transformation of the Spanish industrial sector. Like Industrie du Futur, the approach taken by Industria Conectada is aligned with the German Industrie 4.0. However, it takes a specific business solution approach focusing on big data and analytics, cybersecurity, cloud computing, connectivity and mobility, additive manufacturing, robotics and embedded sensors and systems as the main areas of development.

In Asia, there are several approaches: Made in China 2025, Made in India and ASEAN 4.0 for the Association of Southeast Asian Nations (ASEAN) whose members include technology development leaders like Singapore and Malaysia. All these approaches are aligned with Industry 4.0 and designed to push forward their respective industries in order to increase competitiveness. Japan, on the other hand, has taken a different approach called Society 5.0. Society 5.0 is oriented towards the transformation of society into a super smart society. This policy expects CPS, viewed as the key elements capable of combining cyber and physical space, to bring about a major societal shift. Machines and artificial intelligence will be the main players in this fifth stage of society.

In conclusion, the 4IR is more than technology development: it is an industrial shift involving economic, technical and societal components aimed at improving industrial competitiveness at all levels with a potential impact all over the world. This revolution, and the different adopted policies, is leveraging the smart industry described in Section 1.2.

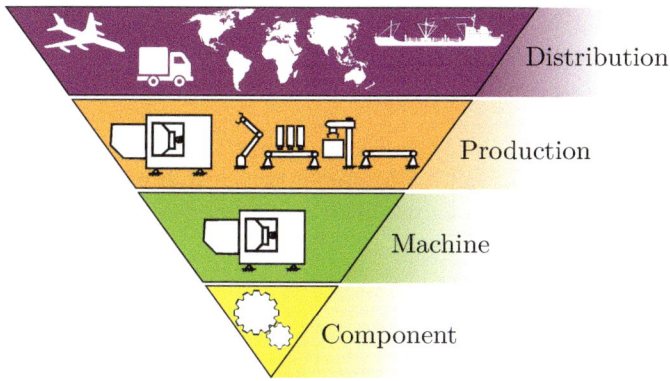

FIGURE 1.3
Different levels of industry smartization.

1.2 Industry Smartization

The word smartization is often used to describe an evolutionary shift towards smart behavior. Technologies related to this evolutionary shift are enabling smart industries at different levels. Smartization is a main thread of this book used to describe how machine learning is applied to provide smart capabilities. Therefore, we define four different levels of abstraction: component (Section 1.2.1), which is part of a machine (Section 1.2.2) within a production (Section 1.2.3) facility that has need of distribution (Section 1.2.4) capabilities to move products to different customers. Figure 1.3 shows a diagram illustrating this approach.

1.2.1 At the Component Level

As explained above, there are different levels of abstraction in industry smartization. At the bottom, we have machine components, e.g., bearings, valves, ball screws, guides and shafts. Component **smartization** refers to the introduction of component **self-awareness** capabilities to provide failure diagnosis and prognosis. This can help to increase the availability of the whole system or subsystem, e.g., machines, air compressors, etc. Components are made self-aware by embedding sensors into the component structure. Sensor complexity is determined by the amount of space available in the component. For example, there may be room for a valve sensor and electronics in its manifold, but a ball-screw sensor needs to be integrated into its structural material.

The main aim of these embedded sensors is to extract data related to phenomena that may cause the component to fail. For example, a sensor built into a bearing might have to measure vibration, temperature, lubrication, humidity, presence of metallic particles, etc. These data can be processed at the sensor or within an upper layer, launching alarms related to potential failures or remaining useful life (RUL). In this case, sensors are referred to as smart sensors.

Component data processing is described in Chapter 4, where ball bearings are used as a testing scenario. Chapter 4 basically illustrates what a smart component is and how it can contribute to the overall industry smartization.

1.2.2   At the Machine Level

The next level of abstraction in industry is the machine. In this case, there are two sources of smart capabilities: (1) self-aware components that are able to provide failure diagnosis and prognosis, (2) data aggregation from different smart components and sensors that are able to supply contextual characteristics, useful for providing actionable insights about the system or subsystem.

Lee et al. (2014) explained that the IoT has enabled data availability, where a machine, with the help of a CPS, is able to extract enough information to be capable of self-assessment. As availability is the most important issue for an industrial machine, self-assessment capabilities can provide the past, current and future conditions of the subsystems to enable tools to improve this issue through maintenance and adaptive control.

Therefore, a self-maintained machine is able to assess its own state of health and level of degradation. This is useful for preventive and **predictive maintenance** in order to reduce machine downtime, increasing its availability. A self-aware machine is able to use the data to monitor the current operating conditions and assess its own best operational state, adjusting process parameters to ensure the highest possible efficiency.

However, the concept of smart machine is broader than the usage of data for self-assessment. As described in Section 1.1, one of the key concepts is data and information sharing. In this respect, **machine-to-machine communication** (M2M) is a concept described by many authors (e.g., Lee et al. (2014), Lin and Chen (2016), Li et al. (2016), Ali et al. (2017) and Tuna et al. (2017)) who highlight data and information sharing between machines in order to perform peer-to-peer comparison. This can be useful for detecting early degradation or any other situation likely to increase machine availability. M2M is also useful for creating a network of cooperative smart machines, where adaptable coordination increases flexibility and productivity, implementing the concept of smart production system.

Chapter 5 describes how machine learning is able to leverage self-awareness capabilities in a machine. In this case, the servomotors moving a machine axis are studied as a use case scenario of a smart machine subsystem.

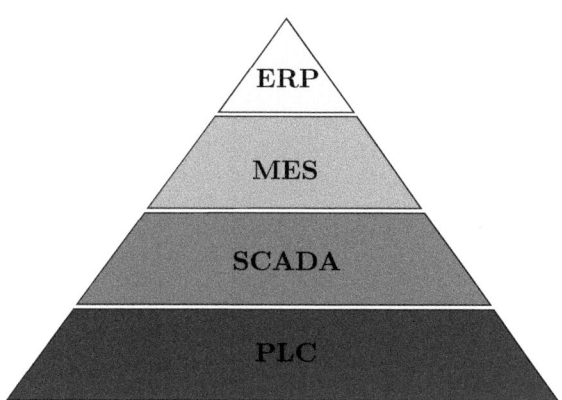

FIGURE 1.4
System integration of a production system.

1.2.3   At the Production Level

As mentioned in Section 1.2.2, a collection of networked smart machines sharing data and information can be defined as a smart production system. Additionally, this machine interconnection provides for asset fleet analytics, such as **overall equipment efficiency** (OEE) defined by availability, productivity, energy efficiency, and manufacturing quality.

At the production level, the abstraction is defined as a smart manufacturing system. This smart system is able to integrate smart machines, but also data coming from other domains such as raw materials behavior, environment, energy, business, material flow and other key performance indicators (KPIs). This integration provides a high-level view of the manufacturing environment, where data could extract added value information that can help to increase system efficiency.

Therefore, as shown in Figure 1.4, a smart factory is able to take advantage of well-established integration systems, such as enterprise resource planning (ERP), which has real-time and synchronized business data: purchasing, sales, distribution, finance, manufacturing, etc. Based on these data, a smart factory should make business-based decisions to increase its competitiveness. Besides, manufacturing execution systems (MES) are a source of useful data for smart factories. In this case, a MES is able to provide data related to the production system, tracking KPIs, raw materials, stock, etc. Programmable logic controllers (PLC) and supervisory control and data acquisition (SCADA) are smart layers on top of machines that are able to provide direct control and supervision of production systems and machines.

To illustrate machine learning-based smartization at the production level, Chapter 6 shows a use case scenario of an automated visual inspection system applied to a heat treatment production system.

1.2.4   At the Distribution Level

The next level of abstraction is distribution, where products are sent to customers or other parent factories. This level is defined as smart logistics. At this point, aggregated data coming from different production systems are mixed with distribution data in order to increase system efficiency, i.e., deliver the product at the right time.

Distribution systems are first and foremost complex combinations of infrastructure and resources with limited availability, and different product destinations and required delivery times. As a result, processes should be highly efficient to avoid bottlenecks and reduce product times to market (length of time that it takes from a product being conceived until it reaches the customer) to prevent a negative impact on company competitiveness.

Therefore, smart distribution systems are complex resource managers that are able to perform three different activities: automated planning, implementation and control. Based on the production data, the smart system defines a delivery plan for the product, including its destination, required infrastructure and resources (e.g., airports, airplanes, etc.) and contingency planning. Planning is performed by searching the optimum path and taking into account other factors, such as different products using the same resources to maximize their usage. Also, the smart system implements or executes the plan, measuring its past, current and future states in order to detect possible deviations and produce the actionable insights based on the contingency plan. If such deviations are detected, the smart system is able to control the situation and take the required actions to guarantee system quality.

Chapter 7 illustrates an application of machine learning to enable smart logistics using a use case related to air freight.

1.3   Machine Learning Challenges and Opportunities within Smart Industries

The Industrial Internet is expected to increase industrial efficiency by 3.3% per year with savings of around 2.6% with respect to cost reduction[11]. These figures will be the result of an overall efficiency increase, leading to higher production with lower raw material and energy usage. As described in Section 1.2, developments are moving towards smartization, where artificial intelligence is a big player.

Additionally, the investment in Industrial Internet applications is measured in billions depending on the region. For example, the expected investment in Europe is around €140 billion per year. This means that industry-oriented

---

[11]Industry 4.0 - Opportunities and challenges of the Industrial Internet. https://www.pwc.nl/en/assets/documents/pwc-industrie-4-0.pdf

artificial intelligence-based products will receive strong support, boosting the adoption rate. Machine learning is an artificial intelligence technology with promising applications enabling smart manufacturing systems within the 4IR. It has a huge potential at all levels: business, technology and people. However, there are some challenges and opportunities related to each level.

In order to understand the challenges and opportunities for machine learning in industry, we should look at how it fits into a 4IR architecture. To do this, we use the reference architecture for IIoT (Lin et al., 2017). This architecture defines three different tiers as follows:

- **Edge tier** collects the data sourced from different industrial levels: component, machine, production line or logistics (see Section 1.2).

- **Platform tier** processes the data from the edge tier and provides a first layer of services and feedback, where time is a critical variable for security and integrity reasons.

- **Enterprise tier** collects information from the platform tier and deploys a second layer of services that provides support for high-level decision making.

Figure 1.5 illustrates an implementation of this architecture. This example addresses predictive asset maintenance, where different component data, such as the computer numerical control (CNC) and smart energy measurement sensors (e.g., Oberon X) among others, are collected, transmitted and synchronized in the edge tier. Then, all the data are sent to the platform tier where a machine learning layer extracts critical actionable insights that can be used to stop the machine in the event of an emergency or to support decision making by the machine operator in the event of a high likelihood of failure. Part of this information is transmitted to the next tier, where another machine learning layer extracts operational or business-oriented insights. In this layer, business decisions are made based on the supplied actionable insights, such as production forecasting or overall factory availability.

A smart industry architecture could be mapped to different impact levels by analyzing the main implications of machine learning. Therefore, the main impact of the machine learning used in the enterprise tier is related to people and business. The machine learning applied in the platform tier will have less impact on business and attach more importance to technology. In the edge tier, machine learning will have a direct impact as the main orchestrator of each smart element within this tier. The following sections give a general idea of the expected impact at each level with their related challenges and opportunities.

1.3.1 Impact on Business

As described above, machine learning will be a key enabler for smart industries with important levels of OEE, which will have a positive impact on business competitiveness. An increase in competitiveness means that the goods produced

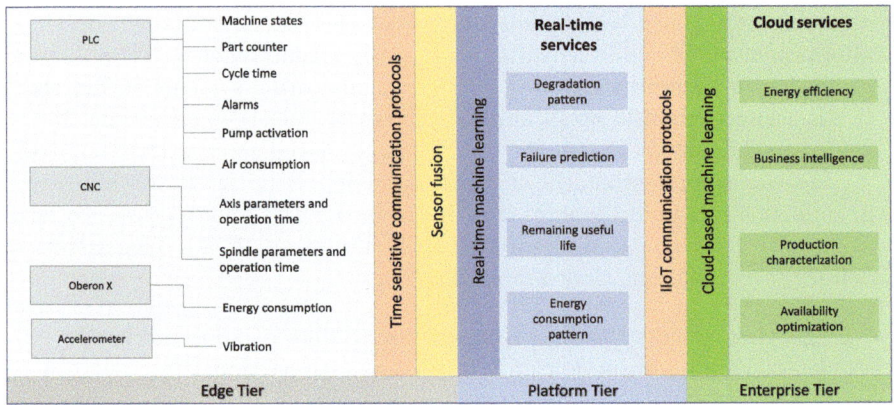

FIGURE 1.5
Role of machine learning within smart factory predictive maintenance[12].

by smart industries have a relatively shorter time-to-market than competitor products, that is, the supply of the right product at the right time and at the right price.

Concepts like mass customization or servitization have emerged to achieve this level of improvement. Mass customization is related to the ability of extremely flexible production systems to provide high volumes of customized products and services. To achieve flexibility, the production system has to be aware of the past and present conditions to monitor actual availability, as well as future conditions in order to predict required production system changes related to a new product customization.

However, asset smartization has a disruptive impact on business, called servitization. As described by Kamp et al. (2017), smartization will leverage new business models such as predictive maintenance, quality control, plant-floor efficiency, etc., which take advantage of predictive analytics output by machine learning. Additionally, increased availability will enable the model of selling uptime instead of machines. Such models are being applied in sectors like the aerospace industry, where airplane turbines are sold by flight time.

There are good opportunities for machine learning to influence and increase business competitiveness, but there are some challenges that it has to overcome. The most important challenge is to understand that machine learning is not a low-cost technology: an elaborate implementation strategy is required to understand how to get the fastest return on investment and make the biggest impact on the enterprise. Nevertheless, efforts are being undertaken from many sides aimed at reducing the expensive resources required by machine learning, such as data storage and training time. Some examples are one-shot algorithms capable of learning from a single example (Fei-Fei et al., 2006), data stream

---

[12]http://www.iiconsortium.org/smart-factory-machine-learning.htm

learning algorithms that learn from the stream and not from databases (Silva et al., 2013) or novelty detection algorithms, capable of performing online learning from unknown situations (Faria et al., 2016).

1.3.2 Impact on Technology

The main impact of machine learning is on technology, as it is the enabler of asset smartization within smart industries, where a component, machine, production line or factory is aware of its condition and has the capability to react because a machine learning algorithm has been trained for the purpose. Chapter 3 discusses several different industrial sectors that actually apply machine learning algorithms to meet specific needs.

Therefore, there are a host of opportunities for different applications requiring smart capabilities. However, as explained in Section 1.3.1, machine learning is not always applicable because it could be expensive or unnecessary if there are traditional engineering-based approaches capable of solving the problem. Machine learning algorithms should be applied to enhance technologies whenever any other traditional engineering approach is unable to provide the required results due to deviations from expected outcomes, accuracy or response time caused by process complexity or specific unknowns.

From the technology development point of view, machine learning is expected to be able to improve asset behavior through increased availability and efficiency and reduced energy consumption. This will bring about an overall productivity increase possibly justifying the introduction of machine learning technologies into smart factories. Less downtime and fewer failures will lead to a sizable reduction in spare parts expenses, boosting the added value of these data-based approaches.

At the same time, machine learning is improving transparency within industry, where the use of knowledge discovery algorithms is leveraging a better understanding of products and processes. This feedback will result in better decisions at product or process design time and even in new products and processes.

From the machine learning point of view, the main technology-related challenge is to devise fast, accurate, efficient and robust algorithms to meet the needs of smart industry. Therefore, there is a need for an approach to move new developments out of the laboratory and into industrial applications faster. Nevertheless, 4IR is prompting industrial companies to provide real applications for use as an algorithm testbed at the research and development stage in order to reduce time-to-market.

1.3.3 Impact on People

As described in Section 1.1.3, Japan's Society 5.0 is the approach that best illustrates the impact of machine learning on people. Therefore, there are many opportunities to use machine learning techniques to replace humans in tedious, stressful and repetitive tasks within the industry.

However, when the terms artificial intelligence, smart manufacturing, self-aware production systems and autonomous machines are mentioned, the first concern raised is that 4IR manufacturing systems will destroy jobs, and an intense man vs. machine battle often ensues. This is the first challenge that machine learning within smart factories has to overcome: prove that it is a support technology and not a threat to employment.

Although smart industries generate negative feelings, the opposite is, in fact, the case. The term intelligence holds the key: it should not be used in connection with a machine. Human beings tend to bend the rules and apply their skills of improvisation to react to disturbances about which they have no previous knowledge. This is why people are able to design machines programmed to do specific tasks. A programmed machine that is good at following rules and capable of reacting to disturbances according to previous training is smart, but not intelligent, because, without specific training, it will fail. For example, if the machine has self-maintenance capabilities enabling predictive maintenance against ball bearing degradation, the system will be useless for predicting linear axis ball screw degradation, no matter how similar the components are.

In this scenario, people are the most important part of smart industries as employees design, program, deploy and monitor the precise rules targeting competitiveness. Therefore, the impact on people will be a primarily educational shift. 4IR employees will be trained to meet the smart industry needs, where intellectual capabilities are more important than physical abilities. As a result, the 4IR will provide better quality jobs involving high-quality and more rewarding tasks, influencing employee professional and personal development. Therefore, low added value and repetitive tasks that compromise ergonomics will be left to machines: smart machines.

1.4   Concluding Remarks

As described in this chapter, the 4IR is the main driving force behind the merger of different available technologies leading to an industrial shift that will affect society at different levels. There are different approaches around the world, all with a common objective: push forward the competitiveness of their country's industrial sector. Although these policies pursue different interests, data are, in all cases, defined as the enabler of the necessary convergence between IT and OT, as the main link for sharing valuable insights between components, machines, production systems and industries with the aim of boosting competitiveness.

Machine learning is the most common technique for extracting actionable insights and implementing smart capabilities. On this ground, machine learning, as a branch of artificial intelligence, is one of the leading 4IR technologies. Therefore, this is a clear opportunity for a technology with a long history (Minsky (1961), Turing (1950)) to take a front seat in industrial development. There is also a chance to take advantage of new edge or cloud computing developments to deploy powerful algorithms and extract valuable information from data.

Smart factories are the goal of the revolution within the industrial sector. They are the result of many years of research and development in different fields of application, which is now moving out of the laboratory and onto the factory shop-floor. More research related to the integration of different technologies at all levels is required to make this move. However, some important steps are being taken.

The rest of the book is organized as follows: Chapter 2 is a compendium of machine learning methods that can be applied for factory smartization. Chapter 3 summarizes actual industrial applications using machine learning. Chapters 4 to 7 show applications of these tools to real-world use cases to illustrate how machine learning is able to provide actionable insights in the 4IR era.

2

Machine Learning

2.1 Introduction

Huge amounts of data have to be visualized, modeled and understood nowadays. Standard descriptive statistics provide a rough overview of the data. Multivariate statistics and machine learning –a burgeoning field of artificial intelligence– are used for data modeling, that is, to transform data into mathematical abstractions of reality that can be manipulated by computers to produce accurate predictions in both static and dynamic scenarios.

Albeit a mathematical discipline, the practice of statistics has become a more computational field since the emergence of computers. Besides, machine learning aims to build algorithm-based systems that learn from data, improving their performance automatically based on experience. Algorithms search within a large space of candidate models to find the one that optimizes a previously specified performance metric (Jordan and Mitchell, 2015).

Statistics and machine learning can be regarded as two different cultures for arriving at useful conclusions from data (Breiman, 2001b). There are three main types of conclusions (Fig. 2.1): (a) clustering, aiming to find groups of similar inputs; (b) prediction, forecasting the response for future inputs; and (c) association discovery, looking for (probabilistic) relationships among input and output variables. In industry, these conclusions mostly have to be drawn from time series or data stream scenarios.

Although complementary, the statistics and machine learning cultures have some differences, summarized as follows:

- Model assumptions. Statistical models are based on strong assumptions like Gaussianity, homoscedasticity, etc., which very often do not hold. These assumptions are not necessary in machine learning algorithms.

- Model selection. The standard criterion for model comparison in statistics is based on the (penalized or marginal) likelihood. Machine learning drives the search for the best model according to more specific scores, e.g., the area under the ROC (receiver operating characteristic) curve (see Section 2.4.1) which focuses on the correct classification rate in supervised classification problems. Searching approaches are also quite different: simple selection methods, like forward selection, backward elimination or stepwise regression, are popular in statistics, whereas a plethora of more sophisticated and

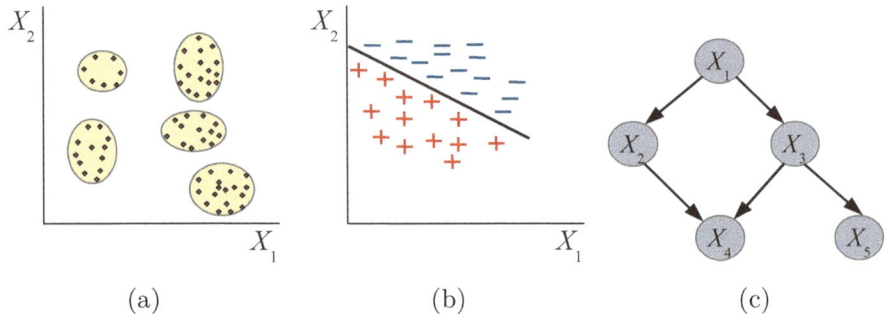

FIGURE 2.1
Three examples of tasks solved by statistics and machine learning methods.
(a) Clustering. (b) Supervised classification. (c) Discovery of associations.

intelligent metaheuristics, such as simulated annealing, tabu search and genetic algorithms, are used in machine learning.

- Feature subset selection. Industrial data suffer from the "curse of dimensionality" (Bellman, 1957), which needs to be addressed by selecting the minimal subset of variables containing the relevant and non-redundant information. Machine learning approaches this challenge using intelligent metaheuristics to move in a space of cardinality 2^n, where n is the number of variables. Statistics assumes a fixed number of variables $k \leq n$ and uses simpler strategies for moving in the search space. For further details, see Section 2.4.2.

Probabilistic graphical models (Koller and Friedman, 2009) that include Bayesian networks (see Section 2.5), Markov networks and hidden Markov models (see Section 2.6) adopt aspects from both cultures, statistics and machine learning. Hence they are considered to lie at the intersection between both disciplines.

Interpretable and easily comprehensible models (those whose decisions are understood by a human expert) are preferred to opaque **blackbox models**. This is essential to gain new insights into and knowledge about the industrial process.

Cross-industry standard process for data mining (CRISP-DM) (Shearer, 2000) is a process that describes commonly used approaches in industry for transforming data into machine learning models. The process is iterative –until achieving a good enough solution–, and interactive –the process flow can move back and forth between different steps depending on the current solution quality. CRISP-DM breaks the process of knowledge discovery into six major steps (Fig. 2.2):

1. Business understanding. This initial step involves understanding the problem objectives and requirements from a business perspective,

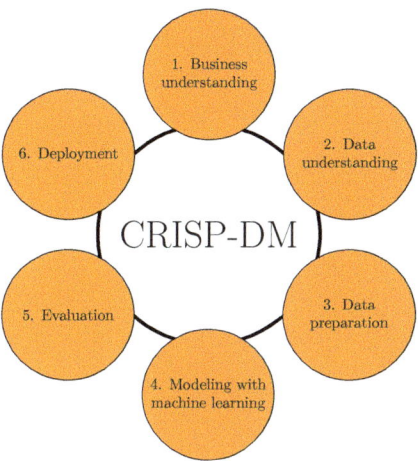

FIGURE 2.2
The six steps of a CRISP-DM process that transforms a dataset into valuable knowledge for a company.

and then considering the problem as a data-driven approach. How and where the data are collected are also decided in this step.

2. Data understanding. The input of this step is a dataset containing information about the problem to be modeled. Then we become familiar with the dataset to discover first insights (via visualization and descriptive statistics), or detect interesting subsets to accept or reject different hypotheses about the data (via hypothesis testing).

3. Data preparation. This step covers all activities to construct the final dataset (that will be modeled in the next step) from the initial raw data. Data preparation tasks are likely to be performed multiple times, and not in any prescribed order. Tasks include outlier detection and any other cleaning aspect, discretization of continuous variables (if necessary), and univariate or multivariate filter feature subset selection.

4. Modeling with machine learning. In this step various machine learning techniques (wrapper and embedded feature subset selection, clustering, supervised classification, association discovery, both in static or data stream environments) are applied. Fig. 2.3 shows all the techniques covered by this chapter.

5. Evaluation. The model in the above step is evaluated by honestly estimating its performance. If the model performance is below our expectation, stepping back to the data preparation step is needed.

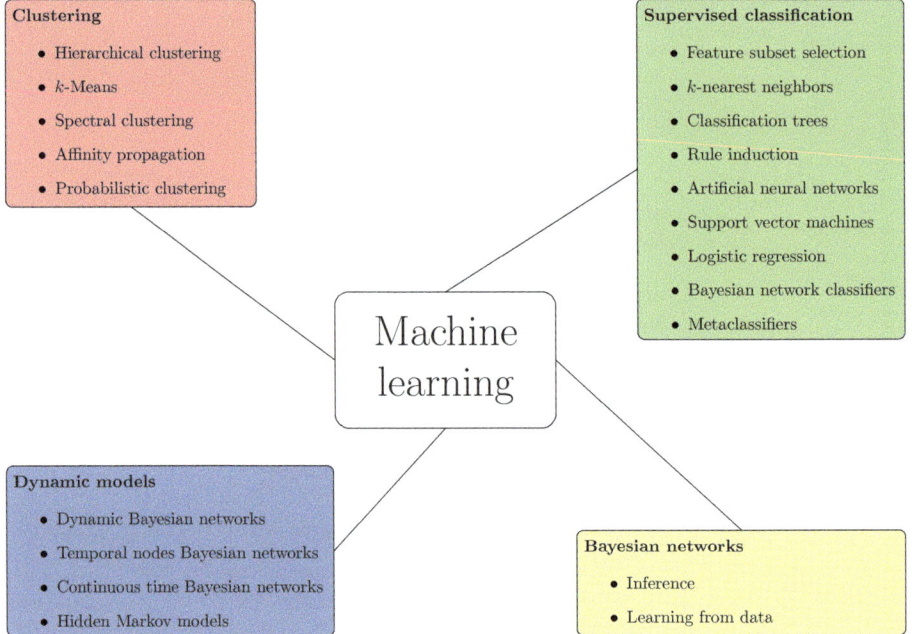

FIGURE 2.3
Machine learning techniques covered in this chapter.

At the end of this step, a decision on the use of the machine learning model should be reached.

6. Deployment. If the decision of the previous step is positive, the model should be implemented in the company. It is important for the customer to understand the actions needed to make use of the created models.

In 2015, IBM corporation extended CRISP-DM by releasing a new methodology called analytics solutions unified method for data mining/predictive analytics (also known as ASUM-DM).

This chapter is organized as follows. Section 2.2 presents basic descriptive and inferential statistical methods. Section 2.3 introduces the concept of clustering, explaining different approaches such as hierarchical clustering, partitional clustering, spectral clustering, affinity propagation and probabilistic clustering. Section 2.4 focuses on supervised classification methods, illustrating non-probabilistic classifiers –k-nearest neighbors, classification trees, rule induction, artificial neural networks and support vector machines–, and probabilistic classifiers –logistic regression and Bayesian classifiers– as well as metaclassifiers. Section 2.5 reviews Bayesian networks which are solid probabilistic graphical models in dynamic scenarios, a common feature in industry, as discussed in Section 2.6. Section 2.7 reviews some machine learning computational tools. The chapter closes with Section 2.8 on open issues in machine learning.

2.2 Basic Statistics

2.2.1 Descriptive Statistics

When analyzing a dataset, we first conduct an **exploratory data analysis** (Tukey, 1977). The main characteristics of the dataset can be summarized using visual graphs and simple measures based on which hypotheses can be stated, e.g., whether two variables are independent of each other or whether the variability of one variable is greater than that of another.

We make a distinction between three basic data types: categorical, discrete numerical and continuous numerical data. **Categorical data** refer to nominal categories based on some qualitative property. **Discrete data** refer to numerical quantities that have an either finite or countably infinite number of values. **Continuous data** can take a continuously infinite range of values, typically an interval of real numbers $\mathbb{R}$. Numerical data are also known as **linear data**, as opposed to directional data, which refer to directions or angles. This book does not deal with directional data.

For any of the different types of data above, let X denote a generic variable of which we have a data sample $\{x_1, ..., x_N\}$ of size N.

2.2.1.1   Visualization and Summary of Univariate Data

A **pie chart** visualizes categorical and discrete data. A circle is divided into sectors, each one representing a category or a value of a discrete variable. Their arc length is proportional to the frequency with which the category has been observed in the data. A **barplot** is a set of rectangular bars with heights proportional to the frequency of each category or value. The bars can be plotted vertically or horizontally. The **histogram** represents the distribution of the data as adjacent rectangles over a set of intervals (bins), with an area proportional to the absolute frequency of the data in the interval. This is the most representative plot for continuous data.

Data visualization plots can be more exactly quantified using descriptive measures called **summary statistics**. These can be grouped into measures of location, measures of dispersion, and measures of the shape of the distribution.

Measures of location or central tendency indicate where the frequency distribution over the set of real numbers, $\mathbb{R}$, is located. A central value between the minimum and the maximum values is chosen as a summary of the data sample. The other data will be distributed around this central point. The **arithmetic mean** $\bar{x}$ of the sample is given by $\bar{x} = \frac{1}{N}\sum_{i=1}^{N} x_i$. The arithmetic mean is not a robust statistic, i.e., it is very much influenced by outliers (abnormally extreme values), and is thus not as representative of the data when such outliers are present. The **geometric mean**, computed as $\bar{x}_G = \sqrt[N]{x_1 x_2 \cdots x_N}$, only applies to data of the same sign and is often used for growth rates, like population growth or interest rates. The **harmonic mean** is the reciprocal of the arithmetic mean of the reciprocals of the data, i.e., $\bar{x}_H = \left(\sum_{i=1}^{N} \frac{x_i^{-1}}{N}\right)^{-1}$. It is appropriate for situations where we are looking for the average rates or ratios. For positive data containing at least two non-equal values, the following inequalities hold: $\bar{x}_H \leq \bar{x}_G \leq \bar{x}$. The **sample median** Me is the numerical value separating the top from the bottom half of the data sample (once the data have been arranged in ascending order of values). Note that it is the sample order rather than the value of each data point that matters. Therefore, the median is better than the mean if the data contain outliers. The median is an appropriate measure for ordinal variables. The **sample mode**, Mo, is the most frequent value in the sample. It is not necessarily unique. The mode is the most representative measure for categorical data.

Dispersion measures provide information about the sparseness of the data around a measure of location. The **sample standard deviation**, s, shows how much variation or "dispersion" there is from the mean $\bar{x}$. s is defined as $s = \sqrt{\frac{1}{N-1}\sum_{i=1}^{N}(x_i - \bar{x})^2}$, and $s \geq 0$. Low values indicate that the data points tend to be very close to the mean, whereas high values indicate that points spread out over a large range of values. The square of s is the **sample variance**, s^2. The **mean absolute deviation** about the mean is defined as $\text{mad} = \frac{1}{N}\sum_{i=1}^{N}|x_i - \bar{x}|$. Since the median is more robust, the **median absolute deviation** about the median is defined as the median of the absolute deviations from the data median, that is, the median of the values $|x_i - Me|, i = 1, ..., N$. A dimensionless measure for eliminating the dependence of the s measurement units is the **coefficient of variation** (CV), the ratio of the standard deviation to the mean, often multiplied by 100 and only defined if $\bar{x} \neq 0$ as CV $= \frac{s}{\bar{x}} 100$. The higher the CV, the greater the dispersion in the variable. The **sample quartiles** are the three points that divide an ordered sample into four groups, each containing a quarter of the points. Thus, the first or lower quartile, denoted Q_1, has the lowest 25% of the data to its left and the highest 75% to its right. The third or upper quartile, denoted Q_3, has 75% of the data to its left and 25% to its right. The second quartile is the median Me, with 50-50% on both sides. A sample with 10 divisions has nine **sample deciles**. With 100 divisions, there are 99 **sample percentiles**. Thus, the first quartile is the 25th percentile. Generally, in a **sample quantile** of order $k \in (0,1)$, a proportion k of the data fall to its left and $1 - k$ to its right. Since quantiles account for the tendency of data to be grouped around a particular point, leaving a certain proportion of data to their left and the rest to their right, they are measures of location but not of centrality. Quantiles are also building blocks of another important dispersion measure: the **interquartile range**, IQR= $Q_3 - Q_1$, i.e., the difference between the upper and lower quartiles. The **range** is the difference between the maximum and minimum value and is also a dispersion measure.

Shape measures characterize the shape of a frequency distribution. They are defined according to the r-th central moments (or moments about the mean) of a data sample, $m_r = \frac{1}{N} \sum_{i=1}^{N} (x_i - \bar{x})^r$. **Skewness** measures the asymmetry of a frequency distribution and is defined as $g_1 = \frac{m_3}{m_2^{3/2}}$. A negative value of g_1 (left-skewed, left-tailed or skewed to the left) indicates that the left tail of the distribution is longer or fatter than the right side and that the bulk of the values lie to the right of the mean, that is, the mean is skewed to the left of a typical central measure of the data. The distribution is usually plotted as a right-leaning curve. A positive g_1 value means the opposite. A zero value corresponds with rather evenly distributed data on both sides of the mean, usually implying a symmetric distribution. Another measure of the shape of the distribution is **kurtosis**, indicating whether the data are peaked or flat relative to a normal (Gaussian) distribution. It is applied to bell-shaped (unimodal symmetric or slightly asymmetric) distributions. Kurtosis is dimensionless and defined as $g_2 = \frac{m_4}{m_2^2} - 3$. Leptokurtic distributions ($g_2 > 0$) are more peaked than normal, platykurtic distributions ($g_2 < 0$) are less peaked than normal and mesokurtic distributions ($g_2 = 0$) have similar, or identical, kurtosis to a normal distribution.

The box-and-whisker plot, or **boxplot**, is a very useful graph as it indicates whether the data are symmetric or have outliers. The spread is shown via the IQR, since a box is drawn with lines at Q_1 and Q_3. Another line is marked inside the box at the median. A "whisker" is drawn from Q_1 to the smallest data value greater than the lower fence, which is defined as $Q_1 - 1.5 \, \text{IQR}$.

Similarly, another whisker is drawn from Q_3 to the largest data value lower than the upper fence, defined as $Q_3 + 1.5\,\text{IQR}$. Any points beyond the whiskers are depicted by points and are, by convention, considered as **outliers**.

Fig. 2.4 shows examples of the above visualization methods for univariate data.

2.2.1.2   Visualization and Summary of Bivariate Data

Now let us look at two variables, X_1 and X_2, of which we have a subsample $\{(x_{11}, x_{12}), ..., (x_{N1}, x_{N2})\}$ (bivariate data) of size N.

If both variables are categorical or discrete, a **two-way contingency table** will report the frequencies of each observed value $(x_{i1}, x_{i2}), i = 1, \ldots, N$. This information can be plotted in a **side-by-side barplot**, where the bars of a variable of interest are grouped by a second variable. If one of the variables is categorical or discrete and the other variable is continuous, histograms and boxplots of the continuous variable can be plotted for each subsample given by a value of the other (categorical or discrete) variable, yielding a **conditional histogram** or **side-by-side boxplot**, respectively. Finally, when both variables are continuous, a **scatterplot** gives an initial idea of their relationship, representing the Cartesian coordinates of the subsample points on the plane.

The strength and direction of the linear relationship between two continuous variables, X_1 and X_2, can be measured by the **sample correlation coefficient**, r_{12}, defined as the **sample covariance**, s_{12}, of the two variables divided by the product of their sample standard deviations, that is, $r_{12} = \frac{s_{12}}{s_1 s_2} = \frac{\frac{1}{N}\sum_{i=1}^{N}(x_{i1}-\bar{x}_1)(x_{i2}-\bar{x}_2)}{s_1 s_2}$, where $\bar{x}_i, s_i, i = 1, 2$, are the sample mean and sample standard deviation of the X_i sample, respectively.

Fig. 2.5 shows examples of the above visualization methods for bivariate data.

2.2.1.3   Visualization and Summary of Multivariate Data

A **scatterplot matrix** represents the scatterplots for all pairs of variables in an array. **3D scatterplots** represent three variables in the three-dimensional space. One solution to avoid overlapping points in a scatterplot is to produce a 2D or **flat histogram**, where the density in each bin is represented by an appropriate color intensity rather than the actual points. **Multipanel 2D boxplots** are useful for visualizing a continuous variable given a discrete or a categorical variable.

The **covariance matrix**, $\mathbf{S}$, whose elements are the covariances of each pair of variables (variances in the diagonal), generalizes the notion of variance to multiple dimensions. The inverse of this matrix, $\mathbf{S}^{-1}$, is known as the **concentration matrix** or **precision matrix**. Accordingly, the elements of the **correlation matrix** $\mathbf{R}$ are pairwise correlations (it has all ones on the diagonal).

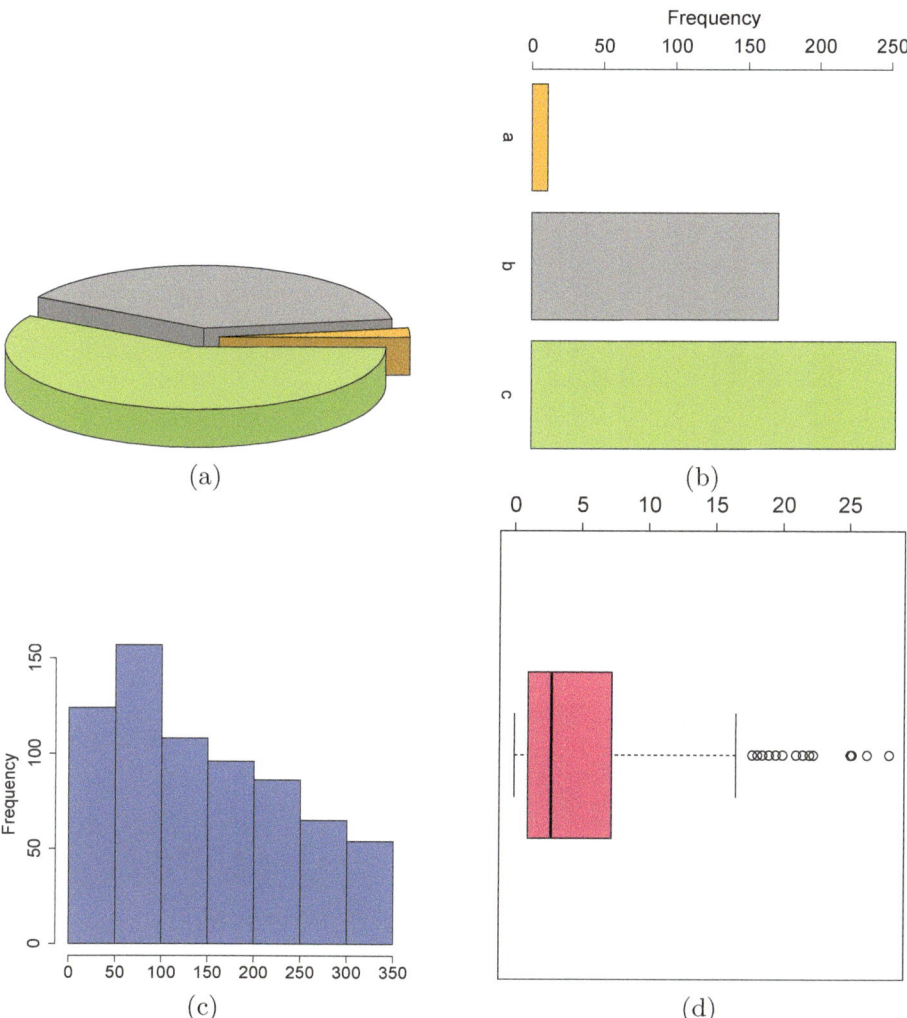

FIGURE 2.4

Plots representing univariate data. (a) Pie charts and (b) barplots are suitable for categorical and discrete data, (c) histograms for continuous data, and (d) boxplots for numerical data.

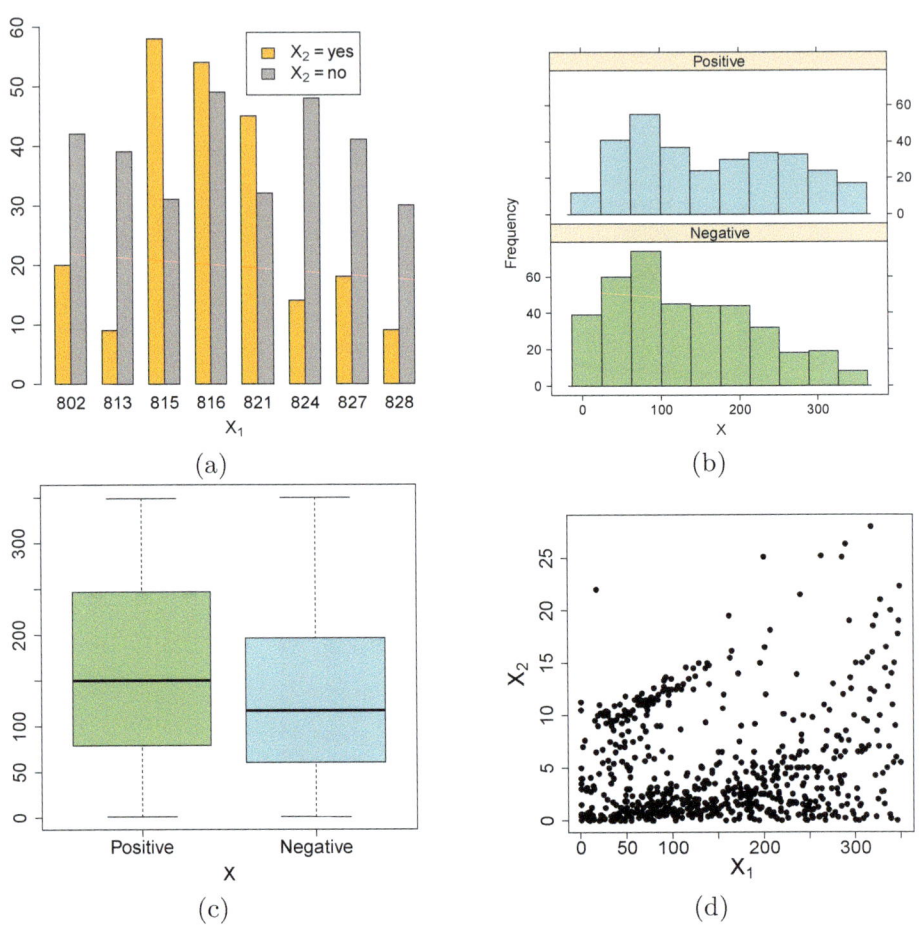

FIGURE 2.5

Plots representing bivariate data. (a) Side-by-side bar plot. (b) Conditional histogram. (c) Side-by-side boxplot. (d) Scatterplot.

Four major approaches for visualizing multivariate data are Chernoff faces, parallel coordinates, principal component analysis and multidimensional scaling. **Chernoff faces** (Chernoff, 1973) display a cartoon human face depicting the size and shape of different facial features according to the variable values. The **parallel coordinate plot** (d'Ocagne, 1885) is a diagram including parallel vertical equidistant lines (axes), each representing a variable. Then each coordinate of each observation point is plotted along its respective axis and the points are joined together with line segments. **Principal component analysis (PCA)** (Jolliffe, 1986) describes the variation in a set of correlated variables in terms of another set of uncorrelated variables, each of which is a linear combination of the original variables. Usually a number of new variables less than n will account for a substantial proportion of the variation in the original variables. Thus, PCA is used for dimensionality reduction but also for data compression, feature extraction and data visualization.

Multidimensional scaling (MDS) (Torgerson, 1952) is a visualization technique that creates a map (that has fewer dimensions than the original data) displaying the relative positions of the data. The map preserves, as closely as possible, the pairwise distances between data points. The map may consist of one, two, three, or even more dimensions.

Fig. 2.6 illustrates visualization methods for multivariate data.

2.2.1.4 Imputation of Missing Data

Data preprocessing is an important step in the data mining process, as the analysis of data that have not been carefully screened can produce misleading results. We focus here on imputation methods able to deal with missing data and also on variable transformation schemes, such as standardization, transformations toward Gaussianity and discretization on further sections.

Missing data are a common problem in industrial datasets. A simple way to remove missing data is to discard the cases with incomplete data from the analysis, working with complete data cases only. This strategy is called **complete-case analysis** and leads to inefficient and biased estimates. The **imputation of missing data** on a variable replaces missing data by a value that is drawn from the probability distribution of this variable.

Single imputation refers to imputing one value for each missing datum. Several methods have been proposed. **Unconditional mean imputation** replaces each missing value with the mean (or median) of the observed values of that variable. In **regression imputation**, the missing values for each variable are replaced with the values predicted from a regression of that variable on other variables. **Hot deck imputation** replaces each missing value with a random draw from a "donor pool", i.e., from a set of variable values for complete cases that have "similar" observed values to the case with missing data. "Similar" can be constructed as exact matching for categorical variables or a small distance for numerical variables. Imputation based on the expectation-maximization algorithm (see Section 2.3.5) is a model-based imputation approach.

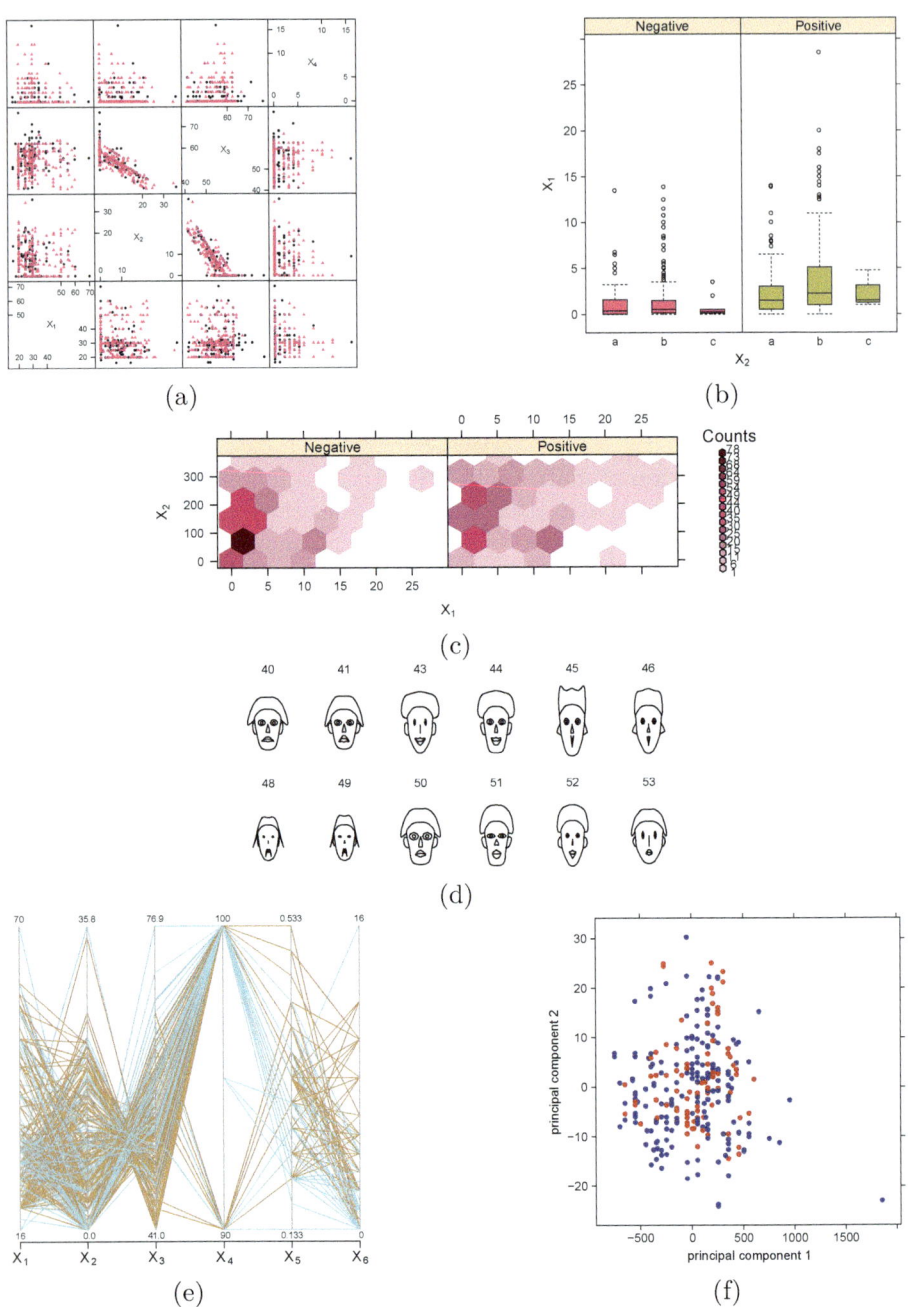

FIGURE 2.6
Multivariate data representation. Discrete or categorical variables are
permitted for multipanels. (a) Scatterplot matrix. (b) Multipanel 2D boxplot.
(c) Flat histogram. (d) Chernoff faces. (e) Parallel coordinates. (f) PCA.

Multiple imputation creates not a single imputed dataset, but several or multiple imputed datasets in which different imputations are based on a random draw from different estimated underlying distributions. Each of the completed datasets is then analyzed and the results are combined (e.g., computing their arithmetic mean) to produce the final imputed value.

2.2.1.5 Variable Transformation

Data transformation means applying a mathematical function to each point in a dataset. This may be necessary because: (a) the measurement units affect the statistical or machine learning procedure to be applied; (b) the transformed data come closer to fulfilling the assumptions of the procedure to be applied (e.g., Gaussianity); (c) the procedure only works for discrete variables.

Variables with different measurement units can pose a problem for some modeling methods. If this is the case, the original data should be transformed such that all new variables share the same mean and standard deviation. This is called **standardization** and consists of subtracting the mean of the original variable from each datum, and dividing the result by the standard deviation. The new mean is 0 and the standard deviation is 1.

Some machine learning methods are based on the assumption that the data follow a Gaussian distribution. However, Gaussianity may not hold for the original data. In this case, special transformations, like the **power transform**, given by $z = x^\lambda, \lambda > 0$, where x is the original variable and z is the transformed variable, can be applied to approximate Gaussianity. According to Tukey (1977), $\lambda > 1$ will extend the right tail of the histogram removing left skewness, whereas $\lambda < 1$ has the opposite effect.

Discretization (Liu et al., 2002) transforms continuous data into categorical data. There are four commonly used methods. **Equal-width discretization** (Catlett, 1991) predefines the value of k, that is, the number of intervals. It then divides the line between the minimum and the maximum value into k intervals of equal width. **Equal-frequency discretization** (Catlett, 1991) divides the sorted values into k intervals so that each interval contains approximately the same number of values. The value of k is given a priori. **Proportional k-interval discretization** (Yang and Webb, 2009) picks the largest integer not greater than the square root of the number of observations, that is, $k = \lceil \sqrt{N} \rceil$, as the number of intervals. In supervised classification settings, the **minimum description length principle-based discretization** (MDLP) algorithm (Fayyad and Irani, 1993) uses information theory-based measures to recursively find the best bins. Each interval should contain only one type of label, that is, the method tries to minimize the entropy of the class variable in each interval. This objective leads to a high number of intervals. The number of intervals is controlled by the MDLP principle. This principle aims to balance minimum entropy and number of bins.

2.2.2 Inference

In industry, it is not usually possible to access all the members of a given target population. For example, it is impossible to access all the pieces produced in a factory during a given year. Therefore, we must be content to analyze the information on a smaller number of pieces. Based on the characteristics of this sample of pieces, we can generalize the results to the annual production of the entire factory. Thanks to this generalization, referred to in statistical jargon as **inference process**, we can estimate parameters from a given probability distribution representing the population, as well as test hypotheses about the values of these parameters or even about the actual distributions. This section introduces the basic concepts of parameter estimation (parameter point estimation and parameter confidence intervals) and hypothesis testing.

There are different random selection methods. However, if standard procedures are followed, mathematical expressions can be used to quantify the accuracy of the estimations. **Cluster sampling** is based on the idea that the whole population can be clustered into smaller subpopulations called clusters. Clusters are homogeneous and are treated as the sampling unit. Suppose that the factory has 1000 machines playing the role of clusters, cluster sampling can select 20 of these machines and inspect all the pieces manufactured by this smaller number of machines. **Stratified sampling** is used when the target population can be easily partitioned into subpopulations or strata. Strata are then chosen to divide the population into non-overlapping and homogeneous regions, where elements belonging to a given stratum are expected to be similar. Stratified sampling assumes that the different strata are very heterogeneous. Simple random samples are taken from each stratum. For example, if our factory has three types of machines, each producing different pieces, stratified sampling will select some pieces at random from each of these subpopulations.

In **systematic sampling**, we have a list of all the members of a given population and we decide to select every k-th value in our sample. The initial starting point is selected at random. The remaining values to be sampled are then automatically determined. For example, suppose we have an ordered list of the 100,000 pieces produced in a factory on a specified day and we plan to use systematic sampling to select a sample of size 200. The procedure is to choose an initial starting point at random between 1 and 500 (since $\frac{100,000}{200} = 500$). If the generated random number is 213, then the units in the sample of size 200 are numbered 213, 713 (213 + 500), 1213 (213 + 2 × 500), ..., and 99,713 (213 + 199 × 500).

2.2.2.1 Parameter Point Estimation

The sample taken from a population will be used to estimate the **parameter** θ of the distribution of the random variable that models that population. For example, we can consider whether or not each manufactured piece is correct (categorical random variable) and its weight (continuous random variable). A Bernoulli distribution, $X \sim \text{Ber}(x|p)$ parametrized with $\theta = p$, which denotes the probability of value 1, is the underlying distribution for the first variable. Its probability mass function is $p(x|p) = p^x(1-p)^{1-x}$ for $x = 0, 1$, where p is unknown and should be estimated from the sample. A **Gaussian distribution**, also called **normal distribution**, $X \sim \mathcal{N}(x|\mu, \sigma)$, or simply $\mathcal{N}(\mu, \sigma)$, is defined by the density function $f(x|\mu, \sigma) = \frac{1}{\sqrt{2\pi\sigma^2}} e^{-\frac{1}{2\sigma^2}(x-\mu)^2}$ for $x, \mu \in \mathbb{R}$ and $\sigma \in \mathbb{R}^+$, and can model the density of the weight of the piece. In this case, $\boldsymbol{\theta}$ is a vector with two components, μ and σ, that should be estimated from the sample.

The observed random sample of size N, that is, the values, $x_1, x_2, ..., x_N$ of the N **independent and identically distributed (i.i.d.)** random variables $X_1, X_2, ..., X_N$, are combined into a function $\hat{\theta} = t(X_1, X_2, ..., X_N)$, known as the **estimator** of θ, which is also a random variable. Its specific value, called an **estimate** of θ, is known after taking a sample. The **sample mean** $\hat{\theta} = \bar{X} = \frac{1}{N}\sum_{i=1}^{N} X_i$ is an estimator for p and also for μ, whereas the **sample variance** $\hat{\sigma}^2 = S_N^2 = \frac{1}{N}\sum_{i=1}^{N}(X_i - \bar{X})^2$ is an estimator for σ^2, the variance of the population.

Computing how close estimates of θ are to the true parameter θ will reveal the goodness of an estimator $\hat{\theta}$. Since θ is unknown, this is approximated under the expectation operator $\mathbb{E}(\cdot)$. The **mean square error** of an estimator $\hat{\theta}$ of θ, defined as $MSE(\hat{\theta}) = \mathbb{E}[(\hat{\theta}-\theta)^2]$, is an important goodness measure. Estimators with small mean square errors will be preferred. The MSE is decomposed as $MSE(\hat{\theta}) = (bias(\hat{\theta}))^2 + Var[\hat{\theta}]$, where **bias**$(\hat{\theta})$, defined as $\mathbb{E}(\hat{\theta}) - \theta$, measures the expected error of the estimator, i.e., how closely its average estimate is able to approximate the target, and its variance, $Var[\hat{\theta}]$, measures how much the estimate fluctuates for different samples (of the same size). Small bias and variance are preferred. Fig. 2.7(a) illustrates these two concepts.

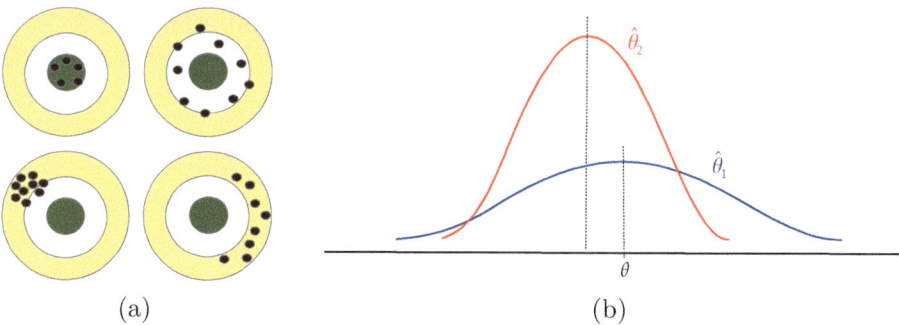

(a)   (b)

FIGURE 2.7

(a) Graphical representation of the concepts of bias and variance: low bias and low variance (top left), low bias and high variance (top right), high bias and low variance (bottom left) and high bias and high variance (bottom right). (b) $\hat{\theta}_1$ is an unbiased estimator of θ and $\hat{\theta}_2$ is a biased estimator of θ. However, $\hat{\theta}_2$ has a smaller variance than $\hat{\theta}_1$.

$\hat{\theta}$ is an **unbiased estimator** of θ if $\mathbb{E}(\hat{\theta}) = \theta$. Otherwise, the estimator is biased. For unbiased estimators, the mean squared error is equal to its variance, that is, $MSE(\hat{\theta}) = Var[\hat{\theta}]$. For a Bernoulli population, the empirical proportion of successes is an unbiased estimator of parameter p. The sample arithmetic mean, $\hat{\mu} = \bar{X}$, and the **sample quasi-variance**, $\hat{\sigma}^2 = S_{N-1}^2 = \frac{1}{N-1} \sum_{i=1}^{N} (X_i - \bar{X})^2$, in a Gaussian density are unbiased estimators of parameters μ and σ^2, respectively.

The variance of any unbiased estimator satisfies the inequality $Var[\hat{\theta}] \geq \frac{1/N}{\mathbb{E}\left[\left(\frac{\partial \ln f(x|\theta)}{\partial \theta}\right)^2\right]}$, known as the **Cramér-Rao inequality**. When the variance of an unbiased estimator equals the Cramér-Rao lower bound, the estimator $\hat{\theta}$ is a **minimum-variance unbiased** estimator of θ, also known as **efficient estimator** of θ.

There are two main methods for deriving estimators with good properties: the method of moments and the maximum likelihood estimation method.

The **method of moments** consists of matching the population moments around the origin, $\alpha_r(\theta_1, ..., \theta_K) = \mathbb{E}[X]^r$, with their corresponding **sample moments** around the origin, $m_r = \frac{1}{N} \sum_{i=1}^{N} x_i^r$ with $r = 1, \ldots, K$. For a probability density function $f(x|\theta_1, ..., \theta_K)$, which depends on K parameters, the system to be solved is

$$\begin{cases} \alpha_1(\theta_1, ..., \theta_K) = m_1 \\ \alpha_2(\theta_1, ..., \theta_K) = m_2 \\ \quad\quad ... \\ \alpha_K(\theta_1, ..., \theta_K) = m_K. \end{cases}$$

For parameter $\theta_1 = p$ of a Bernoulli distribution, the estimator derived from the method of moments is the empirical proportion, that is, $\alpha_1(p) = p = \bar{X} = m_1$. For the parameters of a normal density $\mathcal{N}(\mu, \sigma)$, we solve the following system of two equations:

$$\begin{cases} \alpha_1(\mu, \sigma^2) = \mu = \bar{X} = m_1 \\ \alpha_2(\mu, \sigma^2) = \sigma^2 + \mu^2 = \frac{1}{N} \sum_{i=1}^{N} x_i^2 = m_2. \end{cases}$$

The solution of this system yields $\hat{\mu} = \bar{X}$ and $\hat{\sigma}^2 = \frac{1}{N} \sum_{i=1}^{N} (X_i - \bar{X})^2$.

Maximum likelihood estimation assigns the value that makes the observed data most likely under the assumed probability model to θ. Denoting the **likelihood function** of θ as $\mathcal{L}(\theta|\mathbf{x}) = f(\mathbf{x}|\theta)$ given $\mathbf{x} = (x_1, ..., x_N)$, then $\mathcal{L}(\theta|\mathbf{x}) = f(\mathbf{x}|\theta) = f(x_1|\theta) \cdot f(x_2|\theta) \cdots f(x_N|\theta)$. The value of θ that maximizes $\mathcal{L}(\theta|\mathbf{x})$ is called the **maximum likelihood estimate** of θ, denoted as $\hat{\theta}(x_1, x_2, ..., x_N)$. The **maximum likelihood estimator** (**MLE**) is a statistic denoted as $\hat{\theta}(X_1, X_2, ..., X_N)$. Generally, it tends to be more convenient and easier to use the natural logarithm of $\mathcal{L}(\theta|\mathbf{x})$, called the **log-likelihood function**, $\ln \mathcal{L}(\theta|\mathbf{x})$.

A necessary condition that a MLE must satisfy is $\frac{\partial \ln \mathcal{L}(\theta|\mathbf{x})}{\partial \theta} = 0$. Maximum likelihood estimators have interesting properties. First, MLEs are not necessarily unbiased estimators. However, they are always asymptotically unbiased, i.e., the probability of the MLE differing from the true value of the parameter more than a fixed small value tends to zero, for an increasingly large sample size. Second, MLEs are not necessarily efficient estimators. However, if an efficient estimator of a parameter exists, this efficient estimator is also a MLE.

The MLE for parameter p of a Bernoulli distribution is obtained by equaling the first derivative of the log-likelihood function to zero:

$$\frac{\partial \ln \mathcal{L}(p|\mathbf{x})}{\partial p} = \frac{\sum_{i=1}^{N} x_i}{p} - \frac{N - \sum_{i=1}^{N} x_i}{1 - p} = 0,$$

and checking that its second-order partial derivate is negative. The MLE is given by $\hat{p}(X_1, ..., X_N) = \bar{X}$.

To get the MLE for parameter $\boldsymbol{\theta} = (\mu, \sigma^2)$ of a normal density, we need to compute the log-likelihood function of a sample $x_1, ..., x_N$ taken from a $\mathcal{N}(\mu, \sigma)$ as

$$\ln \mathcal{L}(\mu, \sigma^2|\mathbf{x}) = -\frac{N}{2} \ln(2\pi) - \frac{N}{2} \ln(\sigma^2) - \frac{\sum_{i=1}^{N}(x_i - \mu)^2}{2\sigma^2}.$$

The MLE $(\hat{\mu}, \hat{\sigma}^2)$ is the solution of the following system of equations

$$\begin{cases} \frac{\partial \ln \mathcal{L}(\mu, \sigma^2|\mathbf{x})}{\partial \mu} = \frac{\sum_{i=1}^{N}(x_i - \mu)}{\sigma^2} = 0 \\ \frac{\partial \ln \mathcal{L}(\mu, \sigma^2|\mathbf{x})}{\partial \sigma^2} = -\frac{N}{2\sigma^2} + \frac{\sum_{i=1}^{N}(x_i - \mu)^2}{2\sigma^4} = 0. \end{cases}$$

Solving the system easily yields

$$\hat{\mu}(X_1, ..., X_N) = \frac{\sum_{i=1}^{N} X_i}{N} = \bar{X}, \qquad \hat{\sigma}^2(X_1, ..., X_N) = \frac{\sum_{i=1}^{N}(X_i - \bar{X})^2}{N} = S_N^2.$$

Bayesian estimation considers $\boldsymbol{\theta}$ to be a random variable with a known prior distribution. With the observed sample this distribution is converted, via the Bayes' theorem, to a posterior distribution. Choosing a **conjugate prior**, i.e., the prior and posterior belong to the same family of distributions, simplifies calculation of the posterior distribution. Typical examples are the Dirichlet (Frigyik et al., 2010) and Wishart (Wishart, 1928) distributions. Otherwise, posteriors are often computed numerically or by Monte Carlo techniques.

The posterior distribution is used to perform inferences on $\boldsymbol{\theta}$. Thus, a typical point Bayesian estimation is to choose the value of $\boldsymbol{\theta}$ that maximizes the posterior distribution (i.e., its mode). This is called **maximum a posteriori** (MAP) estimation.

Bayesian estimation is used in Bayesian networks (Section 2.5), both for finding the graph structure and for estimating its parameters. Small sample sizes and data stream scenarios are also suitable for Bayesian estimation.

2.2.2.2   Parameter Confidence Estimation

Parameter confidence estimation can be used to convey the results of the estimation process in terms of a **confidence interval** (CI), whose width (precision) and reliability (confidence) that the true value of the parameter will be found are a more thorough way of estimation.

A $(1 - \alpha)$ confidence interval for a parameter θ, denoted $\text{CI}_{1-\alpha}(\theta)$, is built by first selecting a confidence level, denoted by $(1 - \alpha)$, usually expressed as a percentage $(1 - \alpha) \cdot 100\%$, where $\alpha \in (0, 1]$. The **confidence level** is a measure of the degree of reliability of the procedure used to build the CI. For example, a confidence level of 95% implies that 95% of the samples would provide confidence intervals that would contain the true θ. Although reliability should be high, the width of the CI grows as reliability increases. The CI should verify that $p(L(\mathbf{X}) \leq \theta \leq U(\mathbf{X})) = 1 - \alpha$, where $L(\mathbf{X})$ is its lower bound and $U(\mathbf{X})$ is its upper bound, i.e., $\text{CI}_{1-\alpha}(\theta) = [L(\mathbf{x}), U(\mathbf{x})]$.

The confidence interval for the population mean of a Gaussian distribution with unknown population variance is

$$\text{CI}_{1-\alpha}(\mu) = \left[\bar{X} - t_{1-\alpha/2;N-1} \frac{S}{\sqrt{N}}, \bar{X} + t_{1-\alpha/2;N-1} \frac{S}{\sqrt{N}} \right],$$

where $t_{1-\alpha/2;N-1}$ denotes the quantile of order $1 - \alpha/2$ of a Student's t probability distribution with $N - 1$ degrees of freedom.

Example. Confidence interval

Suppose that we have nine pieces with a mean weight of 100 kilograms and a sample standard deviation of 30 kilograms, the CI for μ with a confidence level of 0.95 is expressed as

$$\text{CI}_{0.95}(\mu) = \left[100 - 2.31\frac{30}{\sqrt{9}}, 100 + 2.31\frac{30}{\sqrt{9}} \right] = [76.9, 123.1]$$

as $t_{0.975;8} = 2.31$. The confidence interval for $N = 900$ pieces with the same confidence level and the same values for $\bar{X}$ and S is expressed by $[98.04, 101.96]$. This illustrates the influence of the sample size on the CI width.   ∎

2.2.2.3   Hypothesis Testing

Hypothesis testing is a method of statistical inference where we first state two hypotheses: a null hypothesis (denoted H_0) and an alternative hypothesis (H_A). The null hypothesis refers to the default belief about the phenomenon under study that is to be rejected. For example, if a new production system is proposed, H_0 will state that the new and old production systems are equally effective, whereas H_A states that the effectiveness of the two production systems is not the same.

Once the hypotheses have been stated, we check whether the data can reject or not H_0. The null hypothesis should be rejected when the difference between the null hypothesis and our observations of the phenomenon under study is statistically significant. Statistical significance means that the differences are due not to chance, but to a real difference between the phenomenon under study and the assumptions of the null hypothesis. For example, differences may be due to chance if they were generated by the observations of the phenomenon (i.e., the differences would perhaps not have arisen using other samples).

Note that when we decide whether or not to reject H_0, we can make two different errors:

- Type I error: we reject H_0 when H_0 is true.

- Type II error: we do not reject H_0 when H_0 is false.

To decide whether or not to reject the null hypothesis, we first select a **significance level**, α, for our hypothesis test. The value of α is equal to the probability of making a type I error. Usually, α is set to 0.05 or 0.01. The use of a lower value $\alpha \in (0, 1)$ reduces the number of type I errors. However, this type I error reduction usually comes at the cost of an increase in type II errors. This behavior has a simple explanation: if we are averse to reject H_0, we will not reject it unless we are very sure about this decision. Additionally, the probability of making a type II error is usually denoted as β. The power of the hypothesis test is usually denoted as $1 - \beta$, and is equal to the probability of rejecting H_0 when we really should reject H_0. In usual hypothesis testing practice, the value of β cannot, unfortunately, be determined in advance as we did with the α value. However, as we just discussed, a reduction in α usually increases the value of β. This reduces the power of the hypothesis test.

After setting the significance level of the test, we are ready to check the data and decide whether or not to reject the null hypothesis. This procedure often involves the computation of a statistic whose distribution is known when H_0 is true. If the value of the statistic output by the data is more extreme than a critical value defined by its distribution, then H_0 is rejected. The critical value has a correspondence with the previously selected α, thus complying with the upper bound on the probability of type I errors. It is also quite common to compute the p-value. The p-**value** is the probability of getting a statistic value that is as extreme as the value yielded by the available data if H_0 is true. Low p-values indicate that H_0 should be rejected. In particular, H_0 is rejected if p-value $\leq \alpha$.

This book discusses two hypothesis tests: the chi-squared test of independence and the Friedman test. These hypothesis tests are used in Section 2.5.3 and Section 7.4.2.2, respectively.

The **chi-squared test of independence** is applied with two categorical variables X and Y with respectively I and J possible values, and a sample of size N with elements that can be categorized according to both categorical variables. The question is whether X and Y can be considered independent variables.

TABLE 2.1
Contingency table

	y_1	$\cdots$	y_j	$\cdots$	y_J	Marginal
x_1	N_{11}	$\cdots$	N_{1j}	$\cdots$	N_{1J}	$N_{1\bullet}$
$\vdots$	$\vdots$	$\ddots$	$\vdots$	$\ddots$	$\vdots$	$\vdots$
x_i	N_{i1}	$\cdots$	N_{ij}	$\cdots$	N_{iJ}	$N_{i\bullet}$
$\vdots$	$\vdots$	$\ddots$	$\vdots$	$\ddots$	$\vdots$	$\vdots$
x_I	N_{I1}	$\cdots$	N_{Ij}	$\cdots$	N_{IJ}	$N_{I\bullet}$
Marginal	$N_{\bullet 1}$	$\cdots$	$N_{\bullet j}$	$\cdots$	$N_{\bullet J}$	N

Table 2.1 contains the number of observations, N_{ij}, in the sample taking the i-th value in X and, at the same time, the j-th value in Y. The total number in the i-th row ($1 \leq i \leq I$) is $N_{i\bullet} = \sum_{j=1}^{J} N_{ij}$, whereas the total number of observations in the j-th column ($1 \leq j \leq J$) is $N_{\bullet j} = \sum_{i=1}^{I} N_{ij}$.

The true probability that an individual falls in cell (i,j) in the contingency table will be denoted θ_{ij}. Under the assumption of independent X and Y, $\theta_{ij} = \theta_{i\bullet}\theta_{\bullet j}$, where $\theta_{i\bullet} = \sum_{j=1}^{J} \theta_{ij}$ and $\theta_{\bullet j} = \sum_{i=1}^{I} \theta_{ij}$, that is, $\theta_{i\bullet}$ is the probability of a produced piece being classified in category i of the row variable and $\theta_{\bullet j}$ is the probability of a piece being classified in category j of the column variable. The null and alternative hypotheses for testing the independence of X and Y is

$$\begin{cases} H_0 : \theta_{ij} = \theta_{i\bullet}\theta_{\bullet j} \\ H_1 : \theta_{ij} \neq \theta_{i\bullet}\theta_{\bullet j} \end{cases}$$

Estimations of $\theta_{i\bullet}$ and $\theta_{\bullet j}$ are given by $\hat{\theta}_{i\bullet} = \frac{N_{i\bullet}}{N}$ and $\hat{\theta}_{\bullet j} = \frac{N_{\bullet j}}{N}$, respectively. The expected number of observations in cell (i,j) is computed as $N\hat{\theta}_{ij}$. Under the assumption of independence, this expected number becomes $N\hat{\theta}_{ij} = N\hat{\theta}_{i\bullet}\hat{\theta}_{\bullet j} = \frac{N_{i\bullet}N_{\bullet j}}{N}$.

The test statistic

$$W = \sum_{i=1}^{I} \sum_{j=1}^{J} \frac{(O_{ij} - E_{ij})^2}{E_{ij}}$$

is used to compare the observed number of cases, $O_{ij} = N_{ij}$, in the sample in each cell (i,j) with the expected number under the null hypothesis, $E_{ij} = \frac{N_{i\bullet}N_{\bullet j}}{N}$. W approximately follows a chi-squared density with $(I-1)(J-1)$ degrees of freedom. The null hypothesis of independence is rejected with a significance level α when the value of W observed in the sample is greater than the quantile $\chi^2_{(I-1)(J-1);1-\alpha}$. The chi-squared approximation is usually satisfactory if E_{ij} are not too small. A conservative rule is to require all E_{ij} to be five or more.

The **Friedman test** (Friedman, 1937) is a non-parametric test associated with a design structure known as randomized complete block design. In this design, there are b blocks[1] corresponding to the observations and $k \geq 2$ treatments are applied to each observation. The aim of the test is to detect differences among the k treatments.

Denoting the measurement for the i-th block in the j-th treatment, with $i = 1, ..., b$ and $j = 1, ..., k$, by x_{ij}, we compute the rank value, r_{ij}, and the sum of the ranks, R_j, for each measurement according to treatment j, finally resulting in an arrangement as shown in Table 2.2.

TABLE 2.2
Blocks, treatments and ranked data in a randomized complete block design

		Treatments					Row totals
		1	$\cdots$	j	$\cdots$	k	
	1	r_{11}	$\cdots$	r_{1j}	$\cdots$	r_{1k}	$k(k+1)/2$
	$\vdots$	$\vdots$	$\ddots$	$\vdots$	$\ddots$	$\vdots$	$\vdots$
Blocks	i	r_{i1}	$\cdots$	r_{ij}	$\cdots$	r_{ik}	$k(k+1)/2$
	$\vdots$	$\vdots$	$\ddots$	$\vdots$	$\ddots$	$\vdots$	$\vdots$
	b	r_{b1}	$\cdots$	r_{b2}	$\cdots$	r_{bk}	$k(k+1)/2$
	Column totals	R_1	$\cdots$	R_j	$\cdots$	R_k	$bk(k+1)/2$

Friedman test assumptions are that all sample populations are continuous and identical, except possibly for location. The null hypothesis is that all populations have the same location. Typically, the null hypothesis of no difference among the k treatments is written in terms of the medians, ψ_i. Both hypotheses, H_0 and H_1, can be written as:

$$\begin{cases} H_0 : \psi_1 = \psi_2 = ... = \psi_k \\ H_1 : \psi_i \neq \psi_j \text{ for at least one pair } (i, j) \end{cases}$$

The standardized test statistic S, defined as

$$S = \left[\frac{12}{bk(k+1)} \sum_{j=1}^{k} R_j^2 \right] - 3b(k+1) \qquad (2.1)$$

is used to evaluate the null hypothesis. Under the assumption that H_0 is true, S is well approximated by a χ_{k-1}^2 distribution. Given a fixed significance level α, we reject H_0 if the value of S observed in the sample is greater than the quantile $\chi_{k-1;1-\alpha}^2$.

---

[1]The name "block" comes from the earliest experimental designs in agriculture, where fields used to be divided into "blocks."

2.3   Clustering

This section develops two different approaches to clustering: the non-probabilistic clustering and the probabilistic clustering. The objective of both approaches is to group or segment a set of objects or instances into subsets or "clusters." Similar objects should be within the same group, whereas very dissimilar objects should be in different groups. For example, groups could be objects corresponding to the same specific state (idle, constant speed, acceleration/deceleration) of servomotors used to position the machine tool axis (see Chapter 5). In non-probabilistic clustering including hierarchical clustering and partitional clustering –such as the K-means algorithm, spectral clustering or affinity propagation– each object belongs to only one cluster. In probabilistic clustering, however, each object can be a member of several clusters at the same time, and they all have a membership probability of each cluster.

Mathematically, the dataset $\mathcal{D} = \{\mathbf{x}^1, ..., \mathbf{x}^N\}$ to be clustered contains N objects, $\mathbf{x}^i = (x_1^i, ..., x_n^i)$, with $i = 1, ..., N$, each of which is characterized by n variables, $\mathbf{X} = (X_1, ..., X_n)$. Hierarchical clustering and K-means clustering work with a **dissimilarity matrix**, which is the result of a transformation of $\mathcal{D}$. The dissimilarity matrix is an $N \times N$ matrix $\mathbf{D} \equiv \left(d(\mathbf{x}^i, \mathbf{x}^j)\right)_{i,j}$, where $d(\mathbf{x}^i, \mathbf{x}^j)$ denotes the dissimilarity between the i-th and the j-th objects.

Standard dissimilarity measures $d(\mathbf{x}^i, \mathbf{x}^j)$ include the **Minkowski distance** for numerical features: $d_{\text{Minkowski}}(\mathbf{x}^i, \mathbf{x}^j) = \left(\sum_{h=1}^n |x_h^i - x_h^j|^g\right)^{1/g}$, with $g \geq 1$. The **Euclidean distance** and the **Manhattan distance** are special cases of the Minkowski distance, when $g = 2$ and $g = 1$, respectively. For binary variables, the dissimilarity between objects can be computed based on a contingency table. For example, in symmetric binary variables, where both states are equally valuable, the dissimilarity can be defined as $d_{\text{binary}}(\mathbf{x}^i, \mathbf{x}^j) = \frac{r+s}{q+r+s+t}$, where q is the number of variables equal to 1 for both objects; t is the number of variables equal to 0 for both objects; and $r + s$ are the total number of variables that are unequal for both objects.

Spectral clustering and the affinity propagation algorithm are based on a **similarity matrix**, with elements $s(\mathbf{x}^i, \mathbf{x}^j)$ for $i, j = 1, ..., N$, denoting the similarity between objects $\mathbf{x}^i$ and $\mathbf{x}^j$. These similarities verify that $s(\mathbf{x}^i, \mathbf{x}^j) > s(\mathbf{x}^i, \mathbf{x}^k)$ iff $\mathbf{x}^i$ is more similar to $\mathbf{x}^j$ than to $\mathbf{x}^k$.

2.3.1   Hierarchical Clustering

Hierarchical clustering algorithms (Gordon, 1987) represent data as a hierarchical structure called **dendrogram** (Fig. 2.8(b)). Each leaf of the dendrogram represents a data object (singleton cluster), whereas all objects are gathered in a single cluster at the top. The intermediate branches show the dissimilarities between two clusters of objects when both start forming a new cluster. The clustering results can be obtained by cutting the dendrogram at different heights.

Agglomerative hierarchical clustering considers that there are initially N singleton clusters, each of which is associated with one of the objects to be grouped. At each stage of the algorithm, the most similar pair of clusters are merged according to a previously defined linkage strategy. This merging process is repeated until the whole set of objects belongs to one cluster (Fig. 2.8).

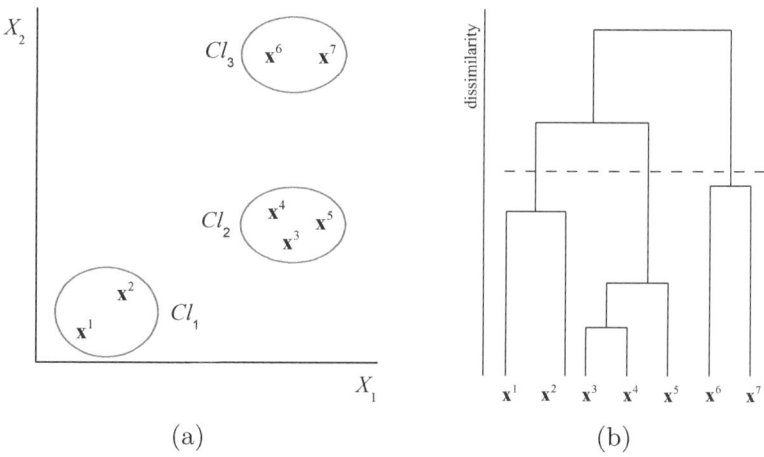

(a)   (b)

FIGURE 2.8
Example of agglomerative hierarchical clustering. (a) Seven points represented in a two-dimensional space with three clusters Cl_1, Cl_2, Cl_3. (b) The corresponding dendrogram. The clusters obtained after cutting the dendrogram at the dotted line are the clusters in (a).

Depending on the dissimilarity definition between two clusters of objects, a distinction is made between different cluster **linkage strategies**. **Single linkage** (Florek et al., 1951) calculates the dissimilarity between two clusters as the minimum distance between all pairs of objects drawn from the two clusters. Single linkage can produce elongated as well as concentric clusters. **Complete linkage** (Sorensen, 1948) takes the maximum distance instead. The resulting clusters tend to be compact. **Average linkage** (Sokal and Michener, 1958) uses the mean distance, and **centroid linkage** (Sokal and Michener, 1958) takes the distance between the cluster centroids. The centroid $\mathbf{c}_i = (c_{i1}, ..., c_{in})$ of cluster Cl_i is defined as the mean position of all the points in all dimensions, i.e., $c_{ir} = \frac{1}{|Cl_i|} \sum_{\mathbf{x}^i \in Cl_i} x_r^i$, $r = 1, ..., n$. Single linkage and centroid linkage have a chaining problem, where objects are assigned to existing clusters rather than being grouped in new clusters. **Ward's method** (Ward, 1963) computes the dissimilarity between two clusters Cl_i and Cl_j as the difference between the summed square distances to the centroid within cluster $Cl_i \cup Cl_j$ and the addition of the summed square distances to the centroid within cluster Cl_i and cluster Cl_j:

$$d_{\text{Ward}}(Cl_i, Cl_j) = \sum_{\mathbf{x}^k \in Cl_i \cup Cl_j} d\left(\mathbf{x}^k, \mathbf{c}^{ij}\right)$$

$$-\left[\sum_{\mathbf{x}^i \in Cl_i} d\left(\mathbf{x}^i, \mathbf{c}^i\right) + \sum_{\mathbf{x}^j \in Cl_j} d\left(\mathbf{x}^j, \mathbf{c}^j\right)\right],$$

where d denotes the squared Euclidean distance and $\mathbf{c}^{ij}$, $\mathbf{c}^i$ and $\mathbf{c}^j$ are the centroids of clusters $Cl_i \cup Cl_j$, Cl_i and Cl_j, respectively.

Average linkage, complete linkage and Ward's method are used when the clusters are expected to be more or less circular clouds.

2.3.2 K-Means Algorithm

The **K-means algorithm** is the most popular partitional clustering method. Partitional clustering aims at partitioning the dataset into clusters without forming a hierarchical structure. Partitional clustering assumes that there is a set of prototypes –the centroids– that represent the dataset. There are two types of partitional clustering methods: **virtual point prototype clustering** and **actual point prototype clustering**. In virtual point prototype clustering, cluster prototypes are not necessarily objects from the original dataset, whereas this is guaranteed to be the case in actual point prototype clustering. The K-means algorithm and spectral clustering are examples of virtual point prototype clustering, whereas affinity propagation is a method belonging to the actual point prototype clustering family.

Partitional clustering methods aim at optimizing a function F, referred to as **partitional clustering criterion**. The function value depends on the current partition $\{Cl_1, ..., Cl_K\}$ of the dataset into K clusters. The cardinality of the number of possible partitions $S(N, K)$ of N objects into K non-empty clusters is given by the **Stirling number of the second kind** (Sharp, 1968):

$$S(N, K) = \frac{1}{K!} \sum_{i=0}^{K} (-1)^{K-i} \binom{K}{i} i^N,$$

with initial conditions $S(0, 0) = 1$ and $S(N, 0) = S(0, N) = 0$. Since this number is huge even for a small N, an exhaustive search for the best clustering partition is infeasible, and heuristics need to be used to approximate the optimum partition.

The **K-means algorithm** (MacQueen, 1967) finds a locally optimal solution for the **square-error-criterion**, that is, the sum of the squared Euclidean distance between each object and its centroid. In mathematical notation, the function to be minimized is given by

$$F_{K-\text{means}}(\{Cl_1, ..., Cl_K\}) = \sum_{k=1}^{K} \sum_{\mathbf{x}^i \in Cl_k} ||\mathbf{x}^i - \mathbf{c}_k||_2^2, \qquad (2.2)$$

where K is the number of clusters, $\mathbf{x}^i = (x_1^i, ..., x_n^i)$ denotes the n components of the i-th object in the original dataset, Cl_k refers to the k-th cluster, and $\mathbf{c}_k = (\mathbf{c}_{k1}, ..., \mathbf{c}_{kn})$ is its corresponding centroid.

Algorithm 2.1 shows the main steps of the K-means algorithm. The K-means algorithm starts with an initial partition of the dataset. After calculating the centroids of these initial clusters, each dataset object is reallocated to the cluster represented by its nearest centroid. Reallocation should reduce the square-error criterion by taking into account the storage ordering of the objects. Whenever the cluster membership of an object changes, the corresponding cluster centroids and the square error should be recomputed. This process is repeated until all object cluster memberships are unchanged.

Algorithm 2.1: Pseudocode of the K-means algorithm (MacQueen, 1967)

> **Input** : An initial partition of the dataset into K clusters $\{Cl_1, ..., Cl_K\}$
> **Output** : Final partition into K clusters as a locally optimal solution of the square-error criterion

> **repeat**
> 1   Calculate cluster centroids: $\mathbf{c}_k = (c_{k1}, ..., c_{kn})$ with $c_{kr} = \frac{1}{|Cl_k|} \sum_{\mathbf{x}^i \in Cl_k} x_r^i, r = 1, ..., n;$
> 2   **for** $i = 1$ **to** N **do**
> 3   Reassign object $\mathbf{x}^i$ to its closest cluster centroid;
> 4   Recalculate centroids for clusters;
>   **endfor**
> **until** Cluster membership is stabilized

Forgy (1965) proposed a partitional clustering algorithm that differs from the above K-means algorithm in terms of how the centroids are updated. Forgy's method only calculates the new centroids once all objects have been assigned to their respective clusters (see Fig. 2.9). This averts the influence of the object storage ordering and speeds up the clustering process.

2.3.3   Spectral Clustering

Spectral clustering (Luxburg, 2007) represents the objects to be clustered as an undirected graph whose associated connectivity matrix is transformed in a sparse description that facilitates their posterior clustering. This sparse description is achieved by means of the eigenvectors of the matrix through

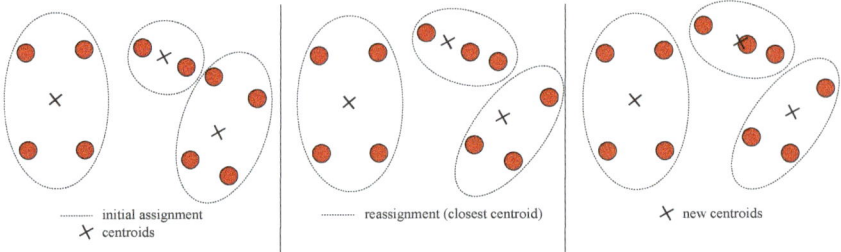

FIGURE 2.9

Example of the evolution of Forgy's method. Ten objects are initially partitioned into three clusters and their corresponding centroids are then computed (left). Reassignments of each object are done according to its nearest centroid (middle). The centroids of the new three clusters are then computed (right). The process ends since no object changes its cluster membership.

a transformation of the similarity matrix. Spectral clustering provides better solutions for datasets with arbitrarily shaped clusters than traditional hierarchical and K-means clustering methods.

The standard spectral clustering algorithm (Algorithm 2.2) starts by computing the similarity matrix $\mathbf{S} \in \mathbb{R}^{N \times N}$ from the N objects, $\mathbf{x}^1, ..., \mathbf{x}^N$, to be clustered. The elements of $\mathbf{S}$ are the similarities $s(\mathbf{x}^i, \mathbf{x}^j)$ between pairs of objects. This matrix is used to output the **similarity graph**, where the weight w_{ij} associated with the edge connecting objects $\mathbf{x}^i$ and $\mathbf{x}^j$ is equal to $s(\mathbf{x}^i, \mathbf{x}^j)$. The similarity graph is commonly transformed by means of one of the following three operations: the ϵ-**neighborhood graph**, where only objects (vertices) whose similarity is greater than ϵ are connected; the k-**nearest neighbor graph**, where one object is connected with another if this second object is one of the k-nearest neighbors of the first object; and the **fully connected graph**, where all pairs of objects (vertices) with positive similarity are connected.

The matrix resulting from this transformation is a non-negative symmetric matrix $\mathbf{W}$, known as the **weighted adjacency matrix**, with elements denoted by w_{ij}, which are equal to zero if their respective objects are not connected. The **degree of a vertex**, denoted by d_i, is defined as the sum of the weights over all adjacent vertices. The **degree matrix $\mathbf{D}$** is a diagonal matrix with degrees $d_1, ..., d_N$ on the diagonal. $\mathbf{W}$ and $\mathbf{D}$ play an important role in defining graph Laplacians. A **graph Laplacian** is a graph whose associated matrix is defined from $\mathbf{W}$ and $\mathbf{D}$ and whose algebraic properties can transform the original objects into a sparse representation according to which they can be easily grouped. The **unnormalized graph Laplacian matrix** is defined as $\mathbf{L} = \mathbf{D} - \mathbf{W}$.

Once the selected operation is carried out and the unnormalized graph Laplacian matrix $\mathbf{L}$ is calculated, the K eigenvectors corresponding to the K smallest eigenvalues of $\mathbf{L}$ are output. These K vectors are organized into a matrix with N rows and K columns. Each row of this new matrix can be interpreted as the transformation of an original object $\mathbf{x}^i$, with $i = 1, ..., N$, into a space where the object grouping is easier than in the original space. Although, in principle, these N transformed objects can be clustered using any clustering method, standard spectral clustering uses the K-means algorithm.

Algorithm 2.2: Pseudocode of the standard spectral clustering

---

Input : Similarity matrix $\mathbf{S} \in \mathbb{R}^{N \times N}$, number of clusters K
Output : Clusters $Cl_1, ..., Cl_K$

1 Construct a similarity graph from one of the three simple transformations: ϵ-neighborhood graph, k-nearest neighbor graph and fully connected graph. Let $\mathbf{W}$ be its weighted adjacency matrix and $\mathbf{D}$ its degree matrix
2 Compute the unnormalized graph Laplacian matrix $\mathbf{L} = \mathbf{D} - \mathbf{W}$
3 Compute the first K eigenvectors $\mathbf{v}_1, ..., \mathbf{v}_K$ corresponding to the K smallest eigenvalues of $\mathbf{L}$
4 Compute $\mathbf{V} \in \mathbb{R}^{N \times K}$, the matrix containing the K vectors $\mathbf{v}_1, ..., \mathbf{v}_K$ as columns
5 Let $\mathbf{y}^i \in \mathbb{R}^K$, with $i = 1, ..., N$, be the vector corresponding to the i-th row of $\mathbf{V}$
6 Cluster the points $\mathbf{y}^1, ..., \mathbf{y}^N$ in $\mathbb{R}^K$ with the K-means algorithm into clusters $Cl_1, ..., Cl_K$

2.3.4 Affinity Propagation

Affinity propagation algorithm (Frey and Dueck, 2007) is based on the concept of message passing between objects. The goal is to find a subset of cluster prototypes, referred here as **exemplars**, that are members of the input dataset. All objects are simultaneously considered as potential exemplars, avoiding the selection of initial cluster prototypes. The number of clusters, K, does not have to be determined before running the algorithm.

The algorithm considers a graph where each vertex is an object. Real-valued messages are recursively sent along edges of the graph until a good set of exemplars and their corresponding clusters emerge. The similarity $s(\mathbf{x}^i, \mathbf{x}^j)$ between objects $\mathbf{x}^i$ and $\mathbf{x}^j$ is an input. The algorithm proceeds by alternating two message-passing steps to update two matrices: the **responsibility matrix**, whose values $r(\mathbf{x}^i, \mathbf{x}^k)$ quantify how well-suited $\mathbf{x}^k$ is to serve as the exemplar for $\mathbf{x}^i$ relative to other candidate exemplars for $\mathbf{x}^i$; and the **availability matrix** with elements $a(\mathbf{x}^i, \mathbf{x}^k)$ representing how appropriate it would be for $\mathbf{x}^i$ to pick $\mathbf{x}^k$ as its exemplar, considering other objects' preference for $\mathbf{x}^k$ as an exemplar. Both matrices are initialized to all zeros. The algorithm then performs the following updates iteratively:

1. Responsibility updates are sent around:

$$r(\mathbf{x}^i, \mathbf{x}^k) \leftarrow s(\mathbf{x}^i, \mathbf{x}^k) - \max_{k' \neq k}\{a(\mathbf{x}^i, \mathbf{x}^{k'}) + s(\mathbf{x}^i, \mathbf{x}^{k'})\}.$$

2. Availabilities are updated:

$$a(\mathbf{x}^i, \mathbf{x}^k) \quad \leftarrow \quad \min\left\{0, r(\mathbf{x}^k, \mathbf{x}^k) + \sum_{i' \notin \{i,k\}} \max\{0, r(\mathbf{x}^{i'}, \mathbf{x}^k)\}\right\}$$

$$a(\mathbf{x}^k, \mathbf{x}^k) \quad \leftarrow \quad \sum_{i' \neq k} \max\{0, r(\mathbf{x}^{i'}, \mathbf{x}^k)\}.$$

The iterations continue until the stopping condition is met. For object $\mathbf{x}^i$, the object $\mathbf{x}^j$ that maximizes $a(\mathbf{x}^i, \mathbf{x}^j) + r(\mathbf{x}^i, \mathbf{x}^j)$ identifies its exemplar. A cluster contains all the objects that have the same exemplar, which is considered as the cluster prototype.

2.3.5 Probabilistic Clustering

Hierarchical and partitional methods are **crisp clustering** approaches, since they assign each object to one and only one cluster. However, cluster solutions assigning to each object a probability of belonging to each of the clusters can be helpful in some practical applications in industry. This is known as **soft clustering** or **probabilistic clustering**.

Probabilistic clustering is based on fitting the density of the dataset to **finite mixture models**. These models fit the density of the data with a weighted finite number of different component densities, usually assumed to be parametric. Fig. 2.10 shows an example of a finite mixture model for fitting the servomotor power consumption density to three standard clusters of patterns of variation (idle, acceleration/deceleration and constant speed). In this example, the three mixture component densities are univariate Gaussians.

The parametric finite mixture model has the form

$$f(\mathbf{x}; \boldsymbol{\theta}) = \sum_{k=1}^{K} \pi_k f_k(\mathbf{x}; \boldsymbol{\theta}_k),$$

where $\boldsymbol{\theta} = (\pi_1, ..., \pi_K, \boldsymbol{\theta}_1, ..., \boldsymbol{\theta}_K)$ denotes the parameter vector, π_k represents the k-th mixing proportion (or component priors) and verifies $0 \leq \pi_k \leq 1$ for all $k = 1, 2, ..., K$ and $\sum_{k=1}^{K} \pi_k = 1$. The functional form of the probability density of the mixture components, $f_k(\mathbf{x}; \boldsymbol{\theta}_k)$, is assumed to be known, although it depends on the unknown parameter $\boldsymbol{\theta}_k$. The number of components of the mixture is K.

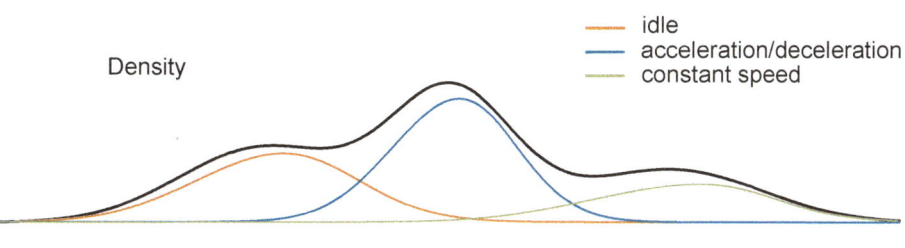

FIGURE 2.10
Example of a finite mixture model with three components for fitting
servomotor power consumption density. The three components correspond to
idle (orange), acceleration/deceleration (blue) and constant speed (green)
states. The density of each component is assumed to follow a univariate
Gaussian.

To fit these finite mixture models, we need to estimate $\boldsymbol{\theta}_k$ parameters
characterizing the component densities and the mixing proportions π_k. Maximum
likelihood estimation sets out likelihood equations with non-closed-form
solutions. Therefore, procedures to approximate these solutions, mainly the
expectation maximization (EM) algorithm (Dempster et al., 1977), are
widely applied.

The **EM algorithm** is an iterative procedure to approximate maximum
likelihood estimations (Section 2.2.2) in the presence of missing (or hidden)
data. In probabilistic clustering with finite mixture models, the assignment of
each data point to a cluster is hidden (missing) and it is encoded by a cluster
random variable. Each iteration of the EM algorithm is a two-step procedure:
the expectation or **E-step** and the maximization or **M-step**. In the E-step, the
missing data are estimated given the observed data and the current estimate
of the finite mixture model parameters. This is achieved using the conditional
expectation of the missing data. The estimation of the missing data provided
by the E-step is used to output a version of the so-called complete data. In
the M-step, the log-likelihood function is maximized under the assumption
that the missing data are known. The EM algorithm is guaranteed to increase
the likelihood at each iteration, ensuring convergence under certain regularity
conditions.

In mathematical notation, given a model that generates a set[2] of observed
data $\mathbf{X}$, a set of unobserved hidden data or missing values $\mathbf{Z}$, and a vector of
unknown parameters $\boldsymbol{\theta}$, and denoting by $\mathcal{L}(\boldsymbol{\theta}; \mathbf{X}, \mathbf{Z})$ the likelihood function,

---

[2]To comply with the standard notation used in EM algorithm literature, the dataset $\mathcal{D}$
possibly containing observed and missing data is not referred to here. $\mathcal{D}$ corresponds to the
concatenation of data $\mathbf{X}$ and $\mathbf{Z}$.

the maximum likelihood estimate of the unknown parameters is determined by the marginal likelihood of the observed data

$$\mathcal{L}(\boldsymbol{\theta}; \mathbf{X}) = p(\mathbf{X}|\boldsymbol{\theta}) = \sum_{\mathbf{Z}} p(\mathbf{X}, \mathbf{Z}|\boldsymbol{\theta}).$$

Maximizing this function is hard and the EM algorithm tries to find the maximum likelihood estimate by iteratively applying two steps:

E-step: Calculate the expected value of the log-likelihood function with respect to the conditional distribution of $\mathbf{Z}$ given $\mathbf{X}$ under the current estimate of the parameters $\boldsymbol{\theta}^{(t)}$. To do this, an auxiliary function $Q(\boldsymbol{\theta}|\boldsymbol{\theta}^{(t)})$ is defined as

$$Q(\boldsymbol{\theta}|\boldsymbol{\theta}^{(t)}) = \mathbb{E}_{\mathbf{Z}|\mathbf{X}, \boldsymbol{\theta}^{(t)}}[\log \mathcal{L}(\boldsymbol{\theta}; \mathbf{X}, \mathbf{Z})].$$

M-step: Maximize the log-likelihood function to find the parameter value

$$\boldsymbol{\theta}^{(t+1)} = \arg \max_{\boldsymbol{\theta}} Q(\boldsymbol{\theta}|\boldsymbol{\theta}^{(t)}).$$

The EM algorithm computes $Q(\boldsymbol{\theta}|\boldsymbol{\theta}^{(t)})$ at each iteration t, operating with expectations of the complete-data log-likelihood, rather than directly improving $\log p(\mathbf{X}|\boldsymbol{\theta})$. This is because improvements to $Q(\boldsymbol{\theta}|\boldsymbol{\theta}^{(t)})$ imply improvements to the $\log p(\mathbf{X}|\boldsymbol{\theta})$. Additionally, the marginal likelihood never deteriorates as the iterations progress, i.e., $\log p(\mathbf{X}|\boldsymbol{\theta}^{(t+1)}) \geq \log p(\mathbf{X}|\boldsymbol{\theta}^{(t)})$ can be proved (McLachlan and Krishnan, 1997). The initialization of the EM algorithm is crucial for the quality of the estimation, but no method uniformly outperforms the others (Figueiredo and Jain (2002)).

The most popular parametric finite mixture model has Gaussian components (Day, 1969), i.e., the **multivariate Gaussian mixture model**, whose density function is

$$f(\mathbf{x}; \boldsymbol{\theta}) = \sum_{k=1}^{K} \pi_k f_k(\mathbf{x}; \boldsymbol{\mu}_k, \boldsymbol{\Sigma}_k),$$

where $\boldsymbol{\mu}_k$ is the mean vector and $\boldsymbol{\Sigma}_k$ is the variance-covariance matrix for the k-th component, a **multivariate normal density** given by

$$f_k(\mathbf{x}; \boldsymbol{\mu}_k, \boldsymbol{\Sigma}_k) = (2\pi)^{-\frac{n}{2}} |\boldsymbol{\Sigma}_k|^{-\frac{1}{2}} \exp\left(-\frac{1}{2}(\mathbf{x} - \boldsymbol{\mu}_k)^T \boldsymbol{\Sigma}_k^{-1}(\mathbf{x} - \boldsymbol{\mu}_k)\right).$$

The parameter vector $\boldsymbol{\theta} = (\pi_1, ..., \pi_K, \boldsymbol{\mu}_1, \boldsymbol{\Sigma}_1, ..., \boldsymbol{\mu}_K, \boldsymbol{\Sigma}_K)$ is composed of the weights of the different clusters, π_k, and of the parameters, $\boldsymbol{\theta}_k = (\boldsymbol{\mu}_k, \boldsymbol{\Sigma}_k)$, of each component of the mixture.

The missing information $\mathbf{z} = (z_1, ..., z_N)$ relates to the assignment (yes/no) of each data point to each cluster. The auxiliary function of the expected complete data log-likelihood is

$$Q(\boldsymbol{\theta}|\boldsymbol{\theta}^{(t)}) = \sum_{i=1}^{N} \sum_{k=1}^{K} r_{ik}^{(t)} \log \pi_k + \sum_{i=1}^{N} \sum_{k=1}^{K} r_{ik}^{(t)} \log f_k(\mathbf{x}; \boldsymbol{\theta}_k),$$

where $r_{ik}^{(t)} = p(Z_i = k|\mathbf{x}_i, \boldsymbol{\theta}^{(t)})$ is the **responsibility** that cluster k takes for the i-th data point, computed in the E-step.

E-step: The responsibility at iteration t has the following simple form:

$$r_{ik}^{(t)} = \frac{\pi_k^{(t)} f_k(\mathbf{x}_i; \boldsymbol{\mu}_k^{(t)}, \boldsymbol{\Sigma}_k^{(t)})}{\sum_{r=1}^{K} \pi_r^{(t)} f_r(\mathbf{x}_i; \boldsymbol{\mu}_r^{(t)}, \boldsymbol{\Sigma}_r^{(t)})}.$$

M-step: We optimize $Q(\boldsymbol{\theta}|\boldsymbol{\theta}^{(t)})$ with respect to $\boldsymbol{\theta}$. For π_k, we get

$$\pi_k^{(t+1)} = \frac{1}{N} \sum_{i=1}^{N} r_{ik}^{(t)}.$$

For $\boldsymbol{\mu}_k$ and $\boldsymbol{\Sigma}_k$,

$$\boldsymbol{\mu}_k^{(t+1)} = \frac{\sum_{i=1}^{N} r_{ik}^{(t)} \mathbf{x}_i}{\sum_{i=1}^{N} r_{ik}^{(t)}}$$

$$\boldsymbol{\Sigma}_k^{(t+1)} = \frac{\sum_{i=1}^{N} r_{ik}^{(t)} (\mathbf{x}_i - \boldsymbol{\mu}_k^{(t+1)})(\mathbf{x}_i - \boldsymbol{\mu}_k^{(t+1)})^T}{\sum_{i=1}^{N} r_{ik}^{(t)}}.$$

These formulas are intuitive: the weight $\pi_k^{(t+1)}$ of each mixture is updated as the average responsibility; the mean of cluster k, $\boldsymbol{\mu}_k^{(t+1)}$, is computed as the weighted average of all data points, where the weights are the responsibilities of cluster k, and, finally, the variance-covariance matrix, $\boldsymbol{\Sigma}_k^{(t+1)}$, is an empirical variance-covariance matrix again weighted using responsibilities. The new estimates

$$\boldsymbol{\theta}^{(t+1)} = (\pi_1^{(t+1)}, ..., \pi_K^{(t+1)}, \boldsymbol{\mu}_1^{(t+1)}, \boldsymbol{\Sigma}_1^{(t+1)}, ..., \boldsymbol{\mu}_K^{(t+1)}, \boldsymbol{\Sigma}_K^{(t+1)})$$

will be used by the E-step in the next iteration of the algorithm.

2.4 Supervised Classification

Supervised classification methods aim to learn models from labeled instances (or cases), i.e., instances with information about predictor variables and the class to which they each belong. The induced model (or classifier) will be used for predicting (inferring) the class value (label) of new instances, each characterized by its predictor variables only.

Three components are fundamental for any supervised classification learning method:

1. An **instance space**, $\Omega_{\mathbf{X}} = \Omega_{X_1} \times \cdots \times \Omega_{X_n}$, containing instances $\mathbf{x} = (x_1, ..., x_n) \in \mathbb{R}^n$ drawn according to some fixed but unknown multivariate probability distribution, $p(\mathbf{x})$. x_i is drawn from the subspace Ω_{X_i} for all $i \in \{1, ..., n\}$, and contains the value of the i-th predictor variable, X_i.

2. A **label space**, Ω_C, containing, for each instance $\mathbf{x} = (x_1, ..., x_n)$, the value, c, of its label, generated from a random variable C. The conditional probability distribution of labels for a given vector of the instance space, $p(c|\mathbf{x})$, and the joint distribution, $p(\mathbf{x}, c)$, of labeled instances are also unknown.

3. A **learning algorithm** able to map instances from the instance space to labels in the label space. Each mapping function refers to a type of supervised classification method. The application of the learning algorithm to a dataset of labeled instances, $\mathcal{D} = \{(\mathbf{x}^1, c^1), ..., (\mathbf{x}^N, c^N)\}$, will provide a **supervised classification model** (or simply a classifier) denoted by ϕ:

$$\begin{aligned} \Omega_{\mathbf{X}} &\xrightarrow{\phi} \Omega_C \\ \mathbf{x} &\to \phi(\mathbf{x}). \end{aligned}$$

This transformation defines a **decision boundary** that partitions the instance space into several subspaces, one for each class. Thus, for binary classification problems, the classifier will classify all the points on one side of the decision boundary as belonging to one class and all the points on the other side as belonging to the other class. If the decision boundary is a hyperplane, and the classifier correctly classifies all instances, then the classification problem is linear, and the classes are linearly separable.

Supervised classification models can be categorized into **non-probabilistic classifiers**, which output a fixed class label for each instance, and **probabilistic classifiers**, which provide an estimation of $p(c|\mathbf{x})$, the conditional probability distribution of labels for a given instance. K-nearest neighbors, classification trees, rule induction, artificial neural networks and support vector machines are examples of non-probabilistic classifiers, whereas logistic regression and Bayesian classifiers belong to the family of probabilistic classifiers.

Example. A binary classification problem

Table 2.3 shows the output of a binary classifier with n predictor variables. Instances 1 and 10 are incorrectly classified. For instance 1, the true class is +, and the classifier output is -. For instance 10, the true class is -, and the classifier output is +. ∎

TABLE 2.3

Output of a binary classifier, $\phi(\mathbf{x})$, on a hypothetical dataset with ten cases and two labels, + and –

Cases	X_1	...	X_n	C	$\phi(\mathbf{x})$
$(\mathbf{x}^1, c^1)$	17.2	...	20.4	+	–
$(\mathbf{x}^2, c^2)$	17.1	...	21.7	+	+
$(\mathbf{x}^3, c^3)$	16.4	...	23.2	+	+
$(\mathbf{x}^4, c^4)$	16.7	...	20.1	+	+
$(\mathbf{x}^5, c^5)$	18.9	...	18.4	–	–
$(\mathbf{x}^6, c^6)$	19.2	...	17.9	–	–
$(\mathbf{x}^7, c^7)$	20.7	...	15.9	–	–
$(\mathbf{x}^8, c^8)$	18.1	...	18.8	–	–
$(\mathbf{x}^9, c^9)$	19.9	...	17.2	–	–
$(\mathbf{x}^{10}, c^{10})$	21.5	...	16.9	–	+

2.4.1 Model Performance Evaluation

2.4.1.1 Performance Evaluation Measures

Performance evaluation measures (Japkowicz and Mohak, 2011) are used as figures of merit for supervised classifiers. There are several measures. Their choice depends on the objective and characteristics of the supervised classification problem, as well as on the type of classifier used. The aim of any supervised classification algorithm is to choose an optimal classifier, i.e., with the optimum value of a selected performance measure[3].

The **confusion matrix** contains the key elements required in most common performance measures. Its (i, j)-th element denotes the number of cases that actually have a class i label and that the classifier ϕ assigns to class j. Standard performance measures are defined as a function of the confusion matrix entries, implicitly using a zero-one loss function. In a zero-one loss function, the cost of a correct classification is zero, while the cost of any type of mistake is one. Cost-specific performance measures are defined based on the confusion matrix and a **cost matrix**, indicating the cost of each possible type of classifier mistake.

In binary classification problems –easily generalized to multiclass classification problems, where there are more than two class values– the four counters for the confusion matrix are the **true positives** (TP), **false positives** (FP), **false negatives** (FN), and **true negatives** (TN), that is, the confusion matrix is

---

[3]This book does not discuss qualitative measures like the transparency, the comprehensibility or the simplicity of the learned model, which are also important in practice.

$$\phi(\mathbf{x})$$

$$C \quad \begin{array}{c} + \\ \\ - \end{array} \begin{pmatrix} \begin{array}{cc} + & - \\ \text{TP} & \text{FN} \\ \\ \text{FP} & \text{TN} \end{array} \end{pmatrix}$$

TP and TN are the number of instances correctly classified as positive and negative, respectively. FN and FP are misclassifications, i.e., positive and negative instances classified as negative and positive, respectively.

Table 2.4 lists eight main performance measures defined from the confusion matrix.

TABLE 2.4

Eight main performance measures in binary classification problems. In the Cohen's kappa statistic, $A = \left(\frac{\text{FN}+\text{TP}}{N}\right)\left(\frac{\text{FP}+\text{TP}}{N}\right) + \left(\frac{\text{FP}+\text{TN}}{N}\right)\left(\frac{\text{FN}+\text{TN}}{N}\right)$

Measure name	Notation	Definition
Accuracy	$\text{Acc}(\phi)$	$\frac{\text{TP}+\text{TN}}{\text{TP}+\text{FN}+\text{FP}+\text{TN}}$
Error rate	$\text{Err}(\phi)$	$\frac{\text{FN}+\text{FP}}{\text{TP}+\text{FN}+\text{FP}+\text{TN}}$
Sensitivity	$\text{Sensitivity}(\phi)$	$\frac{\text{TP}}{\text{TP}+\text{FN}}$
Specificity	$\text{Specificity}(\phi)$	$\frac{\text{TN}}{\text{FP}+\text{TN}}$
Positive predictive value	$\text{PPV}(\phi)$	$\frac{\text{TP}}{\text{TP}+\text{FP}}$
Negative predictive value	$\text{NPV}(\phi)$	$\frac{\text{TN}}{\text{TN}+\text{FN}}$
F_1 measure	$F_1(\phi)$	$\frac{2[\text{PPV}(\phi)\cdot\text{Sensitivity}(\phi)]}{\text{PPV}(\phi)+\text{Sensitivity}(\phi)}$
Cohen's kappa statistic	$\kappa(\phi)$	$\frac{\frac{\text{TP}}{N}+\frac{\text{TN}}{N}-A}{1-A}$

Classification accuracy measures the fraction of instances correctly classified by the classification model. Conversely, error rate measures the proportion of misclassifications. Thus, $\text{Acc}(\phi) + \text{Err}(\phi) = 1$. Sensitivity, also known as **recall** or the **true positive rate** (TPR), represents the proportion of true positives successfully detected by the classifier. Specificity is defined similarly for true negatives. The **false positive rate** (FPR) is one minus specificity. The **positive predictive value**, also known as **precision**, measures the proportion of correctly assigned positive instances. The **negative predictive value** is defined similarly for negative instances. The **F_1 measure** is the harmonic mean of the precision and recall measures. Cohen's kappa statistic (Cohen, 1960) first corrects the accuracy measure considering the result of a chance match between the classifier, $\phi(\mathbf{x})$, and the label generation process, C. The bottom row of Table 2.4 shows the numerator, where the expected proportion of matched instances under the null hypothesis of independence between the true class and the predicted class (mere chance) is subtracted from the classification accuracy. Then the measure is normalized between 0 and 1, as specified in its denominator. All eight performance measures above take values in the interval $[0, 1]$. Values close to 1 are preferred for all the measures, except for error rate. Values close to 0 are better for error rate.

The **Brier score** (Brier, 1950) is very popular for probabilistic classifiers. The Brier score is based on a quadratic cost function and measures the mean square difference (d, the Euclidean distance) between the predicted probability assigned to the possible outcomes for each instance and its actual label. It is defined as

$$\text{Brier}(\phi) = \frac{1}{N} \sum_{i=1}^{N} d^2 \left(p_\phi(\mathbf{c}|\mathbf{x}^i), \mathbf{c}^i \right),$$

where $p_\phi(\mathbf{c}|\mathbf{x}^i)$ is the vector $(p_\phi(\texttt{+}|\mathbf{x}^i), p_\phi(\texttt{-}|\mathbf{x}^i))$ containing the output of the probabilistic classifier, and $\mathbf{c}^i = (1, 0)$ or $\mathbf{c}^i = (0, 1)$ when the label of the i-th instance is **+** or **-**, respectively. The Brier score for a binary classification problem verifies $0 \leq \text{Brier}(\phi) \leq 2$, and values close to 0 are preferred. The Brier score can be regarded as a measure of calibration of a set of probabilistic predictions.

Example. Brier score

Table 2.5 contains the predictions given by a probabilistic classifier ϕ on ten cases. The Brier score is computed as

$$\text{Brier}(\phi) = \frac{1}{10} \left[(0.25 - 1)^2 + (0.75 - 0)^2 + \cdots + (0.08 - 0)^2 + (0.92 - 1)^2 \right]$$
$$= 0.3226.$$

TABLE 2.5

Output of a probabilistic classifier, $p_\phi(\mathbf{c}|\mathbf{x})$, on a hypothetical dataset, with ten cases, and two labels, **+**, and **-**

Cases	X_1	$\ldots$	X_n	C	$p_\phi(\mathbf{c}|\mathbf{x})$
$(\mathbf{x}^1, c^1)$	17.2	$\ldots$	20.4	+	(0.25, 0.75)
$(\mathbf{x}^2, c^2)$	17.1	$\ldots$	21.7	+	(0.95, 0.05)
$(\mathbf{x}^3, c^3)$	16.4	$\ldots$	23.2	+	(0.80, 0.20)
$(\mathbf{x}^4, c^4)$	16.7	$\ldots$	20.1	+	(0.77, 0.23)
$(\mathbf{x}^5, c^5)$	18.9	$\ldots$	18.4	-	(0.65, 0.35)
$(\mathbf{x}^6, c^6)$	19.2	$\ldots$	17.9	-	(0.45, 0.55)
$(\mathbf{x}^7, c^7)$	20.7	$\ldots$	15.9	-	(0.32, 0.68)
$(\mathbf{x}^8, c^8)$	18.1	$\ldots$	18.8	-	(0.02, 0.98)
$(\mathbf{x}^9, c^9)$	19.9	$\ldots$	17.2	-	(0.47, 0.53)
$(\mathbf{x}^{10}, c^{10})$	21.5	$\ldots$	16.9	-	(0.08, 0.92)

A receiver operating characteristic (ROC), or simply **ROC curve** (Lusted, 1960), is defined in a unit square space and shows the binary classifier performance as its discrimination threshold is varied. The discrimination threshold is a cutoff value for the posterior probability $p_\phi(C = +|\mathbf{x})$. Each point of the plot corresponds to a given discrimination threshold. The x- and y-axes are FPR and TPR, respectively. This is why the ROC curve is sometimes called the (1 - specificity) vs. sensitivity plot. The polygonal curve yielded by connecting all pairs of consecutive points shapes the ROC curve.

The point $(0,0)$ denotes the classifier that classifies all instances as negative, yielding FPR=TPR=0. The point $(1,1)$ represents the classifier labeling all instances as positive, hence FPR=TPR=1. Points $(1,0)$ and $(0,1)$ provide the other two end points of the ROC space. The point $(1,0)$ denotes a classifier that makes mistakes in all its predictions. By contrast, the point $(0,1)$ signifies the best, error-free, classifier. The diagonal of the ROC space connecting points $(0,0)$ and $(1,1)$ verifies FPR = TPR at all the points. These points denote **random classifiers**. Classifiers represented by points above (below) the diagonal perform better (worse) than random classifiers. As a rule of thumb, for two points $(\text{FPR}_1, \text{TPR}_1)$ and $(\text{FPR}_2, \text{TPR}_2)$ in the ROC space, $(\text{FPR}_1, \text{TPR}_1)$ represents a better classifier than $(\text{FPR}_2, \text{TPR}_2)$ if $(\text{FPR}_1, \text{TPR}_1)$ is on the left and higher up than $(\text{FPR}_2, \text{TPR}_2)$.

A simple algorithm for the generation of a ROC curve is described in Fawcett (2006), see Algorithm 2.3. Let *min* and *max* be the smallest and largest continuous output values returned by the classifier $\phi(\mathbf{x}^i)$ for instance $\mathbf{x}^i$, i.e., $p(+|\mathbf{x}^i)$ for a probabilistic classifier, and let *incr* be the smallest difference between any two output values. Let N_+ and N_- be the number of real positive and negative cases, respectively. Threshold values t are $min, min + incr, min + 2 \cdot incr, ..., max$. TP and FP are initialized as 0 (Lines 2 and 3). Then if $\phi(\mathbf{x}^i) \geq t$ (Line 5), the TP counter is incremented by one if the case is positive (Line 6); for negative cases (Line 7) the FP counter is incremented by one. TPR and FPR are computed (Lines 8 and 9) and the associated point (FPR, TPR) is added to the ROC curve (Line 10).

Example. ROC curve

Table 2.6 shows the hypothetical outputs $(p(+|\mathbf{x}^i))$ assigned by a probabilistic classifier and the true class labels (c^i) of ten instances $(\mathbf{x}^i)$.

Following Algorithm 2.3, we start with $t = 0.26$. Note that `incr`=0.01. With this threshold, the five positive instances are well classified, but the five negative instances, all with outputs greater than or equal to 0.26, are misclassified. Then point $(1,1)$ is added to the ROC curve, see Fig. 2.11. All thresholds up to 0.29 yield the same results. With $t = 0.29$, instance $\mathbf{x}^{10}$ is correctly classified as $-$, and we get FPR $= 0.80$, and TPR $= 1$. This point $(0.80, 1)$ represents the second point in Fig. 2.11. The next significant threshold is 0.34, which yields the third point, $(0.60, 1)$, on the curve. The other points are generated in a similar fashion. Fig. 2.11 shows the ROC curve produced by drawing a polygonal curve through these points.

Algorithm 2.3: Pseudocode for a simple algorithm for building a ROC curve

---

Input : A classifier ϕ, and constants $min, max, incr, N_+, N_-$
Output: A ROC curve

```
1  for t = min to max by incr do
2  |   TP = 0
3  |   FP = 0
4  |   for xⁱ ∈ 𝒟 do
5  |   |   if φ(xⁱ) ≥ t then
6  |   |   |   if xⁱ is a positive case then
       |   |   |   |   TP = TP +1
7  |   |   |   else
       |   |   |   |   FP = FP +1
       |   |   endif
       |   endfor
8  |   TPR = TP/N₊
9  |   FPR = FP/N₋
10 |   Add point (FPR, TPR) to ROC curve
   endfor
```

TABLE 2.6
Ten hypothetical instances used to generate the ROC curve shown in Fig. 2.11

x^i	1	2	3	4	5	6	7	8	9	10
$p(+|x^i)$	0.98	0.89	0.81	0.79	0.64	0.52	0.39	0.34	0.29	0.26
c^i	+	+	+	−	+	−	+	−	−	−

∎

The **area under the ROC curve** (AUC) is a summary statistic for the ROC curve. For any classifier ϕ, $\text{AUC}(\phi) \in [0, 1]$. $\text{AUC}(\phi) = 1$ in a perfect classifier (FPR = 0, TPR = 1), whereas $\text{AUC}(\phi_{\text{random}}) = 0.5$ for a random classifier. We expect $\text{AUC}(\phi) > 0.5$ for a reasonable classifier. To compute the AUC, a rank is assigned to the classifier output for each instance in the order of decreasing outputs. Then, the AUC is computed as

$$\text{AUC}(\phi) = 1 - \frac{\sum_{i=1}^{N_+}(i - \text{rank}_i)}{N_+ N_-}, \tag{2.3}$$

where rank_i is the rank of the i-th case in the subset of positive labels given by classifier ϕ, and N_+ and N_- denote the number of real positive and negative cases in $\mathcal{D}$, respectively.

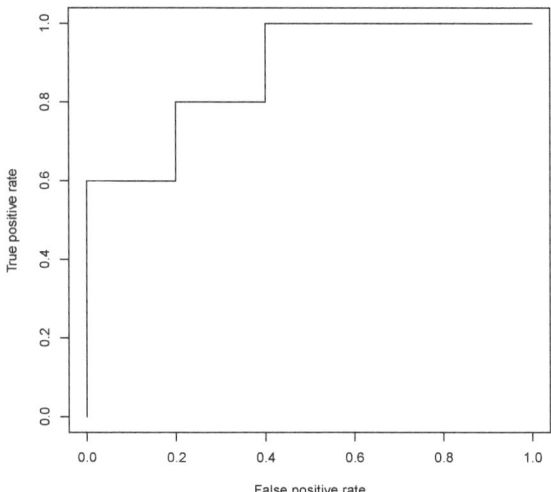

FIGURE 2.11
ROC curve for Table 2.6 data, plotted with the ROCR R package (Sing et al., 2005).

Example. AUC

The result of applying the above formula to the instances in Table 2.6 is:

$$\text{AUC}(\phi) = 1 - \frac{(1-1) + (2-2) + (3-3) + (5-4) + (7-5)}{5 \cdot 5} = 0.88.$$

This is the same result as illustrated in Fig. 2.11:

$$\text{AUC}(\phi) = 0.20 \cdot 0.60 + 0.20 \cdot 0.80 + 0.60 \cdot 1.00 = 0.88.$$

■

For a multiclass problem, the AUC can be obtained as the volume under the ROC surface or, alternatively, as an average AUC of all possible ROC curves obtained from all class pairs.

2.4.1.2 Honest Performance Estimation Methods

This section focuses on how to honestly estimate the performance evaluation measures. A supervised classification model should be able to generalize well on unseen data from the same probability distribution as the training data. **Honest performance estimation methods** estimate the performance measure based on cases that have not previously been seen in the learning phase by the classifier. The **resubstitution method** learns the classifier on a training set that is later used as a testing set. This method is not honest. It usually overfits the data that it was trained on, and its accuracy estimate is optimistically biased.

Fig. 2.12, adapted from Japkowicz and Mohak (2011), shows the honest performance estimation methods explained below. They are grouped into multiple resampling methods, where $\mathcal{D}$ is sampled several times, and single resampling methods, with only one sampling.

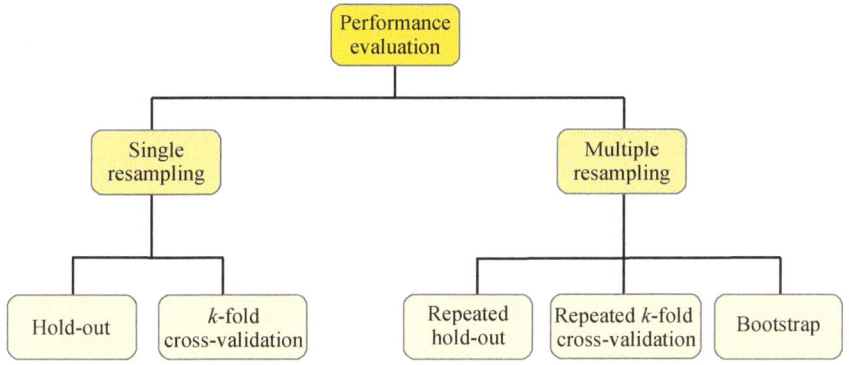

FIGURE 2.12
Honest performance estimation methods.

The **hold-out estimation method** partitions the dataset of cases, $\mathcal{D} = \{(\mathbf{x}^1, c^1), ..., (\mathbf{x}^N, c^N)\}$ into two disjoint data subsets: the **training dataset**, $\mathcal{D}_{\text{training}}$, with N_1 cases and the **test dataset**, $\mathcal{D}_{\text{test}}$, with the other cases. A classifier ϕ_{training} is induced from $\mathcal{D}_{\text{training}}$ by the supervised classification learning algorithm. This model is applied to the unlabeled set of instances of $\mathcal{D}_{\text{test}}$. The performance measures are honestly estimated by comparing true class labels and predictions given by the model ($\phi_{\text{training}}(\mathbf{x})$ or $\hat{c}$) (see Fig. 2.13).

This method is very simple but has several drawbacks. First, the training dataset, instead of the whole dataset, is used to learn the final model. Second, the user has to decide the ratio of the training dataset to the whole dataset (usually 2/3).

k-**fold cross-validation** (Kurtz, 1948) randomly partitions $\mathcal{D}$ into k folds, i.e., subsets of roughly equal sizes. A single fold is held out for testing the model, and the remaining $k-1$ folds are used as training data. This is repeated k times, with each of the k folds. The k results of the performance measure yielded by the testing data are averaged to produce an estimation of the performance of the model induced from $\mathcal{D}$. Unlike hold-out, the final model is learned from the whole dataset, see Fig. 2.14. k must be fixed by the user. The k-fold cross-validation estimator is almost unbiased, but its variance can be large.

The folds in **leave-one-out cross-validation** include only one case, i.e., it is a N-fold cross-validation. Due to its computational burden, it can only be applied to small datasets. In **stratified k-fold cross-validation**, the folds

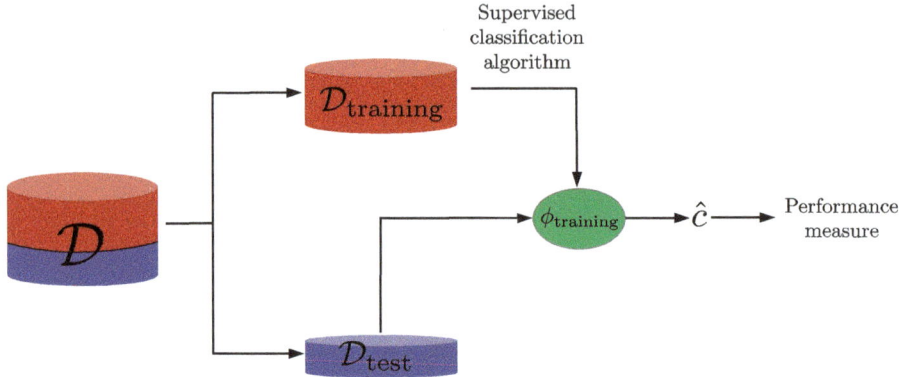

FIGURE 2.13
Hold-out estimation method.

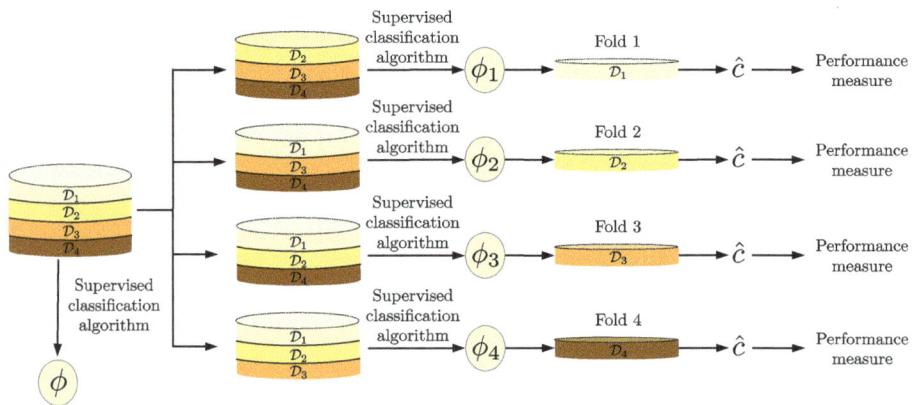

FIGURE 2.14
Four-fold cross-validation method.

are chosen such that the class variable is approximately equally distributed in all folds and similar to the original class distribution in $\mathcal{D}$. Stratification is appropriate for unbalanced datasets, where the class variable is far from being uniformly distributed.

In **repeated hold-out**, the partition in the hold-out scheme is repeated several times. The training and test cases are randomly assigned every time. This resampling has the advantage that estimates are stable (low variance), as a result of a large number of sampling repetitions. A drawback is that there is no control over the number of times each case is used in the training or testing datasets. **Repeated k-fold cross-validation** performs multiple rounds of k-fold cross-validation using different partitions. The most popular version is 10×10 cross-validation (Bouckaert, 2003), which performs 10 repetitions of 10-fold cross-validation, reducing estimator variance.

Bootstrapping (Efron, 1979) generates estimations by sampling from the empirical distribution of the observed data. It is implemented by using random sampling with replacement from the original dataset $\mathcal{D}$ to produce several (B) resamples of equal size N to the original dataset. Thus, all the datasets $\mathcal{D}_b^l$, with $l \in \{1, ..., B\}$, obtained are of size N. As the probability of selection is always the same for each of the N cases (i.e., $1/N$), the probability of a case not being chosen after N selections is $(1 - \frac{1}{N})^N \approx \frac{1}{e} \approx 0.368$. A classifier ϕ_b^l is induced from $\mathcal{D}_b^l$. The l-th test set, $\mathcal{D}_{b\text{-test}}^l$, with $l \in \{1, ..., B\}$, is then formed by all the cases from $\mathcal{D}$ not present in $\mathcal{D}_b^l$, that is, $\mathcal{D}_{b\text{-test}}^l = \mathcal{D} \setminus \mathcal{D}_b^l$. The performance measure of ϕ_b^l is estimated. The average of all B measures is known as the **e0 bootstrap** estimate.

The expected number of distinct instances in each of the B datasets $\mathcal{D}_b^l$ used for training ϕ_b^l is $0.632N$. Hence, the $e0$ bootstrap estimate may be pessimistic. The **.632 bootstrap** estimate addresses this issue by combining the $e0$ bootstrap and the resubstitution estimates with the weights 0.632 and 0.368, respectively (see Fig. 2.15). Bootstrap estimation is asymptotically (large values of B) unbiased with low variance. It is recommended for use with small datasets.

Generally speaking, the honest performance estimation methods described above should be adapted for industrial scenarios where data arrives sequentially, as in time series or in data streams settings (see Section 2.6.1). These adaptations should take into account the data arrival time, that is, none of the instances in the testing dataset should arrive before any of the training dataset instances.

2.4.2 Feature Subset Selection

Feature subset selection or **variable selection** (Lewis, 1962) identifies and removes as many irrelevant and redundant variables as possible. This reduces data dimensionality (n), which may help learning algorithms to induce faster and more effective models. Classifier performance measures may sometimes improve; also, the induced model may be a more compact representation of

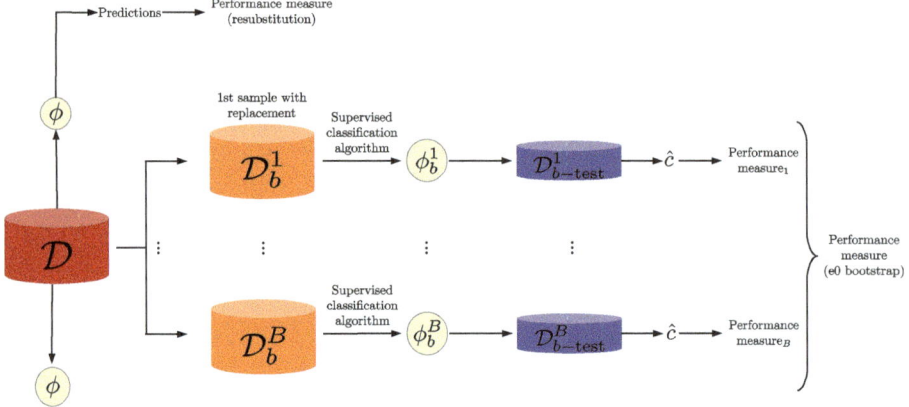

FIGURE 2.15

0.632 bootstrap method. The final performance measure is a weighted sum of the $e0$ bootstrap and the resubstitution estimates, weighted 0.632 and 0.368, respectively.

the target concept. This comes at the expense of increasing the modeling task complexity due to the (added) feature subset selection process, especially if n is large.

A discrete feature X_i is said to be **relevant** for the class variable C if, depending on one of its values, the probability distribution of the class variable changes, i.e., if there exists some x_i and c, for which $p(X_i = x_i) > 0$, such that $p(C = c|X_i = x_i) \neq p(C = c)$. A feature is said to be **redundant** if it is highly correlated with one or more of the other features. Irrelevant and redundant variables affect C differently. While irrelevant variables are noisy and bias the prediction, redundant variables provide no extra information about C.

Feature subset selection can be seen as a combinatorial optimization problem. The optimal subset $\mathcal{S}^*$ of features is sought from the set of predictor variables $\mathcal{X} = \{X_1, ..., X_n\}$, i.e., $\mathcal{S}^* \subseteq \mathcal{X}$. Optimal means with respect to an objective score that, without loss of generality, should be maximized. The search space cardinality is 2^n, which is huge for large values of n. Heuristics are an absolute necessity for moving intelligently in this huge space and provide close to optimal solutions. Fig. 2.16 illustrates a toy example of a search space whose cardinality is 16, with only four predictor variables.

The search is determined by four basic issues:

(a) Starting point. Forward selection begins with no features and successively adds attributes. Backward elimination begins with all features and successively removes attributes. Another alternative is to begin somewhere in the middle and move outwards from this point.

(b) Search organization. An exhaustive search is only feasible for a small

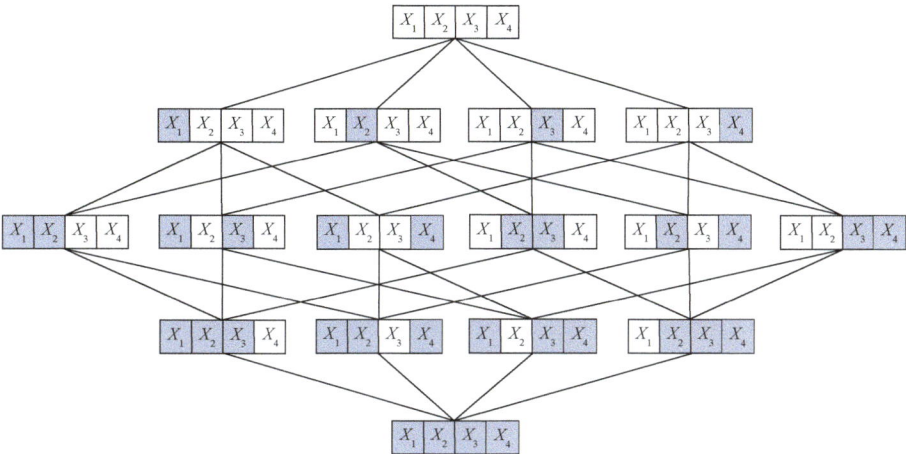

FIGURE 2.16

Each block represents one possible feature subset selection in this problem with $n = 4$. The blue rectangles are variables included in the selected subset. By deletion/inclusion of one feature, we move through the edges.

number of features. Apart from forward and backward searches, heuristics (Talbi, 2009) can achieve good results, although there is no guarantee that the optimal feature subset will be found. A **deterministic heuristic** always finds the same solution to a fixed problem, given the same starting point. Some important deterministic heuristics used in the feature subset selection problem are: sequential feature selection, sequential forward feature selection, sequential backward elimination, greedy hill climbing, best first, plus-L-minus-r algorithm, floating search selection, and tabu search. By contrast, a **non-deterministic heuristic** adds stochasticity into the search process providing varying results depending on different executions. These heuristics can retain a single-solution in each iteration or work with a population of solutions. **Single-solution non-deterministic heuristics** include: simulated annealing, Las Vegas algorithm, greedy randomized adaptive search procedure, and variable neighborhood search. **Population-based non-deterministic heuristics** include: scatter search, ant colony optimization, particle swarm optimization, and evolutionary algorithms like genetic algorithms, estimation of distribution algorithms, differential evolution, genetic programming, and evolution strategies.

(c) Evaluation strategy. How feature subsets are evaluated is the largest differentiating factor of feature selection algorithms for supervised classification. The filter approach, the wrapper approach, embedded methods and hybrid filter and wrapper approaches are different alternatives that are explained below.

(d) Stopping criterion. A feature selector must some time stop searching through the space of feature subsets. A criterion may be to stop when none of the evaluated alternatives improves upon the merit of the current feature subset. Alternatively, the search might continue for a fixed number of iterations.

Filter feature subset selection considers intrinsic data properties to assess the relevancy of a feature, or a subset of features. Filter methods act as a screening step and are independent of any supervised classification algorithm. A popular score in filtering approaches is the mutual information (and related measures) between each predictor variable and the class variable.

The mutual information between two random variables is based on the concept of **Shannon's entropy** (Shannon, 1948), which quantifies the uncertainty of predictions of the value of a random variable. For a discrete variable with l possible values, the entropy is

$$\mathbb{H}(X) = -\sum_{i=1}^{l} p(X = x_i) \log_2 p(X = x_i).$$

The **mutual information** $\mathbb{I}(X, C)$ between a predictor variable X and the class variable C with m possible values is defined as

$$\mathbb{I}(X, C) = \mathbb{H}(C) - \mathbb{H}(C|X) = \sum_{i=1}^{l} \sum_{j=1}^{m} p(x_i, c_j) \log_2 \frac{p(x_i, c_j)}{p(x_i)p(c_j)}.$$

Mutual information is interpreted as the reduction in the uncertainty about C after observing X. It holds $\mathbb{H}(C) \geq \mathbb{H}(C|X)$ (the knowledge of a variable never increases the uncertainty about another) and hence, $\mathbb{I}(X, C) \geq 0$. If X and C are independent, the knowledge of one variable does not have any influence on the uncertainty of the other; hence, mutual information is zero. Features X with high $\mathbb{I}(X, C)$ are preferred over others that have small values for this objective score. In this sense, mutual information can be interpreted as a measure of relevancy.

Univariate filtering evaluates each feature with a feature relevancy score, removing low-scoring features. The selected features are used as input variables for the classification algorithm. Several feature relevancy scores have been proposed in the literature. Mutual information has the disadvantage of preferring features with many different values over features with few different values. A fairer choice is to use **gain ratio** defined as $\frac{\mathbb{I}(X_j, C)}{\mathbb{H}(X_j)}$ or the **symmetrical uncertainty coefficient** defined as $2\frac{\mathbb{I}(X_i, C)}{\mathbb{H}(X_i) + \mathbb{H}(C)}$. In both measures, the denominator normalizes the mutual information.

A clear disadvantage of univariate filtering methods is that they ignore feature dependences as they do not take into account feature redundancy. This redundancy can be detrimental for classification model behavior. Multivariate filtering techniques address this problem. Fig. 2.17 is a diagram showing both univariate and multivariate filtering approaches.

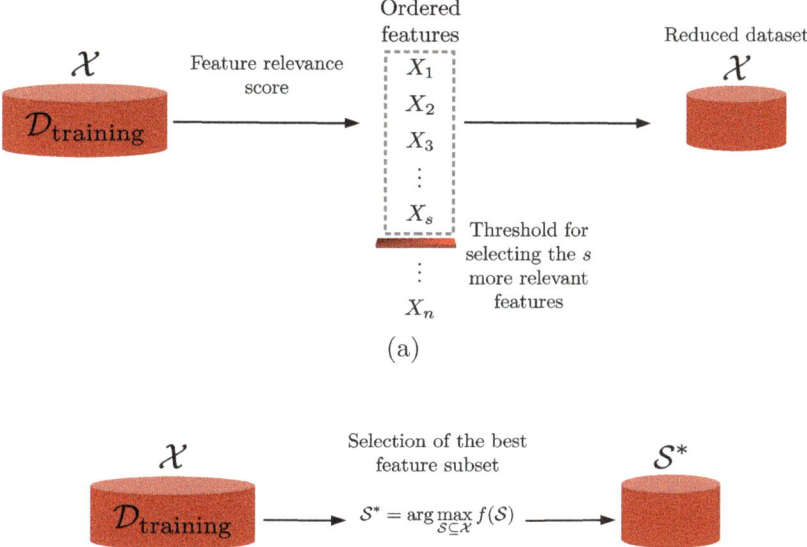

(a)

(b)

FIGURE 2.17

Filtering approaches for feature subset selection. (a) Univariate filter: $X_{(1)}, ..., X_{(n)}$ are the original variables ordered according to a feature relevancy score. The selected feature subset includes the top s variables. (b) Multivariate filter: a 2^n cardinality space is searched for the best subset of features $\mathcal{S}^*$ as an optimization problem. Each subset is evaluated according to a feature relevancy score f.

Multivariate filter methods choose the subset of features according to their relevancy (with respect to the class) and redundancy. **Correlation-based feature selection** (CFS) in Hall (1999) is one of the most widely used methods. The goodness of a feature subset is defined in terms of its correlation with the class (relevancy), and of the lack of correlation between pairs of features in the subset (redundancy). More formally, if $\mathcal{S} \subseteq \mathcal{X} = \{X_1, ..., X_n\}$ denotes a subset of features, CFS searches for $\mathcal{S}^* = \arg\max_{\mathcal{S} \subseteq \mathcal{X}} f(\mathcal{S})$, where

$$f(\mathcal{S}) = \frac{\sum_{X_i \in \mathcal{S}} r(X_i, C)}{\sqrt{k + (k-1) \sum_{X_i, X_j \in \mathcal{S}} r(X_i, X_j)}},$$

and k is the number of selected features, $r(X_i, C)$ is the correlation between feature X_i and class variable C, and $r(X_i, X_j)$ is the correlation between features X_i and X_j. Correlations r are given by the symmetrical uncertainty coefficient. The maximization problem can be solved using any of the above heuristics.

Filtering techniques are easily scalable, computationally simple, and fast; they avoid overfitting problems, and they are independent of the classification algorithm. Filter feature selection needs to be performed only once. This selection is evaluated later using different classification models.

Wrapper methods (John et al., 1994) first build a classifier from a subset of features, which is then evaluated against the estimated classifier performance. These methods are, therefore, classifier dependent and are often impractical for large-scale problems. Any of the criteria introduced in Section 2.4.1 are possible objective functions for driving the search for the best subset of features using any of the above heuristics. Fig. 2.18 illustrates the main characteristics of wrapper approaches for feature subset selection.

Embedded methods include a built-in feature selection mechanism as part of the model training process. The search is carried out in the combined space of feature subsets and models. Like wrapper approaches, embedded approaches depend on the specific learning algorithm but are far less computationally intensive than wrapper methods. **Regularization** (Tikhonov, 1943) can be considered as an embedded feature selection approach. Regularization produces sparse and robust models by introducing additional information usually in the form of a penalty on the likelihood. The **lasso** regularization method (Tibshirani, 1996) is based on a L_1 norm penalty and performs feature subset selection because it converts the coefficients associated with some variables to zero (and the variables can be discarded).

Hybrid feature selection methods combine filter and wrapper approaches. With a big n, the computational burden of wrapper approaches is alleviated by first applying a filter method to dramatically reduce the number of features. In a second stage, the wrapper approach works on the output of

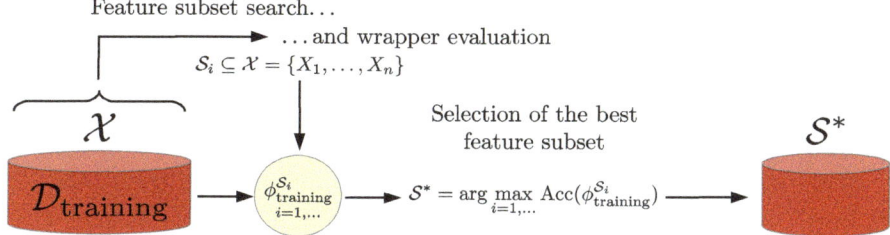

FIGURE 2.18

Wrapper approach for feature subset selection. In this case, each candidate feature subset $S_i \subseteq \mathcal{X} = \{X_1, ..., X_n\}$ is evaluated according to the (estimated) classification accuracy (Acc) of the classifier $\phi_{\text{training}}^{S_i}$ built from S_i in the training set $\mathcal{D}_{\text{training}}$. Any other performance measure could be used instead of accuracy.

the filter method. **Minimal-redundancy-maximal-relevancy** (Peng et al., 2005) is an example of this hybridization. The subset of features maximizing the difference between relevancy and redundancy is selected at the filter stage. A wrapper approach is then applied over this subset in the second stage.

2.4.3 k-Nearest Neighbors

The k-**nearest neighbors classifier** (k-**NN**) (Fix and Hodges, 1951) predicts the unknown class of $\mathbf{x}$ based on the classes associated with the k instances of the training set that are closer to $\mathbf{x}$, using a simple majority decision rule.

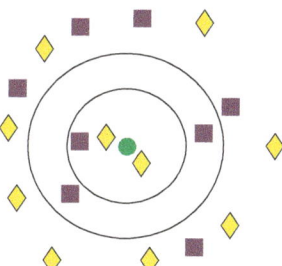

FIGURE 2.19

Example of a k-NN classifier for classifying the green instance in a binary (square, diamond) classification problem.

In Fig. 2.19, the test instance (green circle) should be classified in either the first class (magenta squares) or the second class (yellow diamonds). With $k = 3$ neighbors, the instance is assigned to the second class because there are two diamonds and only one square inside the inner circle. With $k = 5$

neighbors, it is assigned to the first class because there are three squares vs. two diamonds inside the outer circle.

The k-NN algorithm does not have a training phase, nor does it induce a model. Some of the advantages of the k-NN algorithm are that it can learn complex decision boundaries, it is a local method, it uses few assumptions about the data, and it can be easily adapted as an incremental algorithm, especially suitable for data inputs like streams (very common in industrial applications). The main disadvantages are its high storage requirements and its low classification speed. In addition, the algorithm is sensitive to the selected distance (needed to find the neighbors), the value of k, the existence of irrelevant variables, and noisy data. Another disadvantage is that, as there is no model specification, no new knowledge about the problem can be discovered.

Although most implementations of k-NN compute simple Euclidean distances, it has been demonstrated empirically that k-NN classification can be greatly improved by learning an appropriate distance metric from the training data. This is the so-called **metric learning problem**. The neighborhood parameter k plays an important role in k-NN performance (see the example in Fig. 2.19). An increment in k should increase the bias and reduce the classification error variance. The optimum value of k depends on the specific dataset. It is usually estimated according to the available training sample: the misclassification rate is estimated using cross-validation methods for different values of k, and the value with the best rate is chosen. The selection of relevant prototypes is a promising solution for speeding up k-NN in large datasets. These techniques lead to a representative training set that is smaller than the original set and has a similar or even higher classification accuracy for new incoming data. There are three standard categories of **prototype selection methods** (García et al., 2012): condensation methods, edition methods, and hybrid methods. Condensation methods –like, for example, the **condensed nearest neighbors algorithm** (Hart, 1968)– aim to remove superfluous instances (i.e., any that do not cause incorrect classifications). **Edition methods** (Wilson, 1972) are designed to remove noisy instances (i.e., any that do not agree with the majority of their k-nearest neighbors) in order to increase classifier accuracy. Finally, hybrid methods combine edition and condensation strategies, for example, by first editing the training set to remove noise, and then condensing the output of the edition to generate a smaller subset.

Several variants of the basic k-NN have been developed. The **k-NN with weighted neighbors** weighs the contribution of each neighbor depending on its distance to the query instance, i.e., larger weight are given to nearer neighbors. Irrelevant variables can mislead k-NN, and **k-NN with weighted predictor variables** addresses this problem by assigning to each predictor variable a weight that is proportional to its relevancy (mutual information) with respect to the class variable. The distance is thus weighted to determine neighbors. In **k-NN with average distance**, the distances of the neighbors to the query instance are averaged for each class label, and the label associated with the minimum average distance is assigned to the query instance. **k-NN**

with rejection can leave an instance unclassified (and then be dealt by another supervised classification algorithm) if certain guarantees, e.g., a minimum number of votes in the decision rule (much more than $\frac{k}{2}$ in a binary classification problem), are not met.

Instance-based learning (**IBL**) (Aha et al., 1991) extends k-NN by providing incremental learning, significantly reducing the storage requirements and introducing a hypothesis test to detect noisy instances. The first algorithm belonging to this family, **IB1**, includes the normalization of the predictor variable ranges and the incremental processing of instances. Using incremental processing, decision boundaries can change over time as new data arrive.

2.4.4 Classification Trees

Classification trees greedily and recursively partition the instance space into two or more subspaces using the outcome of an input variable splitting function. This function is simply either a value or set of values (for a discrete variable) or a range (for a continuous variable). Nodes are labeled with the variable that they test, and their branches are labeled with their corresponding values. Each node further subdivides the training set into smaller subsets until a stopping criterion is satisfied. At the bottom of the tree, each leaf node is assigned to one class value. Leaves are represented by rectangles; root and internal nodes are depicted by circles.

For classification, unseen instances are sorted down the tree from the root to one of the leaf nodes according to the outcome of the tests along the path. The predicted class is found at the leaf. Each path from the root of a classification tree to one of its leaves can be transformed into a rule (see Section 2.4.5) by simply conjoining the tests along the path to form the antecedent part of the rule and taking the leaf class prediction to form the consequent of the rule. Thus, the tree represents a disjunction of variable value conjunctions.

Example. Classification tree

Fig. 2.20(a) shows the scatterplot of a dataset with two predictor variables, where the dot color distinguishes yes (red) from no (black) instances. Fig. 2.20(b) shows the four-leaf classification tree. The four paths from the root node to a leaf generate four if-then rules:

R_1: IF $X_1 \leq 2.5$ AND $X_2 > 6$ THEN $C =$no
R_2: IF $X_1 \leq 2.5$ AND $X_2 \leq 6$ AND $X_1 > 1.5$ THEN $C =$yes
R_3: IF $X_1 \leq 2.5$ AND $X_2 \leq 6$ AND $X_1 \leq 1.5$ THEN $C =$no
R_4: IF $X_1 > 2.5$ THEN $C =$yes

Thus the instance space is split into four subspaces. ∎

Classification tree algorithms mainly differ with respect to the criterion used to select the nodes, the use of prepruning and/or postpruning strategies

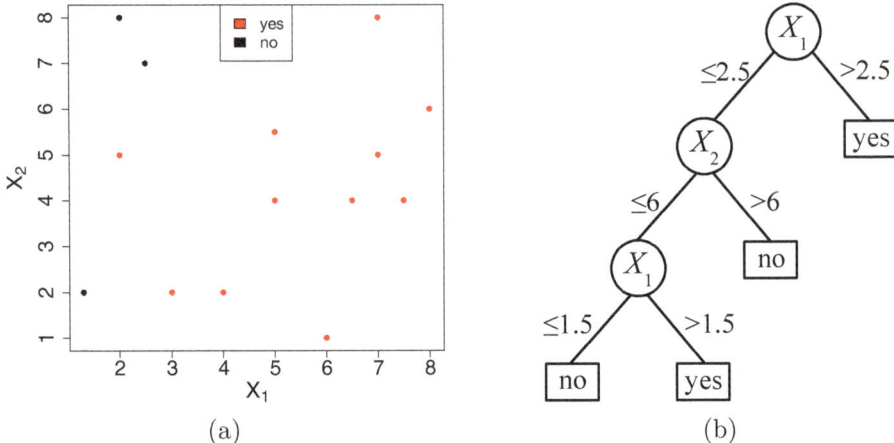

(a)   (b)

FIGURE 2.20
(a) Scatterplot of 14 cases in a classification problem with two predictor variables and two classes: yes (red) and no (black); (b) A classification tree model for this dataset.

and the stopping criteria. The most popular induction algorithms are C4.5 and CART. They can be regarded as variations on a core algorithm called **ID3** (Quinlan, 1986) that stands for **iterative dichotomiser** because the original proposal used only binary variables. The nodes selected by ID3 maximize the mutual information (see Section 2.4.2), called **information gain** in this context, with the class variable C. After selecting the root node, a descendant is created for each value of this variable, and the training instances are sorted to the appropriate descendant node. The best variable at each point of the tree is selected similarly, considering at this stage the as yet unused variables in each path as candidate nodes. ID3 stops at a node when the tree correctly classifies all its instances (all instances are of the same class) or when there are no more variables to be used. This stopping criterion causes overfitting problems, which have been traditionally tackled using pruning methods.

In **prepruning**, a termination condition, usually given by a statistical hypothesis test, determines when to stop growing some branches as the classification tree is generated. In **postpruning**, the full-grown tree is then pruned by replacing some subtrees with a leaf. Postpruning is more widely used, although it is more computationally demanding. A simple postpruning procedure is **reduced error pruning** (Quinlan, 1987). This bottom-up procedure replaces a node with the most frequent class label for the training instances associated with that node as long as this does not reduce tree accuracy. The subtree rooted by the node is removed and converted into a leaf node. The procedure continues until any further pruning would decrease accuracy. Accuracy is estimated with a pruning set or test set.

C4.5 (Quinlan, 1993) is an evolution of ID3 that uses the gain ratio (see Section 2.4.2) as a splitting criterion and can handle continuous variables and missing values. C4.5 stops when there are fewer instances to be split than a given threshold. The set of rules generated from the classification tree are postpruned. Antecedents are eliminated from a rule whenever accuracy increases. The rule is deleted if it has no antecedents. This prunes subpaths rather than subtrees.

The **classification and regression trees (CART)** algorithm (Breiman et al., 1984) builds binary trees. It implements many splitting criteria, mainly the **Gini index** (univariate) and a linear combination of continuous predictor variables (multivariate). The Gini index of diversity aims at minimizing the impurity (not all labels are equal) of the training subsets output after branching the classification tree. It can also be seen as a divergence measure between the probability distributions of the C values. CART adopts cost-complexity pruning and can consider misclassification costs. CART can also generate regression trees, where a real number prediction of a continuous variable C is found at the leaves.

Univariate splitting criteria, where the node is split according to the value of a single variable, like the information gain, gain ratio or Gini index, produce axis-parallel partitions of the feature space. However, **multivariate splitting criteria** –like the linear combination of predictors in CART– result in obliquely oriented hyperplanes. Fig. 2.21 illustrates both types of feature space partitioning.

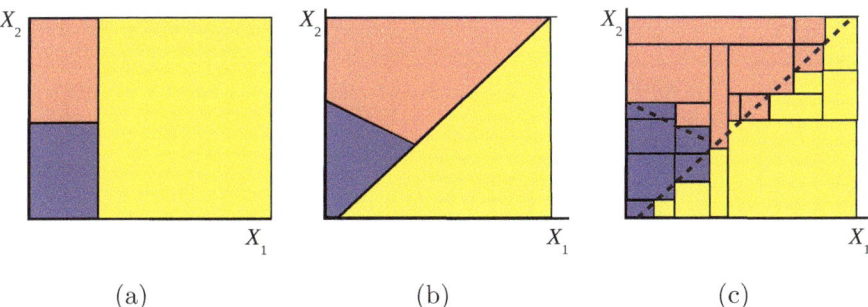

(a)   (b)   (c)

FIGURE 2.21
(a) Hyperrectangle partitioning of a classification tree in the feature space (univariate splitting); (b) Polygonal partitioning produced by an oblique classification tree (multivariate splitting); (c) An axis-parallel tree designed to approximate the polygonal space partitioning of (b). Filling/colors refer to different class labels.

2.4.5   Rule Induction

Rule induction is a supervised classification method that produces models in the form of rules. Rules are expressions like

IF ($X_j = x_j$ AND $X_i = x_i$ AND $\cdots$ AND $X_k = x_k$) THEN $C = c$

where "$X_j = x_j$ AND $X_i = x_i$ AND $\cdots$ AND $X_k = x_k$" is called the **antecedent of the rule**, and "$C = c$" is the **consequent of the rule**. There are other more complex rules, in which some values are negated or only some values are permitted.

Rule induction models are transparent, and easy to understand and apply. They are more general than classification trees, since any classification tree can be transformed into a rule induction model, but the opposite is not always the case.

Repeated incremental pruning to produce error reduction (**RIPPER**$_k$) (Cohen, 1995) is one of the most popular rule induction models. RIPPER$_k$ is based on the **incremental reduced error pruning** (**IREP**) algorithm introduced by Fürnkranz and Widmer (1994).

Algorithm 2.4 shows the IREP pseudocode for a binary classification problem. IREP considers a **rule** as a conjunction of literals. For example, the rule R_j: IF ($X_2 = 5$ AND $X_5 = 6$ AND $X_6 < 0.5$ AND $X_4 > 0.9$) THEN $C = c$ is the conjunction of four literals. A **rule set** is a disjunction of rules: R_1 OR R_2 OR $\cdots$ OR R_k. IREP greedily builds a rule set, one rule at a time. A rule is said to cover an instance of the dataset if its antecedent is true for the instance. When a rule is found, all instances covered by the rule (both positive and negative) are deleted from the growing set (see below). This process is repeated until there are no positive instances or until the rule found by IREP has an unacceptably large error rate.

Algorithm 2.4: Pseudocode for the IREP algorithm

> **Input**   : A split of the dataset on Pos and Neg, an empty Ruleset
> **Output** : A Ruleset
>
> **while** *Pos* $\neq \emptyset$ **do**
> > /* *grow and prune a new rule* */
> > split (Pos, Neg) into (GrowPos, GrowNeg) and (PrunePos, PruneNeg)
> > Rule = GrowRule(GrowPos, GrowNeg)
> > Rule = PruneRule(Rule, PrunePos, PruneNeg)
> > **if** the error rate of Rule on (PrunePos, PruneNeg) exceeds 50% **then**
> > **return** Ruleset
> >
> > **else if then**
> > > add Rule to Ruleset
> > > remove instances covered by Rule from (Pos, Neg)
> > **endif**
> **endwhile**

The strategy used by IREP to build a rule is as follows. First, the positive (Pos) and negative (Neg) instances are randomly partitioned into two subsets, a growing set and a pruning set producing four disjoint subsets: GrowPos and GrowNeg (positive and negative instances used for growing the rule, respectively); PrunePos and PruneNeg (positive and negative instances used for pruning the rule, respectively). Second, a rule is grown. GrowRule starts empty and considers adding any literal of the form $X_i = x_i$ (if X_i is discrete), or $X_i < x_i$, $X_i > x_i$ (if X_i is continuous). GrowRule repeatedly adds the literal that maximizes an information gain criterion called **first-order inductive learner (FOIL)**. FOIL is improved until the rule covers no negative instances from the growing dataset. Let R denote a rule and R' be a more specific rule output from R after adding a literal. The FOIL criterion is defined as:

$$\text{FOIL}\,(R, R', \text{GrowPos, GrowNeg})$$
$$= co\left[-log_2\left(\frac{pos}{pos+neg}\right) + log_2\left(\frac{pos'}{pos'+neg'}\right)\right],$$

where co denotes the percentage of positive instances covered by R and also covered by R' in GrowPos, pos is the number of positive instances covered by R in GrowPos (and similarly for pos' and R'), neg is the number of negative instances covered by R in GrowNeg (and similarly for neg' and R').

The rule is then pruned. Any final sequence of literals from the rule output by the growing phase is considered to be deleted. IREP chooses the deletion that maximizes the function

$$v(R, \text{PrunePos, PruneNeg}) = \frac{pos_R + (|\text{PruneNeg}| - neg_R)}{|\text{PrunePos}| + |\text{PruneNeg}|},$$

where pos_R (neg_R) is the number of instances in PrunePos (PruneNeg) covered by rule R. This process is repeated until no deletion improves v.

RIPPER differs from the original IREP in that it uses another metric for v. It also adds a new heuristic for deciding when to stop adding rules to a rule set and a postpass that improves a rule set. A new instance is classified by finding which rules the instance satisfies. If there is only one rule, this rule assigns its predicted class to the instance. If there is more than one rule, the prediction is the most common class in the training instances covered by those rules. If there are no rules, then the prediction is the most frequent class in the training instances.

AQR and CN2 are other rule induction methods in widespread use. The **AQ rule-generation algorithm (AQR)** (Michalski and Chilausky, 1980) generates several classification rules, one per class. Each rule is of the form "IF *cover* THEN $C = c$", where *cover* is a combination, disjunctions of conjunctions, of variable tests, e.g., $(X_3 = 5 \text{ AND } X_4 > 0.9) \text{ OR } (X_5 = 6 \text{ AND } X_2 < 0.5)$. The associated class value of a cover is the most common class label of the training instances that it covers.

AQR initially focuses on a class and forms the cover to serve as the antecedent of the rule for that class label. AQR generates a conjunction of literals, called a complex, and then removes the instances it covers from the training dataset. This step is repeated until enough complexes have been found to cover all the instances of the chosen class. The score used by AQR to trim the antecedent during the generation of a complex is the maximization of the positive instances covered, excluding the negative instances. The score used to pick the best complex is the maximization of the positive instances covered. The entire process is repeated for each class in turn.

The **CN2 algorithm** (Clark and Niblett, 1989) produces an ordered list of IF-THEN rules. In each iteration, CN2 searches for a complex that covers a large number of instances of a single class and a few other classes. When, according to an evaluation function, the algorithm has found a good complex, it removes the instances that it covers from the training dataset and adds the corresponding rule to the end of the rule list. This process iterates until no more satisfactory complexes can be found. At each stage of the search, CN2 retains a size-limited set of the best complexes found so far. Next, the system considers specializations of this set, i.e., by either adding a new conjunctive term or removing a disjunctive element. CN2 generates and evaluates all possible specializations of each complex. The complex quality is heuristically assessed with the entropy of the class variable, estimated from the instances covered by this complex. Lower entropy is preferred.

A new instance is classified by following the rules in order (from first to last) until we find a rule that the instance satisfies. This rule assigns its predicted class to the instance. If no rules are satisfied, then the prediction is the most frequent class in the training instances.

2.4.6   Artificial Neural Networks

Artificial neural networks (**ANN**s) (McCulloch and Pitts, 1943) are computational models designed to mimic the behavior of biological neural networks. They are extremely simple abstractions of biological systems and are used to approximate functions that can depend on a large number of inputs. ANNs are represented as adaptive systems of interconnected "neurons."

Although the size, ability, and power of ANNs is very limited compared to biological neural networks, they both feature parallel information processing and learning, and generalization from experience. ANNs have the advantage that they do not require a priori assumptions about the underlying data generation process, they are highly adaptive non-linear and non-parametric models and they can handle incomplete and noisy information. Their mathematical properties in accurately approximating functions have been well established. In contrast, ANNs are blackbox models, in which the weights of the incoming and outgoing arcs of the hidden nodes are hard to interpret (see below). Also, ANNs tend to have a high computational burden and are prone to overfitting. These drawbacks should be taken into account when using ANNs in real industrial applications.

Here we focus on the most commonly used ANN model for supervised classification: the multilayer perceptron. The **multilayer feedforward neural network**, also called **multilayer perceptron** (**MLP**) (Minsky and Papert, 1969), consists of a number of interconnected computing units called neurons, nodes, or cells, which are organized in layers. Each neuron converts the received inputs into processed outputs. The arcs linking these neurons have weights representing the strength of the relationship between different nodes. Although each neuron performs very simple computations, collectively an MLP is able to efficiently and accurately implement a variety of (hard) tasks. MLPs are suitable for predicting one or more response (output) variables (discrete or continuous) simultaneously. Here we address standard supervised classification problems with a single-class variable.

Fig. 2.22 shows the architecture of a three-layer MLP for supervised classification. Neurons (represented by circles) are organized in three layers: input layer (circles in yellow), hidden layer (violet), and output layer (red). The neurons in the input layer correspond to the predictor variables, $X_1, ..., X_n$, whereas the output neuron represents the class variable, C. Neurons in the hidden layer are connected to both input and output neurons, and do not have a clear semantic meaning, although they are the key to learning the relationship between the input variables and the output variable. A vector **w** of weights represents the strength of the connecting links. The most commonly used MLP is a fully connected network (any node of a layer is connected to all nodes in the adjacent layers) and includes only one hidden layer.

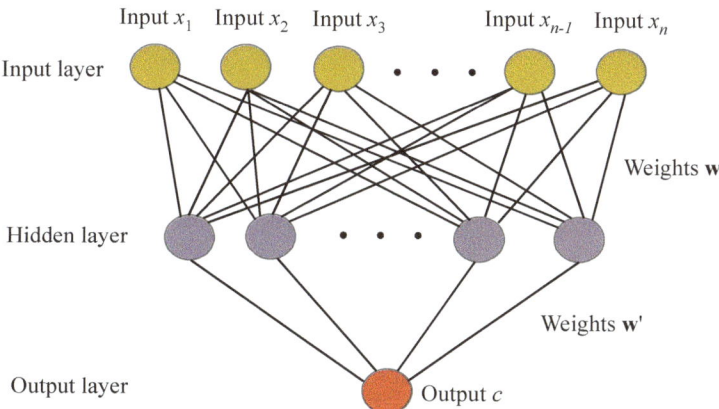

FIGURE 2.22
Structure of a multilayer perceptron for supervised classification, with three types of nodes (input, hidden and output) organized into layers.

In addition to its architecture, the transfer function used in each layer plays an important role in MLPs. Fig. 2.23 shows how the second hidden node processes information from several input nodes and then transforms it into an output. This is a two-step process. In the first step, the inputs, $\mathbf{x} = (x_1, x_2, x_3, ..., x_n)$, are combined with the weights of the connecting links, as a weighted sum, e.g., $\sum_{i=1}^{n} w_{i2}x_i = \mathbf{w}_2^T\mathbf{x}$ for the second hidden neuron. In the second step, the hidden node transforms this to an output via a **transfer function**, $f(\mathbf{w}_2^T\mathbf{x})$. Generally, the transfer function is a bounded non-decreasing function. The sigmoid or logistic function, $f(r) = (1 + \exp(-r))^{-1}$ is one of the most used transfer functions.

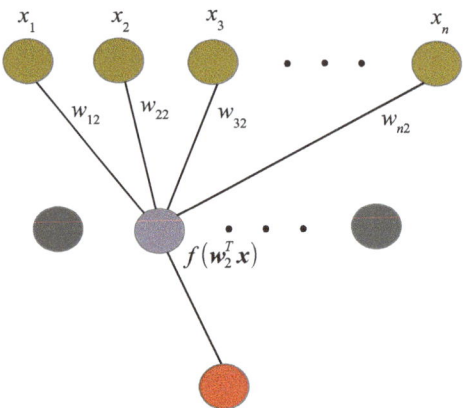

FIGURE 2.23
Transfer function in a hidden node of a multilayer perceptron.

For a three-layer MLP with h hidden neurons, the h outputs, $f(\mathbf{w}_1^T\mathbf{x}), ..., f(\mathbf{w}_h^T\mathbf{x})$, should be weighted with vector $\mathbf{w}'^T = (w_1', ..., w_h')$, yielding the MLP output, that is, $\hat{c} = \sum_{j=1}^{h} w_j' f(\mathbf{w}_j^T\mathbf{x}) = \sum_{j=1}^{h} w_j' f(\sum_{i=1}^{n} w_{ij}x_i)$. This output $\hat{c}$ is compared with the real known label c. All weights of the MLP should be determined such that the predictions $\hat{c}^1, ..., \hat{c}^N$ are as close as possible to the true labels $c^1, ..., c^N$. Training a MLP basically consists of finding $\mathbf{w}$ and $\mathbf{w}'$ that minimize the sum of differences between the MLP output values and the known labels for all training instances.

An error measure $E(\mathbf{w}, \mathbf{w}')$ like the mean squared error, i.e., $E(\mathbf{w}, \mathbf{w}') = \frac{1}{N}\sum_{k=1}^{N}(c^k - \hat{c}^k)^2$, is often used as the objective function to be minimized. The most important method used to solve this unconstrained non-linear optimization problem is the **backpropagation algorithm**. This algorithm is a **gradient method** that finds the best direction in the weight space that most reduces the error measure (see Fig. 2.24). The weight updating from w_{ij}^{old} to w_{ij}^{new} is

$$w_{ij}^{new} = w_{ij}^{old} - \eta\frac{\partial E}{\partial w_{ij}},$$

where $\frac{\partial E}{\partial w_{ij}}$ is the gradient of E with respect to w_{ij} and η is called the **learning rate** and controls the size of the gradient descent step. The backpropagation

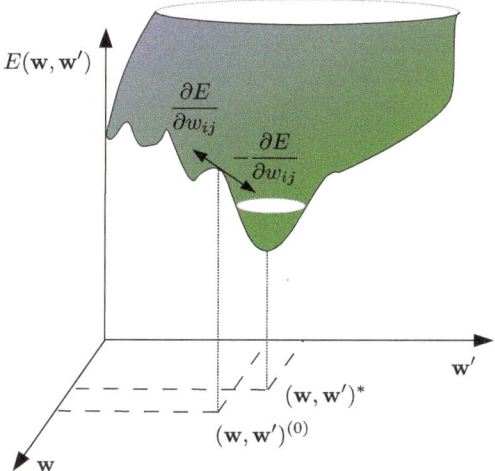

FIGURE 2.24
Multidimensional error space $E(\mathbf{w}, \mathbf{w}')$. The gradient, or steepest, descent method starts with the initialization of weights at $(\mathbf{w}, \mathbf{w}')^{(0)}$. The goal is to find the optimum point $(\mathbf{w}, \mathbf{w}')^*$. Weights are updated according to $\frac{\partial E}{\partial w_{ij}}$, the direction of the partial derivative of the error function with respect to each weight.

algorithm is iteratively run until some stopping criterion is met. Two versions of weight updating schemes are possible. In the batch mode, weights are updated after all training instances are evaluated, while in the online mode, the weights are updated after each instance evaluation. In general, each weight update reduces the total error by only a small amount. Therefore, many passes of all instances are often required to minimize the error until a previously fixed small error value is achieved.

Several aspects should be considered when training ANNs. The most important are: (a) weight values are initialized as random values near zero; (b) overfitting is avoided using **weight decay**, that is, an explicit regularization method that shrinks some of the weights towards zero; (c) input scaling can have a big effect on the quality of the final solution, and it is preferable for inputs to be standardized to mean zero and standard deviation one; (d) the flexibility of the model for capturing data non-linearities depends on the number of hidden neurons and layers, and, in general, it is better to have many hidden units trained with weight decay or another regularization method; (e) a multistart strategy (many different weight initializations) for minimizing the non-convex $E(\mathbf{w}, \mathbf{w}')$ error function is often used.

Recently **deep neural networks** (Schmidhuber, 2015), defined as ANNs with multiple hidden layers, have attracted the attention of many researchers, since their learning process relates to a class of brain development theories proposed by cognitive neuroscientists. Deep neural network implementations have shown outstanding results in several real-world applications.

2.4.7   Support Vector Machines

Support vector machines (SVMs) (Vapnik, 1998) build the classifier by solving a function estimation problem. They can be regarded as an extension of the multilayer perceptron with empirically good performance. We first explain the classical binary SVM, where $\Omega_C = \{-1, +1\}$. The use of label -1 rather than 0 simplifies subsequent formulae.

Fig. 2.25(a) shows a hypothetical dataset with two predictor variables X_1 and X_2. The points can be also considered vectors in $\mathbb{R}^2$ whose tail is point $(0, 0)$ and whose head is at a point with the feature values. Here the data are linearly separable, i.e., we can draw a line (a hyperplane for $n > 2$) separating the two classes. Note that there are infinite possible separating lines and the points of the separate categories are divided by a clear gap or **margin**. A reasonable choice is a line with the largest separation, or margin, between the two classes.

The simplest SVM is the **linear SVM**, a linear classifier with the maximum margin, as this will likely generalize better (see Fig. 2.25(b), where the margin is shown in gray, and it is the line width before hitting a data point). The separating line that is as far as possible from the closest points (the hardest points to be classified) of both classes is sought. The closest points to the separating line are called **support vectors**.

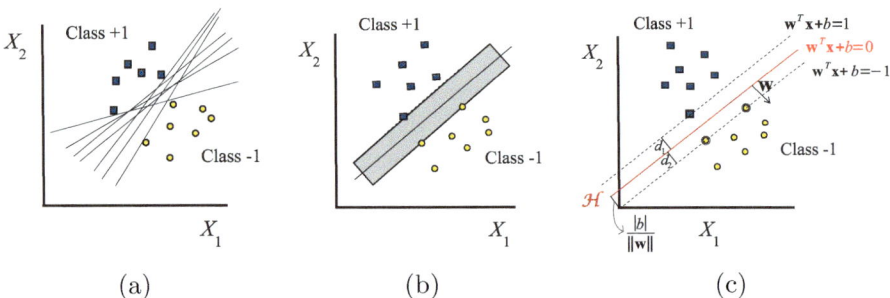

(a)	(b)	(c)

FIGURE 2.25
(a) Many possible separating lines of two linearly separable classes; (b) Linear SVM classifier maximizing the margin around the separating hyperplane; (c) Hyperplane $\mathbf{w}^T\mathbf{x} + b = 0$ for linearly separable data. Its margin is $d_1 + d_2$. The support vectors have double lines.

The hyperplane $\mathcal{H}$ that separates the positive from the negative instances is described by $\mathbf{w}^T\mathbf{x} + b = 0$, where vector $\mathbf{w}$ is normal (perpendicular) to the hyperplane, $|b|/||\mathbf{w}||$ is the perpendicular distance from the hyperplane to the origin and $||\mathbf{w}||$ is the Euclidean norm (length) of $\mathbf{w}$ (Fig. 2.25(c)).

Points above (below) $\mathcal{H}$ should be labeled +1 (-1), that is, the decision rule is $\phi(\mathbf{x}) = \text{sign}(\mathbf{w}^T\mathbf{x} + b)$, and $\mathbf{w}$ and b must be found.

Assume that the data satisfy the constraints $\mathbf{w}^T\mathbf{x}^i + b \geq 1$ for $c^i = +1$ and $\mathbf{w}^T\mathbf{x}^i + b \leq -1$ for $c^i = -1$, which can be combined into

$$c^i(\mathbf{w}^T\mathbf{x}^i + b) \geq 1, \quad i = 1, ..., N. \tag{2.4}$$

The points for which the equality in Eq. 2.4 holds are the points that lie closest to $\mathcal{H}$ (depicted by double lines in Fig. 2.25(c)). These points are the support vectors, the most difficult points to classify. Points that lie on the support hyperplane $\mathbf{w}^T\mathbf{x} + b = -1$ have distance $d_1 = 1/||\mathbf{w}||$ to $\mathcal{H}$, and points that lie on $\mathbf{w}^T\mathbf{x} + b = 1$ have distance $d_2 = 1/||\mathbf{w}||$ to $\mathcal{H}$. $\mathcal{H}$ must be as far from these points as possible. Therefore, the margin, $2/||\mathbf{w}||$, should be maximized.

The linear SVM then finds $\mathbf{w}$ and b satisfying

$$\max_{\mathbf{w},b} \frac{2}{||\mathbf{w}||}$$

subject to

$$1 - c^i(\mathbf{w}^T\mathbf{x}^i + b) \leq 0, \quad \forall i = 1, ..., N.$$

This constrained optimization problem is solved by allocating a Lagrange multiplier $\lambda_i \geq 0, i = 1, ..., N$ to each constraint. Many optimization methods (Fletcher, 2000) can be employed (projection methods, interior point methods, active set methods...), most of which are numerical in real-world cases. The most popular is **sequential minimal optimization** (Platt, 1999). Points $\mathbf{x}^i$ for which $\lambda_i > 0$ are the support vectors. All other points have $\lambda_i = 0$. With the λ_i values, we first calculate

$$\mathbf{w} = \sum_{i \in S} \lambda_i c^i \mathbf{x}^i, \tag{2.5}$$

where S denotes the set of indices of the support vectors (for which $\lambda_i > 0$). Finally, offset b is calculated as

$$b = \frac{1}{|S|} \sum_{s \in S} (c^s - \sum_{i \in S} \lambda_i c^i (\mathbf{x}^i)^T \mathbf{x}^s). \tag{2.6}$$

Each new point $\mathbf{x}$ will be classified as

$$c^* = \phi(\mathbf{x}) = \text{sign}(\mathbf{w}^T\mathbf{x} + b). \tag{2.7}$$

Note that the support vectors completely determine the SVM classifier. The other data points can be disregarded when the learning phase is over. Since there are not usually too many support vectors, classification decisions are reached reasonably quickly.

For non-linearly separable data, e.g., outliers, noisy or slightly non-linear data, the constraints of Eq. 2.4 can, provided that we are still looking for a linear decision function, be relaxed slightly to allow for misclassified points, although at a cost. The constraints now come with non-negative slack variables ξ_i (Cortes and Vapnik, 1995):

$$c^i(\mathbf{w}^T\mathbf{x}^i + b) \geq 1 - \xi_i,$$
$$\xi_i \geq 0, \quad \forall i = 1, ..., N.$$

The opposite to the above **hard-margin linear SVM** is called a **soft-margin linear SVM**, where points on the wrong side of $\mathcal{H}$ have a penalty that increases with the distance from $\mathcal{H}$. ξ_i can be regarded as the distance from the support hyperplane for misclassified instances and 0 for correct classifications. ξ_i thereby measures the degree of misclassification of $\mathbf{x}^i$. The solution is again given by Eq. 2.5 and Eq. 2.6, but S is determined by finding the indices where $0 < \lambda_i < M$, where M is the cost parameter to be tuned by the user. A large M heavily penalizes errors, and the SVM will try to find a hyperplane and margin with very few points within the margin. This could mean that there is a small margin if the points are not easily separable. A small M does not exclude misclassifications, but finds a larger margin. Thus, M controls the trade-off between errors and the margin size.

In the **non-linear SVM**, suitable for general non-linearly separable data (Fig. 2.26(a)), the data is mapped to a much higher-dimensional space where a linear decision rule is found (Fig. 2.26(b)). The theoretical motivation is **Cover's theorem** (Cover, 1965). Cover's theorem states that a set of training data that are not linearly separable are very likely (high probability) to be made linearly separable if they are mapped to a higher-dimensional space using a non-linear transformation.

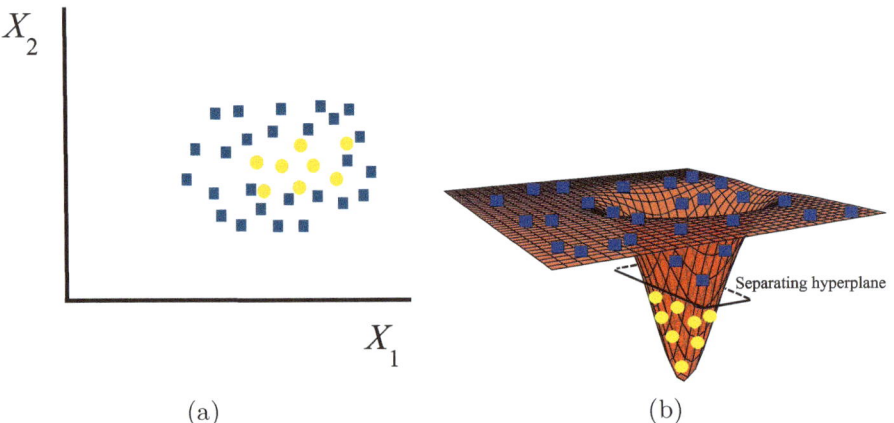

(a)   (b)

FIGURE 2.26
(a) Example with two non-linearly separable classes. (b) Both classes become linearly separable after the data are mapped to a higher-dimensional space.

Thus, if we use a non-linear transformation to map the data to some other feature space $\mathcal{F}$

$$\boldsymbol{\psi} : \mathbb{R}^n \mapsto \mathcal{F}$$

$$\mathbf{x} \mapsto \boldsymbol{\psi}(\mathbf{x})$$

formulating the non-linear SVM is equivalent to all $\mathbf{x}$ in Eq. 2.5-2.7 being replaced by their mapped versions $\boldsymbol{\psi}(\mathbf{x})$. Note, however, that Eq. 2.7 requires only the inner product of mapped points, i.e., products $\boldsymbol{\psi}(\mathbf{x}^i)^T \boldsymbol{\psi}(\mathbf{x}^s)$, to classify new instances (after substituting the $\mathbf{w}$ expression in Eq. 2.5), and $\boldsymbol{\psi}(\mathbf{x}^i)$ alone is not used. This is where a clever mathematical projection called **kernel trick** enters into play. The kernel trick computes such inner products and avoids specifying the (unknown) mapping $\boldsymbol{\psi}$ that produces a linearly separable problem.

A **kernel function** or simply a **kernel** K is defined as a symmetric function of two arguments (i.e., $K(\mathbf{x}, \mathbf{x}') = K(\mathbf{x}', \mathbf{x})$) that returns the value of the inner product of the two mapped arguments in $\mathbb{R}$, that is, $K(\mathbf{x}, \mathbf{x}') = \boldsymbol{\psi}(\mathbf{x})^T \boldsymbol{\psi}(\mathbf{x}')$.

The classification problem is then recast in terms of a kernel, and a new point $\mathbf{x}$ will be classified as

$$c^* = \phi(\mathbf{x}) = \text{sign}(\sum_{i \in S} \lambda_i c^i K(\mathbf{x}^i, \mathbf{x}) + b),$$

where $b = \frac{1}{|S|} \sum_{s \in S}(c^s - \sum_{i \in S} \lambda_i c^i K(\mathbf{x}^i, \mathbf{x}^s))$, and S are the indices i of support vectors such that $0 < \lambda_i < M$.

It can be less costly to compute $K(\mathbf{x}^i, \mathbf{x}^j)$ than to use $\boldsymbol{\psi}(\mathbf{x}^i)^T \boldsymbol{\psi}(\mathbf{x}^j)$, and there is no need to know $\boldsymbol{\psi}$ explicitly. The user specifies the kernel function. See Table 2.7 for typical kernels.

TABLE 2.7
Typical kernel functions

Name	$K(\mathbf{x}, \mathbf{x}')$	Parameters
Linear	$\mathbf{x}^T \mathbf{x}' + c$	$c \in \mathbb{R}$
Homogeneous polynomial	$(a\mathbf{x}^T \mathbf{x}')^p$	$a \in \mathbb{R}$, degree $p \in \mathbb{N}$
Inhomogeneous polynomial	$(a\mathbf{x}^T \mathbf{x}' + c)^p$	$a, c \in \mathbb{R}$, degree $p \in \mathbb{N}$
Gaussian	$e^{-\frac{1}{2\sigma^2}\|\mathbf{x}-\mathbf{x}'\|^2}$	width $\sigma > 0$
Exponential	$e^{-\frac{1}{2\sigma^2}\|\mathbf{x}-\mathbf{x}'\|}$	width $\sigma > 0$
Sigmoidal	$\tanh(a\mathbf{x}^T \mathbf{x}' + c)$	$a, c \in \mathbb{R}$

Polynomial kernels are appropriate when the training data are normalized. The Gaussian kernel is an example of a radial basis function (RBF) kernel. σ must be carefully tuned: when σ is decreased, the curvature of the decision boundary increases (the decision boundary is very sensitive to noise) and overfitting may occur. With a high σ, the exponential will behave almost linearly, and the higher-dimensional projection will start to lose its non-linear power. The exponential kernel is closely related to the Gaussian kernel, merely omitting the square of the norm. It is also an RBF kernel. The sigmoid (or hyperbolic tangent) kernel is equivalent to a two-layer perceptron ANN. A common choice for a here is $1/N$.

An appropriate selection of M and the kernel is a key issue for achieving good performance. The user often selects both using a grid search with exponentially growing sequences. A validation dataset serves to estimate the accuracy for each point on the grid. For a user's guide to SVM, see Ben-Hur and Weston (2010).

The **multiclass SVM** extends the binary SVM to class variables with more than two categories. The most used option is to combine many binary SVMs (Hsu and Lin, 2002). For instance, we can train an SVM on each pair of labels. A new instance is then classified by voting, i.e., by selecting the label most frequently predicted by these binary SVMs.

2.4.8 Logistic Regression

Logistic regression (Hosmer and Lemeshow, 2000) is a probabilistic classification model that can include continuous and categorical predictor variables and does not make any assumptions about their distributions. We explain the classical binary logistic regression. Its generalization to the multiclass case is quite straightforward.

The binary logistic regression model is formulated as

$$p(C = 1|\mathbf{x}, \boldsymbol{\beta}) = \frac{e^{\beta_0 + \beta_1 x_1 + \cdots + \beta_n x_n}}{1 + e^{\beta_0 + \beta_1 x_1 + \cdots + \beta_n x_n}} = \frac{1}{1 + e^{-(\beta_0 + \beta_1 x_1 + \cdots + \beta_n x_n)}},$$

implying that

$$p(C = 0|\mathbf{x}, \boldsymbol{\beta}) = \frac{1}{1 + e^{\beta_0 + \beta_1 x_1 + \cdots + \beta_n x_n}},$$

where $\boldsymbol{\beta} = (\beta_0, \beta_1, ..., \beta_n)^T$ are the parameters to be estimated from the data.

Despite being a classifier and not a regression model, this classification method is termed regression due to the presence of linear combinations of variables in both models. Logistic comes from the sigmoid or logistic function (Section 2.4.6).

One of the main reasons for its popularity is the interpretability of the $\boldsymbol{\beta}$ parameters. The **logit**[4] **form** of the logistic regression model states the difference between the probabilities of belonging to both classes:

$$logit\ (p(C = 1|\mathbf{x}, \boldsymbol{\beta})) = \ln \frac{p(C = 1|\mathbf{x}, \boldsymbol{\beta})}{1 - p(C = 1|\mathbf{x}, \boldsymbol{\beta})} = \beta_0 + \beta_1 x_1 + \cdots + \beta_n x_n$$

and makes it easier to interpret. Let $\mathbf{x}$ and $\mathbf{x}'$ be vectors such that $x_l = x'_l$ for all $l \neq j$ and $x'_j = x_j + 1$, then $logit\ p(C = 1|\mathbf{x}', \boldsymbol{\beta}) - logit\ p(C = 1|\mathbf{x}, \boldsymbol{\beta}) =$

---

[4]The term *logit* stands for logistic probability unit.

$\beta_0 + \sum_{l=1}^{n} \beta_l x_l' - (\beta_0 + \sum_{l=1}^{n} \beta_l x_l) = \beta_j x_j' - \beta_j x_j = \beta_j$. Therefore, coefficient β_j represents the logit change when X_j ($j = 1, \ldots, n$) increases by one unit, if the other variables are unchanged. The logistic regression coefficients should then be interpreted with respect to their effects on the log of the odds.

The parameter estimates, $\hat{\boldsymbol{\beta}}$, are computed by maximum likelihood estimation (Section 2.2.2). Assuming that all the N instances are independent and identically distributed (i.i.d.), the log-likelihood function, $\ln \mathcal{L}(\boldsymbol{\beta}|\mathbf{x}^1, \ldots, \mathbf{x}^N)$, is given by

$$\sum_{i=1}^{N} c^i (\beta_0 + \beta_1 x_1^i + \cdots + \beta_n x_n^i) - \sum_{i=1}^{N} \ln(1 + e^{\beta_0 + \beta_1 x_1^i + \cdots + \beta_n x_n^i}). \qquad (2.8)$$

For simplicity's sake, we write $\ln \mathcal{L}(\boldsymbol{\beta})$ rather than $\ln \mathcal{L}(\boldsymbol{\beta}|\mathbf{x}^1, \ldots, \mathbf{x}^N)$. $\hat{\boldsymbol{\beta}}$ is the result of maximizing Eq. 2.8. The first-order derivatives of the equation with respect to each X_j are set to zero and the resulting system with $n + 1$ equations has to be solved:

$$\begin{cases} \dfrac{\partial \ln \mathcal{L}(\boldsymbol{\beta})}{\partial \beta_0} = \displaystyle\sum_{i=1}^{N} c^i - \sum_{i=1}^{N} \dfrac{e^{\beta_0 + \beta_1 x_1^i + \cdots + \beta_n x_n^i}}{1 + e^{\beta_0 + \beta_1 x_1^i + \cdots + \beta_n x_n^i}} = 0 \\[3mm] \dfrac{\partial \ln \mathcal{L}(\boldsymbol{\beta})}{\partial \beta_j} = \displaystyle\sum_{i=1}^{N} c^i x_j^i - \sum_{i=1}^{N} x_j^i \dfrac{e^{\beta_0 + \beta_1 x_1^i + \cdots + \beta_n x_n^i}}{1 + e^{\beta_0 + \beta_1 x_1^i + \cdots + \beta_n x_n^i}} = 0, \quad j = 1, \ldots, n. \end{cases}$$

The system cannot be solved analytically, because there are non-linear functions in β_js. Hence $\hat{\boldsymbol{\beta}}$ is approximated using iterative techniques such as the **Newton-Raphson method**. This method requires the first and second derivatives (Hessian matrix), and $\hat{\boldsymbol{\beta}}^{\mathrm{old}}$ is updated to $\hat{\boldsymbol{\beta}}^{\mathrm{new}}$ by

$$\hat{\boldsymbol{\beta}}^{\mathrm{new}} = \hat{\boldsymbol{\beta}}^{\mathrm{old}} - \left(\frac{\partial^2 \ln \mathcal{L}(\boldsymbol{\beta})}{\partial \boldsymbol{\beta} \partial \boldsymbol{\beta}^T} \right)^{-1} \frac{\partial \ln \mathcal{L}(\boldsymbol{\beta})}{\partial \boldsymbol{\beta}},$$

where the derivatives are evaluated at $\hat{\boldsymbol{\beta}}^{\mathrm{old}}$. The formula is initialized arbitrarily, e.g., $\hat{\boldsymbol{\beta}}^{\mathrm{old}} = \mathbf{0}$. Its choice is not relevant. The procedure is stopped when there is a negligible change between successive parameter estimates or after running a specified maximum number of iterations.

As with linear regression, multicollinearity among predictor variables must be removed, since it produces unstable β_j estimates. Again as in linear regression, the statistical significance of each variable can be assessed based on hypothesis tests on the β_j coefficients. Testing the null hypothesis $H_0 : \beta_r = 0$ against the alternative hypothesis $H_1 : \beta_r \neq 0$ amounts to testing the elimination of X_r, a way of performing feature selection. Two nested models are used, i.e., all terms of the simpler model occur in the complex model. Most standard approaches are sequential: forward or backward. In a backward elimination process, we can test the hypothesis that a simpler model M_0 holds against a more complex alternative M_1, where M_0 contains the same terms as M_1, except variable X_r. M_0 and M_1 are compared by means of their deviances. The **deviance** D_M of model M is defined in logistic regression as

$$D_M = -2 \sum_{i=1}^{N} \left[c^i \ln \left(\frac{\hat{\theta}_i}{c^i} \right) + (1 - c^i) \ln \left(\frac{1 - \hat{\theta}_i}{1 - c^i} \right) \right],$$

where $\hat{\theta}_i = p(C = c^i | \mathbf{x}, \boldsymbol{\beta})$). Note that the first (second) term is considered zero when $c^i = 0$ ($c^i = 1$). The statistic for testing that M_0 holds against M_1 is $D_{M_0} - D_{M_1}$, which behaves like an approximate chi-squared statistic χ_1^2. If H_0 is rejected, then we select the complex model (M_1) over the simpler model (M_0). In general, several terms can likewise be eliminated from M_1 to yield M_0, although the degrees of freedom of the chi-squared distribution are equal to the number of additional parameters that are in M_1 but not in M_0 (Agresti, 2013). A forward inclusion process works similarly, albeit starting from the null model and including one variable at a time.

Regularization (Section 2.4.2) can also be used for modeling purposes in logistic regression (Shi et al., 2010), especially when $N \ll n$ (i.e., the so-called "large n, small N" problem). L_1-regularization, known as lasso, is designed to solve $\max_{\boldsymbol{\beta}} \left(\ln \mathcal{L}(\boldsymbol{\beta}) - \lambda \sum_{j=1}^{n} |\beta_j| \right)$, where $\lambda \geq 0$ is the penalization parameter that controls the amount of shrinkage (the larger the λ, the greater the shrinkage and the smaller the β_js). The solution includes coefficients that are exactly zero, thus performing feature subset selection.

2.4.9   Bayesian Network Classifiers

Bayesian network classifiers create a joint model $p(\mathbf{x}, c)$ (**generative model**) that is then used to output $p(c|\mathbf{x})$. Note that logistic regression modeled $p(c|\mathbf{x})$ directly (**discriminative model**). These classifiers are probabilistic graphical models offering an interpretable representation of uncertain knowledge. Moreover, their semantics is based on the sound concept of conditional independence (Section 2.5.1), since they are particular cases of Bayesian networks (see Section 2.5.2-2.5.3). The algorithms are computationally efficient. We make a distinction between discrete and continuous domains for predictor variables, resulting in discrete and continuous Bayesian network classifiers, respectively.

2.4.9.1   Discrete Bayesian Network Classifiers

Discrete Bayesian network classifiers (Bielza and Larrañaga, 2014b) model $p(\mathbf{x}, c)$ according to a factorization given by a Bayesian network. The Bayesian network structure is a **directed acyclic graph** (**DAG**) whose vertices correspond to the random discrete variables $X_1, ..., X_n, C$ and whose arcs encode the probabilistic (in)dependences (see Section 2.5.1) among triplets of variables. Each factor is a categorical distribution $p(x_i | \mathbf{pa}(x_i))$ or $p(c | \mathbf{pa}(c))$, where $\mathbf{pa}(x_i)$ is a value of the set of variables $\mathbf{Pa}(X_i)$, which are parents of

X_i in the DAG. The same applies for $\mathbf{pa}(c)$. Thus,

$$p(\mathbf{x}, c) = p(c|\mathbf{pa}(c)) \prod_{i=1}^{n} p(x_i|\mathbf{pa}(x_i)).$$

With sparse $\mathbf{Pa}(X_i)$, this factorization saves many parameters to be estimated.

The standard decision rule finds c^* such that $c^* = \arg\max_c p(c|\mathbf{x}) = \arg\max_c p(\mathbf{x}, c)$.

If C has no parents, then $c^* = \arg\max_c p(c)p(\mathbf{x}|c)$. In this case, different factorizations of $p(\mathbf{x}|c)$, starting from the simplest naive Bayes model, produce a family of **augmented naive Bayes models** (Fig. 2.27, left).

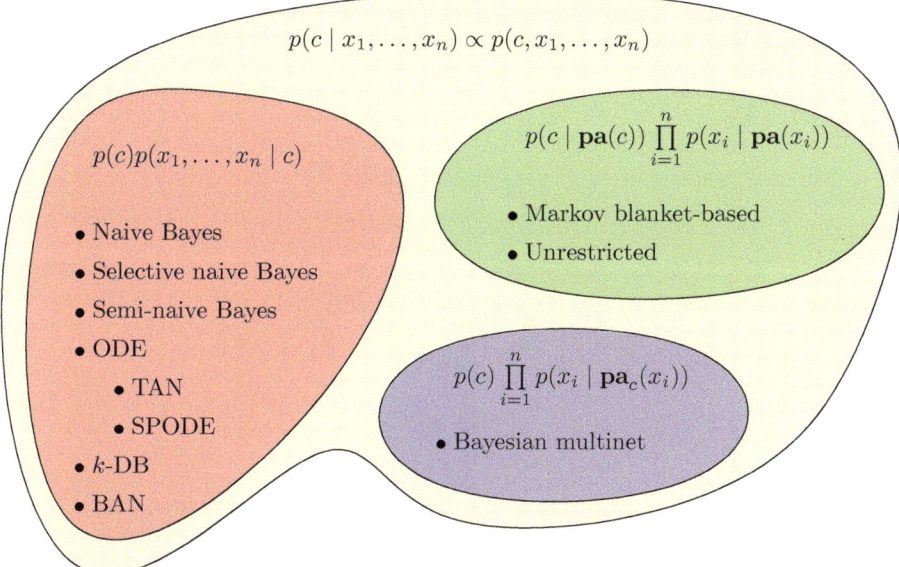

FIGURE 2.27
Taxonomy of discrete Bayesian network classifiers according to three different factorizations of $p(\mathbf{x}, c)$. The group to the left contains the augmented naive Bayes models.

When C has parents, we have Markov blanket-based and unrestricted Bayesian network classifiers (Fig. 2.27, top right), whereas the more complex Bayesian multinets model the conditional independence relationships for different c values (Fig. 2.27, bottom right). Examples of these three families of Bayesian network classifiers are explained below.

Besides the Bayesian network classifier structure, the probabilities $p(x_i|\mathbf{pa}(x_i))$ of the factorization must be estimated from $\mathcal{D}$ by standard methods like maximum likelihood or Bayesian estimation. If X_i takes values $\{1, 2, ..., R_i\}$, the maximum likelihood estimate of $p(X_i = k|\mathbf{Pa}(X_i) = j)$

is given by $\frac{N_{ijk}}{N_{\cdot j}}$, where N_{ijk} is the frequency in $\mathcal{D}$ of cases with $X_i = k$ and $\mathbf{Pa}(X_i) = j$ and $N_{\cdot j}$ is the frequency in $\mathcal{D}$ of cases with $\mathbf{Pa}(X_i) = j$. In Bayesian estimation, assuming a Dirichlet prior distribution over $(p(X_i = 1|\mathbf{Pa}(X_i) = j), ..., p(X_i = R_i|\mathbf{Pa}(X_i) = j))$ with all hyperparameters equal to α, then the posterior distribution is Dirichlet with hyperparameters equal to $N_{ijk} + \alpha$, $k = 1, ..., R_i$. Hence, $p(X_i = k|\mathbf{Pa}(X_i) = j)$ is estimated by $\frac{N_{ijk} + \alpha}{N_{\cdot j} + R_i \alpha}$. This is called the **Lindstone rule**. Special cases are **Laplace estimation** (see Section 2.2.2.1) and the **Schurmann-Grassberger rule**, with $\alpha = 1$ and $\alpha = \frac{1}{R_i}$, respectively.

Naive Bayes (Minsky, 1961) is the simplest Bayesian network classifier, where all predictive variables are assumed to be conditionally independent given the class. When n is high and/or N is small, $p(\mathbf{x}|c)$ is difficult to estimate and this strong assumption is useful. The conditional probabilities for each c given $\mathbf{x}$ are computed as

$$p(c|\mathbf{x}) \propto p(c) \prod_{i=1}^{n} p(x_i|c).$$

Fig. 2.28 shows an example of naive Bayes with five predictor variables.

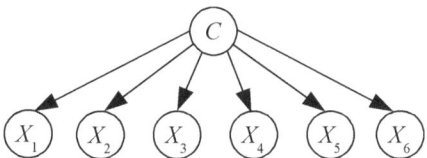

FIGURE 2.28
Naive Bayes: $p(c|\mathbf{x}) \propto p(c)p(x_1|c)p(x_2|c)p(x_3|c)p(x_4|c)p(x_5|c)p(x_6|c)$.

Naive Bayes will improve its performance if only relevant, and especially non-redundant, variables are selected to be in the model. In the **selective naive Bayes**, probabilities are

$$p(c|\mathbf{x}) \propto p(c|\mathbf{x}_F) = p(c) \prod_{i \in F} p(x_i|c),$$

where $F \subseteq \{1, 2, ..., n\}$ denotes the indices of the selected features. Filter (Pazzani and Billsus, 1997), wrapper (Langley and Sage, 1994) and hybrid approaches (Inza et al., 2004) have been used for selective naive Bayes models.

The **semi-naive Bayes** model (Fig. 2.29) relaxes the conditional independence assumption of naive Bayes trying to model dependences between the predictor variables. To do this, it introduces new features that are the Cartesian product of two or more original predictor variables. These new predictor variables are still conditionally independent given the class variable. Thus,

$$p(c|\mathbf{x}) \propto p(c) \prod_{j=1}^{K} p(\mathbf{x}_{S_j}|c),$$

where $S_j \subseteq \{1, 2, ..., n\}$ denotes the indices in the j-th feature (original or Cartesian product), $j = 1, ..., K$ (K is the number of nodes), $S_j \cap S_l = \emptyset$, for $j \neq l$.

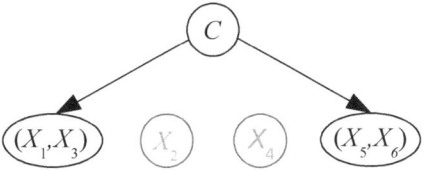

FIGURE 2.29
Semi-naive Bayes: $p(c|\mathbf{x}) \propto p(c)p(x_1, x_3|c)p(x_5, x_6|c)$.

The objective function driving the standard algorithm for learning a semi-naive Bayes model (Pazzani, 1996) is classification accuracy. The **forward sequential selection and joining** algorithm starts from an empty structure. The accuracy is computed after assigning the most frequent label to all instances. Then the algorithm chooses the best option (in terms of classification accuracy) between (a) adding a variable not yet used as conditionally independent of the already included features (original or Cartesian products), and (b) joining a variable not yet used with each feature (original or Cartesian products) present in the classifier. The algorithm stops when accuracy does not improve.

In **one-dependence estimators** (**ODE**s), each predictor variable depends on at most one other predictor variable apart from the class variable. Tree-augmented naive Bayes and superparent-one-dependence estimators are two types of ODEs.

The predictor variables of the **tree-augmented naive Bayes** (**TAN**) form a tree. Thus, all have one parent, except for one variable, called the root, which is parentless (Fig. 2.30). Then

$$p(c|\mathbf{x}) \propto p(c)p(x_r|c) \prod_{i=1, i \neq r}^{n} p(x_i|c, x_{j(i)}),$$

where X_r denotes the root node and $\{X_{j(i)}\} = \mathbf{Pa}(X_i) \setminus C$, for any $i \neq r$.

The mutual information of any pair of predictor variables conditioned on C, $\mathbb{I}(X_i, X_j|C)$, is first computed to learn a TAN structure (Friedman et al., 1997). This measures the information that one variable provides about the other variable when the value of C is known. Second, a complete undirected graph with nodes $X_1, ..., X_n$ is built. The edge between X_i and X_j is annotated with a weight equal to the above mutual information of X_i and X_j given C. Third, Kruskal's algorithm (Kruskal, 1956) is used to find a **maximum weighted spanning tree** in that graph, containing $n - 1$ edges. This algorithm selects a subset of edges from the graph such that they form a tree and the sum of their weights is maximized. This is performed by sequentially choosing the edge with the heaviest weight, provided this does not yield a cycle. We then select

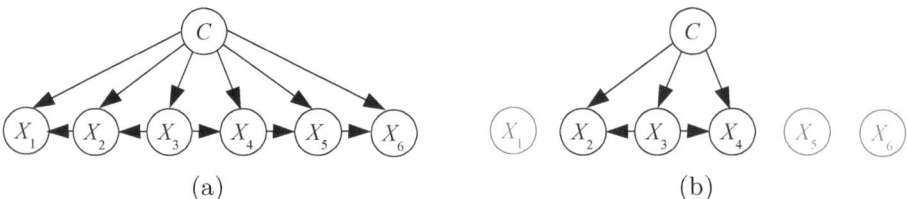

FIGURE 2.30

(a) TAN with X_3 as root node:
$p(c|\mathbf{x}) \propto p(c)p(x_1|c, x_2)p(x_2|c, x_3)p(x_3|c)p(x_4|c, x_3)p(x_5|c, x_4))p(x_6|c, x_5)$. (b)
Selective TAN: $p(c|\mathbf{x}) \propto p(c)p(x_2|c, x_3)p(x_3|c)p(x_4|c, x_3)$.

any variable as the root node and set the direction of all edges as outgoing
from this node to make the undirected tree directed. This tree including only
predictor variables is added to a naive Bayes structure to produce the final
TAN structure.

If the weights are first filtered with a χ^2 test of independence, the resulting
classifier is the **selective TAN** (Blanco et al., 2005) (Fig. 2.30(b)). This may
yield a forest (i.e., a disjoint union of trees) rather than a tree because there
are many root nodes.

Superparent-one-dependence estimators (Keogh and Pazzani, 2002)
(**SPODE**s) are an ODE where all predictors depend on the same predictor
called the superparent as well as the class. Note that this is a particular case
of a TAN model. Classification is given by

$$p(c|\mathbf{x}) \propto p(c)p(x_{sp}|c) \prod_{i=1, i \neq sp}^{n} p(x_i|c, x_{sp}),$$

where X_{sp} denotes the superparent node.

The **averaged one-dependence estimator** (**AODE**) (Webb et al., 2005)
is a widely used variant of SPODE. This model averages the predictions of
all SPODEs for which the probability estimates are accurate, i.e., where the
training data contain more than m cases verifying $X_{sp} = x_{sp}$. Webb et al.
(2005) suggest fixing $m = 30$. The average prediction is given by

$$p(c|\mathbf{x}) \propto p(c, \mathbf{x}) = \frac{1}{|\mathcal{SP}_{\mathbf{x}}^m|} \sum_{X_{sp} \in \mathcal{SP}_{\mathbf{x}}^m} p(c)p(x_{sp}|c) \prod_{i=1, i \neq sp}^{n} p(x_i|c, x_{sp}), \quad (2.9)$$

where $\mathcal{SP}_{\mathbf{x}}^m$ denotes for each $\mathbf{x}$ the set of predictor variables qualified as
superparents and $|\cdot|$ is its cardinal. AODE is, in fact, a collection of classifiers
(i.e., a metaclassifier, see Section 2.4.10). Fortunately, AODE avoids model
selection, and the structure is fixed.

In the k-**dependence Bayesian classifier** (k-**DB**) (Sahami, 1996), each
predictor variable has, apart from the class variable, at most k parents

(Fig. 2.31). Then

$$p(c|\mathbf{x}) \propto p(c) \prod_{i=1}^{n} p(x_i|c, x_{i_1}, ..., x_{i_k}),$$

where $X_{i_1}, ..., X_{i_k}$ are parents of X_i.

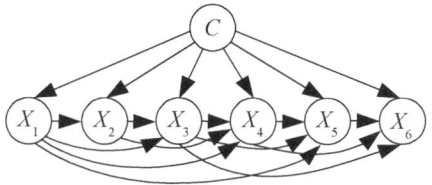

FIGURE 2.31
3-DB structure: $p(c|\mathbf{x}) \propto$
$p(c)p(x_1|c)p(x_2|c, x_1)p(x_3|c, x_1, x_2)p(x_4|c, x_1, x_2, x_3)p(x_5|c, x_1, x_3, x_4)$
$p(x_6|c, x_3, x_4, x_5)$.

X_i enters the model according to the value of $\mathbb{I}(X_i, C)$, starting with the highest. When X_i enters the model, its parents are selected by choosing the k variables X_j that are already in the model and have the highest values of $\mathbb{I}(X_i, X_j|C)$.

In the **Bayesian network-augmented naive Bayes (BAN)** (Ezawa and Norton, 1996), the predictor variables can form any Bayesian network structure (Fig. 2.32). Probabilities are now given by

$$p(c|\mathbf{x}) \propto p(c) \prod_{i=1}^{n} p(x_i|\mathbf{pa}(x_i)).$$

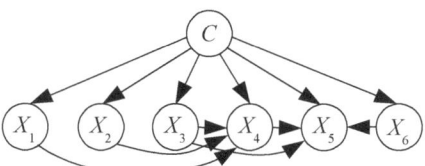

FIGURE 2.32
Bayesian network-augmented naive Bayes:
$p(c|\mathbf{x}) \propto p(c)p(x_1|c)p(x_2|c)p(x_3|c)p(x_4|c, x_1, x_2, x_3)p(x_5|c, x_3, x_4, x_6)p(x_6|c)$.

A BAN learning process first ranks all n predictor variables based on $\mathbb{I}(X_i, C)$ and then selects the minimum number k of predictor variables verifying $\sum_{j=1}^{k} \mathbb{I}(X_j, C) \geq t_{CX} \sum_{j=1}^{n} \mathbb{I}(X_j, C)$, where $0 < t_{CX} < 1$ is the threshold. Second, $\mathbb{I}(X_i, X_j|C)$ is computed for all pairs of selected variables. The process now selects the minimum number e of edges $X_i - X_j$ verifying

$\sum_{i<j}^{e} \mathbb{I}(X_i, X_j | C) \geq t_{XX} \sum_{i<j}^{k} \mathbb{I}(X_i, X_j | C)$, where $0 < t_{XX} < 1$ is the threshold. Edges are oriented according to the variable ranking in the first step: higher-ranked variables point towards lower-ranked variables.

If C has parents,

$$p(c|\mathbf{x}) \propto p(c|\mathbf{pa}(c)) \prod_{i=1}^{n} p(x_i|\mathbf{pa}(x_i)).$$

A **Markov blanket-based Bayesian classifier** should identify the Markov blanket of the class variable. The **Markov blanket** of C is the set of variables $\mathbf{MB}_C$ which make C conditionally independent of the other variables in the network, given the Markov blanket. Therefore, they are the only variables needed to predict C (since $p(c|\mathbf{x}) = p(c|\mathbf{mb}_C)$), and these classifiers are designed to search for this Markov blanket. Under certain conditions, the Markov blanket of C is the set of its parents, its children and the parents of its children. (Fig. 2.33).

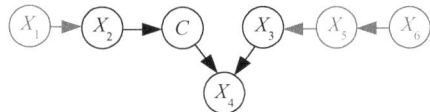

FIGURE 2.33
Markov blanket-based Bayesian classifier:
$p(c|\mathbf{x}) \propto p(c|x_2)p(x_2)p(x_3)p(x_4|c, x_3)$. The Markov blanket of C is
$\mathbf{MB}_C = \{X_2, X_3, X_4\}$.

In Koller and Sahami (1996), this is stated as a feature selection problem. Their proposal starts from the set of all the predictor variables and eliminates a variable at each step (backward greedy strategy) until it gets a good enough approximation of $\mathbf{MB}_C$. The algorithm eliminates feature by feature, trying to keep $p(C|\mathbf{MB}_C^{(t)})$, the conditional probability of C given the current estimation of the Markov blanket at step t, as close to $p(C|\mathbf{X})$ as possible.

In **unrestricted Bayesian classifiers**, C is not considered a special variable and any existing Bayesian network structure learning algorithm (Section 2.5.3) can be applied. The corresponding Markov blanket of C is used later for classification purposes, i.e., $p(c|\mathbf{mb}_C)$ rather than $p(c|\mathbf{x})$.

Finally, **Bayesian multinets** (Geiger and Heckerman, 1996) can represent conditional independence relationships that hold for only some but not all the values of the variables involved. They include several (local) Bayesian networks, each representing a joint probability of all variables conditioned on a specific subset of values of a variable H, called the hypothesis or distinguished variable. The class variable C is the distinguished variable of **Bayesian multinets based classifiers**. The subsets of values of C are usually singletons. Thus, conditioned on each c, the predictors can form different local networks with different structures, where trees or forests are the most common (see Fig. 2.34).

Therefore, the relations among variables do not have to be the same for all c:

$$p(c|\mathbf{x}) \propto p(c) \prod_{i=1}^{n} p(x_i|\mathbf{pa}_c(x_i)),$$

where $\mathbf{Pa}_c(X_i)$ is the parent set of X_i in the local Bayesian network associated with $C = c$.

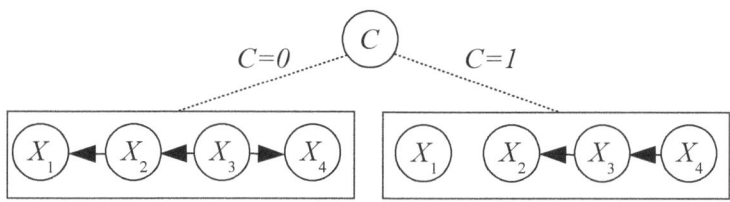

FIGURE 2.34
Bayesian multinet as a collection of trees: $p(C = 0|\mathbf{x}) \propto p(C = 0)p(x_1|C = 0, x_2)p(x_2|C = 0, x_3)p(x_3|C = 0)p(x_4|C = 0, x_3)$ and $p(C = 1|\mathbf{x}) \propto p(C = 1)p(x_1|C = 1)p(x_2|C = 1, x_3)p(x_3|C = 1, x_4)p(x_4|C = 1)$.

2.4.9.2   Continuous Bayesian Network Classifiers

Some Bayesian classifiers assume conditional Gaussian densities for continuous predictor variables. Thus, the **Gaussian naive Bayes classifier** (Friedman et al., 1998a) assumes that the conditional density of each predictor variable, X_i, given a value of the class variable, c, follows a Gaussian distribution, that is, $X_i|C = c \sim \mathcal{N}(x_i|\mu_{c,i}, \sigma_{c,i})$ for all $i = 1, \ldots, n$; $c = 1, ..., R$. The prediction is computed as

$$c^* = \arg\max_c p(c) \prod_{i=1}^{n} \left[\frac{1}{\sqrt{2\pi}\sigma_{c,i}} e^{\frac{-1}{2}\left(\frac{x_i - \mu_{c,i}}{\sigma_{c,i}}\right)^2} \right].$$

The parameters to be estimated are the a priori probabilities $p(c)$ and the mean $\mu_{c,i}$ and standard deviation $\sigma_{c,i}$ of each predictor variable X_i for each c value of the class variable. Maximum likelihood is usually employed for estimations.

The **Gaussian semi-naive Bayes classifier, Gaussian tree-augmented naive Bayes classifier** and **Gaussian k-dependence Bayesian classifier** were proposed by Pérez et al. (2006) as adaptations of the respective discrete classifiers to continuous domains under Gaussianity assumptions.

For non-Gaussian predictors, **kernel-based Bayesian classifiers** (Pérez et al., 2009) use non-parametric kernel density estimation (Silverman, 1986), whereas Rumí et al. (2006) and Flores et al. (2011) used a **mixture of truncated exponentials** in naive Bayes and AODEs, respectively.

2.4.10   Metaclassifiers

Metaclassifiers (Kuncheva, 2004) have featured prominently in machine learning since the 1990s and have been used in successful real-world applications. Metaclassifiers use multiple classification models, called **base classifiers**, to make the final decision. The base classifiers are first generated and then combined.

The main grounds underlying this idea is the **no free lunch theorem** (Wolpert and Macready, 1997), whereby a general-purpose (and universally good) classification algorithm is theoretically impossible. Combining multiple algorithms, the overall performance is expected to improve; the variance of the metaclassifier (Section 2.2.2) has shown to be reduced. Diversity in the base classifiers is believed to be a good property for a metaclassifier. Base classifiers should make mistakes in different instances and specialize in problem subdomains. This resembles the behavior of a patient visiting more than one doctor to get a second opinion before making a (better) final decision about his or her health.

The possible ways of combining the outputs of L base classifiers $\phi_1, ..., \phi_L$ in a metaclassifier depend on whether or not base classifiers are probabilistic. A non-probabilistic classifier outputs predicted class labels, whereas probabilistic classifiers produce, for each instance, a distribution with the estimated posterior probabilities of the class variable conditioned on $\mathbf{x}$. In each case we have, respectively, methods of fusion of label outputs and methods of fusion of continuous-valued outputs.

The **fusion of label outputs** defines different voting rules for decision making. Examples include unanimity vote, majority vote, simple majority vote, thresholded majority vote and weighted majority vote. In the **fusion of continuous-valued outputs**, the estimated posterior probabilities of c_j conditioned on $\mathbf{x}$ for classifier ϕ_i, i.e., $p_i(c_j|\mathbf{x})$, can be interpreted as the confidence in label c_j. As with label outputs, there are multiple options for summarizing all the outputs given by the L classifiers. Examples are the simple mean, the minimum, the maximum, the median, the trimmed mean[5], and the weighted average.

Besides this plethora of combiners, there are popular metaclassifiers, namely, stacking, cascading, bagging, random forests, boosting and hybridizations, all described below.

Stacked generalization (Wolpert, 1992) is a generic methodology, where the outputs of the base classifiers, $\phi_1, ..., \phi_L$, are combined through another classifier ϕ^*. In its simplest version, two layers are stacked. The base classifiers form layer-0, which are usually different classification algorithms. Their predictions (output by honest estimation methods) along with the true class labels are the inputs for the layer-1 classifier, which makes the final decision.

Cascading (Kaynak and Alpaydin, 2000) sorts the L classifiers in increas-

---

[5]The trimmed mean calculates the mean after discarding equal parts from both extremes of the probability distribution or sample.

ing order of complexity in terms of either space, time or representation cost (Fig. 2.35). Given an instance, a classifier is only used if the preceding classifiers are not sufficiently confident for that instance. This confidence is related to its output. Thus, a probabilistic classifier that makes a decision based on the maximum a posteriori class value, $c^* = \arg\max_c p(c|\mathbf{x})$, could require a specific threshold θ^* for the maximum posterior probability. If the probability is not high enough, then the classifier is not considered confident and the next classifier is applied. To limit the number L of classifiers, the few instances not covered by any classifier are treated by a non-parametric classifier, like the k-NN algorithm.

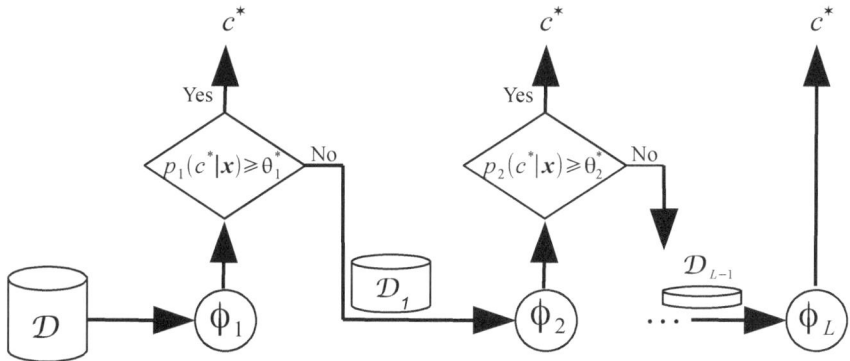

FIGURE 2.35
Cascading metaclassifier. The prediction of an instance $\mathbf{x}$ by classifier ϕ_i is $c^* = \arg\max_c p_i(c|\mathbf{x})$ whenever $p_i(c^*|\mathbf{x}) \geq \theta_i^*$ (and $\mathbf{x}$ is a correct classification). Otherwise, if $\mathbf{x}$ is a misclassification or $p_i(c^*|\mathbf{x}) < \theta_i^*$, $\mathbf{x}$ is passed on to ϕ_{i+1}, probably with a different threshold θ_{i+1}^*.

Bootstrap AGGregatING, also known as **bagging**, generates multiple versions of the same classification algorithm, each built from bootstrap replicates of the original dataset $\mathcal{D}$ of size N (Breiman, 1996). Bootstrapping (Section 2.4.1) randomly samples with replacement N cases from $\mathcal{D}$. Bagging (Fig. 2.36) repeats the bootstrapping L times to yield replicate datasets $\mathcal{D}_b^l$, $l = 1, ..., L$, all of size N. About 63.2% of the original examples in each dataset are chosen during this process. Then a classifier ϕ_l is learned from $\mathcal{D}_b^l$, $l = 1, ..., L$. The goodness of each base classifier can be estimated using the non-selected cases (about 36.8% of the original dataset), known as **out-of-bag** cases. Thus, the out-of-bag prediction for an instance $\mathbf{x}$ will only involve classifiers that have not been trained on $\mathbf{x}$. The final decision is made using the majority vote rule (for label outputs) or the average/median combiner (for continuous-valued outputs). Bagging works well for **unstable classifiers**, where a small change in the input data can produce large changes in their outputs. Bootstrap replicates entail small changes in $\mathcal{D}$. Therefore, if the base classifier is unstable, bagging will provide diversity in the metaclassifier. Classification trees, rule induction and ANNs are unstable and hence appropriate for bagging implementation.

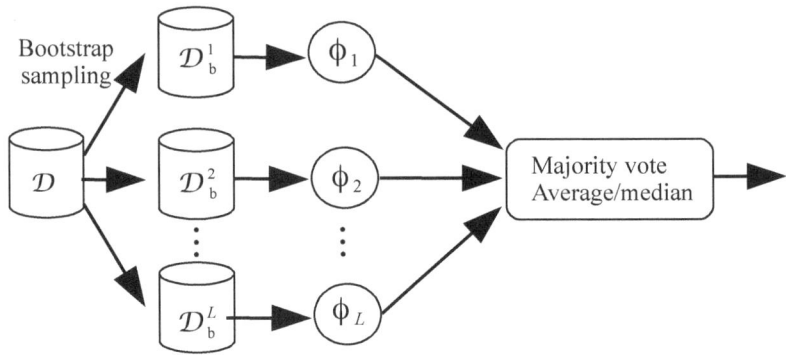

FIGURE 2.36
Bagging metaclassifier. The same type of classifier is trained from bootstrap replicates. The final decision uses majority vote (label outputs) or average/median (continuous outputs).

A **random forest** (Breiman, 2001a) is a variant of bagging where base classifiers are classification trees. It is termed 'random' because besides randomizing the dataset instances (as in bagging), we can use random feature selection or even randomly vary some tree parameter. By combining these sources of diversity we get different versions of random forests. The bagged trees are combined at the end by majority vote.

Boosting (Freund and Schapire, 1997) incrementally builds the metaclassifier, adding one base classifier at a time. The classifier added at step i is trained on a dataset sampled from $\mathcal{D}$. In the first step, all instances have the same probability of being selected (uniform distribution). Then the distribution shifts to increase the likelihood of "difficult" instances, i.e., instances where the preceding classifiers failed. The main algorithm is called **AdaBoost**, which stands for **ADAptive BOOSTing**, initially proposed for binary classes. Algorithm 2.5 shows the **AdaBoost.M1** pseudocode, which is the most straightforward extension of AdaBoost to the multiclass case.

Step 2a corresponds to the initial uniform sampling when $i = 1$. The resulting dataset $\mathcal{D}_i$ of size N is the input for learning classifier ϕ_i (Step 2b). The weighted error of ϕ_i is computed as the sum of the misclassification weights (Step 2c). If this error is greater than 0.5 or zero, ϕ_i is ignored and the process ends with $i - 1$ base classifiers (Step 2d). Otherwise, the weights are updated (Step 2f). The effect is that instances correctly classified by ϕ_i have lower weights, whereas misclassifications have greater weights, since $\beta_i \in (0, 0.5)$. The denominator is a normalization factor. Finally, decisions are combined in the classification phase (Steps 3 and 4) using a weighted majority vote, where

---

Algorithm 2.5: AdaBoost.M1

Input : A dataset $\mathcal{D} = \{(\mathbf{x}^1, c^1), ..., (\mathbf{x}^N, c^N)\}$, a base classifier and L
Output: A metaclassifier $\{\phi_1, ..., \phi_L\}$

1 Initialize weights $w_j^1 = \frac{1}{N}, j = 1, ..., N$

2 **for** $i = 1, ..., L$ **do**

2a   Draw a sample $\mathcal{D}_i$ from $\mathcal{D}$ with replacement using the probability distribution $(w_1^i, ..., w_N^i)$

2b   Learn a classifier ϕ_i using $\mathcal{D}_i$ as the training set

2c   Compute the weighted error ϵ_i at step i by $\epsilon_i = \sum_{j=1}^{N} w_j^i l_j^i$ ($l_j^i = 1$ if ϕ_i misclassifies $\mathbf{x}^j$ and $l_j^i = 0$ otherwise)

2d   **if** $\epsilon_i = 0$ *or* $\epsilon_i \geq 0.5$ **then**
        | Ignore ϕ_i, set $L = i - 1$, and stop
        else

2e   Set $\beta_i = \frac{\epsilon_i}{1 - \epsilon_i}$

2f   Update weights: $w_j^{i+1} = \frac{w_j^i \beta_i^{1 - l_j^i}}{\sum_{k=1}^{N} w_k^i \beta_i^{1 - l_k^i}}$, for $j = 1, ..., N$

        end

    end

3 For an instance $\mathbf{x}$ to be classified, calculate the support for class c_k by $\mu_k(\mathbf{x}) = \sum_{\phi_i(\mathbf{x}) = c_k} \ln(1/\beta_i)$

4 Select the class with the maximum support as the label for $\mathbf{x}$

---

each classifier's vote is a function of its accuracy in the training set, given by $\ln(1/\beta_i)$. Note that a zero error ($\epsilon_i = 0$ in Step 2d) is a potential overfitting. In this case, $\beta_i = 0$, $\ln(1/\beta_i) = \infty$ and ϕ_i has an infinite voting-weight that should be avoided (despotic classifier). Classifiers with $\epsilon_i < 0.5$ are called **weak classifiers**, they are AdaBoost targets. Fig. 2.37 is a flowchart showing how AdaBoost.M1 works.

Hybrid classifiers hybridize two (or more) classification algorithms to leverage their strengths. **Naive Bayes tree (NBTree)** (Kohavi, 1996) combines classification trees and naive Bayes. NBTree recursively splits the instance space into subspaces, and a (local) naive Bayes classifier is built in each subspace. It is this local model that predicts the class label of the instances that reach the leaf. **Lazy Bayesian rule learning algorithm (LBR)** (Zheng and Webb, 2000) combines naive Bayes and rules. To classify a test instance, LBR generates a rule whose antecedent is a conjunction of predictor-value pairs and whose consequent is a local naive Bayes classifier created from the training cases satisfying the antecedent. **Logistic model trees** (Landwehr et al., 2003) are classification trees with logistic regression models at the leaves, applied to instances that reach such leaves.

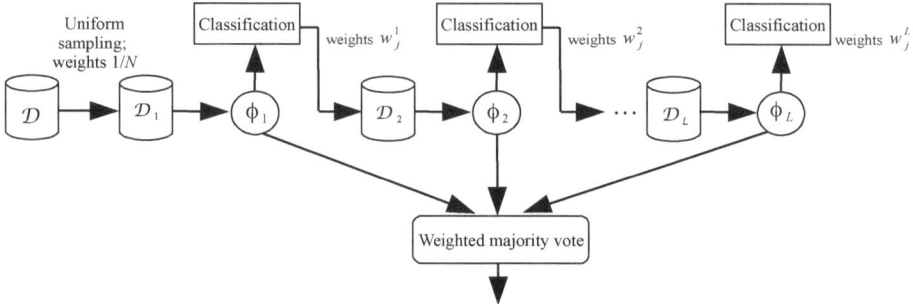

FIGURE 2.37
Boosting metaclassifier. The base classifiers are all of the same type. The training set $\mathcal{D}_i$ of size N sampled from $\mathcal{D}$ focuses more on the mistakes of ϕ_{i-1}. The final decision uses the weighted majority vote.

2.5   Bayesian Networks

This section reviews Bayesian networks. Bayesian networks are models that have many advantages with respect to their representation and usability. They are intuitive probabilistic graphical models of dependence relationships among the variables of a domain under uncertainty. They can accommodate both continuous and discrete variables, and even temporal variables. The model can be learned automatically from data and/or with the aid of a domain expert. Moreover, Bayesian networks can support all machine learning tasks (Section 2.1): clustering, supervised classification and association discovery.

2.5.1   Fundamentals of Bayesian Networks

A **Bayesian network** (BN) (Pearl, 1988; Koller and Friedman, 2009) is a compact representation of the joint probability distribution (JPD) $p(X_1, ..., X_n)$ over a set of discrete random variables $X_1, ..., X_n$. Once the JPD is found, all the information is known, and any probabilistic question can be answered. However, the JPD requires all configurations of $X_1, ..., X_n$, which is an exponentially growing number on n (e.g., we need 2^n values if all X_i are binary), to be determined. Bayesian networks solve this problem by using the concept of conditional independence between triplets of variables.

Two random variables X and Y are **conditionally independent** (c.i.) given another random variable Z if $p(x|y, z) = p(x|z) \ \forall x, y, z$ values of X, Y, Z, that is, whenever $Z = z$, the information $Y = y$ does not influence the probability p of x. An equivalent definition is $p(x, y|z) = p(x|z)p(y|z) \ \forall x, y, z$ values of X, Y, Z. Let $I_p(X, Y|Z)$ denote this condition. X, Y, Z can even be disjoint random vectors.

If conditional independence is exploited, we can avoid intractability because we use fewer parameters (probabilities) and a compact expression. Suppose that we find, for each X_i, a subset $\mathbf{Pa}(X_i) \subseteq \{X_1, ..., X_{i-1}\}$ such that given $\mathbf{Pa}(X_i)$, X_i is conditionally independent of all variables in $\{X_1, ..., X_{i-1}\} \setminus \mathbf{Pa}(X_i)$, i.e., $p(X_i|X_1, ..., X_{i-1}) = p(X_i|\mathbf{Pa}(X_i))$. This is what a BN does. Then the JPD factorizes as

$$p(X_1, ..., X_n) = p(X_1)p(X_2|X_1)p(X_3|X_1, X_2) \cdots p(X_n|X_1, ..., X_{n-1})$$
$$= p(X_1|\mathbf{Pa}(X_1)) \cdots p(X_n|\mathbf{Pa}(X_n)). \tag{2.10}$$

The first equality is the application of the chain rule. In the second equality, we use the previous assumption. The resulting expression will (hopefully) have fewer parameters. Furthermore, this modularity makes the maintenance and reasoning easier, as explained below.

A BN represents this factorization of the JPD with a directed acyclic graph (DAG). This is the qualitative component of a BN, called the **BN structure**. A graph $\mathcal{G}$ is a pair (V, E), where V is the set of nodes and E is the set of edges between the nodes in V. Nodes are the domain random variables $X_1, ..., X_n$. If the edges are directed –called arcs– from one node to another, $\mathcal{G}$ is directed. The **parent nodes $\mathbf{Pa}(X_i)$** of a node X_i are all the nodes pointing at X_i as given by the arcs. Similarly, X_i is their **child node**. An **acyclic** graph contains no cycles, that is, following the direction of the arcs, there is no sequence of nodes (directed path) starting and ending at the same node.

The other component of the BN is quantitative and is a collection of conditional probability distributions. They form the **BN parameters**. For each node X_i, the distributions are $p(X_i|\mathbf{Pa}(X_i))$, one per $\mathbf{Pa}(X_i)$ value. These conditional probabilities are multiplied as indicated by the arcs to output the JPD (see Eq. 2.10). In discrete variables, BN parameters can be arranged tabularly, yielding a **conditional probability table (CPT)**.

Example. Factory production

Fig. 2.38 shows a hypothetical example of a BN, modeling factory production. All variables are binary. Years Y is the factory's age, where y denotes 'more than 10 years' and $\neg y$ denotes 'less than 10 years'. Employees E represents the number of employees: more (e) or less ($\neg e$) than 100 employees. Machines M has two values: m and $\neg m$ for 'more than 20 machines' and 'less than 20 machines', respectively. Pieces P also has two options: more (p) or less ($\neg p$) than 10,000 produced pieces per year. Finally, the variable Failures F includes f that stands for 'more than two failures on average per month' and otherwise the state is $\neg f$. As for the arcs, factory age influences its manpower (E) and size (M), each of which determines production (P). Failures depend on how many machines there are in the factory. As regards the specific BN parameters, note, for example, that if a factory has more than 100 employees and more than 20 machines, there is a 0.96 probability that the factory will manufacture more than 10,000 pieces: $p(p|e, m) = 0.96$. However, if the factory has fewer than 100 employees and fewer than 20 machines, this probability is only 0.10, i.e., $p(p|\neg e, \neg m) = 0.10$.

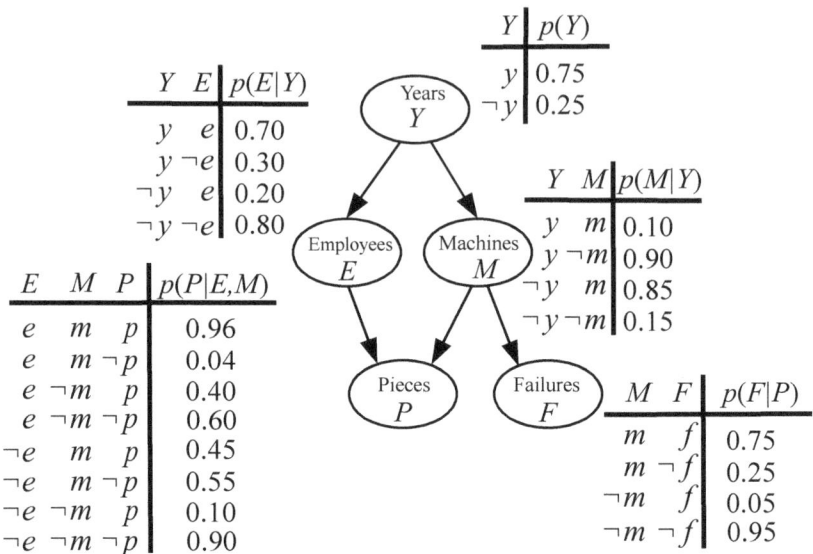

FIGURE 2.38
Hypothetical BN modeling factory production.

The JPD is factorized as

$$p(Y, E, M, P, F) = p(Y)p(E|Y)p(M|Y)p(P|E, M)p(F|M).$$

To fully specify the JPD, we require $2^5 = 32$ parameters. However, the BN representing the above JPD factorization requires 22 input probabilities, as shown in Fig. 2.38 (or, in actual fact, 17, since complementary probabilities can be derived). ∎

The **descendant nodes** of X_i are the nodes reachable from X_i by repeatedly following the arcs. Let $\mathbf{ND}(X_i)$ denote the **non-descendant nodes** of X_i. Following the arcs in the opposite direction, we find the **ancestors**. In a BN, each node is conditionally independent of its non-descendants, given its parents, or $I_p(X_i, \mathbf{ND}(X_i)|\mathbf{Pa}(X_i))$ for short. This is the **local directed Markov property** or **Markov condition**.

Apart from the Markov condition, there is a graphical criterion for finding additional conditional independences. If $\mathbf{X}$ is **u-separated** (Lauritzen et al., 1990) from $\mathbf{Y}$ given $\mathbf{Z}$, then $\mathbf{X}$ and $\mathbf{Y}$ are c.i. given $\mathbf{Z}$, for any $\mathbf{X}, \mathbf{Y}, \mathbf{Z}$ disjoint random vectors (sets of nodes in the BN)[6]. Checking whether **X** and **Y** are u-separated by **Z** is a three-step procedure:

1. Get the smallest subgraph containing **X**, **Y**, and **Z** and their ancestors (this is called the **ancestral graph**).

2. Moralize the resulting subgraph, i.e., add an undirected link between parents having a common child and then drop directions on all arcs.

3. **Z** u-separates **X** and **Y** whenever **Z** is in all paths between **X** and **Y**.

Example. Factory production (u-separation)

All nodes are descendants of Y. The descendants of M are P and F. The Markov condition for M states that E and M are c.i. given Y. All nodes are non-descendants of P and hence P and $\{Y, F\}$ are c.i. given $\{E, M\}$.

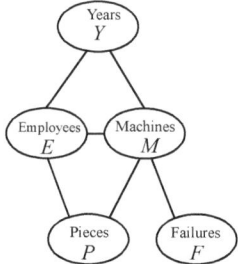

FIGURE 2.39
Moralized ancestral graph of the factory production BN in Fig. 2.38.

Let us check whether P and F are u-separated by $\{E, M\}$. The ancestral subgraph is the whole DAG. Edge E-M is now added because E and M have P as a child. The moralized ancestral graph after dropping arc directions is shown in Fig. 2.39. Since E or M is always found in every path from P to F, P and F are u-separated by $\{E, M\}$. Hence P and F are c.i. given $\{E, M\}$. However, Y and F are not u-separated by P because we can go from F to Y through M, without crossing P. ∎

Because in BNs separation implies conditional independence, BNs are said to be an **independence map** of p, or **I-map** for short. In **perfect maps**, the reverse also holds since conditional independences also imply separations and then all the independences in the distribution are read directly from the DAG, which is not always the case in BNs (in BNs p may have some independences that are not reflected in $\mathcal{G}$ by u-separations).

BNs are, in fact, a **minimal I-map** of p, i.e., an I-map where if some arc is

---

[6]There is an equivalent criterion to u-separation, called d-separation, because it is applied to directed graphs, that is perhaps harder to verify, but also implies conditional independence (Verma and Pearl, 1990a).

removed it is no longer an I-map. A domain expert helping to build a minimal I-map starts by considering an **ancestral ordering** of nodes (i.e., parents come before children in the order), say $X_1, X_2, \cdots, X_n$. Then the minimal subset of nodes in $\{X_1, ..., X_{i-1}\}$ that renders X_i c.i. of $\{X_1, ..., X_{i-1}\} \backslash \mathbf{Pa}(X_i)$ are selected as parents of X_i, $\mathbf{Pa}(X_i)$, see Eq. 2.10. As the ancestral ordering is unknown, we can, in practice, take an arbitrary ordering or use a causal order if there is one. The resulting DAG and its corresponding factorization will be an I-map of the independence statements for the JPD.

Two BNs with the same set of nodes are **Markov equivalent** (Chickering, 1995) if both DAGs induce the same set of conditional independence statements among variables. Two DAGs are Markov equivalent if and only if they have the same skeleton and the same **immoralities**, also called **v-structures** (Verma and Pearl, 1990b). An immorality is a structure $X \rightarrow Y \leftarrow Z$, where X and Z are not connected.

The space of DAGs partitions into a set of equivalence classes, since the equivalence relation is reflexive, symmetric and transitive. The **complete partially DAG (CPDAG)** or **essential graph** uniquely represents all members of an equivalence class. It has an arc $X \rightarrow Y$ if it appears in every DAG of the same equivalence class or else a link $X - Y$ (meaning that either direction $X \rightarrow Y$ or $X \leftarrow Y$ is possible in the DAGs within the equivalence class, see Fig. 2.40(a)-(b)). The DAG members of an equivalence class can be derived from an essential graph by assigning any direction to the undirected edges, provided that this does not introduce any cycle or immorality into the graph (see Fig. 2.40(c)-(e)).

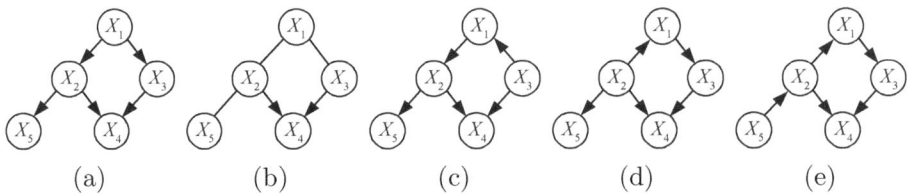

| (a) | (b) | (c) | (d) | (e) |

FIGURE 2.40
(a) A DAG with five variables. There is one immorality at X_4. (b) Its essential graph. (c)-(e) The three DAGs equivalent to the DAG in (a). DAGs (a),(c)-(e) form the equivalence class, represented by the essential graph (b).

In the world of continuous random variables, **Gaussian BNs** (Shachter and Kenley, 1989) assume that the JPD for $\mathbf{X} = (X_1, ..., X_n)$ is a multivariate normal distribution (see Section 2.3.5), $\mathcal{N}(\boldsymbol{\mu}, \boldsymbol{\Sigma})$, given by

$$f(\mathbf{x}; \boldsymbol{\mu}, \boldsymbol{\Sigma}) = \frac{1}{(2\pi)^{n/2}|\boldsymbol{\Sigma}|^{1/2}} \exp\left(-\frac{1}{2}(\boldsymbol{x} - \boldsymbol{\mu})^T \boldsymbol{\Sigma}^{-1}(\boldsymbol{x} - \boldsymbol{\mu})\right), \quad (2.11)$$

where $\boldsymbol{\mu} = (\mu_1, ..., \mu_n)^T$ is the vector of means, $\boldsymbol{\Sigma}$ is the $n \times n$ covariance matrix and $|\boldsymbol{\Sigma}|$ is its determinant. Its inverse is the precision matrix $\mathbf{W} = \boldsymbol{\Sigma}^{-1}$

(see Section 2.2.1). The required parameters are then $\boldsymbol{\mu}$ and $\boldsymbol{\Sigma}$. An interesting property is that a variable X_i is conditionally independent of X_j given the other variables iff $w_{ij} = 0$, where w_{ij} is the (i,j)-entry of $\mathbf{W}$.

The JPD in a Gaussian BN can be equivalently defined by the product of n univariate (linear) Gaussian conditional densities

$$f(\mathbf{x}) = f_1(x_1)f_2(x_2|x_1)\cdots f_n(x_n|x_1, ..., x_{n-1}), \tag{2.12}$$

each given by

$$f_i(x_i|x_1, ..., x_{i-1}) \sim \mathcal{N}(\mu_i + \sum_{j=1}^{i-1} \beta_{ij}(x_j - \mu_j), v_i), \tag{2.13}$$

where μ_i is the unconditional mean of X_i (i.e., the i-th component of $\boldsymbol{\mu}$), v_i is the conditional variance of X_i given values for $x_1, ..., x_{i-1}$ and β_{ij} is the linear regression coefficient of X_j in the regression of X_i on $X_1, ..., X_{i-1}$. Thus, the parameters that determine a Gaussian BN in this factorized form are $\boldsymbol{\mu} = (\mu_1, ..., \mu_n)^T$, $\mathbf{v} = (v_1, ..., v_n)^T$ and $\{\beta_{ij}, j = 1, ..., i-1; i = 1, ..., n\}$.

Example. Gaussian Bayesian network

Fig. 2.41 shows the structure of a Gaussian BN. Its distributions are

$$
\begin{aligned}
f_1(x_1) &\sim \mathcal{N}(\mu_1, v_1) \\
f_2(x_2) &\sim \mathcal{N}(\mu_2, v_2) \\
f_3(x_3) &\sim \mathcal{N}(\mu_3, v_3) \\
f_4(x_4|x_1, x_2) &\sim \mathcal{N}(\mu_4 + \beta_{41}(x_1 - \mu_1) + \beta_{42}(x_2 - \mu_2), v_4) \\
f_5(x_5|x_2, x_3) &\sim \mathcal{N}(\mu_5 + \beta_{52}(x_2 - \mu_2) + \beta_{53}(x_3 - \mu_3), v_5).
\end{aligned}
$$

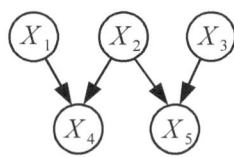

FIGURE 2.41
A Gaussian Bayesian network.

We can choose between any of the two representations, Eq. 2.11 or Eq. 2.13, since both are equivalent. There are formulas to transform one into the other. First, the unconditional means μ_i are the same in both representations. Second, matrix $\mathbf{W}$ of the multivariate Gaussian density can be built recursively from

v_i and β_{ij} of a given Gaussian BN using the formula

$$\boldsymbol{W}(i+1) = \begin{pmatrix} \boldsymbol{W}(i) + \dfrac{\boldsymbol{\beta}_{i+1}\boldsymbol{\beta}_{i+1}^T}{v_{i+1}} & \dfrac{-\boldsymbol{\beta}_{i+1}}{v_{i+1}} \\[2mm] \dfrac{-\boldsymbol{\beta}_{i+1}^T}{v_{i+1}} & \dfrac{1}{v_{i+1}} \end{pmatrix},$$

where $\boldsymbol{W}(i)$ denotes the $i \times i$ upper-left submatrix of $\boldsymbol{W}$, $\boldsymbol{\beta}_i$ is the $(i-1)$-dimensional vector of coefficients $(\beta_{i1}, ..., \beta_{ii-1})$, and $\boldsymbol{W}(1)=1/v_1$. Note that vector $\boldsymbol{\beta}_i$ contains $\beta_{i1}, ..., \beta_{ii-1}$, the coefficients in the regression of X_i on $X_1, ..., X_{i-1}$ and, accordingly, incoming arcs (from parents) to X_i in the graph. For the opposite transformation, other formulae can be used to derive β_{ij} and v_i of the Gaussian BN from matrix $\boldsymbol{\Sigma}$ of the multivariate Gaussian density.

Gaussianity may not hold in practice. Due to its compact representation and computational tractability, Gaussianity is sometimes assumed even if it only roughly approximates the true distribution. Alternatively, Gaussianity can be relaxed, mainly with non- and semi-parametric density estimation techniques: kernel-based densities, Gaussian process networks, non-parametric regression models, copula density functions, mixtures of truncated exponentials, mixtures of polynomials and general mixtures of truncated basis functions. Nevertheless, the use of these models for learning and simulation is still in its infancy, with many open issues to be solved.

Hybrid BNs refer to BNs with both discrete and continuous random variables. In **conditional linear Gaussian networks** (CLGs) (Lauritzen and Wermuth, 1989), a continuous variable X_i can have continuous $V_1, ..., V_k$ and discrete $U_1, ..., U_m$ parents. For each configuration $\mathbf{u} = (u_1, ..., u_m)$ of its discrete parents, its conditional probability distribution is the so-called conditional linear Gaussian on its continuous parents, i.e., Eq. 2.13 is now

$$f_i(x_i|\mathbf{u}, v_1, ..., v_k) \sim \mathcal{N}(\mu_i^{\mathbf{u}} + \sum_{j=1}^{k} \beta_{ij}^{\mathbf{u}}(v_j - \mu_j), v_i^{\mathbf{u}}).$$

Discrete variables cannot have continuous parents in CLG networks.

2.5.2   Inference in Bayesian Networks

2.5.2.1   Types of Inference

Inference, or **probabilistic reasoning**, refers to the computation of the conditional probability distribution of a query variable X_i (or set of variables) of interest given the values of some other variables, called the **observed evidence** $\mathbf{E} = \mathbf{e}$, i.e., $p(x_i|\mathbf{e})$, or, more generally, the conditional probability distribution $p(X_i|\mathbf{e})$. There are three kinds of variables in $\mathbf{X}$: a query variable X_i (a variable or a vector), the evidence variables $\mathbf{E}$ and the other unobserved variables $\mathbf{U}$. If there is no evidence, probabilities of interest are prior distributions $p(X_i)$.

BN inference can combine evidence from any part of the network and perform any kind of query.

Abductive inference is an important type of inference that finds the values of a set of variables that best explain the observed evidence. In **total abduction**, we solve $\arg\max_{\mathbf{U}} p(\mathbf{U}|\mathbf{e})$, i.e., we find the most probable explanation (MPE), whereas **partial abduction** solves the same problem for a subset of variables in $\mathbf{u}$ (the explanation set), referred to as the partial maximum a posteriori (MAP). Note that both probabilities are computed, together with an optimization problem. Solving a supervised classification problem, i.e., $\max_r p(C = c_r|\mathbf{x})$ is a particular case of finding the MPE.

Example. Factory production (probabilistic reasoning)

The bar charts in Fig. 2.42(a) show the prior probabilities of the factory production example (Fig. 2.38). Note, for instance, that the probability of producing many pieces, $p(p)$, is 0.39. All the inferences and figures were output using GeNIe[7] (see Section 2.7).

Now suppose that we have a factory with many machines ($M = m$). The updated probabilities given this evidence, i.e., $p(x_i|m)$ for any state x_i of nodes Y, E, P or F, are shown in Fig. 2.42(b). The probability of the state m for `Machines` is fixed at 100%. The probability of producing many pieces is now higher: $p(p|m) = 0.62$. For a factory with few machines, $p(p|\neg m) = 0.30$ (not shown). This is an example of **predictive reasoning**, where we predict the effect (produced pieces) given a cause (machines).

(a)   (b)

FIGURE 2.42
Exact inference on the factory production example. (a) The bar charts show the prior distributions $p(X_i)$ of each node X_i. (b) The evidence of observing a factory with many machines ($M = m$) is propagated through the network to yield the resulting updated (posterior) distributions $p(X_i|m)$.

Given the effect $F = f$ at `Failures`, the probability of the cause being many machines is high, $p(m|f) = 0.86$. This is an example of **diagnostic reasoning**, where we diagnose the causes given the effects. Also, E and M are

---

[7]`https://www.bayesfusion.com`

independent in the v-structure $E \rightarrow P \leftarrow M$ and have $p(e) = 0.57, p(m) = 0.29$ (Fig. 2.42(a)). However, if P is observed, e.g., $P = p$, they become dependent, that is, when the effect P is known, the presence of one explanatory cause renders the alternative cause less likely (it is explained away). Thus, if we know that the factory has many employees $(E = e)$, this would explain the observed high number of pieces produced p and would lower the probability of `Machines` being the cause, i.e., $p(m|p, e) = 0.32 < p(m|p) = 0.45$. This is an example of **intercausal reasoning**, which is unique to BNs.

Besides, we can find the MPE for a factory with failures, that is, we solve $\arg\max_{\{Y,E,M,P\}} p(Y, E, M, P|f)$ and get $(\neg y, \neg e, m, \neg p)$, with a probability of 0.28, that is, failures are explained by the factory not being old, and the number of employees, machines and piece production being low. The other possible configurations are less likely. Finally, again given f, we can search for the (reduced) explanation set (Y, M). Thus, $\arg\max_{\{Y,M\}} p(Y, M|f)$ is $(\neg y, m)$, with a probability of 0.63. This partial abduction indicates that failures are (partially) explained by the factory not being old and having many machines. ∎

2.5.2.2   Exact Inference

The exact computation of any probability is by definition

$$p(X_i | \mathbf{E} = \mathbf{e}) = \frac{p(X_i, \mathbf{e})}{p(\mathbf{e})} \propto \sum_{\mathbf{U}} p(X_i, \mathbf{e}, \mathbf{U}). \qquad (2.14)$$

However, this **brute-force approach** is not efficient, since the source of the terms $p(x_i, \mathbf{e}, \mathbf{U}) = p(\mathbf{x})$ that have to be summed out is the JPD, which was output by multiplying the factors in Eq. 2.10. It would probably take exponential time to use the full JPD rather than exploiting the factorization encoded by the BN. In fact, **exact inference** in graphical models is NP-hard (Cooper, 1990). Fortunately, many cases can be tackled very efficiently using the algorithms shown below. In these algorithms, the local distributions of the BN are viewed as functions, also called **potentials**. Thus, $p(E|Y)$ is a function $f_E(E, Y)$, and, generally, $p(X_i|\mathbf{Pa}(X_i)) = f_i(X_i, \mathbf{Pa}(X_i))$.

The **variable elimination algorithm** (Zhang and Poole, 1994) uses the distributive law performing (local) summations on the necessary factors. This way, sums are "pushed in" as far as possible when summing out (marginalizing) irrelevant terms.

Example. Factory production (brute-force inference)

Using the brute-force approach, we compute $p(P)$ as

$$
\begin{aligned}
p(P) &= \sum_{Y,E,M,F} p(Y, E, M, F, P) \\
&= \sum_{Y,E,M,F} p(Y)p(E|Y)p(M|Y)p(P|E, M)p(F|M).
\end{aligned}
$$

However, this expression can be rearranged more efficiently as

$$p(P) = \sum_Y p(Y) \sum_E p(E|Y) \sum_M p(M|Y)p(P|E,M) \sum_F p(F|M),$$

where the distributive law is used to avoid repeated calculations. ∎

With this idea in mind, the variable elimination algorithm applied to compute $p(X_i)$ first selects an elimination ordering containing all the variables but X_i. It then follows the order and, for each $X_k, k \neq i$, computes $g_k = \sum_{X_k} \prod_{f \in \mathcal{F}_k} f$, where the summation (marginalizing out X_k) is computed after taking the product of all functions f involving X_k (the set $\mathcal{F}_k$). The whole process should be repeated for a different target distribution $p(X_j)$.

Example. Factory production (inference with variable elimination)

Let us take the elimination ordering F-M-E-Y. For F, we compute $g_1(M) = \sum_F p(F|M)$. For M, $g_2(Y,E,P) = \sum_M p(M|Y)p(P|E,M)g_1(M)$. Next function $g_3(Y,P) = \sum_E p(E|Y)g_2(Y,E,P)$ eliminates E. Finally, we eliminate Y, and $\sum_Y p(Y)g_3(Y,P)$ yields the final result, that is,

$$
\begin{aligned}
p(P) &= \sum_Y p(Y) \sum_E p(E|Y) \sum_M p(M|Y)p(P|E,M)g_1(M) \\
&= \sum_Y p(Y) \sum_E p(E|Y)g_2(Y,E,P) \\
&= \sum_Y p(Y)g_3(Y,P).
\end{aligned}
$$

In numerical terms, $g_1(M) \equiv 1$, $g_2(y,e,p) = 0.456, g_2(y,\neg e,p) = 0.135, g_2(\neg y,e,p) = 0.876, g_2(\neg y,\neg e,p) = 0.399, g_3(y,p) = 0.359$ and $g_3(\neg y,p) = 0.494$. This yields $p(p) = 0.39$, and, similarly, $p(\neg p) = 0.61$ (Fig. 2.42(a)). Fewer operations (multiplications and additions) are required than for the brute-force approach. ∎

Any other elimination ordering different from F-M-E-Y would have achieved the same result but possibly at a different computational cost. Many heuristics have been proposed to find good orderings, since it is NP-hard to find the optimal elimination ordering (Bertelè and Brioschi, 1972).

The above example computes prior distributions without any observed evidence. To get $p(X_i|\mathbf{e})$, we can compute the non-normalized distribution $p(X_i, \mathbf{e})$ by applying the variable elimination algorithm to the functions instantiated by $\mathbf{E} = \mathbf{e}$ and eliminating the variables different from X_i and $\mathbf{E}$. Then the conditional probability is output by renormalizing by $p(\mathbf{e})$ (Eq. 2.14). Thus, if X_i is binary, $p(x_i|\mathbf{e}) = \frac{p(x_i, \mathbf{e})}{p(x_i, \mathbf{e}) + p(\neg x_i, \mathbf{e})}$, where these probabilities are all in $p(X_i, \mathbf{e})$, yielded by the variable elimination algorithm.

An alternative implementation of variable elimination is the **junction tree algorithm** (Shafer and Shenoy, 1990; Lauritzen and Spiegelhalter, 1988), which runs a **message passing algorithm** on an auxiliary structure called **junction tree, clique tree** or **join tree**. This is applicable to general BNs or **multiply connected BNs**, where more than one undirected path can exist between any pair of nodes. The factory production BN is multiply connected, since nodes P and Y, for example, are linked by two paths: Y-E-P and Y-M-P.

The junction tree algorithm on multiply connected BNs is a four-step procedure:

1. Moralize the BN and output the moral graph.

2. Triangulate the moral graph and output the cliques (nodes of the junction tree).

3. Create the junction tree and assign initial potentials to each clique.

4. Apply the message passing algorithm to the junction tree.

Moralize the BN (Step 1) means connecting ("marrying") all parents with a common child. The undirected graph after dropping arc directions is the **moral graph** (see Fig. 2.43(b)).

A **triangulated graph** or **chordal graph** is an undirected graph where all cycles of four or more vertices have a chord, which is an edge that is not part of the cycle but connects two vertices of the cycle. In **singly connected BNs**, also called **polytrees**, i.e., a DAG with no loops (cycles in the undirected graph), triangulation is unnecessary because their moral graphs are always triangulated. Polytrees were very popular in the early days of BNs because the first inference algorithm was Pearl's message passing algorithm for simple trees (Pearl, 1982), also called **belief propagation** or **sum-product message passing**, later extended to polytrees (Kim and Pearl, 1983).

The basic technique for triangulating a graph (Step 2) iteratively eliminates nodes following an elimination ordering. Eliminating node X means: (1) adding edges so that all nodes adjacent to X become pairwise adjacent (if they are not already), and (2) deleting node X and its adjacent edges. The added edges are called **fill-in edges**. An optimal triangulation should add the fewest fill-in edges, which is an NP-hard problem (Arnborg et al., 1987). Many heuristics have been proposed to find good triangulations (see Flores and Gámez (2007) for a review). A set of vertices $\mathbf{C}$ that is complete (all nodes are pairwise linked) and maximal (it is not a subset of another complete set) is called a **clique**. The term clique may also directly refer to the subgraph. Cliques are the nodes of the junction tree and can be retrieved from the fill-in process, since, when eliminating X, edges are added to make the subgraph given by X and its neighbors complete.

The junction tree is then created (Step 3), with cliques $\mathbf{C}_j$ as nodes and satisfying the **running intersection property**: given two nodes $\mathbf{C}_j$ and $\mathbf{C}_k$, then all nodes included in the path between $\mathbf{C}_j$ and $\mathbf{C}_k$ must contain $\mathbf{C}_j \cap \mathbf{C}_k$. A **separator** $\mathbf{S}_{jk}$ of two adjacent cliques $\mathbf{C}_j$ and $\mathbf{C}_k$ is its intersection: $\mathbf{C}_j \cap \mathbf{C}_k = \mathbf{S}_{jk}$. Fig. 2.43(c) shows a junction tree for the factory production example. The potential ψ_j assigned to each clique $\mathbf{C}_j$ must be identified in the

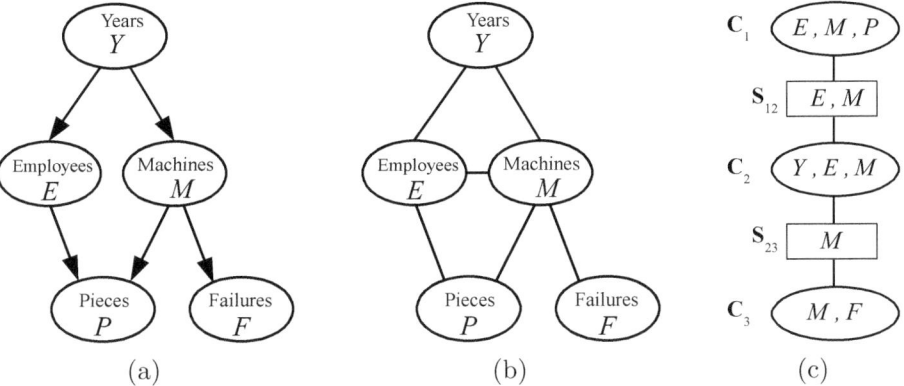

FIGURE 2.43
(a) Structure of the BN modeling factory production. (b) Its moral graph, where a new edge has been added to marry two parents, E and M, with a common child. (c) Its junction tree, with three cliques $\mathbf{C}_1 = \{E, M, P\}$, $\mathbf{C}_2 = \{Y, E, M\}$ and $\mathbf{C}_3 = \{M, F\}$, and their corresponding separators. The potentials assigned to each clique are $\psi_1(E, M, P) = p(P|E, M)$, $\psi_2(Y, E, M) = p(E|Y)p(M|Y)p(Y)$, $\psi_3(M, F) = p(F|M)$.

new structure. Each potential in the BN is attached to a clique that contains its domain. If there is more than one potential attached to the same clique, the potential at this clique is the product of these potentials. If a clique has no attached potentials, the constant function 1 is attached.

In the message passing algorithm (Step 4), a node collects the incoming messages (factors) from its neighboring nodes, performs some multiplications and additions, and sends results as an outgoing message to its neighboring nodes. Any node is selected as the root node, and all messages flow "upward" from the leaves to the root along the (unique) path towards the root –first round of messages, called 'collect evidence'. Then a second round of messages is passed from the root to the leaves. This step is called 'distribute evidence'. The process is complete when all leaves have received their messages. A message $M^{j \to k}(\mathbf{S}_{jk})$ from clique $\mathbf{C}_j$ to clique $\mathbf{C}_k$ is defined over $\mathbf{S}_{jk}$ as

$$M^{j \to k}(\mathbf{S}_{jk}) = \sum_{\mathbf{C}_j \setminus \mathbf{S}_{jk}} \psi_j \prod_{l \in (\mathrm{Nb}_j \setminus \{k\})} M^{l \to j}(\mathbf{S}_{lj}), \qquad (2.15)$$

where Nb_j is the set of indices of nodes that are neighbors of $\mathbf{C}_j$. Thus, at clique $\mathbf{C}_j$, all the incoming messages $M^{l \to j}$ are multiplied by its own potential ψ_j. When the message passing ends, each clique $\mathbf{C}_i$ contains

$$p(\mathbf{C}_i, \mathbf{e}) = \psi_i \prod_{l \in \mathrm{Nb}_i} M^{l \to i}(\mathbf{S}_{li}), \qquad (2.16)$$

that is, the clique marginals. To compute the marginal (unnormalized) distribution over a particular variable X, we can select a clique containing X and sum out the other variables in the clique.

In short, the junction tree algorithm is based on the same principle as the variable elimination algorithm, albeit with a sophisticated strategy for caching computations. Thanks to this strategy, multiple variable elimination runs can be performed much more efficiently than performing each run separately.

Example. Factory production (exact inference with the junction tree algorithm)

Suppose that our target distribution is $p(P|m)$, i.e., the probability of piece production (many, p, or few, $\neg p$) if the factory has many machines. The application of Eq. 2.16 followed by Eq. 2.15 yields

$$
\begin{aligned}
p(\mathbf{C}_1, e) &= p(E, m, P) \\
&= \psi_1(E, m, P) M^{2 \to 1}(E, m) \\
&= p(P|E, m) \sum_Y \psi_2(Y, E, m) M^{3 \to 2}(m) \\
&= p(P|E, m) \sum_Y \psi_2(Y, E, m) \sum_F p(F|m) \\
&= p(P|E, m) \sum_Y p(E|Y) p(m|Y) p(Y),
\end{aligned}
$$

since $\sum_F p(F|m) \equiv 1$. According to the calculations, $M^{2 \to 1}(e, m) = 0.095$, $M^{2 \to 1}(\neg e, m) = 0.019$, and hence $p(E, m, P)$ is derived. Now we can compute $p(P|m)$ as $\frac{\sum_E p(E, m, P)}{\sum_{E,P} p(E, m, P)}$, which results in $p(p|m) = 0.62$ and $p(\neg p|m) = 0.38$.

If we are looking for all $p(X_i|m)$, we set a node, say $\mathbf{C}_1$, as the root. Then the upward pass would include messages $M^{1 \to 2}$ and $M^{2 \to 3}$ and the downward pass, $M^{3 \to 2}$ and $M^{2 \to 1}$. After these two rounds, we get $p(\mathbf{C}_i, e)$ for all $i = 1, 2, 3$, and $p(X_i|m)$ is derived by marginalization, as for $p(P|m)$. All the results are shown in Fig. 2.42(b). ■

Inference is straightforward in Gaussian BNs, since any conditional and marginal distribution is still Gaussian. Thus, the updated parameters, mean and variance, of the density function $f(x_i|\mathbf{e})$ have closed-form expressions (Lauritzen and Jensen, 2001):

$$
\text{mean} = \mu_i + \mathbf{\Sigma}_{X_i \mathbf{E}} \mathbf{\Sigma}_{\mathbf{EE}}^{-1} (\mathbf{e} - \boldsymbol{\mu}_{\mathbf{E}})
$$
$$
\text{variance} = v_i - \mathbf{\Sigma}_{X_i \mathbf{E}} \mathbf{\Sigma}_{\mathbf{EE}}^{-1} \mathbf{\Sigma}_{X_i \mathbf{E}}^T,
$$

where $\mathbf{\Sigma}_{X_i \mathbf{E}}$ is the vector with the covariances of X_i, and each variable in $\mathbf{E}$, $\mathbf{\Sigma}_{\mathbf{EE}}$ is the covariance matrix of $\mathbf{E}$, and $\boldsymbol{\mu}_{\mathbf{E}}$ is the unconditional mean of $\mathbf{E}$.

In general BNs using non-parametric density estimation techniques, inference has been performed on networks with a small number of nodes only (see, e.g., Shenoy and West (2011)). The problem is that the intermediate factors generated by multiplying or marginalizing factors during the inference process using distributions $p(X_i|\mathbf{Pa}(X_i))$ from one distribution family will not necessarily be members of the same family. The solution in such cases is to use approximate inference methods.

2.5.2.3 Approximate Inference

Approximate inference methods balance the accuracy of the results and the capability to deal with complex models, where exact inference is intractable. Like exact inference, approximate inference is also NP-hard in general BNs (Dagum and Luby, 1993). The most successful idea is to use stochastic simulation techniques based on Monte Carlo methods. The network is used to generate a large number of cases (full instantiations) from the JPD. The probability is then estimated by counting observed frequencies in the samples. As more cases are generated, the exact probability will be better approximated (by the law of large numbers).

Probabilistic logic sampling (Henrion, 1988) is a well-known method that works by following an ancestral node ordering (forward sampling). It first samples from parentless nodes and then, after drawing samples from all parents of a child node, samples from the child node. The values for each node are fixed and used for the conditioning parts of the next samplings. After sampling from all nodes, we have a sample of $p(\mathbf{X})$, the JPD. Then we repeat the process a great many times and approximate the probability by the relative observed frequency. It is straightforward to sample from a discrete distribution $p(X|\mathbf{pa}(X))$, whereas there are efficient, but complex, methods for continuous distributions $f(X|\mathbf{pa}(X))$ (Law and Kelton, 1999).

Example. Factory production (approximate inference with probabilistic logic sampling)

Suppose again that we have a factory with many machines ($M = m$). Then the target distributions to be estimated are $p(X_i|m)$ for all X_i different from M.

Probabilistic logic sampling would start by simulating from $p(Y)$ (which has a 0.75 probability of taking the value y, see Fig. 2.38). Suppose that this yields y. Now we simulate from $p(E|y)$ (which has a 0.70 probability of taking the value e) and yields $\neg e$. Then we simulate from $p(M|y)$ (with a 0.10 probability of $M = m$), which results in m. Next we generate from $p(P|\neg e, m)$, which has a 0.45 probability of taking the value p, producing p. Finally, by simulating from $p(F|m)$, $\neg f$ is returned. Therefore, the generated sample is $(y, \neg e, m, p, \neg f)$ for (Y, E, M, P, F). By repeating the process a large number of times, the probabilities $p(X_i|m)$ are estimated by their relative observed frequencies. Thus, for instance, a simulation yields $p(p|m) \approx 0.733$ with 100 samples, $p(p|m) \approx 0.656$ with 1,000 samples, and $p(p|m) \approx 0.618$ with 10,000 samples. The exact value is $p(p|m) = 0.62$ (see Fig. 2.42(b)). Note that samples including $M = \neg m$ are rejected and discarded, since they are not compatible with the evidence $M = m$.   ∎

Hence, if **e** is very unlikely, probabilistic logic sampling wastes many samples. The **likelihood weighting** method addresses this problem (Fung and Chang, 1990; Shachter and Peot, 1989). Other powerful techniques are **Gibbs sampling** (Pearl, 1987) and, more generally, **Markov chain Monte Carlo** (MCMC) methods. MCMC methods build a Markov chain, the stationary distribution of which is the target distribution of the inference process. Thus, the states of the chain (when converged) are used as a sample from the desired distribution. They are easy to implement and widely applicable to very general networks (undirected networks included) and distributions.

2.5.3   Learning Bayesian Networks from Data

The learning task involves learning the two components of a BN $\mathcal{B} = (\mathcal{G}, \boldsymbol{\theta})$: its structure $\mathcal{G}$ (a DAG) and its parameters $\boldsymbol{\theta}$ (entries in the CPTs).

2.5.3.1   Learning Bayesian Network Parameters

For parameter learning, we need to have the structure. Let R_i be the cardinality of Ω_{X_i}, the number of possible values of variable X_i. Let $q_i = |\Omega_{\mathbf{Pa}(X_i)}|$ be the number of possible combinations, each denoted $\mathbf{pa}_i^j$, of the values of X_i parents, i.e., $\Omega_{\mathbf{Pa}(X_i)} = \{\mathbf{pa}_i^1, ..., \mathbf{pa}_i^{q_i}\}$. Then the CPT of X_i contains the parameters $\theta_{ijk} = p(X_i = k|\mathbf{Pa}(X_i) = \mathbf{pa}_i^j)$, the conditional probability that X_i takes its k-th value given that its parents take their j-th value. Therefore, the CPT of X_i requires the estimation of parameters $\boldsymbol{\theta}_i$, a vector of $R_i q_i$ components. $\boldsymbol{\theta} = (\boldsymbol{\theta}_1, ..., \boldsymbol{\theta}_n)$ includes all the parameters in the BN, i.e., $\theta_{ijk}, \forall i = 1, ..., n, j = 1, ..., q_i, k = 1, ..., R_i$, and hence it is a vector with $\sum_{i=1}^{n} R_i q_i$ components.

Parameters θ_{ijk} are estimated from the dataset $\mathcal{D} = \{\mathbf{x}^1, ..., \mathbf{x}^N\}$, where $\mathbf{x}^h = (x_1^h, ..., x_n^h)$, $h = 1, ..., N$. Let N_{ij} be the number of cases in $\mathcal{D}$ in which $\mathbf{Pa}(X_i) = \mathbf{pa}_i^j$ has been observed, and N_{ijk} be the number of cases in $\mathcal{D}$ where $X_i = k$ and $\mathbf{Pa}(X_i) = \mathbf{pa}_i^j$ have been observed at the same time $(N_{ij} = \sum_{k=1}^{R_i} N_{ijk})$.

The maximum likelihood estimation (Section 2.2.2) finds $\widehat{\boldsymbol{\theta}}^{\mathrm{ML}}$ such that it maximizes the likelihood of the dataset given the model:

$$\widehat{\boldsymbol{\theta}}^{\mathrm{ML}} = \arg\max_{\boldsymbol{\theta}} \mathcal{L}(\boldsymbol{\theta}|\mathcal{D}, \mathcal{G}) = \arg\max_{\boldsymbol{\theta}} p(\mathcal{D}|\mathcal{G}, \boldsymbol{\theta}) = \arg\max_{\boldsymbol{\theta}} \prod_{h=1}^{N} p(\mathbf{x}^h|\mathcal{G}, \boldsymbol{\theta}).$$

(2.17)

In BNs, probabilities $p(\mathbf{x}^h|\mathcal{G}, \boldsymbol{\theta})$ in Eq. 2.17 are factorized according to $\mathcal{G}$, that is, $p(\mathbf{x}^h|\mathcal{G}, \boldsymbol{\theta}) = \prod_{i=1}^{n} p(x_i^h|\mathbf{pa}_i^h, \boldsymbol{\theta})$. We now use the assumptions of **global parameter independence** and **local parameter independence** (Spiegelhalter and Lauritzen, 1990). Global parameter independence states that the parameters associated with each variable in a network structure are independent, whereas, in local parameter independence, the parameters associated with each state of the parents of a variable are independent. Hence we have

$$\mathcal{L}(\boldsymbol{\theta}|\mathcal{D}, \mathcal{G}) = \prod_{i=1}^{n} \prod_{j=1}^{q_i} \prod_{k=1}^{R_i} \theta_{ijk}^{N_{ijk}}. \tag{2.18}$$

The parameters maximizing the likelihood function of Eq. 2.18 can be estimated via relative frequencies:

$$\widehat{\theta}_{ijk}^{\text{ML}} = \frac{N_{ijk}}{N_{ij}}.$$

With sparse datasets, a smoothing technique is usually implemented to address situations where N_{ij} can be zero or even when the estimation is based on very few cases. For instance, the **Laplace estimator** (which is in fact a Bayesian estimation, see Section 2.2.2.1) yields

$$\widehat{\theta}_{ijk}^{\text{Lap}} = \frac{N_{ijk} + 1}{N_{ij} + R_i}.$$

If $\mathcal{D}$ has incomplete instances (with missing values), the estimations can be calculated with the EM algorithm (Section 2.3.5) first applied in BNs by Lauritzen (1995). A more elaborate version is the **structural EM** (Friedman, 1998), where not only parameters but also structures can be updated at each EM iteration.

Gaussian BNs represented as a multivariate Gaussian, see Eq. 2.11, have $\boldsymbol{\theta} = (\boldsymbol{\mu}, \boldsymbol{\Sigma})$ as parameters. Their maximum likelihood estimates are, respectively, the sample mean vector $\frac{1}{N} \sum_{i=1}^{N} \mathbf{x}^i$ of the data and the sample covariance matrix $\mathbf{S} = \frac{1}{N} \sum_{i=1}^{N} (\mathbf{x}^i - \bar{\mathbf{x}})(\mathbf{x}^i - \bar{\mathbf{x}})^T$. In Gaussian BNs represented as the product of conditional Gaussian densities, see Eq. 2.13, parameters v_i and β_{ij} are estimated, respectively, with the sample conditional variance and with the coefficients of X_j in the regression of X_i on $X_1, ..., X_{i-1}$.

Example. Parameters θ_{ijk} in a BN and their estimates

Fig. 2.44(a) shows a BN structure with four nodes and $\Omega_{X_i} = \{1, 2\}, i = 1, 3, 4$, $\Omega_{X_2} = \{1, 2, 3\}$. As per the graph, $q_1 = q_2 = 0, q_3 = 6, q_4 = 2$.

All 21 parameters θ_{ijk} are shown in Table 2.8.

Suppose that we have a dataset (Fig. 2.44(b)) to estimate these parameters. To estimate $\theta_{1-1} = p(X_1 = 1)$, we find four out of six instances in the X_1 column, and hence, $\widehat{\theta}_{1-1}^{\text{ML}} = 2/3$ (Fig. 2.44(b)). To estimate $\theta_{322} = p(X_3 = 2|X_1 = 1, X_2 = 2)$, we find that neither of the two instances with $X_1 = 1, X_2 = 2$, include either $X_3 = 2$ or $\widehat{\theta}_{322}^{\text{ML}} = 0$ (this is a case where $N_{ijk} = 0$). To estimate $\theta_{361} = p(X_3 = 1|X_1 = 2, X_2 = 3)$, we find that $\widehat{\theta}_{361}^{\text{ML}}$ is undefined since there are no instances with $X_1 = 2, X_2 = 3$ (i.e., $N_{ij} = 0$). However, the Laplace estimates yield $\widehat{\theta}_{322}^{\text{Lap}} = 1/4, \widehat{\theta}_{361}^{\text{Lap}} = 1/2$. ∎

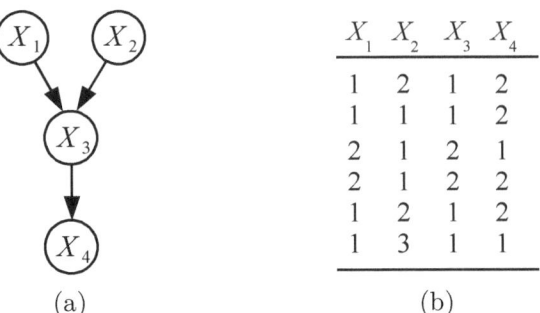

(a)   (b)

FIGURE 2.44
(a) A BN with four nodes. (b) A dataset with $N = 6$ for $\{X_1, ..., X_4\}$ from which the BN in (a) has been learned.

TABLE 2.8
Parameters θ_{ijk} of the BN in Fig. 2.44

Parameters	Meaning
$\boldsymbol{\theta}_1 = (\theta_{1-1}, \theta_{1-2})$	$(p(X_1 = 1), p(X_1 = 2))$
$\boldsymbol{\theta}_2 = (\theta_{2-1}, \theta_{2-2}, \theta_{2-3})$	$(p(X_2 = 1), p(X_2 = 2), p(X_2 = 3))$
$\boldsymbol{\theta}_3 = (\theta_{311}, \theta_{312}, \ldots, \theta_{361}, \theta_{362})$	$(p(X_3 = 1\|X_1 = 1, X_2 = 1),$
	$p(X_3 = 2\|X_1 = 1, X_2 = 1), \ldots$
	$p(X_3 = 1\|X_1 = 2, X_2 = 3),$
	$p(X_3 = 2\|X_1 = 2, X_2 = 3))$
$\boldsymbol{\theta}_4 = (\theta_{411}, \theta_{412}, \theta_{421}, \theta_{422})$	$(p(X_4 = 1\|X_3 = 1), p(X_4 = 2\|X_3 = 1),$
	$p(X_4 = 1\|X_3 = 2), p(X_4 = 2\|X_3 = 2))$

2.5.3.2 Learning Bayesian Network Structures

There are two main ways of approaching structure learning. One type of algorithms is based on testing conditional independences between triplets of variables. The second approach scores the goodness of each candidate structure and searches for the best-scoring candidate.

Constraint-based methods use the data to statistically test conditional independences among triplets of variables. The goal is to build a DAG that represents a large percentage (and whenever possible all) of the identified conditional independence constraints (the minimal I-map). The **PC algorithm** (Spirtes and Glymour, 1991) is the most outstanding procedure. The data-generating distribution is assumed to be faithful to the DAG, that is, both conditional independence and d- or u-separation are equivalent (i.e., the DAG is a perfect map of p). PC starts with all nodes connected by edges and follows three steps. Step 1 outputs the adjacencies in the graph, i.e., the skeleton of the learned structure. Step 2 identifies **colliders** (a collider or converging connection at node X is $Y \to X \leftarrow Z$). Step 3 orients the edges and outputs the CPDAG, the Markov equivalence class of DAGs. Here we explain Step 1, see Algorithm 2.6, where Adj_i denotes the adjacency set of X_i. Steps 2 and 3 are described elsewhere (Spirtes and Glymour, 1991).

Algorithm 2.6: Step 1 of the PC algorithm: estimation of the skeleton

---

    Input   : A complete undirected graph and an ordering σ on the variables $\{X_1, ..., X_n\}$

    Output : Skeleton $\mathcal{G}$ of the learned structure

1 Form the complete undirected graph $\mathcal{G}$ on nodes $\{X_1, ..., X_n\}$
2 $t = -1$
3 **repeat**
    $t = t + 1$
    repeat
4   Select a pair of adjacent nodes $X_i - X_j$ in $\mathcal{G}$ using ordering σ
5   Find $\mathbf{S} \subset Adj_i \setminus \{X_j\}$ in $\mathcal{G}$ with $|\mathbf{S}| = t$ (if any) using ordering σ
6   Remove edge $X_i - X_j$ from $\mathcal{G}$ iff X_i and X_j are c.i. given $\mathbf{S}$
    until all ordered pairs of adjacent nodes have been tested
  until all adjacent pairs $X_i - X_j$ in $\mathcal{G}$ satisfy $|Adj_i \setminus \{X_j\}| \leq t$

Under faithfulness, conditional independence and d- or u-separation are equivalent. Therefore, if we find by hypothesis testing (like χ^2 tests, Section 2.2.2) that $I_p(X_i, X_j|\mathbf{S})$ holds for some $\mathbf{S}$, then edge $X_i - X_j$ can be removed. If $\neg I_p(X_i, X_j|\mathbf{S})$ for all $\mathbf{S}$, then we conclude that X_i and X_j are directly connected. Fortunately, not all possible sets $\mathbf{S}$ have to be checked. Rather, it is enough to condition on variables adjacent to X_i or X_j.

Thus, the first iteration of PC checks all pairs of nodes (X_i, X_j) for marginal independence, i.e., $\mathbf{S} = \emptyset$. The cardinality t of $\mathbf{S}$ is increased one by one ($\mathbf{S}$ with two nodes, then three nodes, etc.) to check whether, for each ordered pair (X_i, X_j) still adjacent in $\mathcal{G}$ and any $\mathbf{S}$ of size t of $Adj_i \setminus \{X_j\}$, the null hypothesis of independence $I_p(X, Y|\mathbf{S})$ is not rejected. The edge $X_i - X_j$ is removed if and only if we find a set $\mathbf{S}$ that renders X_i and X_j conditionally independent. The search for $\mathbf{S}$ with $t + 1$ variables does not start until the search of all sets with t variables fails. The graph is progressively thinned out until all possibilities (up to $n - 2$ variables) are exhausted, and there are no more adjacency sets to check. Note that as the PC algorithm progresses and $\mathbf{S}$ includes more variables, the reliability of the statistical tests checking conditional independences drops (there will be fewer instances on which to apply the tests).

Score and search-based methods measure the goodness of each candidate BN with a score function relative to data. An optimal structure maximizes the scoring function. Three main characteristics of these methods are: (a) the search space where the BN structure should be found, (b) the score used for assigning the goodness of each structure, and (c) the search method that enables intelligent movements in the search space (see Fig. 2.45).

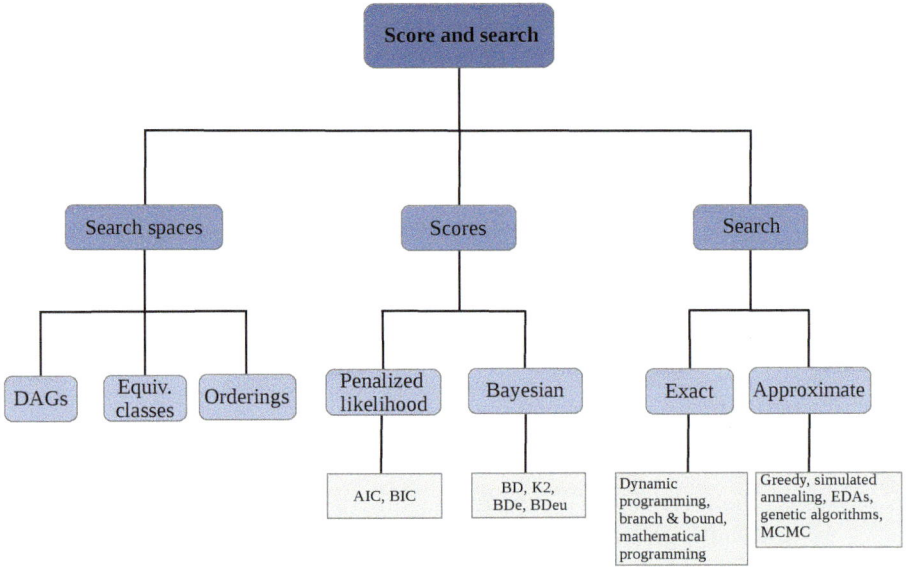

FIGURE 2.45
Methods for BN structure learning based on score and search.

There are three possible structure spaces: (a) the space of DAGs; (b) the space of Markov equivalent classes; and (c) the space of orderings. The cardinality of the **space of DAGs** is super-exponential in the number of nodes: the number $f(n)$ of possible BN structures with n nodes is given by the recurring formula

$$f(n) = \sum_{i=1}^{n} (-1)^{i+1} \binom{n}{i} 2^{i(n-i)} f(n-i), \text{ for } n > 2,$$

which is initialized with $f(0) = f(1) = 1$ (Robinson, 1977). Finding a network structure that optimizes a score is an NP-hard combinatorial optimization problem even if we restrict the number of parents of each node to at most two (Chickering, 1996). The impossibility of evaluating all possible structures makes the use of heuristic search algorithms very appropriate as discussed below.

The **space of Markov equivalence classes** is smaller than the space of DAGs because all Markov equivalent DAGs are represented by a unique structure, the CPDAG or essential graph. Moving within this new space avoids jumping from one DAG to another within the same equivalence class, which is useless when all DAGs within the same equivalence class are equally scored (the function is score equivalent). Simulation results have found that the #DAGs/#CPDAGs ratio approaches an asymptote of about 3.7 (Gillispie and Perlman, 2002), which indicates that the reduction in the space size is only moderate. Moreover, time has to be spent checking whether or not a structure belongs to an equivalence class when moving in this space.

The rationale behind moving in the **space of orderings** of the variables is that some learning algorithms only work with a fixed order, assuming that only the variables that come before a given variable in the ordering can be its parents (e.g., the K2 algorithm explained below). The score of the best network consistent with an ordering is the score of that ordering. Given an ordering, there are $2^{n(n-1)/2}$ possible BN structures. Also, $n!$ possibilities have to be searched to find a good ordering. It is advantageous to work in the space of orderings because each step makes more global modifications than in the space of DAGs, and there is, therefore, a lower probability of getting trapped in local optima.

A score $Q(\mathcal{D}, \mathcal{G})$ measures the goodness of fit of a BN structure $\mathcal{G}$ to the dataset $\mathcal{D}$. We are looking for $\mathcal{G}$ that maximizes the score. One simple score is the estimated **log-likelihood of the data given the BN**:

$$\log \mathcal{L}(\widehat{\boldsymbol{\theta}}|\mathcal{D}, \mathcal{G}) = \log p(\mathcal{D}|\mathcal{G}, \widehat{\boldsymbol{\theta}}) = \log \prod_{i=1}^{n} \prod_{j=1}^{q_i} \prod_{k=1}^{R_i} \widehat{\theta}_{ijk}^{N_{ijk}} = \sum_{i=1}^{n} \sum_{j=1}^{q_i} \sum_{k=1}^{R_i} N_{ijk} \log \widehat{\theta}_{ijk},$$

where $\widehat{\theta}_{ijk}$ is usually taken as the maximum likelihood estimate, i.e., $\widehat{\theta}_{ijk} = \widehat{\theta}_{ijk}^{\text{ML}} = \frac{N_{ijk}}{N_{ij}}$, the frequency counts in $\mathcal{D}$.

One problem is that this score increases monotonically with the complexity of the model (known as **structural overfitting**), as shown in Fig. 2.46. The optimal structure would be the complete graph. A family of **penalized log-likelihood** scores addresses this issue by penalizing network complexity. Their general expression is

$$Q^{Pen}(\mathcal{D}, \mathcal{G}) = \sum_{i=1}^{n}\sum_{j=1}^{q_i}\sum_{k=1}^{R_i} N_{ijk} \log \frac{N_{ijk}}{N_{ij}} - dim(\mathcal{G})pen(N),$$

where $dim(\mathcal{G}) = \sum_{i=1}^{n}(R_i - 1)q_i$ denotes the model dimension (number of parameters needed in the BN), and $pen(N)$ is a non-negative penalization function. The scores differ depending on $pen(N)$: if $pen(N) = 1$, the score is called **Akaike's information criterion** (AIC) (Akaike, 1974) and if $pen(N) = \frac{1}{2}\log N$, the score is the **Bayesian information criterion** (BIC) (Schwarz, 1978).

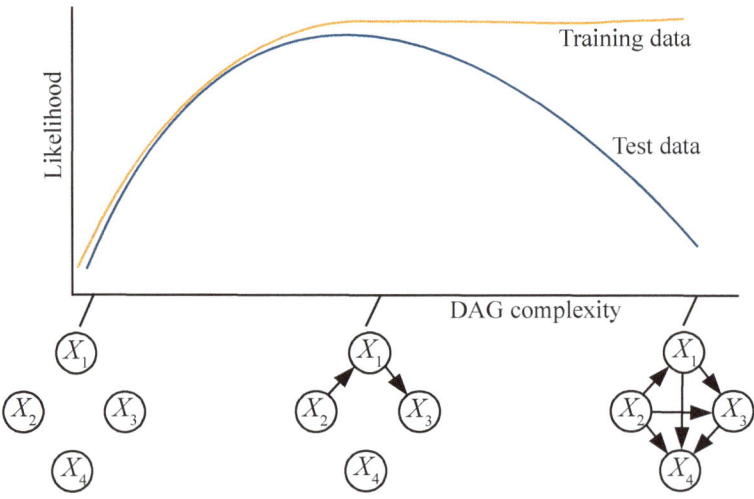

FIGURE 2.46
Structural overfitting: the likelihood of the training data is higher for denser graphs, whereas it degrades for the test data.

The BN structure can also be estimated using a Bayesian approach. The goal is to find $\mathcal{G}$ that maximizes its posteriori probability given the data, i.e., find $\arg\max_{\mathcal{G}} p(\mathcal{G}|\mathcal{D})$. Using Bayes' formula, $p(\mathcal{G}|\mathcal{D}) \propto p(\mathcal{D},\mathcal{G}) = p(\mathcal{D}|\mathcal{G})p(\mathcal{G})$. The second factor, $p(\mathcal{G})$, is the prior distribution over structures. The first factor, $p(\mathcal{D}|\mathcal{G})$, is the **marginal likelihood** of the data, defined as

$$p(\mathcal{D}|\mathcal{G}) = \int p(\mathcal{D}|\mathcal{G}, \boldsymbol{\theta})f(\boldsymbol{\theta}|\mathcal{G})d\boldsymbol{\theta},$$

where $p(\mathcal{D}|\mathcal{G}, \boldsymbol{\theta})$ is the likelihood of the data given the BN (structure $\mathcal{G}$ and parameters $\boldsymbol{\theta}$), and $f(\boldsymbol{\theta}|\mathcal{G})$ is the prior distribution over the parameters. Depending on $f(\boldsymbol{\theta}|\mathcal{G})$, we have different scores. If a Dirichlet distribution is set, i.e., $(\boldsymbol{\theta}_{ij}|\mathcal{G})$ follows a Dirichlet of parameters $\alpha_{ij1}, ..., \alpha_{ijR_i}$, we have the **Bayesian**

Dirichlet score (BD score). A Dirichlet distribution is determined by hyperparameters α_{ijk} for all i, j, k. The K2 score, the BDe score and the BDeu score are instantiations of this score.

The **K2 score** (Cooper and Herskovits, 1992) uses the uninformative assignment $\alpha_{ijk} = 1$, for all i, j, k, resulting in

$$Q^{K2}(\mathcal{D}, \mathcal{G}) = p(\mathcal{G}) \prod_{i=1}^{n} \prod_{j=1}^{q_i} \frac{(R_i - 1)!}{(N_{ij} + R_i - 1)!} \prod_{k=1}^{R_i} N_{ijk}!.$$

The **K2 algorithm** uses a greedy search method and the K2 score. The user gives a node ordering and the maximum number of parents that any node is permitted to have. Starting with an empty structure, the algorithm incrementally adds, from the set of nodes that precede each node X_i in the node ordering, the parent whose addition most increases the function:

$$g(X_i, \mathbf{Pa}(X_i)) = \prod_{j=1}^{q_i} \frac{(R_i - 1)!}{(N_{ij} + R_i - 1)!} \prod_{k=1}^{R_i} N_{ijk}!.$$

When the score does not increase further with the addition of a single parent, no more parents are added to node X_i, and we move on to the next node in the ordering.

The **likelihood-equivalent Bayesian Dirichlet score (BDe score)** (Heckerman et al., 1995) sets the hyperparameters as $\alpha_{ijk} = \alpha\, p(X_i = k, \mathbf{Pa}(X_i) = \mathbf{pa}_i^j | \mathcal{G})$. The equivalent sample size α expresses the user's confidence in the prior network. In the **BDeu score** (Buntine, 1991), $\alpha_{ijk} = \alpha \frac{1}{q_i R_i}$.

The huge search space has led to propose many heuristics for structure learning, including greedy search, simulated annealing, estimation of distribution algorithms (EDAs), genetic algorithms, and MCMC methods.

2.6 Modeling Dynamic Scenarios with Bayesian Networks

2.6.1 Data Streams

In recent years, advances in hardware technology have facilitated new ways of collecting data continuously. In many applications, the volume of such data is so large that it may be impossible to store the data on disk. Furthermore, even when the data can be stored, the volume of incoming data may be so large as to be impossible to process. Therefore, the development of machine learning algorithms becomes significantly more challenging in this context.

Internet traffic, multiple satellites continuously gathering multiple terrestrial, atmospheric and ocean surface observations of the entire Earth, the stream of financial transactions related to securities and options, and sensor-based data collection related to continuous physical observations such as temperature, pressure, human EMG/ECG/EEG signals or vibrations in manufacturing industries, are typical data streaming scenarios. For example, Google handles several billion searches and NASA satellites generate images containing terabytes of information on a daily basis. These datasets are too large to fit in main memory and are stored in alternative secondary storage devices. Therefore, random access to these datasets is prohibitively expensive. One goal of data stream mining (Gama, 2010) is to create a learning process that linearly increases according to the number of instances. Moreover, as data supplying new information arrive continuously, the previously induced model does not only need to incorporate new information, but also eliminates the effects of outdated data.

Data streams have intrinsic characteristics, such as possibly infinite volume, chronological order, and dynamical changes. Machine learning methods for static datasets are able to scan datasets many times with unlimited time and memory resources and produce fairly accurate results. On the other hand, machine learning methods for data streams may produce approximate results and have to satisfy constraints, such as single-pass, real-time response, bounded memory, and concept drift detection (Nguyen et al., 2015). Each instance in a data stream is examined at most once and cannot be backtracked. This **single-pass** constraint can be relaxed slightly to allow an algorithm to remember instances in the short term. Many data stream applications require a **real-time** data processing and decision-making response. The **bounded memory** constraint relates to the fact that only a small summary of the data streams can be stored and computed, and the rest of the data possibly have to be removed. Finally, **concept drift** refers to the situation when the underlying data distribution changes over time invalidating the current model which has to be updated.

As data streams are potentially infinite, it is common in real-world applications to process only a portion of the entire data stream. This portion is defined as a time window of the data instances. There are four possible types of time windows: (i) **landmark window**, covering the entire data stream from the starting to the current time; (ii) **sliding window**, which considers only the most recent instances; (iii) **fading window**, where a different decreasing weight is progressively assigned to the instances according to arrival time from the newest to the oldest; and (iv) **tilted-time window**, which divides the timescale into different sections from the most recent to the oldest, where the most recent sections are rendered in more detail.

Apart from these time window variants, there are two main computational approaches to modeling data streams: incremental learning and online-offline learning. **Incremental learning** modeling incrementally evolves to adapt to concept drifts in incoming data. The adaptation of the model can follow a data instance or a time window strategy. **Online-offline learning** divides the modeling process into two phases. In the online phase, a synopsis of the data is updated in real time. In the offline phase, the modeling is performed on-demand on the stored synopsis.

Supervised classification data stream models should be validated by adapting the performance evaluation methodology explained in Section 2.4.1 to the temporal scenario of data streams. Thus, the adaptation of the hold-out validation method considers that data instances are clustered into chunks. Each data chunk is first used as a test instance (if it belongs to the future with respect to the training data chunks) and, once this chunk belongs to the past, it is then used to update the model. A special case of this hold-out adaptation method, where chunk size is equal to one instance, is called **prequential validation** (Gama et al., 2013).

Nguyen et al. (2015) report a survey of data stream clustering and supervised classification methods. Here we briefly present some techniques. With regard to clustering methods, **STREAM** (O'Callaghan et al., 2002) is a partitional clustering method for data streams, which extends the K-medians algorithm[8] using a divide-and-conquer strategy and performing clustering incrementally. The data stream is broken down into chunks, each with a manageable size for storage in main memory. For each chunk, STREAM uses a K-medians algorithm to select K representatives (medians) which it stores. The process is repeated for the next chunks. When the number of representative points exceeds the main memory storage, a second level of clustering is applied, that is, STREAM operates in a multilevel manner. **CluStream** (Aggarwal et al., 2004) is a hierarchical clustering method (Section 2.3.1) for data streams that uses micro-clusters, a temporal extension of the clustering feature vector, to capture the summary information about the data stream. CluStream adopts an online-offline learning approach. In the online phase, it continuously maintains a set of micro-clusters in the data stream. When a new micro-cluster is created, an outlier micro-cluster is deleted or two neighboring micro-clusters are merged. In the offline phase, it runs the K-means algorithm to cluster the stored micro-clusters. **SWEM** (Dang et al., 2009) is a probabilistic clustering method for data streams based on finite mixture models (see Section 2.3.5) that uses a fading window. SWEM represents each Gaussian mixture as a vector of parameters containing the weights of the mixture, and its mean and covariance matrix. For the first data window, SWEM applies the EM algorithm until parameter convergence. In the incremental phase, SWEM uses the converged parameters from the previous window of data instances as the initial values for the parameters of the new mixture model. Table 2.9 shows the reviewed data stream clustering algorithms.

As far as supervised classification is concerned, **on-demand-stream** (Aggarwal et al., 2006) is a k-nearest neighbor classifier (Section 2.4.3) that extends the CluStream method and works with the micro-cluster structure, the tilted time window, and the online-offline approach. A micro-cluster is extended

---

[8]K-medians is a variation of the K-means algorithm (Section 2.3.2), where the median of a cluster, instead of the mean, is calculated as its centroid.

TABLE 2.9
Data stream clustering algorithms outline

Data stream clustering	
Algorithm	Method
STREAM (O'Callaghan et al., 2002)	k-medians
CluStream (Aggarwal et al., 2004)	Hierarchical
SWEM (Dang et al., 2009)	Probabilistic

with a class label, and it only takes instances with the same class label. Its offline classification process starts to find a good window of data instances. On-Demand-Stream performs 1-NN classification and assigns the label of the closest micro-cluster to a testing instance. The **Hoeffding tree** (Domingos and Hulten, 2000) is a classification tree (Section 2.4.4) for data streams. A Hoeffding tree uses the Hoeffding bound to choose an optimal splitting variable within a sufficient amount of received instances. The Hoeffding bound provides some probabilistic guarantees about this splitting variable selection. The algorithm is incremental, which satisfies the single-pass constraint. For each new data item received, it uses Hoeffding bounds to check whether the best splitting variable is confident enough to create the next-level tree node. A **granular artificial neural network** (Leite et al., 2010) has been proposed to classify data streams. This is built by augmenting the structure of an ANN (Section 2.4.6) with granular connections formed as intervals. There are two model learning phases. In the first phase, information granules of incoming data are constructed. In the second phase, the neural network is built on the information granules rather than on the original data. Support vector machines (Section 2.4.7) have also been adapted for data stream scenarios. The **core vector machine** algorithm (Tsang et al., 2007) uses minimum enclosed balls, basically hyperspheres, to represent the data instances that they contain, thereby extending the support vector machine method. The algorithm first finds a representative minimum enclosing ball set as a good approximation of the original dataset. This set is then optimized to find the maximum margin directly. **RGNBC** (Babu et al., 2017) is a rough Gaussian naive Bayes classifier (Section 2.4.9) for data stream classification with recurring concept drift. Rough set theory is used to detect concept drifts, and then the current Gaussian naive Bayes classifier is modified to handle the new underlying data distribution. The **online bagging** and **online boosting** algorithms (Oza and Russell, 2005) are adaptations of traditional bagging and boosting methods (Section 2.4.10). In online bagging, each data instance is resampled according to a Poisson distribution whose parameter is equal to one rather than using the uniform distribution of the bootstrapping. The Poisson distribution is the result of considering unlimited data instances. In online boosting, the weights of incoming data instances and the base classifier are adjusted according to

TABLE 2.10
Data stream supervised classification algorithms outline

Data stream supervised classification	
Algorithm	Method
On-demand-stream (Aggarwal et al., 2006)	k-nearest neighbors
Hoeffding tree (Domingos and Hulten, 2000)	Classification tree
Granular artificial neural network (Leite et al., 2010)	Artificial neural networks
Core vector machine (Tsang et al., 2007)	Support vector machine
RGNBC (Babu et al., 2017)	Gaussian naive Bayes
Online bagging and boosting (Oza and Russell, 2005)	Bagging and boosting

the current classifier error rates. Table 2.10 shows the reviewed data stream supervised classification algorithms.

2.6.2 Dynamic, Temporal and Continuous Time Bayesian Networks

There are three basic types of Bayesian network models for dynamic processes (Barber and Cemgil, 2010): dynamic Bayesian networks, temporal nodes Bayesian networks and continuous time Bayesian networks.

Dynamic Bayesian networks (Dean and Kanazawa, 1989) are state-based models that represent the state of each variable at discrete time intervals. The structure consists of a series of time slices, where each slice contains the value of each variable at a given time. Time is discretized, and the same Bayesian network model is repeated for each time slice. Arcs may connect nodes within the same time slice, called **instantaneous arcs**. Also, arcs between nodes of different time slices are **transition arcs** that specify how variables change from one time point to another. Transition arcs can only go forward in time, since a variable state at one time point is determined by the states of other variables at previous time points. This also guarantees the acyclicity of the graph. A prior Bayesian network specifies the initial conditions.

Formally, a dynamic Bayesian network represents a discrete-time **stationary stochastic process**[9] for a vector of n variables, $\mathbf{X}[t] = (X_1[t], ..., X_n[t])$ at each time $t = 1, ..., T$. For example, the statistical measures extracted from the pixel values at time t in an automated visual inspection system for the in-process quality control of the laser surface heat treatment of steel cylinders depend on the values at previous times (see Chapter 6 for details). A common

---

[9]A stationary process is a stochastic process whose joint probability distribution does not change over time.

assumption is to consider a **first-order Markovian transition model**, i.e., $p(\mathbf{X}[t] \mid \mathbf{X}[t-1], ..., \mathbf{X}[1]) = p(\mathbf{X}[t] \mid \mathbf{X}[t-1])$. For this sparse dynamic Bayesian network, we obtain

$$p(\mathbf{X}[1], ..., \mathbf{X}[T]) = p(\mathbf{X}[1]) \prod_{t=2}^{T} p(\mathbf{X}[t] \mid \mathbf{X}[t-1]).$$

$p(\mathbf{X}[1])$ are the initial conditions, factorized according to the prior Bayesian network structure. $p(\mathbf{X}[t] \mid \mathbf{X}[t-1])$ is also factorized over each $X_i[t]$ as $\prod_{i=1}^{n} p(X_i[t] \mid \mathbf{Pa}[t](X_i))$, where the parent variables of X_i, $\mathbf{Pa}[t](X_i)$, may be in the same or in the previous time slice. In continuous domains, a multivariate Gaussian distribution is mostly assumed for $p(\mathbf{X}[1])$ and univariate conditional Gaussian distributions for $p(X_i[t] \mid \mathbf{Pa}[t](X_i))$.

Higher-order Markov models (the probability at time t depends on two or more previous time slices) fit more complex temporal processes, although they pose challenges for structure and parameter estimation.

Example. Structure of a dynamic Bayesian network

Fig. 2.47 illustrates the structure of a dynamic Bayesian network with a first-order Markovian transition model assumption, four variables and three time slices.

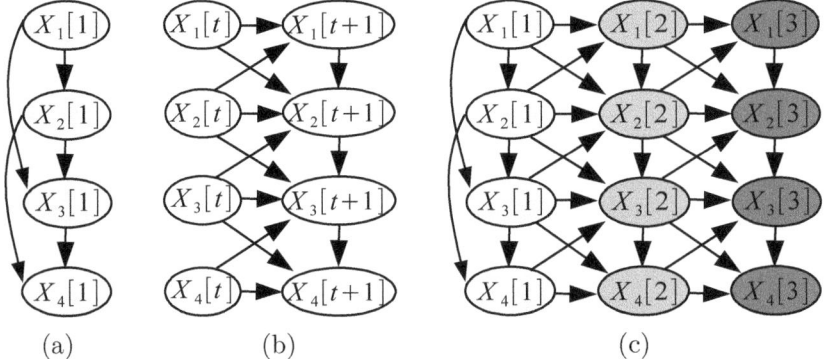

     (a)   (b)   (c)

FIGURE 2.47
A dynamic BN structure with four variables X_1, X_2, X_3 and X_4 and three time slices ($T = 3$): (a) prior BN; (b) transition network, with the first-order Markovian transition assumption; (c) dynamic BN unfolded in time for three time slices.

Inference with dynamic Bayesian networks is easier if the transition network is unfolded in time to constitute a single network. The JPD for $T = 3$ in Fig. 2.47(c) factorizes as

$$p(\mathbf{X}[1], \mathbf{X}[2], \mathbf{X}[3], \mathbf{X}[4])$$
$$= p(X_1[1])p(X_2[1] \mid X_1[1])p(X_3[1] \mid X_2[1], X_1[1])p(X_4[1] \mid X_3[1], X_2[1])$$
$$\prod_{t=2}^{3} \Big(p(X_1[t] \mid X_1[t-1], X_2[t-1])$$
$$\cdot p(X_2[t] \mid X_1[t], X_1[t-1], X_2[t-1], X_3[t-1])$$
$$\cdot p(X_3[t] \mid X_2[t], X_2[t-1], X_3[t-1], X_4[t-1])$$
$$\cdot p(X_4[t] \mid X_3[t], X_3[t-1], X_4[t-1]) \Big).$$

■

The constraint-based and the score and search learning methods presented in Section 2.5.3 can be adapted to learn first-order Markovian dynamic Bayesian networks. The prior network can be learned from a dataset containing instances at time $t = 1$, whereas the transition network can be learned from a dataset including $2n$ variables, instances from times $t - 1$ and also from t ($t = 2, ..., T$).

Friedman et al. (1998b) developed an adaptation of score and search learning methods to dynamic environments. The **dynamic hill-climbing (DHC)** algorithm is based on a hill-climbing search procedure that iteratively improves the BIC score of the prior and transition networks. Trabelsi (2013) adapted the **max-min hill-climbing (MMHC)** (Tsamardinos et al., 2006), a constraint-based learning algorithm, to dynamic settings, developing the **dynamic max-min hill-climbing (DMMHC)**. DMMHC consists of three stages. In the first stage, the algorithm tests conditional independences to identify, for each node, the sets of candidate parent and child nodes (neighbors). In the second stage, the candidate neighbors for each node are identified in a three-step procedure: (a) candidate neighbors of variables in the same time slice t; (b) candidate parents in the past time slice $t-1$ of variables in time slice t; and (c) candidate children in the future time slice $t + 1$ of variables in time slice t. In the final stage, a restricted hill-climbing search is run considering the temporal constraints.

Temporal nodes Bayesian networks (Galán et al., 2007) include two types of nodes: instantaneous nodes and temporal nodes. A temporal node is defined by a set of states, where each state is determined by an ordered pair (λ, τ), with λ denoting the value of a random variable and $\tau = [a, b]$ the time interval in which the state change occurs. Nodes with no intervals defined for any of their states are called instantaneous nodes.

Example. Structure of a temporal nodes Bayesian network

Suppose that at time $t = 0$ a failure F in a machine is detected. There are three possible failure types: `mild`, `moderate` or `severe`. Let us consider that the machine has two components C_1 and C_2. The failure can trigger an incorrect response of C_1, of C_2 or of both, C_1 and C_2. Therefore, the possible values for C_1 and C_2 are `correct` and `incorrect`. These three nodes, F, C_1 and C_2, are instantaneous nodes that may generate subsequent changes in other two nodes. The incorrect response of the first component may produce oil O and/or water W leaks, whereas the malfunction of the second component may cause oil O leaks. The severity of the failure and the correctness of the first component influence the time that it takes for water leaks to occur. The time taken for oil leaks to occur depends on the three instantaneous nodes. Fig. 2.48 shows the structure of this temporal nodes Bayesian network.

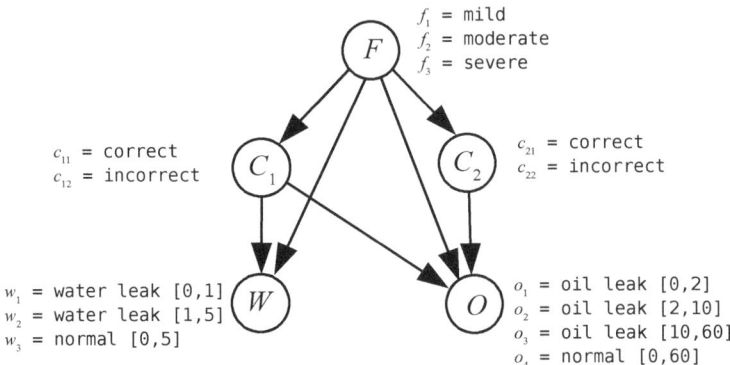

FIGURE 2.48

Example of a temporal nodes Bayesian network. F, C_1 and C_2 are instantaneous nodes, whereas W and O denote temporal nodes.

■

Temporal nodes Bayesian networks can be learned from data (Hernández-Leal et al., 2013).

Continuous time Bayesian networks (Nodelman et al., 2002) overcome the main limitations of dynamic Bayesian networks and temporal nodes Bayesian networks by explicitly representing the dynamics of the process by computing the probability distribution over time when specific events occur. The nodes of a continuous time Bayesian network represent random variables whose state evolves continuously over time. Thus, the evolution of each variable depends on the state of its parents in the graph structure.

A continuous time Bayesian network over $X_1, X_2, ..., X_n$ consists of two components: (a) an initial probability distribution $p^0(X_1, X_2, ..., X_n)$ specified as a Bayesian network; and (b) a continuous transition model specified as a directed (possibly cyclic) graph and, for each variable X_i (with possible values $x_{i1}, ..., x_{iR_i}$), a set of conditional intensity matrices, defined as

$$
\mathbf{Q}_{X_i}^{\mathbf{pa}(x_i)} = \begin{pmatrix}
-q_{x_{i1}}^{\mathbf{pa}(x_i)} & q_{x_{i1},x_{i2}}^{\mathbf{pa}(x_i)} & \cdots & q_{x_{i1},x_{iR_i}}^{\mathbf{pa}(x_i)} \\
q_{x_{i2},x_{i1}}^{\mathbf{pa}(x_i)} & -q_{x_{i2}}^{\mathbf{pa}(x_i)} & \cdots & q_{x_{i2},x_{iR_i}}^{\mathbf{pa}(x_i)} \\
\vdots & \vdots & \ddots & \vdots \\
q_{x_{iR_i},x_{i1}}^{\mathbf{pa}(x_i)} & q_{x_{iR_i},x_{i2}}^{\mathbf{pa}(x_i)} & \cdots & -q_{x_{iR_i}}^{\mathbf{pa}(x_i)}
\end{pmatrix}
$$

for each instantiation $\mathbf{pa}(x_i)$ of the parent variables $\mathbf{Pa}(X_i)$ of node X_i. The diagonal elements, $q_{x_{ik}}^{\mathbf{pa}(x_i)} = \sum_{x_{ij} \neq x_{ik}} q_{x_{ik},x_{ij}}^{\mathbf{pa}(x_i)}$ are interpreted as the instantaneous probability of X_i departing from x_{ik} for a specific instantiation $\mathbf{pa}(x_i)$ of $\mathbf{Pa}(X_i)$. The non-diagonal elements, $q_{x_{ik},x_{ij}}^{\mathbf{pa}(x_i)}$, represent the instantaneous probability of transitioning from the k-th possible value of X_i, x_{ik}, to its j-th possible value, x_{ij}, for a specific instantiation $\mathbf{pa}(x_i)$ of $\mathbf{Pa}(X_i)$.

Continuous time Bayesian networks can deal with both point evidence and continuous evidence. Point evidence refers to the observation of the value of a variable at a particular instant in time, whereas continuous evidence refers to the value of a variable over an entire time interval. Shelton et al. (2010) developed inference and learning from data algorithms.

2.6.3 Hidden Markov Models

Hidden Markov models (HMMs) (Rabiner and Juang, 1986) are one of the most important sequence processing machine learning models. They are based on **Markov chains** that are usually specified by the following components: (a) a set of N states $\{q_1, q_2, ..., q_N\}$; (b) a transition probability matrix $\mathbf{A}$ with elements a_{ij} each representing the probability of moving from state q_i to state q_j, that is, $a_{ij} = p(q_j|q_i)$, with $\sum_{j=1}^{N} a_{ij} = 1$; and (c) special start, q_0, and final, q_F, states that are not associated with observations.

Example. Markov chain graph

Fig. 2.49 shows a Markov chain for assigning probabilities to sequences denoting the quality of the pieces produced by a machine in a factory. The four possible values of these qualities are `very high`, `high`, `medium` and `low`. These four states, as well as the start and final states, are represented as nodes in the graph. The annotated arcs between nodes represent transition probabilities. ∎

In a **first-order Markov chain**, the probability of a particular state depends exclusively on the previous state. An alternative representation that is sometimes used for Markov chains does not rely on a start or final state, but instead represents the probability distribution over initial states and a set of accepting states. A Markov chain is useful when we need to compute a probability for a sequence of events that we can observe in the real world. However, the events of interest are often not directly observable in the real

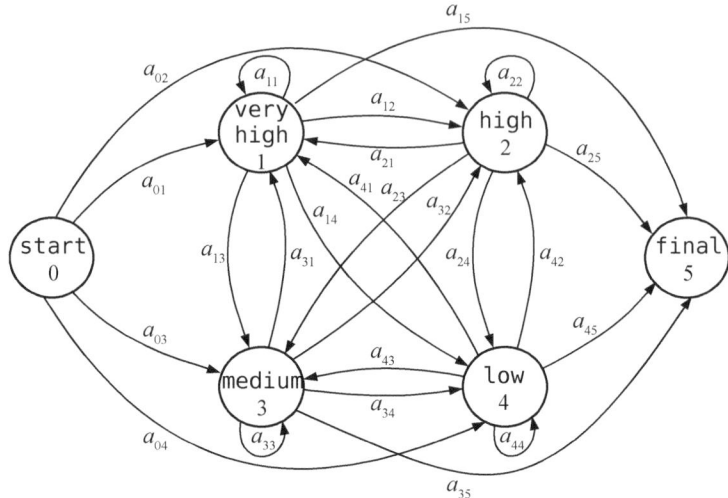

FIGURE 2.49

Example of a Markov chain represented as a graph. In addition to the start state (node 0) and final state (node 5), the other four states are represented by nodes 1 to 4. A transition probability is associated with each arc in the graph.

world. Using a hidden Markov model, we can compute probabilities for both observed and hidden events that we consider to be causal factors in our probabilistic model.

An HMM is specified by the following components: (a) a set of h hidden states $\{1, 2, ..., h\}$ of a hidden variable H; (b) an $h \times h$ transition probability matrix $\mathbf{A}$ with elements a_{ij}, each representing the probability of moving from state i to state j, that is, $a_{ij} = p(H_t = j|H_{t-1} = i)$, with $\sum_{j=1}^{h} a_{ij} = 1$; (c) a sequence of T observations $\mathbf{o} = (o_1, ..., o_T)$; (d) a sequence of emission probabilities $b_i(o_t)$ expressing the probability of an observation o_t being generated from a hidden state i, that is, $b_i(o_t) = p(O_t = o_t|H_t = i)$ for all $t = 1, ..., T$. These $b_i(o_t)$ are the elements of an $h \times K$ emission probability matrix $\mathbf{B}$, where K denotes the number of different possible observation values; (e) an initial probability distribution over initial states $\boldsymbol{\pi} = (\pi_1, \ldots, \pi_h)$. The HMM can be described by a parameter vector, $\boldsymbol{\theta} = (\mathbf{A}, \mathbf{B}, \boldsymbol{\pi})$.

A **first-order hidden Markov model** is based on two simplifying assumptions. First, as a first-order Markov chain, the probability of a particular hidden state depends only on the previous state: $p(H_t|H_{t-1}, \ldots, H_1) = p(H_t|H_{t-1})$. Second, the probability of an output observation $O_t = o_t$ depends only on the hidden state $H_t = h_t$ (with $h_t \in \{1, 2, \ldots, h\}$)that produced the observation and not on any other states or any other observations: $p(o_t|h_1, \ldots, h_t, \ldots, h_T, o_1, \ldots, o_t, \ldots, o_T) = p(o_t|h_t)$.

Example. First-order hidden Markov model

Fig. 2.50 shows an example of a first-order hidden Markov model with two hidden states representing the correctness of a machine component (`correct`, `noncorrect`) whose initial probability distribution is $(0.97, 0.03)$; the elements of the transition matrix are $a_{11} = 0.95, a_{12} = 0.05, a_{21} = 0.10, a_{22} = 0.90$; and the emission probabilities are given by $b_1(o_1) = 0.80, b_1(o_2) = 0.20, b_2(o_1) = 0.08, b_2(o_2) = 0.92$, with o_1 and o_2 denoting a `normal speed` and a `slow speed` of the machine, respectively.

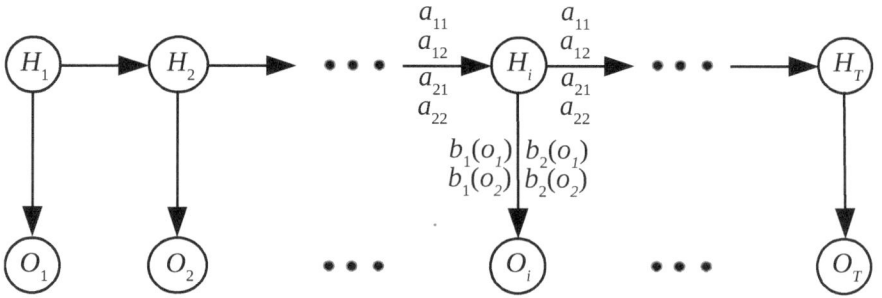

FIGURE 2.50
Example of a first-order hidden Markov model.

◼

Given an observation sequence $\mathbf{o} = (o_1, ..., o_T)$, HMMs have to solve three fundamental problems: (i) evaluate its likelihood; (ii) discover the optimal hidden state sequence; and (iii) learn the HMM parameters, $\boldsymbol{\pi}$, a_{ij} and $b_i(o_t)$. This is explored below.

2.6.3.1 Evaluation of the Likelihood of an Observation Sequence

Following on with the above example, we want to compute the probability of the observation sequence "`normal speed, slow speed, normal speed`", but we do not know what the hidden state sequence is. For a given hidden state sequence (e.g., "`correct, noncorrect, correct`"), we can easily compute the likelihood of the above observation sequence. Thus, taking into account that $p(\mathbf{o}|\mathbf{h}) = \prod_{i=1}^{T} p(o_i|h_i)$, we have that

$p(\texttt{normal speed}, \texttt{slow speed}, \texttt{normal speed}|\texttt{correct}, \texttt{noncorrect}, \texttt{correct})$
$= p(\texttt{normal speed}|\texttt{correct})$
$\quad \cdot p(\texttt{slow speed}|\texttt{noncorrect})$
$\quad \cdot p(\texttt{normal speed}|\texttt{correct}).$

The joint probability of a particular hidden state sequence $\mathbf{h}$ generating a particular observation sequence $\mathbf{o}$ is computed as

$$p(\mathbf{o}, \mathbf{h}) = p(\mathbf{o}|\mathbf{h})p(\mathbf{h}) = \prod_{i=1}^{T} p(o_i|h_i) \prod_{i=1}^{T} p(h_i|h_{i-1}).$$

We can compute the total probability of the sequence of observations by just summing over all possible hidden state sequences:

$$p(\mathbf{o}) = \sum_{\mathbf{h}} p(\mathbf{o}, \mathbf{h}) = \sum_{\mathbf{h}} p(\mathbf{o}|\mathbf{h})p(\mathbf{h}). \qquad (2.19)$$

However, this procedure is extremely inefficient and computationally expensive. For an HMM with h hidden states and a sequence of T observations, there are h^T possible hidden sequences. This number can be huge if h and T are both large, making it infeasible to compute the likelihood of an observation sequence by computing and then summing all the separate observation likelihoods for each hidden state sequence.

The **forward algorithm** only requires $h^2 T$ operations to compute the likelihood of an observation sequence. This algorithm stores intermediate values as it builds the probability of the observation sequence. The term $\alpha_t(j) = p(o_1, ..., o_t, H_t = j)$ represents the probability of being in hidden state j after considering the first t observations. $\alpha_t(j)$ is computed by summing over the probabilities of every path that could lead to this observation sequence and hidden value. The computation of $\alpha_t(j)$ takes advantage of the following recursion equation:

$$\alpha_t(j) = \sum_{i=1}^{h} \alpha_{t-1}(i)a_{ij}b_j(o_t). \qquad (2.20)$$

Denoting by 0 and F the initial and final states, respectively, the initialization of the forward algorithm is given by $\alpha_1(j) = \pi_j b_j(o_1)$, and $a_{0j} = \pi_j$, for $j = 1, ..., h$. The termination of the recursion corresponds to $\alpha_T(h_F) = \sum_{i=1}^{h} \alpha_T(i)a_{iF}$. This represents $p(o_1, ..., o_T, H_T = h_F)$, which would be introduced in Eq. 2.19.

2.6.3.2 Decoding

For any model containing hidden variables, the task of determining which sequence of hidden variables is (has the highest probability of being) the underlying source of some sequence of observations is a problem called the **decoding task**. Given the observation sequence "`normal speed, slow speed, normal speed`", the task of the decoder is to find the best (most probable) hidden machine quality sequence that can be seen as its underlying source.

A naive approach for solving this problem is to run the forward algorithm for each possible hidden state sequence and select the sequence with the highest probability. As explained above, the number of possible hidden sequences is h^T, and the forward algorithm requires $h^2 T$ operations for each sequence.

The most common decoding algorithm for HMMs is the **Viterbi algorithm** (Viterbi, 1967). Like the forward algorithm, the Viterbi algorithm is a kind of dynamic programming procedure. $v_t(j)$ represents the probability that the HMM is in its j-th hidden state after considering the first t observations and passing through the most probable state sequence $h_0, h_1, ..., h_{t-1}$. Formally,

$$v_t(j) = \max_{h_0, h_1, ..., h_{t-1}} p(h_0, h_1, ..., h_{t-1}, o_1, o_2, ..., o_t, H_t = j).$$

The most probable path is represented by taking the maximum of all the possible previous state sequences. The Viterbi algorithm computes the value of $v_t(j)$ recursively as

$$v_t(j) = \max_{i=1,...,h} v_{t-1}(i) a_{ij} b_j(o_t).$$

Note that the Viterbi algorithm is identical to the forward algorithm, except that it takes the max of the previous path probabilities, whereas the forward algorithm takes the sum.

2.6.3.3 Hidden Markov Model Training

The third problem is to learn the HMM parameters $\theta = (\mathbf{A}, \mathbf{B}, \pi)$ given an observation sequence and a set of possible states. The standard algorithm for training HMMs is the **forward-backward algorithm**, also known as the **Baum-Welch algorithm** (Baum et al., 1970), which is a special case of the EM algorithm (Section 2.3.5). The Baum-Welch algorithm finds a local maximum $\theta^* = \arg\max_{\theta} p(o_1, o_2, ..., o_T | \theta)$. The algorithm starts by computing an initial estimate for the probabilities, which it then uses to improve the estimate, repeating this scheme iteratively.

Thus, the algorithm initializes $\theta = (\mathbf{A}, \mathbf{B}, \pi)$ randomly, although the use of prior information about the parameters (if available) is recommendable, as this knowledge can speed up algorithm convergence and steer it toward a local maximum. Each iteration of the Baum-Welch algorithm is based on two procedures: forward and backward. Parameters $\theta = (\mathbf{A}, \mathbf{B}, \pi)$ are updated after applying both procedures.

The forward procedure finds recursively the probability of the observation sequence $o_1, ..., o_t$ and being in the hidden state i at time t, i.e., $\alpha_t(i) = p(o_1, ..., o_t, H_t = i)$, like the forward algorithm (Eq. 2.20): $\alpha_t(i) = \sum_{j=1}^{h} \alpha_{t-1}(j) a_{ji} b_i(o_t)$. This formula is initialized with $\alpha_1(i) = a_{0i} b_i(o_1)$, and $a_{0i} = \pi_i$.

The backward procedure computes $\beta_t(i) = p(o_{t+1}, ..., o_T | H_t = i)$ in a similar manner to the forward procedure, using the following recursion formulas: $\beta_T = 1$ and $\beta_t(i) = \sum_{j=1}^{h} \beta_{t+1}(j) a_{ij} b_j(o_{t+1})$. To update θ, we need to introduce two auxiliary variables:

$$\gamma_t(i) = p(H_t = i | o_1, ..., o_T) = \frac{p(H_t = i, o_1, ..., o_T)}{p(o_1, ..., o_T)} = \frac{\alpha_t(i) \beta_t(i)}{\sum_{j=1}^{h} \alpha_t(j) \beta_t(j)},$$

which is the probability of being in state i at time t given the observed sequence $(o_1, ..., o_T)$ and parameters $\boldsymbol{\theta} = (\mathbf{A}, \mathbf{B}, \boldsymbol{\pi})$, and

$$
\begin{aligned}
\xi_t(ij) &= p(H_t = i, H_{t+1} = j | o_1, ..., o_T) \\
&= \frac{p(H_t = i, H_{t+1} = j, o_1, ..., o_T)}{p(o_1, ..., o_T)} \\
&= \frac{\alpha_t(i) a_{ij} \beta_{t+1}(j) b_j(o_{t+1})}{\sum_{k=1}^{h} \sum_{l=1}^{h} \alpha_t(k) a_{kl} \beta_{t+1}(l) b_l(o_{t+1})},
\end{aligned}
$$

which is the probability of being in the hidden state i and j at times t and $t+1$, respectively, given the sequence of observations $o_1, ..., o_T$. The denominators of $\gamma_t(i)$ and $\xi_t(ij)$ are the same. They represent the probability of the observed sequence $o_1, ..., o_T$ (given the parameters $\boldsymbol{\theta} = (\mathbf{A}, \mathbf{B}, \boldsymbol{\pi})$).

The parameters of the HMM model can now be updated:

- $\pi_i = \gamma_1(i)$ represents the expected frequency of being in the hidden state i at time 1.

- $a_{ij} = \frac{\sum_{t=1}^{T-1} \xi_t(ij)}{\sum_{t=1}^{T-1} \gamma_t(i)}$ which is the expected number of transitions from state i to state j compared to the expected total number of times the hidden state i is observed in the sequence from $t = 1$ to $t = T - 1$.

- $b_i(o_t) = \frac{\sum_{t=1}^{T} \mathbb{I}(O_t = o_t) \gamma_t(i)}{\sum_{t=1}^{T} \gamma_t(i)}$, where $\mathbb{I}(O_t = o_t)$ is an indicator function, that is,

$$
\mathbb{I}(O_t = o_t) = \left\{ \begin{array}{ll} 1 & \text{if } O_t = o_t \\ 0 & \text{otherwise} \end{array} \right.
$$

and $b_i(o_t)$ is the expected number of times that the observed sequence is equal to o_t while being in hidden state i over the expected total number of times that it is in hidden state i.

These three steps (forward and backward procedures and the updating of $\boldsymbol{\theta} = (\mathbf{A}, \mathbf{B}, \boldsymbol{\pi})$ parameters) are repeated iteratively until the convergence criterion is met.

2.7   Machine Learning Tools

This section describes the characteristics of some of the most popular machine learning software tools for clustering, supervised classification, Bayesian networks and dynamic environments.

For clustering and supervised classification, we have selected the following five software tools: WEKA[10], R[11], scikit-learn[12], KNIME[13] and RapidMiner[14]. **WEKA** (Hall et al., 2009) is a Java-based open-source machine learning platform developed at the University of Waikato, New Zealand. The software is free under the GNU/GPL 3 license for non-commercial purposes. It is popular mainly because it is user friendly and a large number of implemented algorithms are available. WEKA offers four user interface options: command-line interface, Explorer, Experimenter and Knowledge Flow. The preferred option is Explorer, which can be used to define the data source, data preparation, machine learning algorithm execution, and visualization. Experimenter is mainly used for comparing the performance of different algorithms on the same dataset. Knowledge Flow is useful for specifying the dataflow using connected visual components. **Massive Online Analysis (MOA)** (Bifet et al., 2012) is based on the WEKA framework and includes many online learning algorithms for evolving data streams.

The open-source tool and programming language **R** (Lafaye de Micheaux et al., 2013) is the successor of S, a statistical language originally developed by Bell Labs in the 1970s. The source code of R is written in C++, Fortran and in R itself. It is an interpreted language and is optimized for mostly matrix-based calculations. The tool offers only a simple GUI with a command-line shell for input. As all the commands have to be entered in the R language, it is not a user-friendly environment, although code editors like RStudio make R easier to use. For machine learning projects, Rattle (Williams, 2009) offers a decent GUI for R similar to Weka's Explorer. There is a wealth of online documentation for all algorithms.

scikit-learn (Pedregosa et al., 2011) is a free Python package. It has a command-line interface and requires some Python programming skills. One of its main strong points is its well-written online documentation.

KNIME (Berthold et al., 2008) is the acronym of Konstanz Information Miner and is developed and maintained by a Swiss company based on initial developments at the University of Konstanz, Germany. KNIME is open-source, although commercial licenses exist for companies requiring professional technical support. One of the greatest strengths of KNIME is its integration with WEKA and R.

RapidMiner (Hofmann and Klinkenberg, 2013) is a Java-based tool currently under development by the company RapidMiner, Germany. Previous versions were open source. RapidMiner offers an integrating environment with a visually appealing and user-friendly GUI. RapidMiner also offers the option of application wizards that construct the machine learning process automatically based on the required project goals.

---

[10]https://www.cs.waikato.ac.nz/ml/weka/

[11]https://www.r-project.org/

[12]http://scikit-learn.org/stable/

[13]https://www.knime.com/

[14]https://rapidminer.com/

Table 2.11 lists the clustering and supervised classification methods supported by the five tools.

TABLE 2.11
Machine learning tools for clustering and supervised classification

	WEKA	R	scikit-learn	KNIME	RapidMiner
Hierarchical clustering	√	√	√	√	√
K-means	√	√	√	√	√
Spectral clustering		√	√		
Affinity propagation		√	√		
Probabilistic clustering	√	√	√		√
Feature subset selection	√	√	√	√	√
k-nearest neighbors	√	√	√	√	√
Classification tree	√	√	√	√	√
Rule induction	√	√			√
Artificial neural networks	√	√	√	√	√
Support vector machines	√	√	√	√	√
Logistic regression	√	√	√	√	√
Bayesian network classifiers	√	√	√	√	√
Metaclassifiers	√	√	√	√	√

[*]The symbol √ denotes that the machine learning method is available in the respective software.

For Bayesian networks, we have selected the following five software tools: HUGIN[15], GeNIe, Open-Markov[16], gRain[17] and bnlearn[18]. **HUGIN** (Madsen et al., 2005) is a software package –developed by HUGIN EXPERT, a company located in Aalborg, Denmark– for building and deploying decision support systems for reasoning and decision making under uncertainty. HUGIN software is based on Bayesian network and influence diagram technology. The HUGIN software package consists of the HUGIN Decision Engine (HDE), a GUI and application program interfaces (APIs) to facilitate the integration of HUGIN into applications. **GeNIe modeler** (Druzdzel, 1999) is a GUI providing an interactive model for building and learning Bayesian networks and it is connected with SMILE (Structural Modeling Inference and Learning Engine), which provides exact and approximate inference algorithms. It is based on research at the University of Pittsburgh, USA. Nowadays, it is developed by BayesFusion, LLC. **Open-Markov** (Arias et al., 2012) is a software tool that implements both constraint-based and score+search learning algorithms and approximate inference methods. It is under development at the National University for Distance Education in Madrid. **gRain** (Højsgaard, 2012) is an R

---

[15]https://www.hugin.com/
[16]http://www.openmarkov.org/
[17]https://CRAN.R-project.org/package=gRain
[18]http://www.bnlearn.com/

package for evidence propagation in probabilistic graphical models developed at Aalborg University. **bnlearn** (Scutari, 2010) is an R package that includes several algorithms for learning the structure and parameters of Bayesian networks from data with either discrete or continuous variables. It implements both constraint-based and score-based algorithms and also includes parallel computing functionalities.

Table 2.12 lists the methods for Bayesian network inference and learning from data supported by the five tools.

TABLE 2.12

Software for Bayesian networks

	HUGIN	GeNIe	Open-Markov	gRain	bnlearn
Exact inference:					
Junction tree	√	√		√	
Approximate inference:					
Probabilistic logic sampling	√	√	√		√
Constraint-based learning:					
PC algorithm	√	√	√		√
Score+search:					
K2 algorithm	√	√	√		√

*The symbol √ denotes that the inference or structure learning method is available in the respective software

2.8 The Frontiers of Machine Learning

A recent meeting between researchers of the National Academy of Sciences and The Royal Society (National Academy of Sciences and The Royal Society, 2017) on machine learning has reached some conclusions about what the future holds for this artificial intelligence discipline. The main open issues that will condition the way machine learning will be applied in our lives are summarized below.

One of the main challenges that society has to face is the ethic of using certain types of data, and managing them in different ways. This is, for example, the case in criminal justice, where scoring systems based on machine learning have been applied to predict the likelihood of repeat offending. It is assumed that the algorithm should be designed free of societal assumptions about factors such as race, gender, or socioeconomic status. However, the outputs of these systems reflect the data on which they are trained. If these data embody current societal biases or inequality, then a machine learning system will replicate these biases.

Questions arise about how humans and machine learning systems interact as well as the societal challenges of adapting to a world where these systems are increasingly pervasive. During the first industrial revolution, individuals had to adapt to new ways of communicating, traveling, and working. Nowadays we wonder if humans will be able to adapt to changes in almost all aspects of life as a consequence of advances in machine learning.

Educational barriers are avoiding the ubiquity of machine learning systems in society. As early as the elementary school level, students could benefit from greater encouragement to develop a science, technology, engineering, and mathematics skill set. In postsecondary curricula, it is common to only emphasize traditional mathematics, excluding any kind of computing and communication skills. Although companies are aggressively hiring new talent in machine learning, there are relatively few people trained in data science, statistics and machine learning. In this sense, experiences, like the **automatic statistician project**[19] that aims to build an artificial intelligence for data science, helping people make sense of their data, are more than welcome.

The modeling capabilities provided by machine learning pose new challenges to managing privacy. Sometimes, machine learning will use data containing sensitive information, whereas in other cases machine learning might create sensitive insights from seemingly irrelevant data. Machine learning tools should have the potential to provide new kinds of transparency about data and inferences, and should be applied to detect, remove, or reduce human bias, rather than reinforcing it. Transparency and interpretability of predictive machine learning models are a must, as one needs to understand what the predictive model is doing, and will do in the future, in order to trust and deploy it.

To push forward the boundaries of machine learning, statisticians, engineers, data scientists, computer scientists and mathematicians can benefit from different key stakeholders: sociologists, to discuss the ethical and societal technological issues; psychologists, who could offer valuable insights into the ways humans interact with technology; unions and industrial psychologists, as voices of workforce changes from continued development of machine learning methods; policy makers and regulators, who could contribute to a dialogue about autonomy and fair information principles; and historians, whose knowledge about past eras of rapid technological change can be very useful.

Regulating machine learning activities (and artificial intelligence in general) governance seems feasible and desirable. However, risks and considerations are disparate in different domains. Policy markers should recognize that to varying degrees and over time, various industries will need distinct, appropriate, regulations.

---

[19]https://www.automaticstatistician.com/index/

3

Applications of Machine Learning in Industrial Sectors

The detailed and comprehensive structure for sector and industry analysis called Industry Classification Benchmark[1] of FTSE Russell is used in this chapter.

3.1 Energy Sector

Machine learning is now an integral part of the operations of most oil and gas companies, which they use to translate datasets including large volumes of real-time information into actionable insights. Low commodity price environment, time savings, cost reductions, efficiency boosts and safety improvements are all crucial outcomes that can be achieved using machine learning in oil and gas operations[2].

A common problem in the oil and gas industries is to find a non-invasive technique to estimate the ratio of oil or gas transferred through pipelines from offshore **drilling** activities. One way to do this is by passing a beam of gamma rays through the pipe and looking at the beam attenuation as it interacts with the material. This provides information about the material density. Typically, multiple beams at different wavelengths, energies and geometries are used. The machine learning model needs to predict properties about the material based on the data provided by the beams. If the number of beams in the machine learning model matches the number of beams in the new material, the problem can be solved by the supervised classification methods described in Section 2.4. However, if the data of new and unlabeled material are based on a different number of beams, these methods need to be adapted. Closely related to this issue, artificial neural networks have been developed to locate and size different defect types in the oil and gas pipelines from sensors measuring magnetic flux leakage signals (Mohamed et al., 2015).

Another common problem refers to the uncertainties in **reservoir exploitation**. These uncertainties are high when trying to figure out how a tight

---

[1]http://www.ftse.com/products/downloads/ICB_Rules.pdf
[2]https://www.machinelearning-oilandgas.com/

133

rock formation responds to an induced hydraulic fracture treatment. This process can be modeled by making appropriate use of complex and historical reservoir data through machine learning.

Modern drilling is based on real-time information about ongoing operations produced by rigs containing a huge number of sensors that actively measure numerous parameters related to vessel operation, as well as information about the down-hole drilling environment. Using machine learning facilities for advanced computer-based video interpretation, many different phenomena can be continuously, robustly, and accurately assessed.

The use of machine learning in the oil and gas industries is not limited to exploration and production, as many operators in the petrochemical refining sector now rely on these algorithms to continuously improve the overall performance of their facilities and more effectively maintain their equipment.

3.1.1   Oil

Crude oil is today the world's leading fuel, and its price has a big impact on the global environment, economy, and oil exploration and exploitation activities. **Oil price forecasts** are very useful for industries, governments and individuals. Major factors affecting the oil market are demand, supply, population, geopolitical risks and economic issues. Crude oil price prediction is a very challenging problem for machine learning methods due to its high volatility. Several machine learning techniques have been proposed for oil price prediction.

Nwiabu and Amadi (2017) develop a naive Bayes classifier containing demand and supply variables to predict upward or downward price movements. Xie et al. (2006) apply support vector machines to this problem. They are empirically compared with multilayer perceptron artificial neural networks and autoregressive integrated moving average (ARIMA) models on the monthly spot prices of West Texas Intermediate (WTI) crude oil from 1970 to 2003. Yu et al. (2008) estimate crude oil prices based on an ensemble of artificial neural networks. First, the original crude spot price series is decomposed into a finite number of chunks. Then, a one hidden layer perceptron is used to model each of the dataset chunks. Finally, the prediction results of all the models are combined using another artificial neural network. The WTI crude oil price and Brent crude oil price series are used to test the effectiveness of the proposal. Gao and Lei (2017) noticed that crude oil price series are not necessarily the result of a stationary process and proposed the use of data stream learning algorithms in the WTI benchmark dataset.

In recent years, pirate attacks against shipping and oil field installations have become more frequent and more serious. Bouejla et al. (2012) provide an innovative solution that addresses the problem from the perspective of the entire processing chain, that is, from the detection of a potential threat to the implementation of a response. Bayesian networks are used to discover the relationships between 20 variables concerning the characteristics of the threat and the potential target, existing protection tools, environmental constraints, etc. The initial Bayesian network is automatically induced from the International Maritime Organization's Piracy and Armed Robbery database that contains historical (dating back to 1994) data on pirate attacks in the maritime environment. This initial model is later improved with the contribution of knowledge from domain experts.

Bayesian networks have also been applied to **drilling rig operation management** (Fournier et al., 2010). Drilling rigs are operated by contractors who hire out their services to oil companies for both exploration and exploitation. Drilling rig operation is extremely expensive. Typically an offshore rig in the Gulf of Mexico can cost from $400,000 to $600,000 per day to operate. The dataset used was sourced by ODS-Petrodata Ltd and covers over 25 years of historical rig activity. Each rig record is characterized by around 1,000 variables ranging from operational data (water depth, footage drilled, durations, etc.) to technical data (cantilever capacity, water depth rating, age, etc.). Domain experts selected 17 key variables from this huge dataset. A score (K2 metric) and search (genetic algorithm) approach is used to induce a Bayesian network model from this smaller dataset.

3.1.2 Gas

Abstract dissolved gas analysis (DGA) of the insulation oil of power transformers is a research tool to monitor their health and to detect impending failures by recognizing anomalous patterns of DGA concentrations. The failure prediction problem can be seen as a machine learning task on DGA samples, optionally exploiting the transformer age, nominal power and voltage. There are two approaches: binary classification for detecting failure and regression of time to failure. Mirowski and LeCun (2018) review and evaluate 15 classification and regression models for this problem, like k-nearest neighbors, classification trees, artificial neural networks and support vector machines.

Pipelines are one of the most popular and effective ways of transporting hazardous materials, especially natural gas. However, the rapid development of **gas pipelines** and stations in urban areas poses a serious threat to public safety and assets. A comprehensive methodology for accident scenario and risk analysis of gas transportation systems, especially in natural gas stations, has been developed using Bayesian networks (Zarei et al., 2017). The Bayesian network for failure mode and effect analysis is provided by expert domains that consider a total of 43 variables containing information about failure modes, causes and effects on the system, severity of effects, detection level and risk priority number.

3.2　Basic Materials Sector

This sector includes chemicals and basic resources (see Fig. 3.1).

3.2.1　Chemicals

Like other industries, the chemical industry operates in a competitive global market, where mergers and acquisitions designed to reinforce company position are commonplace. This industrial sector can expect big opportunities by embracing machine learning.

Four major application areas of machine learning in the chemical industry are: (a) manufacturing, (b) drug design, (c) toxicity prediction, and (d) compound classification. The volume of data that has to be handled in **chemical manufacturing** to tackle optimization, monitoring, and control problems is increasing (Wuest et al., 2016). Machine learning can contribute significantly to speeding up the processes, finding more sustainable and cost-effective solutions, and making room for innovations. Thus, Ribeiro (2005) used support vector machines and artificial neural networks for monitoring the quality of in-process data in a plastic injection molding machine.

The aim in **drug design** is to identify lead compounds with significant activity against a selected biological target. The drug target is a protein whose activity is modulated by its interaction with a chemical compound and may thus control a disease. Lead compounds are identified at the drug discovery stage. They are then optimized in the drug development phase, resulting in a small number of chemicals that are evaluated in human clinical trials. Machine learning has been used at the drug discovery stage to build functions that rank the probability that a chemical will have activity against a known target and to predict ligand-receptor affinity, target structure and the side-effects of new drugs, as well as for target screening on cells and even in drug delivery systems (Bernick, 2015). The review by Lima et al. (2016) mentions random forests, decision trees, artificial neural networks and support vector machines as the main techniques in new drug discovery, whereas Lavecchia (2015) adds k-nearest neighbors, and naive Bayes. Another important use of machine learning is to predict the pharmacokinetic and toxicological profile of compounds, i.e., the so-called ADME-Tox (absorption, distribution, metabolism, excretion and toxicity) (Maltarollo et al., 2015).

Machine learning is used in many aspects of **toxicity detection and prediction**. Predicting chemical toxicity is an important issue in both the environmental and drug development fields. In vitro bioassay data are often used to predict in vivo chemical toxicology. Judson et al. (2008) compare k-nearest neighbors, artificial neural networks, naive Bayes, classification trees and support vector machines with filter-based feature selection. Machine learning is used in drug development to detect toxicities, such as hepatotoxicity,

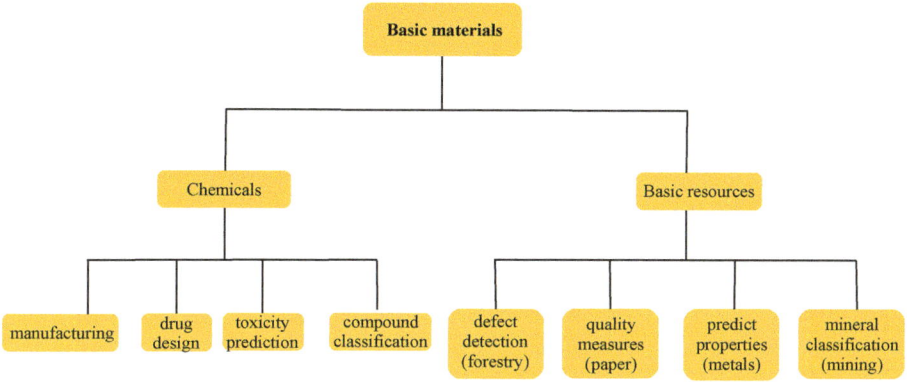

FIGURE 3.1
Applications of machine learning in the basic materials sector.

nephrotoxicity, and ototoxicity. Few researchers have addressed cardiotoxicity and neurotoxicity, which are fields where there are new research opportunities (Bernick, 2015). REACH is the European regulation on registration, evaluation, authorization and restriction of chemicals. This new legislation has led to an increase in the in silico prediction of toxicity data on chemicals produced in or imported into the European Union (EU). A widely used predictive method is a QSAR (quantitative structure-activity relationships) approach based on artificial neural networks (Dearden and Rowe, 2015).

Machine learning techniques are faster and cheaper than in vivo experimental tests at predicting **genotoxicity**. The aim is to detect compounds that have an adverse effect on the process of heredity in human beings. They can collect many different chemicals whose molecules are represented by both fingerprints and molecular descriptors. Fan et al. (2018) used six classifiers for this purpose: naive Bayes, k-nearest neighbors, C4.5 classification tree, artificial neural networks, support vector machines and random forests.

Finally, thousands of chemical compounds can be automatically categorized into different classes using supervised classification methods for **compound classification**. Smusz et al. (2013) use WEKA to compare 11 classifiers (including four metaclassifiers), whereas Lang et al. (2016) use active machine learning to reduce the required number of training compounds. Active machine learning iteratively processes labeled data to avoid the costly, error-prone and time-consuming process of manually gathering class information usually supplied by chemists or sourced from experiments. Li et al. (2009) use support vector machines to classify polymers. Böcker et al. (2005) choose hierarchical clustering and K-means to analyze large compound libraries.

More practical goals within the chemical industry are to help create new and novel fragrances that perform well technically (do not irritate the skin, do not change color after a few months), smell good and are unique in the marketplace. Master perfumers typically train for ten years before they become proficient. Goodwin et al. (2017) use different classifiers to predict target gender and average rating for unseen fragrances, all characterized by a set of fragrance notes. Also, the data are projected in a 2D space using t-distributed stochastic neighbor embedding (t-SNE) (van der Maaten and Hinton, 2008), a non-linear dimensionality reduction technique. This discovers clusters of perfumes and free spaces without data, which could suggest combinations of as yet unexplored but promising fragrance notes. Xu et al. (2007) design a new pigment mixing method based on an artificial neural network to emulate real-life pigment mixing, as well as to support the creation of new artificial pigments.

3.2.2   Basic Resources

In **forestry**, internal defect detection in hardwood logs is important with regard to the commercial value of resulting boards and finished wood products. Sarigul et al. (2005) build an artificial neural network from computed tomography images of hardwood logs for a preliminary classification of every pixel according to labels such as "knot," "split," and "bark."

In **paper production**, the so-called Kappa number is an interesting quality measure of the paper pulp, which is, however, hard to measure directly using online sensors. Li and Zhu (2004) found that support vector machines outperform artificial neural networks as a means of inferring the Kappa number from measurements of surrounding sensors. Iglesias et al. (2017) use a MLP, support vector machines and CART to predict some pulp properties, i.e., pulp yield, Kappa number, ISO brightness, fiber length and fiber width, using the proportion of sapwood and heartwood in the raw material.

In **industrial metals**, Pardakhti et al. (2017) take chemical and structural descriptors to predict methane adsorption of metal organic frameworks. To do this, they use classification trees, support vector machines and random forests. Rosenbrock et al. (2017) examine atomic structures called grain boundaries (GB) that have a major influence on many physical properties of crystalline materials (strength, ductility, corrosion resistance, crack resistance, and conductivity). Support vector machines and classification trees are trained to (independently) predict three different properties of GBs: GB energy, temperature-dependent mobility, and shear-coupled GB migration. This contributes to producing stronger, less corrosive metals. Defect detection machine learning tools are also found in the steel, as well as the wood, industry (Bürger et al., 2014), where data are first preprocessed with PCA and then support vector machines with different kernels, random trees and artificial neural networks are learned. Besides, Bayesian networks (Section 2.5) predict the change tendency of silicon content in hot metals (Wang, 2007). Gosangi and Gutierrez-Osuna (2011) use dynamic Bayesian networks (Section 2.6.2) to model the transient response of metal-oxide sensors modulated with a sequence of voltage steps. This characterizes the dynamic relationship between sensor inputs and outputs in order to understand the underlying operating principles.

Finally, there is a plethora of machine learning applications in the **mining industry** for assessing ore fragmentation in underground and open-pit operations and for recognizing spalling, cracked shotcrete, and plate deformation. Carey et al. (2015) use machine learning for mineral classification. Harvey and Fotopoulos (2016) build geological maps using naive Bayes, k-nearest neighbors, random forests and support vector machines to correctly identify geological rock types in an area with complete ground validation information. This improves the tedious conventional field expedition techniques.

3.3   Industrials Sector

The industrials sector covers the design, manufacturing, assembly, distribution and retail of industrial materials, goods and services. In this wide-ranging industrial sector, machine learning technique applications mainly target industrial products and processes (see Fig. 3.2).

Industrial goods manufacturing industries are mainly related to heavy duty and, sometimes, highly automated and integrated processes as in the aerospace industry. Consequently, almost all the industries in this sector require large amounts of raw materials and resources to be able to provide added value. To be profitable, companies need to operate efficiently in terms of low downtimes (i.e., machines are not functioning because of an unexpected failure or long maintenance times), high availability (i.e., the machine production time is as close as possible to the total machine uptime) and scrap minimization (i.e., the percentage of parts with quality problems is significantly lower than the total number of produced parts). For example, heavy duty manufacturing machinery used to produce cement and other building aggregates requires large amounts of energy resulting in high production costs. If the production is stopped due to a failure, the production cost will increase due to the maintenance cost, drastically reducing the profit margin. On the other hand, aircraft manufacturing uses large amounts of raw materials, some of which are extremely expensive. If there is a high scrap ratio during aircraft component manufacturing, the final cost of the aircraft could be prohibitive.

As robustness and efficiency are key requirements, these industries share a common need to get actionable insights from the product and process data to ensure profitable products and processes. Traditionally, the insights are gained by means of tedious statistical tools or statistical process control techniques whose application is limited by the amount of data that they handle. With increased computing power, however, machine learning techniques are starting to be successfully applied in many industrial sectors. Nevertheless, there are some obstacles to the deployment of machine learning techniques coming out of labs or from other industrial sectors, as there are several critical issues to be solved, including harsh environments, limited access to communication infrastructures and so on.

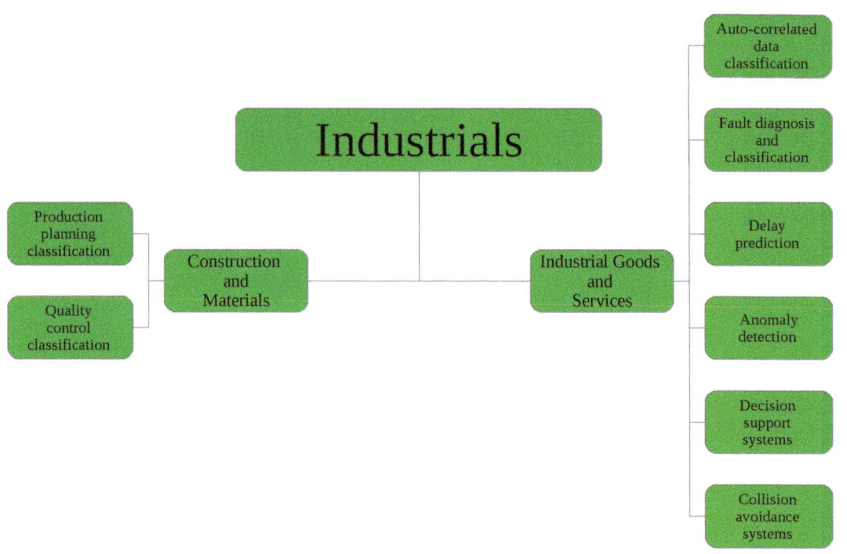

FIGURE 3.2
Applications of machine learning in the industrials sector.

From this general point of view, Hansson et al. (2016) investigate different machine learning tools that can be applied to heavy industry. They analyze feature subset selection (see Section 2.4.2), clustering (Section 2.3), artificial neural networks (Section 2.4.6), support vector machines (Section 2.4.7), classification trees (Section 2.4.4) and metaclassifiers (Section 2.4.10) with respect to their industrial applications. Additional techniques from those explained in this work could have been applied, as it is possible to obtain similar actionable insights with all of them. However, there is also a real challenge related to the deployment of the algorithms into real working environments, where other restrictions define the optimal algorithm depending on its communications, data storage, computing power, among other needs at the application field. These integration challenges found between algorithms and their infrastructure needs are being solved by the Fourth Industrial Revolution, which is introducing machine learning applications to the industrials sector through IT and OT integration. Some examples are summarized below.

3.3.1 Construction and Materials

With regard to **industrial materials production**, there are different manufacturing stages in which machine learning is applied, as there are different chemical processes related to the actual materials and the end-user application. For example, **structural steel** is one of the most commonly used materials for construction and other applications. However, according to the World Steel Association, there are more than 3,500 grades of steels with different mechanical and chemical properties[3]. Accordingly, the steel manufacturing industry needs to correctly identify the processing routes depending on the steel grade, width, thickness, special requirements and related tolerances. For this reason, Stirling and Buntine (1988) describe how a steel manufacturer applies machine learning techniques to acquire knowledge about steel mill processing routes. In this case, the company receives more than 60 orders per day with around 7,500 entries related to the product description that define the different process combinations to get the required product. The total number of different route combinations exceeds 10,000. For this reason, the company has developed a system that uses rule induction (see Section 2.4.5) and ID3 and C4.5 (see Section 2.4.4), mixed with operational expertise, to get the best manufacturing route in terms of quality and delivery rates. Again within structural steel manufacturing, Halawani (2014) describe how classification tree ensembles, such as random forests, are applied to fault detection during the manufacturing process. Additionally, feature subset selection techniques are used to find the most significant features.

3.3.2 Industrial Goods and Services

The most representative example in **industrial electronics manufacturing** is related to electronic semi-conductor manufacturing, where machine learning applications address a number of challenges, such as final product dispatching rules at testing stage. Wang et al. (2005) apply a mixture of classification trees and artificial neuronal networks to find the rules that drive the company testing procedures. Also, Hsu and Chien (2007) apply an artificial neural network to improve the yield in semi-conductor manufacturing.

As explained above, the industrials sector has been traditionally based on statistical process control. However, Chinnam (2002) explains that statistical tools are not applicable in highly automated manufacturing, such as electric and electronic equipment, because there are autocorrelated data (data with a delayed copy of itself as a function of delay). Autocorrelated data can generate false alarms or low true positive detection rates in process control. These limitations may cause a severe production deviation, especially in systems whose control system is able to stop production based on alarms. As a result, Chinnam (2002) demonstrates that support vector machines are an effective

---

[3]https://www.worldsteel.org/media-centre/about-steel.html

technique for minimizing errors related to false alarms and true positive detection rates with an increase in accuracy.

Within the **industrial engineering** sector, applications are related to industrial equipment or components, such as pumps, engines, compressors, bearings and elevators. In this scenario, Kowalski et al. (2017) describe a marine engine application based on a single-hidden layer feedforward neural network oriented to fault diagnosis. Another example is the application of anomaly detection techniques from data streams (see Section 2.6.1) to assist elevator manufacturing and maintenance (Herterich et al., 2016).

With regard to the **aerospace industry**, there are two levels of applications: component manufacturing and solutions, such as flight control, or decision support systems. Machine learning is mainly applied for quality control in aerospace component manufacturing, where high accuracy rates on 100% inspection are required. In this case, the applications are similar to other component manufacturing in terms of methodology. However, there are some interesting applications such as an automatic horizon detection device to assist the pilot during flight. Fefilatyev et al. (2006) describe the use of support vector machines, C4.5 classification tree and naive Bayes classifiers. In this case, accuracy is very high using only a small set of images. Apart from classification tasks, feature subset selection techniques based on image transformation and ranking depending on the pixel value are used.

In **defense equipment manufacturing**, industry efforts focus on the **cyber defense industry**. Firewalls and other devices are being designed to detect evolving threats at different levels. The most useful cyber defense approach is anomaly detection (deviations from normal behavior), where different variations have been implemented using machine learning techniques. Communication signal anomalies are detected by learning normal signals traffic. However, there are some improvements, such as anomaly detection related to different user profiles described by Lane and Brodley (1997). In this case, the user profile is learned from characteristic sequences of actions performed by different users. To detect anomalies, the system first computes the sequence similarity in order to classify user behavior. However, other machine learning techniques, such as artificial neural networks, naive Bayes, k-nearest neighbors and support vector machines, are applied in cyber defense depending on the threat (Buczak and Guven, 2016).

Like cyber defense, **industrial services**, such as financial administration, mainly use machine learning for fraud detection. Bose and Mahapatra (2001) analyze the most common techniques such as rule induction, artificial neuronal networks and case-based reasoning, all of which are used as data mining techniques to predict or classify different types of fraud and threats in electronic transactions.

For **industrial transportation**, machine learning is mainly applied to manage traffic at ports and airports where there is a critical mixture between high-volume traffic, tight scheduling and large vessels with potential hazardous content. For marine ports, some of the collision avoidance systems are developed based on artificial neural networks, as described by Simsir et al. (2014), which, in this case, works as a decision support system helping the traffic managers to avoid accidents. For airports, Zonglei et al. (2008) describe a large-scale alarm for delayed flights that uses clustering techniques (Section 2.3) to reduce the amount of data coming from a Chinese airport in order to be able to process the available data faster. In this case, the K-means algorithm (Section 2.3.2) is used to find the cluster of each record. Supervised classification models, such as Bayesian classifiers, classification trees, artificial neuronal networks and rule of induction, were tested on the detected clusters to create the alarm system.

3.4 Consumer Services Sector

This section contains examples of machine learning application in retail, media and tourism (see Fig. 3.3).

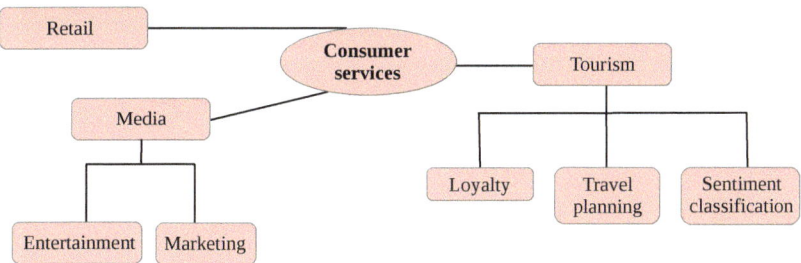

FIGURE 3.3
Applications of machine learning in the consumer services sector.

3.4.1 Retail

Machine learning methods can provide **grocers** with competitive advantages by avoiding costly problems of having too much or too little fresh food in stock and as they are the secret to smarter fresh-food replenishment. In addition, they can make demand forecasts based not just on historical sales data but on other influential factors such as advertising campaigns, store opening times, local weather and public holidays.

3.4.2   Media

Entertainment, broadcasting, cinema and television are other fields where machine learning can help. Examples include: (i) video analysis tracking for emotions, eeriness, frights and loving, alongside audio analysis of music and tone of voice; (ii) real-time indexing and analysis of broadcast programming to provide advertising partners with increased visibility, transparency and accountability; (iii) development of systems that learn about audience interests and recommend television programs and movies based on taste; (iv) video encoder improvement to provide incredible picture quality on a 4-inch and 5-inch screen.

An example of (iii) is the Netflix Prize[4], an open competition for the best algorithm to predict user ratings for films. It was launched in 2006 and in September 2009 the grand prize of $1,000,000 was given to a team which improved Netflix's own algorithm by 10%.

Marketing can also take advantage of the real-time analysis of tons of data (Sterne, 2017). Tableau[5] and Qlikview[6] provide a rich palette of data visualization widgets widely used in marketing research. For a marketing campaign to be successful, understanding which words, phrases, sentences and even content formats resonate with particular members of the audience is key. Machine learning algorithms can be applied to the data from all campaigns to deduce the best textual introduction for emails sent to an audience or even to an individual, thereby increasing likelihood of success. Other examples include the analysis of mobile customer behavior to help app publishers identify the most loyal users and predict customer churn. Armed with this insight, marketers can take actions across digital channels to deepen customer engagement or invest more in retaining specific customer segments.

3.4.3   Tourism

Loyalty is one of the strategic marketing targets as companies can thus enhance competitive advantages with clear benefits: customer willingness to repurchase and promote products can lead to company revenue growth and increased market share, costs reduction, and increased employee job satisfaction. **Tourism** loyalty is influenced by several factors, including customer service offered by employees, tour website functions, consumer perception of the characteristics of local tourism and customer loyalty in terms of revisiting a destination. Hsu et al. (2009) apply Bayesian networks to data collected from tourists with a tour experience. They conclude that tourism loyalty is greater for tourists that have a better perception of customer service, web functions and local characteristics of the destination, which may lead them to revisit the destination or recommend it to others. Wong and Chung (2008) apply classification trees to

---

[4]http://www.netflixprize.com/
[5]https://www.tableau.com
[6]https://www.qlik.com

passenger loyalty for people on a domestic airline, identifying several groups of loyal and disloyal passengers.

Selecting tourist attractions to visit at a destination is an important part of planning a trip. Although various online travel recommendation systems have been developed to provide support for users with travel planning over the last decade, few systems focus on recommending customized tourist attractions. Huang and Bian (2009) provide personalized recommendations of tourist attractions in an unfamiliar city based on a Bayesian network that takes into account the travel behavior of both the user and other users.

The rapid growth in Internet tourism applications has led to an enormous amount of personal comments for travel-related information on the Web. These reviews can take different forms like blogs, wikis or forum websites. The information in these reviews is valuable for travel planning. Sentiment classification techniques are used for mining personal comments from travel blogs. Ye et al. (2009) compare naive Bayes and support vector machines for sentiment classification of the reviews on travel blogs for seven popular travel destinations in the USA and Europe.

Other important problems in the tourism sector are the estimation of tourist arrivals, hotel rates and seasonal prices, and the determination of which factors influence customer satisfaction in a restaurant.

3.5 Healthcare Sector

The explosive growth of health-related data presents unprecedented opportunities for improving patient health. Health-related data arise from diverse sources including, but not limited to, individual patient health records, genomic data, data from wearable health monitors, online reviews of physicians, clinical literature, and medical imagery. Machine learning in the context of **healthcare** applications (Dua et al., 2013; Jothi et al., 2015; Wiens and Wallace, 2016; Jiang et al., 2017; Khare et al., 2017; Natarajan et al., 2017) is especially challenging due to a combination of issues. First, there is the sheer volume and variety of data types, from waveforms to unstructured text. Second, research in this area spans the entire learning pipeline from problem formulation, to feature selection, model learning, and output. At each stage along the pipeline, there are challenges related to a variety of issues including: missing data, class imbalance, temporal consistency, and task heterogeneity. Finally, it is not enough to develop accurate models; the technology must be adopted by clinicians and/or biomedical researchers if it is to have impact.

The advantages of living with sophisticated algorithms to learn models from a large volume of healthcare data, and then use the resulting insights to assist clinical practice are significant. Machine learning can help reduce diagnosis and therapeutic errors that are unavoidable in human clinical practice.

Moreover, a machine learning system can extract useful information from a large patient sample to provide support for real-time inferences for health risk alerts and health outcome prediction. According to Darcy et al. (2016), there is a tremendous opportunity to oversee the application of machine learning in patient care. Medicine, which is only just getting used to the electronic medical record, needs to forge ahead with the digital revolution.

According to PubMed-listed references (Jiang et al., 2017), supervised machine learning algorithms are ranked by popularity as follows: support vector machines, neural networks, logistic regression, discriminant analysis, random forests, naive Bayes, k-nearest neighbors, classification trees, and finally, hidden Markov models.

This section is organized around the following topics: cancer, nervous system, cardiovascular disease, diabetes and obesity, see Fig. 3.4. The use of bioinformatics as a prediction tool is crossdisciplinary.

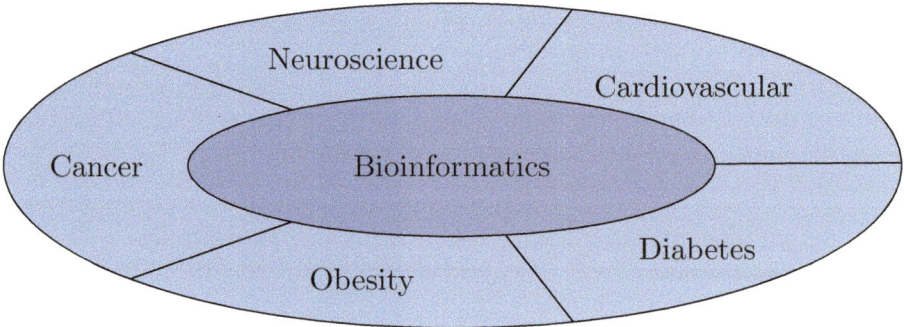

FIGURE 3.4
Healthcare applications of machine learning.

3.5.1   Cancer

Cancer has been characterized as a heterogeneous disease consisting of many different subtypes. The early cancer diagnosis and prognosis is a necessity in cancer research, as it can facilitate the subsequent clinical management of patients. The importance of classifying cancer patients into high- or low-risk groups is evident for diagnosis and prognosis, as well as for modeling the progression and treatment of cancerous conditions (Kourou et al., 2015).

Three important problems that have been addressed using machine learning methods are (i) the prediction of cancer susceptibility (risk assessment) like breast cancer risk estimation (Ayer et al., 2010), where artificial neural networks have been applied to a dataset with more than 48,000 mammographic findings, as well as demographic risk factors and tumor characteristics. The area under the ROC curve was used in order to assess the model discriminative power; (ii) the prediction of cancer recurrence in oral cancer (Exarchos et al., 2012) with clinical, imaging tissue, and genomic data comparing Bayesian classifiers with artificial neural networks, support vector machines, classification trees and random forests in combination with multivariate filter and wrapper approaches for feature subset selection; (iii) the prediction of cancer survival (Park et al., 2013), evaluating the survival of women who have been diagnosed with breast cancer, with survivability as the class variable referring to patients who have and have not survived.

Bayesian networks have been intensively applied in cancer research. Sesen et al. (2013) have performed personalized lung cancer survival prediction estimates and treatment selection recommendations using Bayesian networks, based on the English Lung Cancer Database, which includes more than 126,000 patients who were diagnosed between 2006 and 2010. The model was constructed on a set of relevance variables available when a new patient came in for a treatment decision. Structure learning was carried out both manually (elicited by experts) and automatically (with a score and search approach that uses the K2 metric in combination with simulated annealing). The automatic approach outperformed the manual method. Cruz-Ramírez et al. (2007) study the effectiveness of several Bayesian networks classifiers (naive Bayes and several variants, and unrestricted Bayesian network classifiers) for accurately diagnosing breast cancer. Gevaert et al. (2006) learn a Bayesian network classifier from data for predicting breast cancer prognosis by integrating clinical (including age, diameter, tumor grade, estrogen and progesterone receptor status, and the presence of angioinvasion and lymphocytic infiltration) and microarray data (mRNA expression levels of approximately 25,000 genes for each patient). The two class variable values correspond to poor and good prognosis. Poor prognosis refers to recurrence within fives years after diagnosis and good prognosis corresponds to a disease-free interval of at least five years. The Markov blanket-based classifier structure was built using the K2 search algorithm in combination with the Bayesian Dirichlet scoring metric. Parameters were estimated assuming a Dirichlet prior distribution.

Onisko and Austin (2015) develop a dynamic Bayesian network for predicting the risk of developing cervical precancer and invasive cervical cancer. The aim is to identify women that are at higher risk of developing cervical cancer and who should be screened differently than indicated in the guidelines. The data were collected over an eight-year period (2005-2012) and contain two screening tests (Pap and hrHPV) for more than 790,000 patients. The other collected variables are diagnostic or therapeutic procedures, patient history findings, and demographic variables. Some variables are temporal, i.e., they are repeated for each time step. According to USA cervical cancer guidelines, the time step chosen for this model was one year.

3.5.2   Neuroscience

Neuroscience studies the nervous system. It is a multidisciplinary branch of biology, which deals with the anatomy, biochemistry, molecular biology, and physiology of neurons and neural circuits. Recent technological advances have led, for example, to high spatial and temporal resolution recordings of the activity of hundreds of cells located in a relatively small region of the brain using either imaging approaches or electrodes. These big data offer an opportunity for machine learning to provide a better understanding of both the healthy and diseased brain, leading to more successful treatments in the future (Landhuis, 2017). Bielza and Larrañaga (2014a) review the use of Bayesian networks in neuroscience.

Some important works in the literature on machine learning applications for neuroanatomy, neurosurgery, neuroimaging, and neurodegenerative diseases follow.

In neuroanatomy, DeFelipe et al. (2013) apply machine learning methods to gain new insights into the classification of cortical GABAergic interneurons to produce an accepted nomenclature of neuron types, not currently available. A web-based interactive system was used that collected data from several experts in the neuroanatomy field about the terminological choices (common type, horse-tail, chandelier, Martinotti, common basket, arcade, large basket, Cajal-Retzius, neurogliaform or other) for a set of cortical interneurons. The 3D reconstructions of these neurons were used to measure a large number of morphological features of each neuron. All the supervised classification methods introduced in Section 2.4 were applied, with the exception of logistic regression. Univariate and multivariate filtering were the chosen feature subset selection approaches. Additionally, experts' opinions were modeled using Bayesian networks.

Celtikci (2017) reviews more than 50 studies on neurosurgery classified according to the following topics: hydrocephalus, deep brain stimulation, neurovascular, epilepsy, glioma, radiosurgery, spine, and traumatic brain injury. Six supervised classification methods (neural networks, Bayesian classifiers, support vector machines, classification trees, logistic regression and discriminant analysis) are applied.

Neuroimaging is a widespread technique in cognitive neuroscience. Several imaging techniques are available. They differ in anatomical coverage, temporal sampling and imaged hemodynamic properties. The most used modalities are: fMRI, MRI, and EEG. Abraham et al. (2014) report the use of scikit-learn software (see Section 2.7) in different neuroimaging tasks. The facilities provided by the software are illustrated on several problems: decoding the mental representations of objects in the brain, encoding brain activity and decoding images and functional connectivity analysis at resting-stage. They use methods like independent component analysis (a variant of PCA) univariate filtering for feature subset selection, hierarchical clustering and K-means, and logistic regression and support vector machines to tackle these problems.

Bielza and Larrañaga (2014a) review more than 40 papers on Bayesian network applications in neuroimaging. Dynamic Bayesian networks have been applied to different problems in fMRI (dyslexia, Parkinson's disease, schizophrenia, dementia in elder subjects), MRI (mild cognitive impairment) and EEG (motor task).

Neurodegenerative diseases and brain disorders cost the economy of the developed countries a huge amount of money. For example, brain disorders cost Europe an estimated €798 billion in 2010 (Olesen et al., 2012). Parkinson's disease and Alzheimer's disease are the two neurodegenerative diseases that account for the highest financial expenditure. The K-means algorithm has recently been applied to search for patient subtypes from a large, multicenter, international, and well-characterized cohort of Parkinson's disease patients across all motor stages, using a combination of motor features (bradykinesia, rigidity, tremor, axial signs) and specific validated rater-based non-motor symptom scales (Mu et al., 2017). Multi-dimensional Bayesian network classifiers (Bielza et al., 2011) are used in Borchani et al. (2014) to simultaneously predict the five items (mobility, self-care, usual activities, pain/discomfort and anxiety/depression) of the European quality of life-5 dimensions (EQ-5D) from the Parkinson's disease questionnaire (PDQ-39). PDQ-39 is a 39-item self-report questionnaire, which assesses Parkinson's disease-specific health-related quality, containing questions about mobility, activities of daily living, emotional well-being, social support, cognition, communication, bodily discomfort and stigma. Transcript interaction networks induced by ensembles of Bayesian classifiers have provided new candidate transcripts in the study of Alzheimer's disease (Armañanzas et al., 2012). Bind et al. (2015) review supervised machine learning methods (artificial neural networks, k-nearest neighbors, support vector machines, naive Bayes classifier, random forest, bagging and boosting) for Parkinson's disease prediction, whereas Tejeswinee et al. (2017) apply univariate and multivariate feature subset selection methods in combination with classification trees, naive Bayes classifiers, support vector machines, k-nearest neighbors, random forest and boosting in Alzheimer's and Parkinson's disease datasets.

3.5.3 Cardiovascular

Cardiovascular medicine generates a plethora of biomedical, clinical and operational data as part of patient care delivery. These data are often stored in diverse data repositories which are not readily usable for cardiovascular research. However, the application of machine learning techniques in cardiovascular diseases is not new, although there has been an exponential growth in the number of PubMed-listed publications including "cardiology" and "machine learning" terms over the last few years (Shameer et al., 2018). Datasets in cardiology can contain variables from cardiac imaging modalities like echocardiography, magnetic resonance imaging, single-photon emission, computed tomography, near-infrared spectroscopy, intravascular ultrasound, optical coherence tomography in combination with molecular entities (genomics, transcriptomics, proteomics) and data from clinical trials. Clustering methods can help to subtype chronic complex diseases common in cardiovascular medicine, whereas supervised classification is useful to discriminate between physiological and pathological hearts. Real-time prediction of acute cardiovascular events from input signals such as temperature, blood pressure, pulseoxymetry, echocardiography and impedance cardiography, using hardware-implemented Bayesian networks has been developed by Tylman et al. (2016).

3.5.4 Diabetes

Diabetes mellitus is defined as a group of metabolic disorders exerting significant pressure on human health worldwide. Machine learning has been applied in the field of diabetes mellitus to address issues like prediction and diagnosis, diabetes complications, genetic background and environment, and healthcare and management with prediction and diagnosis being the most popular category. According to the review by Kavakiotis et al. (2017), 85% of the applications used supervised classification algorithms and 15% clustering methods. Support vector machines are the most successful and widely used algorithm.

3.5.5 Obesity

Nowadays **obesity** researchers have access to a wealth of data. Sensor and smartphone app data, electronic medical records, large insurance databases and publicly available national health data provide input that machine learning algorithms can transform into mathematical models. DeGregory et al. (2006) show an empirical comparison of logistic regression, artificial neural networks and classification trees to predict high levels of body fat percentage from anthropometric predictor variables taken from a sample of more than 25,000 patient records extracted from the National Health and Nutrition Examination Survey (NHANES) dataset.

3.5.6 Bioinformatics

Larrañaga et al. (2006) review applications of machine learning to different **bioinformatics** topics, where bioinformatics is regarded as an interdisciplinary field that develops methods and software tools for understanding biological data. The topics covered in the review are genomics, proteomics, systems biology, text mining and other applications. Filter, wrapper and hybrid feature subset selection methods are discussed. The reviewed clustering methods include hierarchical, K-means and probabilistic clustering. All supervised classification approaches presented in Section 2.4, except rule induction, are reviewed. Bayesian networks and hidden Markov models are also accounted for.

3.6 Consumer Goods Sector

The applications of machine learning to consumer goods fall into three main categories: automobiles, food and beverages, and personal and household goods (see Fig. 3.5).

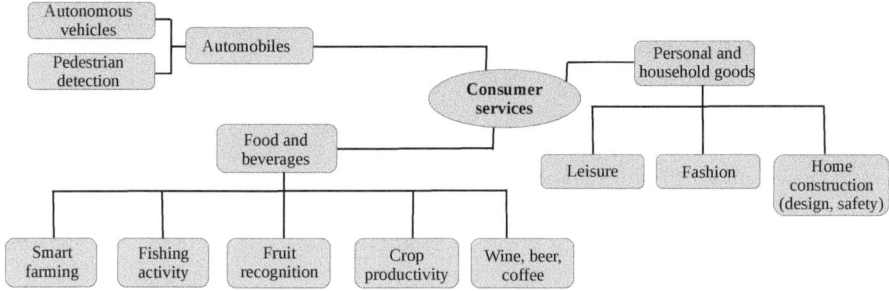

FIGURE 3.5
Applications of machine learning in the consumer goods sector.

3.6.1 Automobiles

Americans drive nearly three trillion miles, which translates into many hours spent in traffic, and the number grows significantly considering the entire planet. The time spent in traffic is potentially dangerous, considering that more than 3,000 lives are lost every day and most accidents are due to human error. **Autonomous vehicles** have the potential to improve the quality and productivity of the time spent in cars, increase the safety and efficiency of the transportation system, and transform transportation into a utility available to anyone, anytime. This requires technical advances in many aspects of vehicle autonomy, ranging from vehicle design to control, perception, planning, coordination, and human interaction. Schwarting et al. (2018) review recent advances in planning and decision-making for autonomous vehicles, focused on: (a) how vehicles decide where to go next; (b) how vehicles use the data provided by their sensors to make decisions with short and long time horizons; (c) how interaction with other vehicles affects what they do; (d) how vehicles can learn how to drive from their history and from human driving; (e) how to ensure that the vehicle control and planning systems are correct and safe; and (f) how to ensure that multiple vehicles on the road at the same time are coordinated and managed to most effectively move people and packages to their destinations. The review contains some approaches to perception based on machine learning methods, mainly convolution neural networks and Bayesian deep learning methods (a paradigm at the intersection between deep learning and Bayesian probability theory). Probabilistic approaches like partially observable Markov decision processes are included among the methods used in behavior-aware motion planning. In addition, the authors conclude that machine learning approaches for planning and decision-making need to be developed, evaluated, and integrated.

Driving in dynamically changing traffic scenarios is a challenging task for autonomous vehicles, especially on urban roadways. Prediction of surrounding vehicle driving behaviors plays a crucial role in such scenarios. Geng et al. (2017) apply hidden Markov models to the driving behavior for each possible traffic scenario from an ontology of scenarios. The ontology considers road elements, traffic participants, and their interrelationships. The continuous features of each driving behavior are learned by hidden Markov models with field data based on a priori knowledge (traffic rules, driving experience). A rule-based reasoning method is designed to specify each candidate model, input features, and a priori probabilities for different scenarios. The future behavior of each target vehicle is predicted taking into account both the a priori probabilities and the testing results of trained hidden Markov models (the a posteriori probabilities).

Pedestrian detection based on an automated sensor-based system is a challenging application for an autonomous vehicle. Navarro et al. (2017) present an application focused on processing the information generated by a Velodyne HDL-64E LIDAR. This sensor is designed for obstacle detection and navigation of autonomous ground vehicles and marine vessels and provides a 360-degree field of view and a very high data points rate (more than one million points per revolution). Pedestrians are detected by selecting cubic shapes and applying machine vision and machine learning algorithms to the XY, XZ, and YZ projections of the points contained in the cube. k-nearest neighbors, naive Bayes classifiers, and support vector machines are the supervised classification methods used.

3.6.2   Food and Beverages

In the food sector, we discuss some examples from farming, fishery, and the fruit, vegetables and tea markets.

Wolfert et al. (2017) review state of the art of big data applications in **smart farming**. The review aims to identify the related socioeconomic challenges to be addressed. It shows that the scope of big data applications in smart farming goes beyond primary production and is influencing the entire food supply chain. Big data are used to provide predictive insights in farming operations, drive real-time operational decisions, and redesign business processes for game-changing business models. Additionally, it is expected that big data will cause major shifts in roles and power relations among different players in current food supply chain networks. According to the authors, the future of smart farming may unravel along a continuum between two extreme scenarios: (a) closed, proprietary systems in which the farmer is part of a highly integrated food supply chain, and (b) open, collaborative systems in which the farmer and every other stakeholder in the chain network are flexible about choosing business partners for both technology and food production.

Based on their previous experiences, Shakoor et al. (2017) develop an intelligent system for prediction analysis on farming in Bangladesh. The system suggests area-based beneficial crop rank before the cultivation process. Six major crops are considered: Aus rice, Aman rice, Boro rice, potato, jute and wheat. The prediction is made by analyzing a dataset sourced from the Yearbook of Agricultural Statistics and the Bangladesh Agricultural Research Council for the above crops according to the area and using classification trees and k-nearest neighbors as machine learning models.

The impact of fishing on ecology and conservation has to be studied to gain a better understanding of the behavior of the global fishing fleets in order to prioritize and enforce fisheries management and conservation measures worldwide. Satellite-based automatic information systems (S-AIS) are now commonly installed on most ocean-going vessels and have been proposed as a novel tool to explore the movements of fishing fleets in near-real time. de Souza et al. (2016) present approaches to identify **fishing activity** from S-AIS data for three dominant fishing gear types: trawl, longline and purse seine. Using a large dataset containing worldwide fishing vessel tracks from 2011 to 2015, hidden Markov models were developed to detect and map fishing activities.

Automatic fruit recognition using machine vision is considered as a challenging task as fruits exist in various colors, sizes, shapes and textures. Shukla and Desai (2016) recognize nine different classes of fruits. First, the fruit images are preprocessed to subtract the background and extract the blob representing the fruit. Then, visual characteristics, combination of colors, shapes and textures are used as predictor variables. k-nearest neighbors and support vector machines were applied.

Crop productivity plays a significant role in India's economy. Vegetables are grown throughout the year under particular climatic conditions and culti-vation periods. The vegetables may be affected by bacteria, viruses or insects. It is important to monitor the crops to control the spreading of disease, and thus Tippannavar and Soma (2017) propose a machine learning technique for vegetable leaf identification and abnormality detection from leaf images. The leaf part is segmented from the background by threshold and morphological operations, and then texture and color features are extracted by fractal features and color correlogram, respectively. Two classification tasks such as vegetable identification (six different types of vegetables) and disease identification (dis-order or normal leaf) are carried out using k-nearest neighbors and artificial neural networks.

Bakhshipour et al. (2018) classify different classes of black tea, including orange pekoe, flowery orange pekoe, flowery broken orange pekoe, and pekoe dust one, from three types of predictor variables (18 color variables, 13 gray image texture variables, and 52 wavelet texture variables), acquired and pro-cessed using a computer vision system. Correlation-based feature selection with simulated annealing like heuristic search in combination with classification trees, Bayesian network classifiers and support vector machines are applied.

Machine learning has been applied in the beverages sector mainly in the wine, beer and coffee industries for quality and price prediction, identification of their designation of origin, backorder prediction, and identification of diseases in coffee plants.

Nowadays, the **wine industry** is using product quality certifications to promote its products. This is a time-consuming process and requires the assessment of human experts, which makes the process very expensive. Gupta (2018) explores the use of machine learning techniques such as linear regression, artificial neural networks and support vector machines for predicting wine quality in two stages. First, linear regression is used for the selection of key predictor variables. These selected variables are the inputs for artificial neural networks and support vector machines for wine quality prediction. The experiments were carried out on the Wine dataset, a collection of white (about 5,000 samples) and red (more than 1,500 samples) wines. Each sample of both types of wine consists of twelve physiochemical variables: fixed acidity, volatile acidity, citric acid, residual sugar, chlorides, free sulfur dioxide, total sulfur dioxide, pH, sulphates, alcohol, and quality rating. The quality rating is based on a sensory test carried out by at least three sommeliers and scaled according to eleven quality classes from 0 (very bad) to 10 (excellent).

Yeo et al. (2015) apply **Gaussian process**[7] regression and **multi-task learning**[8] in the area of wine price prediction. The experiments used historical price data of the 100 wines in the Liv-Ex 100 index. First, the wines are grouped into two clusters based on autocorrelation. Second, Gaussian process regression and ARIMA models are compared in each cluster. Multi-task learning with kernels as models for each cluster provides competitive results compared with the Gaussian process. Acevedo et al. (2007) discriminate wines according to their designation of origin using direct UV-visible spectrophotometric variables output by a Shimadzu UV-vis (UV-160A) spectrophotometer. The dataset includes a large number of Spanish red and white wines. k-nearest neighbor, artificial neural networks and support vector machines in combination with a sequential backward feature selection method are applied to this problem.

Beer quality is mainly defined by its color, foamability and foam stability. These properties are influenced by the chemical composition of the product, such as proteins, carbohydrates, pH and alcohol. Traditional methods for assessing specific chemical compounds are usually time-consuming and costly. Gonzalez-Viejo et al. (2018) apply machine learning methods to predict beer quality based on 15 foam and color-related variables output by a robotic pourer and chemical fingerprinting using near infrared spectroscopy. Artificial

---

[7]A Gaussian process is a stochastic process, that is, a collection of random variables indexed by time or space, such that every finite collection of these random variables has a multivariate normal distribution.

[8]Multi-task learning is a subfield of machine learning in which multiple learning tasks are solved at the same time, while exploiting commonalities and differences across tasks.

neural networks predict chemometric targets such as pH, alcohol and maximum volume of foam. Also, Li (2017) proposes the backorder prediction of Danish brewery craft beer in the early stage of the supply chain based on historical data. These historical data contain information on the orders for the eight weeks prior to the week to be predicted. Less than one percent of the products in the dataset went on backorder. This leads to a big imbalance in the binary classes. k-nearest neighbors, classification trees, logistic regression, support vector machines and an ensemble of k-nearest neighbors were applied.

Coffee is a plant whose seeds called coffee beans are grown all over the world, particularly in Ethiopia. There are three major types of **coffee disease** affecting the leaves of a coffee plant: coffee leaf rust, coffee berry disease, and coffee wilt disease. Mengistu et al. (2016) develop an automatic system for the recognition of these diseases using imaging and machine learning techniques. More than 9,000 coffee plant images were preprocessed by removing low frequency background noise, normalizing the intensity of the image, removing reflection and applying filters to reduce image noise. Genetic algorithms were applied for multivariate filtering feature selection showing that color features are generally more relevant than texture features for this recognition problem. k-nearest neighbors, artificial neural networks, and naive Bayes were the supervised classification models used.

3.6.3   Personal and Household Goods

Finally, we conclude this section with some machine learning applications for home construction, leisure and personal goods.

The field of construction is well placed to benefit from the advent of machine learning. The BIM 360 Project IQ Team at Autodesk has integrated machine learning methods for generative design, risk evaluation and mitigation and construction safety. The aim of **generative design** is to mimic nature's evolutionary approach within design. Genetic algorithms are used to explore a huge number of feasible design solutions and find the best option. Risk evaluation and mitigation happen every day on a construction site. There are hundreds of subcontractors working on different trades simultaneously; there are thousands of issues that get created and managed, and everything is changing constantly. The BIM 360 IQ project focuses on understanding the challenges that construction managers, project managers and superintendents deal with on a daily basis in order to manage these issues and explore the ways in which the process might be improved using machine learning methods exploiting historical data. It also assigns a "risk score" to each subcontractor in the project, a metric to indicate the amount of risk to which they are currently exposing the project. This helps construction managers to better prioritize their time and work closer with these teams. **Construction safety** is the number one priority across all job sites. BIM 360 IQ focuses on understanding the behavior and context regarding safety issues, which they then bring to the attention of safety managers. The application automatically scans all safety issues on a job site to which it then attaches a tag indicating whether they could lead to a potential fatality. Special attention is given to issues related to the "fatal four" –fall, struck by, caught between, and electrocution– as they are the causes behind a high percentage of accidents.

The **video game market** has become an established and ever-growing global industry in the leisure goods sector. Serious games are one of its most interesting fields. A serious game should be educational and, at the same time, fun and entertaining. A serious game is thus designed to be both attractive and appealing to a broad target audience and to meet specific educational goals. Frutos-Pascual and García-Zapirain (2017) review the use of decision making and machine learning techniques in serious games published in journal papers between January 2005 and September 2014. A total of 129 papers are reviewed. From the point of view of machine learning, naive Bayes (13 papers), artificial neural networks (12 papers), k-nearest neighbors (10 papers), and support vector machines (5 papers) had the highest inclusion rate.

Machine learning-based predictions in the **fashion industry** have been carried out by Dadoun (2017) analyzing Apprl's dataset. Apprl's network consists of bloggers and online magazines, monitoring hundreds of thousands of visitors to online retailers per month, each generating unique pieces of data. Apprl started collecting this data in 2012 and now stores more than three million records. The variables in this dataset include the product brand, the category (shoes, shirts, etc.), the color, currency of the payment, gender of the client, stock (whether or not the product was in stock), vendor selling the product, name of the product, product regular price, name of the publisher who published the product, date when the product was sold, sale amount by product, number of clicks a product generated, and a popularity rate calculated by product. The last three variables are the targets to be predicted by the machine learning model. k-nearest neighbors, classification trees, logistic regression, random forest and boosting were applied in these three prediction problems.

3.7   Telecommunications Sector

The telecommunications sector is a key industry in the 21st century because it enables information exchange. The growth of machine learning is particularly important in the telecommunications sector which now needs to process large amounts of data. The signs of expansion are, for example, the increment in smartphone use or the steady evolution of other technologies such as wearables or the Internet of Things, none of which would be possible without continuous improvements in telecommunications. Other industrial sectors will also benefit from improved data sharing, like the coordination of supply chains or easily accessible cloud analytics. Fig. 3.6 shows a summary of the machine learning applications in telecommunications.

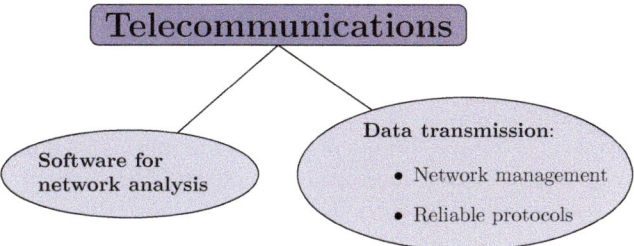

FIGURE 3.6
Applications of machine learning in the telecommunications sector.

3.7.1 Software for Network Analysis

One of the oldest applications in the telecommunications sector is the **detection of spam emails**. The naive Bayes classifier (Section 2.4.9) is one of the most used machine learning algorithms in spam filtering applications. One often cited example of an anti-spam application is the Apache SpamAssasin project. This project combines the naive Bayes approach with a set of common rules in spam messages to compute a spam score. If the spam score is greater than a specified threshold, the email is considered as spam. One of the main email providers, Google, uses its own spam filter (Taylor et al., 2007), combining classification tree (Section 2.4.4), logistic regression (Section 2.4.8) and optimization method features. Google's spam filter has very strict requirements:

- It should classify millions of messages a day, and the algorithm therefore has to scale properly.

- It should work with different languages.

- It should be interpretable in order to understand the underlying decision criteria of the classifier.

- It should detect not only spam, but also other malicious intents such as phishing attacks.

3.7.2 Data Transmission

Another application of machine learning in telecommunications is the **management of wireless mobile networks**. As the demand for fast, secure and reliable mobile network access increases with the deployment of new wireless networks (such as 5G), network management for mobile network operators is also expected to become more complex. One of the main approaches for improving network management is to deploy self-organizing networks (SONs) (Klaine et al., 2017). The 3rd Generation Partnership Project and the Next Generation Mobile Networks association encourage the use of SONs in 3G and Long Term Evolution (LTE) networks. SONs can automatically take the necessary actions to maintain network operation at near optimal levels. Taking the correct actions involves the construction of more intelligent systems that can be addressed using machine learning techniques. These machine learning models can be trained using huge amounts of data that are regularly collected by network operators to monitor the state of the mobile network. Multiple machine learning techniques have been applied to the SON model:

- Unsupervised classification (Section 2.3) for configuration of operational parameters, caching, resource optimization, load balancing, fault detection, etc.

- Supervised classification (Section 2.4) for user mobility prediction, resource allocation, load balancing, fault classification, etc.

- **Reinforcement learning** is a machine learning area where the system learns to decide which is the best action to take. However, it is not trained with data in which a supervisor (as in supervised learning) indicates the best action for a set of situations. Instead, the machine learning algorithm receives a reward or penalty after the action has been taken depending on whether or not the action is successful. The system should learn to make the best decisions given the reward and penalties of previous actions. Reinforcement learning has been used in SONs for parameter configuration, caching, resource optimization, load balancing, resource optimization, backhaul optimization, etc.

- Markov models (such as Markov chains and hidden Markov models, see Section 2.6.3) for fault detection, resource optimization, etc.

- **Transfer learning** is a machine learning area where a model learned using a known dataset is applied to a different (but similar) application. Transfer learning has been applied in SONs for caching, resource optimization, fault classification, etc.

Another interesting problem in telecommunications is to ensure a **reliable connection during data transmission**. A common technique in the telecommunications sector is to use forward error correction codes. Forward error correction codes encode the message including redundant information so that the receiver can detect any errors during the transmission. A well-known instance of forward error correction codes is Turbo codes, which have been used in the Digital Video Broadcasting - Return Channel Satellite (DVB-RCS) standard. The DVB-RCS standard enables satellite communications to provide Internet access. It has been shown (McEliece et al., 1998) that Turbo codes are an instance of the Bayesian network belief propagation algorithm (see Section 2.5.2).

3.8   Utilities Sector

The utilities sector comprises the generation and distribution of utilities such as gas, electricity or water to end users. Machine learning can be applied to solve some important problems in this sector, such as utility demand and production forecasting, power plant fault monitoring and distribution network design (see Fig. 3.7).

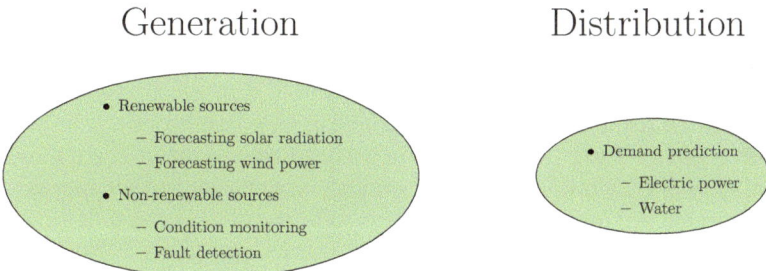

FIGURE 3.7
Applications of machine learning in the utilities sector.

3.8.1   Utilities Generation

In the generation-related activities, one of the main utilities is electricity. Note that it is always necessary to maintain a good balance between energy demand and production in this industry because electricity cannot be easily stored. There is extensive literature about the use of machine learning techniques in the electricity generation process. We can divide electricity generation based on the type of generation source: renewable and non-renewable sources of energy. The performance of renewable source electricity generation systems is usually more dependent on external factors, especially the weather. For this reason, it is not surprising that a sizable number of papers focus on forecasting with renewable sources.

For example, **solar radiation** forecasting (Voyant et al., 2017; Inman et al., 2013) tries to predict the production of solar power stations. Usually, solar radiation forecasting involves some types of weather forecasting, such as the cloud formation and movement guided by satellites images and ground measurements. Traditionally, this problem has been solved using dynamic atmospheric models, but machine learning algorithms have performed well.

Supervised (k-nearest neighbors, classification trees, artificial neural networks, support vector machines, Bayesian classifiers) and unsupervised classification algorithms (K-means, hierarchical clustering) have been applied to this problem.

Wind power generation forecasting (Foley et al., 2012; Zhang et al., 2014) is another application of machine learning to renewable sources of energy. As with solar radiation, wind is another atmospheric phenomenon that sometimes needs to be predicted to estimate power production. Furthermore, the relationship between wind speed and electricity generation is usually non-linear and bounded (Marvuglia and Messineo, 2012). For this reason, wind power production forecasting can be challenging even if accurate atmospheric information is available. Artificial neural networks and support vector machines are the most common techniques for wind power generation forecasting, sometimes combined with traditional atmospheric models to predict the expected wind speed.

The main non-renewable sources of energy for power generation are usually fossil fuels and nuclear energy. As for renewable sources of energy, some papers have tried to predict the power production in a combined cycle power plant (Tüfekci, 2014) using different machine learning algorithms, such as artificial neural networks, support vector machines, bagging and other regression methods. However, given the greater predictability of this type of power plants, the main issue addressed by machine learning algorithms is **fault detection** and **condition monitoring**. For example, support vector machines have been applied to fault detection in a thermal power plant (Chen et al., 2011). In addition, a probabilistic variant of support vector machines has been applied to condition monitoring in a nuclear power plant (Liu et al., 2013).

3.8.2   Utilities Distribution

As far as distribution-related activities are concerned, the utilities have to be distributed to end users. To offer a good quality of service, production and demand should be balanced. We reviewed some machine learning algorithms applied to the prediction of the production above. However, demand estimation is also important and a key problem to be solved in the distribution phase. Niu et al. (2010) propose to forecast **electric power demand**. A support vector machine-based solution is used and compared against basic support vector machines and artificial neural network algorithms.

Similarly, **water demand** has also been forecast. Water demand prediction is necessary for the correct planning and scheduling of water supply and treatment plants. Tiwari and Adamowski (2015) predict the water demand for urban zones using artificial neural networks in combination with bootstrap samples to yield confidence intervals. Also, Herrera et al. (2010) apply several machine learning algorithms (e.g., using artificial neural networks and random forests) to the prediction of water demand in urban zones.

3.9   Financial Services Sector

Over the last few years, a range of technological developments in the financial sector have led to the creation of infrastructure and rather large datasets. The proliferation of electronic trading platforms has been accompanied by an increase in the availability of high-quality market data mostly stored in structured formats. This scenario has resulted in the computerization of the markets, where machine learning algorithms can directly interact with them, placing complex buy and sell orders in real time based on sophisticated automated decision making, very often with minimal human intervention.

Following a recent publication by the Financial Stability Board[9] on the use of artificial intelligence and machine learning in financial services, this section divides the different applications into four types (see Figure 3.8): (a) customer-focused, including credit-scoring, insurance, and client-facing chatbots; (b) operations-focused, including capital optimization, model risk management and market impact analysis; (c) trading and portfolio management in financial markets; and (d) uses of machine learning by financial institutions for regulatory compliance or by public authorities for supervision (Fig. 3.8).

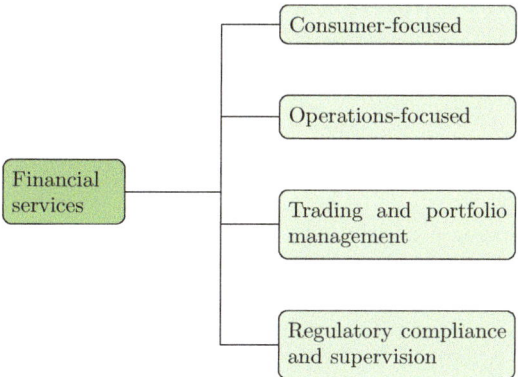

FIGURE 3.8
Financial applications of machine learning.

3.9.1   Customer-Focused Applications

Machine learning methods have been applied in the front office of financial institutions. Client data are fed into machine learning algorithms to assess credit quality and thus price loan contracts. Risk assessment for selling and

---

[9]http://www.fsb.org/2017/11/artificial-intelligence-and-machine-learning-in-financial-service/

pricing insurance policies can be carried out automatically. Finally, chatbots can increase client interactions, providing virtual assistance for users in natural language.

Credit-scoring tools based on machine learning should speed up lending decisions, while potentially limiting incremental risks. Structured data from financial institution transaction and payment histories have served as the foundation of most credit-scoring models in the past. Nowadays, however, banks and other lenders are increasing the use of unstructured and semi-structured data sources, such as social media, text message activities and mobile phone use to capture other aspects of creditworthiness. A clear advantage of the use of machine learning techniques for credit scoring is that they can analyze massive amounts of data very quickly, lowering the cost of assessing credit risks and increasing the number of individuals whose credit risk can be measured. The main disadvantage is that some machine learning paradigms are not transparent, which makes it impossible to provide appropriate explanations of the resulting credit decision. Lessmann et al. (2015) report an extensive comparison of machine learning classifiers (41 classification methods across eight credit-scoring datasets) on this issue. It includes all supervised classification paradigms explained in Section 2.4, with the exception of rule induction and wrapper feature subset selection.

The **insurance industry** can take advantage of machine learning natural language processing to improve the underwriting process, identify higher-risk cases and potentially reduce claims and improve profitability, determine repair costs, categorize the severity of vehicle accident damage, as well as prevent car accidents (Chong et al., 2005).

Chatbots are virtual assistants that interact with customers in natural language (by text or voice) to help solve problems with transactions. Chatbots use machine learning algorithms to improve over time. Although the generation of chatbots now in use by financial service companies is simple, there is potential for growth as their use becomes more widespread, especially among the younger generations, and they become more sophisticated. Chatbots are increasingly moving toward providing real-time insurance advice.

3.9.2   Operations-Focused Applications

Financial institutions have used machine learning techniques for a number of operational (or back-office) applications. These applications include capital optimization by banks, model risk management and market impact analysis.

Capital optimization, that is, profit maximization given capital scarcity, is an issue where metaheuristic optimization techniques (see Section 2.4.2) have been applied. Evolutionary computation approaches, such as genetic algorithms[10], have been used in the area of derivatives margin optimization,

---

[10]http://dx.doi.org/10.2139/ssrn.2921822

such as margin valuation adjustment (MVA). MVA is designed to determine the funding cost of the initial margin posted for a derivation transaction.

Model risk management is an application that has posed challenges to banks as a result of the increased use of stress testing in the wake of the financial crisis. Also, supervised machine learning methods have the potential to accurately assess financial credit risks and predict business failures. See Chen et al. (2016) for a recent review of this topic.

Market impact analysis involves evaluating the effect of a company's own trading on market prices and liquidity. This cost prediction has been carried out recently using artificial neural networks and support vector machines (Park et al., 2016). Clustering methods have been used to identify groups of bonds that behave similarly to each other.

3.9.3 Trading and Portfolio Management Applications

Financial firms also use machine learning to devise trading and investment strategies.

Trading execution applies machine learning for making decisions and executing trades faster than any human can. In addition, the impact of human emotions on trading decisions is avoided (Kearns and Nevmyvaka, 2013).

Portfolio management was established by Markowitz (1952)[11] and can be regarded as a process of deciding which proportions of various assets make a portfolio better than any other according to a particular criterion. Regularization (Section 2.4.2) has been applied to portfolio optimization by Ban et al. (2016).

3.9.4 Regulatory Compliance and Supervision Applications

Regulated institutions and authorities are using machine learning for regulatory compliance and supervision, respectively.

Regulatory compliance concerns the monitoring of trader behavior and communications with regard to transparency and market conduct. Machine learning can help in this issue by interpreting data inputs such as emails, spoken words, instant messages, documents and metadata.

Supervision of transactions is a field where statistical (Bolton and Hand, 2002) and supervised machine learning methods, i.e., naive Bayes, logistic regression and k-nearest neighbors (Awoyemi et al., 2017) have been applied to detect fraudulent operations. This problem is challenging on two grounds. First, the profiles of normal and fraudulent behavior change constantly (requiring concept drift detection, see Section 2.6.1), and, second, credit card fraud datasets are highly imbalanced.

---

[11]Markowitz was awarded the 1990 Nobel Memorial Prize in Economic Sciences.

3.10   Information Technology Sector

The information technology sector includes multiple industries, usually associated with the field of computer science, such as computer hardware, software, Internet, semi-conductors and office/telecommunications equipment (see Fig. 3.9). As some of the tasks in this industry (e.g., Internet applications) are rather data centric, machine learning techniques are quite well adapted to the information technology sector.

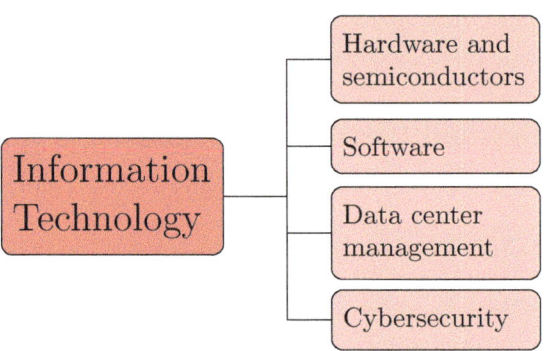

FIGURE 3.9
Applications of machine learning in the information technology sector.

3.10.1   Hardware and semi-conductors

Semi-conductor production is a rather sensitive process that involves hundreds of processes. Faulty wafers can increase production costs if they are not detected early on during the manufacturing stage. Some papers (Kim et al., 2012; Lee et al., 2017) have highlighted the usefulness of machine learning techniques for detecting **faulty wafers**. Intel, one of the major semi-conductor manufacturing companies, has designed an intelligent system relying on deep learning (specifically, convolutional neural networks) to detect **silicon packaging faults**. Silicon packaging is a complex and expensive process, and Intel's approach has achieved a near-human false negative rate.

In a similar vein, **hardware failure** detection has been explored in the literature (Murray et al., 2005). Western Digital, a major hard disk producer, has reported its use of machine learning to detect faulty hard disks and find errors as early as possible during production.

3.10.2 Software

Software developers can also improve their results using machine learning techniques. Zhang and Tsai (2003) provide an overview of the problems in **software engineering** that could be tackled using machine learning. Machine learning can address the following tasks:

- Prediction/estimation of a software project progress: software quality, development cost, maintenance effort, software reliability, reusability. This problem has been addressed using artificial neural networks, k-nearest neighbors, classification trees and Bayesian networks.

- Property and model discovery: identify properties of software entities. Artificial neural networks have been used in this use case.

- Transformation: automatically modify software to achieve a benefit, for example, assist developers by converting serial programs to parallel programs. This problem has been tackled using artificial neural networks and a nearest neighbor-based clustering algorithm.

- Reuse/maintenance: help with maintenance efforts in a software project, for example, by finding reusable components in the software. k-nearest neighbors and classification trees have been the main algorithms to solve this task.

A specific software engineering use case is systems development. This area is usually concerned with very low-level software projects, such as the development of operating systems, compilers or networking where performance is an important issue. Recently, Kraska et al. (2017) proposed possibly replacing traditional data structures with faster and memory saving **learned index structures** based on artificial neural networks.

3.10.3 Data Center Management

The management of large computer systems can also be optimized using machine learning. Google reduced its **data center cooling** bill by 40% by training artificial neural networks. The artificial neural networks were trained using historical data from thousands of sensors within the data center (containing temperatures, power, pump speeds, etc.). Then, they trained three ensembles of artificial neural networks. An artificial neural network ensemble tries to predict the average future power usage effectiveness. Another two artificial neural network ensembles are responsible for predicting the future temperature and pressure in the data center. These artificial neural network ensembles can simulate the data center behavior in order to find the best set of parameters for the cooling system while maintaining correct data center operating conditions.

3.10.4 Cybersecurity

Cybersecurity is a prominent example of machine learning applications in a more connected world. In this field, one of the most common solutions is the use of antivirus software. Kasperksy, a cybersecurity and antivirus provider, is using decision tree ensembles to improve the detection performance of its products. These ensembles are trained in-lab on constantly renewed selections of files. The same company, also announced the use of deep learning models to analyze execution logs of suspicious files to detect malware.

Another cybersecurity-related activity is **fraud detection** in Internet applications, especially applications that make use of credit card payments (Dorronsoro et al., 1997; Srivastava et al., 2008). PayPal is one of the most important companies managing online payments and uses machine learning techniques, such as artificial neural networks and deep learning. Visa, one of the largest card payment organizations, is reported to be using machine learning systems (such as artificial neural networks and other self-improving algorithms) for fraud detection.

4

Component-Level Case Study: Remaining Useful Life of Bearings

4.1 Introduction

As mentioned in Section 3.3, bearings (see Fig. 4.1) play a major role in industry and many mechanical processes, and constitute the weakest servomotor component. The useful life of a bearing depends on many factors like mechanical load, fatigue, resonance, heat loads, quality of the materials and many more. If a bearing inside a complex mechanical system fails, the losses in terms of production line, time and money are substantial. On this ground, accurate bearing **remaining useful life** (RUL) estimations are important.

If the RUL of a bearing is known, its replacement can be planned to avoid possible accidents. If the RUL is incorrectly predicted though, there are two scenarios both of which have associated costs: a failure might occur before the bearing is replaced or the bearing might be replaced earlier than required leading to an unnecessary stoppage of a mechanical process. Therefore, it is important to accurately predict the RUL.

Nowadays, vibrational and thermal sensor readings supply data on the current state of a bearing. From these fingerprints and previous sensor readings, it is possible to constantly predict bearing RUL. However, the use of the raw signal may lead to intractable datasets. To overcome this problem, feature extraction methodologies can be applied to reduce the size of the datasets.

This chapter is divided into four sections. In Section 4.2, we outline current data-driven prognosis techniques for ball bearing, together with the bearing dataset selected for this case study. In Section 4.3, we examine which features can be extracted from the raw signal, the role of the frequency domain in sampling vibrational phenomena, how to filter raw signals and how these filtering techniques can be useful for the feature extraction. We also explain the chosen degradation model and its parameters, and the theoretical background of RUL estimation and its assumptions. In Section 4.5, we report and discuss the results of the proposed model. Finally, the conclusions of this case study are outlined, together with gaps and future research directions in this area, in Section 4.6.

(a)

(b)

FIGURE 4.1
Image from two bearings. (a) Healthy bearing. (b) Damaged roller bearing
(bottom part). Image by xersti at Flickr.

4.2   Ball Bearing Prognostics

4.2.1   Data-Driven Techniques

Suppose that a doctor receives a visit from a patient who has a number of
symptoms. The doctor examines the patient with the appropriate instruments
and, based on his or her experience and knowledge, gives the patient an
estimation of the likelihood that he or she is suffering from a particular illness.
This is what we call a **diagnosis**. In an industrial setting, the patient in this
example is the bearing, and the instruments used to determine its state of
health are sensors and signal analysis tools. Now any good doctor informs his or
her patients of the consequences of not receiving correct and timely treatment:
how and when their state of health will deteriorate into a critical condition.
This is what we call a **prognosis**. In an industrial setting, the time until the
condition of the patient (ball bearing) becomes critical and is its RUL. A good
diagnosis and prognosis can fully determine the current and future condition
of the bearing. In this section, we briefly introduce the existing data-driven
techniques for determining RUL.

We can divide RUL data-driven techniques into two categories: statistical
and machine learning models. The statistical models for estimating RUL are:

- Markov models, which assume that machinery degradation processes evolve in a finite state space assuming the Markovian property. Whereas these models assume that the health states can be observed directly, this is not usually possible in machine tools. To describe the degradation processes of these unobserved states, hidden Markov models (HMMs) (Section 2.6.3) are applied to machinery prognostics (Tobon-Mejia et al., 2012).

- Autoregressive models (AR), which assume that a machine's future state is a linear function that depends on past states. Qian et al. (2014) compute RUL value using an AR model.

- Random coefficient models, which describe the stochasticity of degradation processes by adding random coefficients to degradation models that are generally assumed to be normally distributed. Lu and Meeker (1993) estimate RUL value in this manner.

- Gaussian processes for regression purposes. Gaussian processes are cumulative damage processes of random variables with joint multivariate Gaussian distributions. Saha et al. (2010) use a GPR to estimate RUL values.

- Inverse Gaussian process models (IGPM), which assume that machinery degradation process increments are independent and follow an inverse Gaussian distribution. Wang and Xu (2010) use an IGPM to predict RUL.

- Gamma process models, which assume that degradation process increments at disjoint time intervals that are independent random variables with a gamma distribution. van Noortwijk (2009) apply a gamma process model to degradation estimation.

- Wiener process models, which generally take the form of a drift term plus a diffusion term following a Brownian motion. They are one of the most commonly used stochastic process models. Doksum and Hbyland (1992) use a Wiener process to predict RUL.

Existing machine learning models are:

- Artificial neural networks (Section 2.4.6). Feed-forward neural networks are the most common for RUL estimation. Sbarufatti et al. (2016) use an ANN with a Monte Carlo method to estimate RUL values.

- Neural fuzzy networks (FN), which are fuzzy logic[1] systems whose inference structures are determined by expertise and whose membership functions are optimized by ANNs. Wang et al. (2004) use FNs to predict RUL values.

- Support vector machines (SVMs) (Section 2.4.7). Dong and Luo (2013) use a SVM to estimate degradation process of a system.

---

[1]Fuzzy logic extends classical Boolean logic by assigning any real number between 0 and 1 to propositional variables.

For this case study, we use HMMs, which are able to represent the bearings degradation evolution through hidden states which facilitates the comprehension of the estimated parameters. The fact that the bearings health is not observable fits perfectly with the idea of hidden states.

4.2.2 PRONOSTIA Testbed

In 2012 the IEEE Reliability Society in collaboration with FEMTO-ST Institute, launched the IEEE Prognostics and Health Management (PHM) 2012 Data Challenge. The challenge consisted of estimating ball bearing RUL under constant and non-constant conditions. The experiments were carried out on the PRONOSTIA experimental platform. The platform is a shaft bearing system driven by an AC motor which rotates the operating system to a certain angular speed, a pneumatic jack amplified by a level arm to exert a radial force on the ball bearing in order to reduce its life duration, accelerometers and resistance temperature detector to extract vibrational and thermal information respectively, see Nectoux et al. (2012) for more details. Participants were provided with run-to-failure datasets, including the ball bearing failures when the accelerometers register a force greater or equal to 20 g. The symbol g denotes the standard gravity, that is 1 g = 9.80665 m/s^2. For this context, vibration and temperature signals for three operating conditions were included:

1. Operating condition 1: 1800 rpm and 4000 N.

2. Operating condition 2: 1650 rpm and 4200 N.

3. Operating condition 3: 1500 rpm and 5000 N.

The datasets do not include information about the failure mode. There are two training datasets and five test datasets for operating conditions 1 and 2, and there are two training datasets but only one test dataset for operating condition 3. The original dataset labels are shown in Table 4.1.

A sample of vibration signals (vertical and horizontal) were recorded during 0.1 seconds with a sampling frequency of 25.6 kHz. Thus, each sample consists of 2,560 data (measured in gravities g), and was recorded within a 10-second period. Table 4.2 shows the actual RUL values for the test datasets.

4.3 Feature Extraction from Vibration Signals

In this section, several commonly used techniques to analyze vibration signals are reviewed. When a sensor is used to measure a physical event, the output is a signal that carries relevant information. At first glance, this raw signal may not provide any insight into what is happening, and therefore features capturing the underlying physical phenomenon have to be extracted.

TABLE 4.1
Training and test datasets for evaluating the RUL method

Dataset	Operating conditions	Label	Purpose	# Samples	# Data
1	1	Bearing1_1	Training	2,803	7,188,231
2	1	Bearing1_2	Training	871	2,228,889
3	1	Bearing1_3	Testing	1,802	4,613,120
4	1	Bearing1_4	Testing	1,139	2,915,840
5	1	Bearing1_5	Testing	2,302	5,893,120
6	1	Bearing1_6	Testing	2,302	5,893,120
7	1	Bearing1_7	Testing	1,502	3,845,120
8	2	Bearing2_1	Training	911	2,331,249
9	2	Bearing2_2	Training	797	2,039,523
10	2	Bearing2_3	Testing	1,202	3,077,120
11	2	Bearing2_4	Testing	612	1,566,720
12	2	Bearing2_5	Testing	2,002	5,125,120
13	2	Bearing2_6	Testing	572	1,464,320
14	2	Bearing2_7	Testing	172	440,320
15	3	Bearing3_1	Training	515	1,317,885
16	3	Bearing3_2	Training	1,637	4,189,083
17	3	Bearing3_3	Testing	352	901,120

Let us first make some observations about the time and frequency domains. Suppose that we have a signal $f(t)$ with period $T \in \mathbb{R}$. This signal is composed of several frequency components that contain important information about it. However, those frequency components are not explicit in $f(t)$, so a transformation is needed to identify and measure them. Therefore, the **Fourier transform** is commonly used to perform the decomposition of the signal in frequency components. Eq. 4.1 defines the Fourier transform $\hat{f}(z)$ of the signal[2]:

$$\hat{f}(z) = \int_{-\frac{T}{2}}^{\frac{T}{2}} f(t)e^{-2\pi i z t}dt. \qquad (4.1)$$

We also assume that $f(t)$ satisfies the following condition $\int_{-\frac{T}{2}}^{\frac{T}{2}} |f(t)|^2 dt < \infty$. As a result, we are sure that $f(t)$ belongs to a special vector space called $L^2([-\frac{T}{2}, \frac{T}{2}])$ or the square-integrable functions in the interval $[-\frac{T}{2}, \frac{T}{2}]$. This space includes a special set of functions $E = \{e^{2\pi i \frac{n}{T} t}\}_{n \in \mathbb{Z}}$, which can generate any vector $g \in L^2([-\frac{T}{2}, \frac{T}{2}])$. This vector is generated by means of a linear combination (Rudin, 1976) of numbers $\{c_n\}_{n \in \mathbb{Z}}$ such that:

---

[2]i denotes the number that solves $x^2 + 1 = 0$ or simply $i = \sqrt{-1}$.

TABLE 4.2
Actual RUL values for the reported datasets

Dataset	Actual RUL
3	5,730 s
4	339 s
5	1,610 s
6	1,460 s
7	7,570 s
10	7,530 s
11	1,390 s
12	3,090 s
13	1,290 s
14	580 s
17	820 s

$$f(t) = \sum_{n \in \mathbb{Z}} c_n e^{2\pi i \frac{n}{T} t}. \tag{4.2}$$

The right-hand side of this equation is known as the **Fourier series** of $f(t)$. On the other hand, Euler's formula indicates that $e^{i\theta} = \sin(\theta) + i\cos(\theta)$, which implies that $f(t)$ can be decomposed into periodic functions. The coefficients $\{c_n\}_{n \in \mathbb{Z}}$ denote which periodic functions or frequencies play a more important role in $f(t)$. Notice that the function $f(t)$ can be reconstructed only if we know the coefficients $\{c_n\}_{n \in \mathbb{Z}}$. Therefore, these coefficients fully determine $f(t)$.

We want to find the value of the coefficients $\{c_n\}_{n \in \mathbb{Z}}$. The space $L^2([-\frac{T}{2}, \frac{T}{2}])$ has an inner product[3] which is[4] $\langle f, g \rangle = \frac{1}{T} \int_{-\frac{T}{2}}^{\frac{T}{2}} f(t)g^*(t)dt$. According to this inner product, any two different vectors $f, g \in E$ must have the following properties: $\langle f, g \rangle = 0$ and $\langle f, f \rangle = 1$. It follows from the above properties that each coefficient c_n can be expressed as:

$$c_n = \langle f(t), e^{2\pi i \frac{n}{T} t} \rangle = \frac{1}{T} \int_{-\frac{T}{2}}^{\frac{T}{2}} f(t) e^{-2\pi i \frac{n}{T} t} dt. \tag{4.3}$$

Note also that c_n can be computed as the Fourier transform of $f(t)$ evaluated

---

[3]An inner product on a vector space L^2 is a bilinear function $\langle \cdot, \cdot \rangle$ with the following properties:

  1. $\langle \lambda u + v, w \rangle = \lambda \langle u, w \rangle + \langle v, w \rangle$
  2. $\langle u, \lambda v + w \rangle = \lambda \langle u, v \rangle + \langle u, w \rangle$
  3. $\langle u, u \rangle = 0$ if and only if $u = 0$
  4. $\langle u, u \rangle \geq 0$

for any $u, v, w \in L^2$ and $\lambda \in \mathbb{R}$.
[4]$g^*(t)$ is the complex conjugation of $g(t)$. If $g(t) = x(t) + iy(t)$, then $g^*(t) = x(t) - iy(t)$.

at n/T, i.e., $c_n = \frac{1}{T}\hat{f}(\frac{n}{T})$. We conclude that the coefficients $\{c_n\}_{n\in\mathbb{Z}}$ can be computed directly using the Fourier transforms. Fig. 4.2 illustrates the relationship between $\hat{f}(z)$ and $f(t)$, showing how $f(t)$ is decomposed into simpler periodic functions.

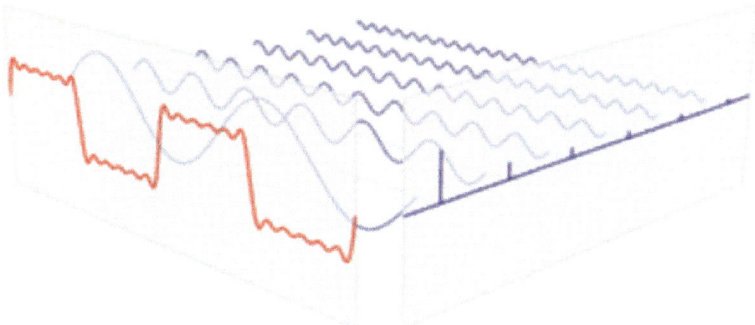

FIGURE 4.2

The red plot is the signal $f(t)$ and the blue plot is $\hat{f}(z)$. $f(t)$ can be decomposed into simple periodic functions. The amplitude of each simple periodic function determines the relevancy of its frequency.

At this point, we should mention the **Nyquist-Shannon sampling theorem** (Shannon, 1949). This theorem establishes a criterion for defining the sampling frequency of a periodic physical phenomenon. Suppose that $f(t)$ is a signal and $\hat{f}(z)$ is non-zero for the frequency domain $[-W, W] \subset \mathbb{R}$, fixed with a finite frequency W. Therefore, $f(t)$ is completely determined if it is sampled at a frequency of at least $(2W)^{-1}$. Without applying the sampling theorem, feature extraction will be poor due to problems like aliasing and the information captured by sensors will be neither useful nor reliable.

Now that we understand the interactions between the frequency and time domains clarified by the Nyquist-Shannon sampling theorem and the Fourier series decomposition, we are ready to extract features from the raw signal.

It is important to take into account the statistical features of the time domain like variance, skewness and kurtosis. These features were described in Section 2.2.1. Another important time feature is the **root mean square value** (RMS). The RMS value transforms a non-constant into a constant signal. Suppose that $f(t)$ is a function defined in the time interval $[T_1, T_2] \subset \mathbb{R}$, the mathematical formulation of RMS is expressed as:

$$\text{RMS}(f(t)) = \sqrt{\frac{1}{T_2 - T_1} \int_{T_1}^{T_2} |f(t)|^2 dt}. \tag{4.4}$$

Note that a ball bearing is a rotating machine element. Any fault in a bearing component will cause characteristic frequencies, namely FTF, BPFI,

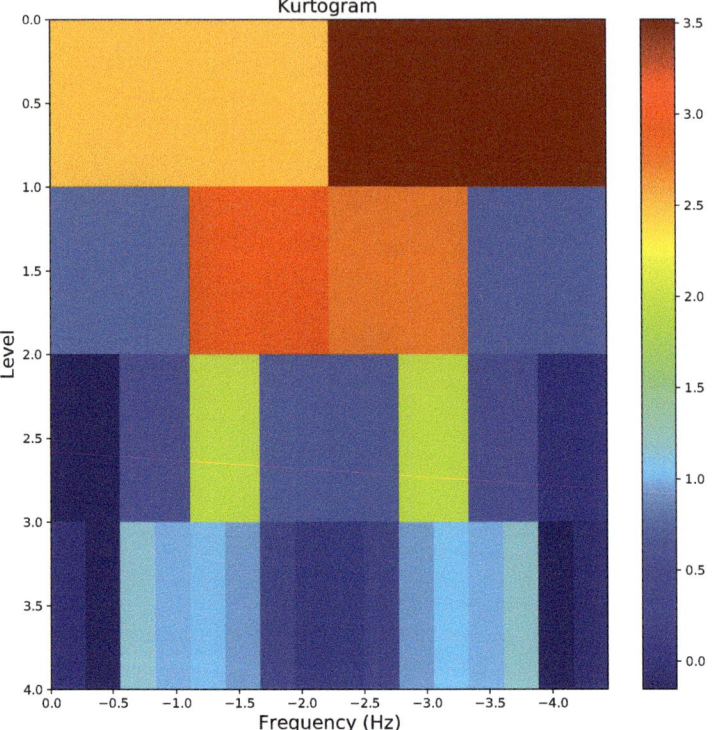

FIGURE 4.3
Example of a fast kurtogram. The frequency spectrum is divided into a factor of 2^k parts, where $k \in \mathbb{N}$ is the level of decomposition. A pass-band filter is applied to filter each region of the 2^k parts. Kurtosis is calculated for each filtered signal, and the filter of the signal with the highest kurtosis value is chosen.

BPFO, and BSF, discussed in Section 5.2.2. Therefore spectral (frequency-based) features can provide information about the current health state of a bearing and the possible failure mode.

As in the time domain, statistical features can be extracted from the frequency spectrum. However, deeper transformations and treatments can be applied to the signal spectrum to gain a better understanding of the failure modes and their evolution. For example, digital and analogical filters can be applied to the raw signal in order to remove noise or highlight frequencies. Another important method is **spectral kurtosis** which is used to clean the raw signal. When a periodic transient force is detected in a signal, the kurtosis value increases. Therefore, the idea is to find the optimal filter which highlights the highest time kurtosis in time domain. Some traditional strategies like the fast kurtogram (Fig. 4.3) are used to design this filter.

The main problem with the Fourier transform is that it assumes that the input signal is stationary or that its intrinsic parameters are always constant. However, this assumption does not hold in real-world applications. This has led to the development of time-frequency representations. For example, the **short-time Fourier transform** (STFT)[5] which is, for a signal $f(t)$, $\tilde{f}(t, z) = \int_{-\infty}^{\infty} x(\tau)w(\tau - t)e^{-2\pi iz\tau}d\tau$. This transform should extract the frequencies at each point in time, as shown in Fig. 4.4. When a non-stationary signal is being studied, its frequencies will change over time. The STFT can identify and track these frequencies.

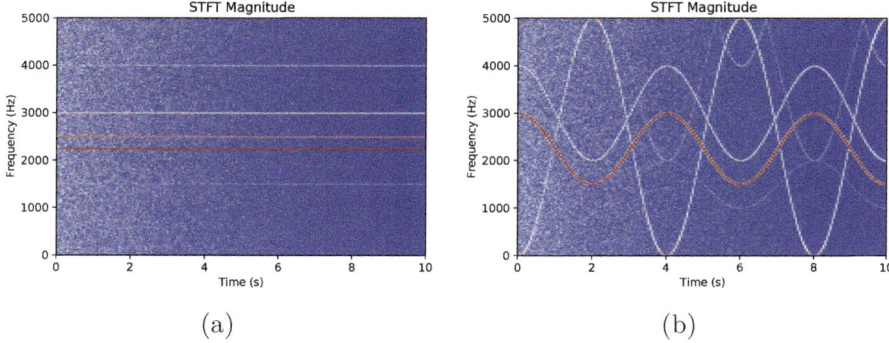

(a)   (b)

FIGURE 4.4

The Fourier transform is computed for short times, as a result of which we get the frequencies over time. (a) A stationary signal, whose frequencies do not change over time. (b) A non-stationary signal, whose principal frequencies change over time.

4.4 Hidden Markov Model-Based RUL Estimation

In this section, we introduce HMMs to model the operating conditions for RUL estimation. We present the learned models with the codification of their hidden states, followed by the strategy and assumptions used to compute the RUL (Le et al., 2015). Finally, we report on and discuss the results of the RUL estimation.

Imagine that we can run a machine as many times as desired. If in each trial, we run the machine to failure and measure the RUL value, we will find, at the end of the process, that the RUL is a random variable D, and the expected

---

[5]$w(t)$ is called a window function. Commonly used window functions are the Gaussian or the Hann windows.

RUL value will thus be $\mathbb{E}[\text{RUL}] = \mathbb{E}[D]$, where $\mathbb{E}$ is the expectation operator. The random variable D can be decomposed into its h hidden states. Suppose also that, in each trial of our machine, we can also determine the time spent in each of the hidden states. Therefore, each state will have a random variable D_i. Then the decomposition is $D = \sum_{i=1}^{h} D_i$, and the expected RUL value will be $\mathbb{E}[D] = \sum_{i=1}^{h} \mathbb{E}[D_i]$.

Now, in order to determine the RUL at each time point, we assume that the hidden states form a total order. In other words, given any two hidden states, we can always say which represent a worse situation for the bearing. Let $S = \{1, 2, ..., i, i+1, .., h\}$ be the ordered set of hidden states. Given that the current hidden state is i, the RUL value at time t will be a random variable:

$$\text{RUL}(t) = D_i^t + \sum_{j=i+1}^{h} D_j, \tag{4.5}$$

where D_i^t is a random variable defined as $D_i^t = D_i - D_i(t)$. D_i^t expresses the difference between the total time for state i (D_i) and the time spent in state i up to timepoint t ($D_i(t)$). If we also assume that each $D_i \sim \mathcal{N}(\mu_{D_i}, \sigma_{D_i})$, then we can deduce that D_i^t follows a Gaussian distribution with mean $\mu_{D_i} - D_i(t)$, standard deviation σ_{D_i}, which is truncated to the left of zero (Le et al., 2015). To conclude, the expected RUL value at time t given that the current hidden state is i can be computed according to:

$$\mathbb{E}[\text{RUL}(t)] = \mu_{D_i} - D_i(t) + \sum_{j=i+1}^{h} \mu_{D_j}. \tag{4.6}$$

As we are dealing with distributions, the RUL estimation can be given as a confidence interval. We introduce $\mathbb{E}[\text{RUL}_u(t)]$ and $\mathbb{E}[\text{RUL}_b(t)]$, as its upper and lower bounds:

$$\mathbb{E}[\text{RUL}_u(t)] = \mu_{D_i} - \bar{D}_i + \sum_{j=i+1}^{h} \mu_{D_j} + \eta \sum_{k=i}^{h} \sigma_{D_k}, \tag{4.7}$$

$$\mathbb{E}[\text{RUL}_b(t)] = \mu_{D_i} - \bar{D}_i + \sum_{j=i+1}^{h} \mu_{D_j} - \eta \sum_{k=i}^{h} \sigma_{D_k}. \tag{4.8}$$

These bounds consider the mean deviations from the time duration of each hidden state. As Eq. 4.7 overestimates, and Eq. 4.8 underestimates, the RUL, a confidence parameter η (Tobon-Mejia et al., 2012) is added to both equations. For this case study, this parameter is set to $\eta = 0.5$.

In Eq. 4.7 – Eq. 4.8 we need to find μ_{D_i} and σ_{D_k} for each hidden state. It is here that we use the learned HMMs. Suppose that we have M training datasets. For each dataset, we use the Viterbi algorithm to estimate the hidden states and, therefore calculate the duration d_{ij}, for each hidden state i and every dataset j. We can estimate μ_{D_i} and σ_{D_i} using Eq. 4.9 and Eq. 4.10, respectively:

$$\hat{\mu}_{D_i} = \frac{1}{M} \sum_{j=1}^{M} d_{ij}, \tag{4.9}$$

$$\hat{\sigma}_{D_i} = \sqrt{\frac{1}{M-1} \sum_{j=1}^{M} (d_{ij} - \hat{\mu}_{D_i})^2}. \tag{4.10}$$

4.4.1 Hidden Markov Model Construction

The Python `hmmlearn` library was used for this case study. Using this library, we can build, define and sample HMMs and use the forward-backward, Viterbi and Baum-Welch algorithms (Section 2.6.3).

Recall that an HMM is a tuple $(\mathbf{A}, \mathbf{B}, \boldsymbol{\pi})$, where $\mathbf{A}$ is the transition matrix, $\mathbf{B}$ is a vector of parameters that characterizes the emission densities[6] and $\boldsymbol{\pi}$ are the initial probabilities of the hidden states. In the context of the RUL problem, the hidden states are interpreted as the bearing health states. We assume that the emission densities for each state $i \in \mathbf{B}$ follow a normal distribution, each with its own mean and standard deviation $\mathcal{N}(\mu_i, \sigma_i)$. Thus, $\mathbf{B} = (\mu_1, \ldots, \mu_h, \sigma_1, \ldots, \sigma_h)$. For the proposed dataset, we have three different operating conditions. Therefore, we need a model for each condition. For this case study, we are going to use the RMS values (Section 4.3) to have a good and clear interpretation of the learned parameters. The RMS values are important for determining RUL because their values increase as a bearing fault evolves (Caesarenda and Tjahjowidodo, 2017). Recall that the $f(t)$ is a vibration signal whose value increases as a bearing fault evolves. Therefore, each sample from each dataset is turned into its RMS value to output a sequence of RMS values for each training set. Notice that with these calculations we reduce the amount of observations that feed the HMM because a RMS value is extracted from each sample. For instance, dataset 1 is reduced from 7,188,231 data to 2,803 RMS values.

For our model, we use three states, $S = \{\texttt{good}, \texttt{fair}, \texttt{bad}\}$. Taking these hidden states into account, the model parameters $\mathbf{A}$, $\mathbf{B}$ and $\boldsymbol{\pi}$ are determined using the Baum-Welch algorithm introduced in Section 2.6.3. In theory, it would be better to have many hidden states to represent the dynamic evolution of bearing degradation (Rabiner, 1989). Due to computational constraints, however, we opt for a limited set of states.

Eq. 4.11 shows the learned parameters for the HMM describing operating condition 1.

---

[6]The emission probabilities defined in Section 2.6.3 are now emission densities as the observed variables are continuous.

$$\mathbf{A}_1 = \begin{pmatrix} 0.953 & 0.044 & 0.002 \\ 0.037 & 0.961 & 0.002 \\ 0.000 & 0.010 & 0.990 \end{pmatrix}$$

$$\boldsymbol{\pi}_1^T = \begin{pmatrix} 1 & 0 & 0 \end{pmatrix} \tag{4.11}$$

$$\boldsymbol{\mu}_1^T = \begin{pmatrix} 0.578 & 0.375 & 1.291 \end{pmatrix}$$

$$(\boldsymbol{\sigma}_1^2)^T = \begin{pmatrix} 0.012 & 0.001 & 0.634 \end{pmatrix}.$$

These matrices and vectors do not immediately indicate which parameters correspond to each hidden state. We have to decode the learned parameters to identify the hidden states. Notice that the probability of the first entry in vector $\boldsymbol{\pi}_1$ is one. This means that if we sample from this model, it will always begin with this state; hence, it is classified as the **good** state. Now if we take a look at the transition matrix $\mathbf{A}_1$, the probability of the bearing remaining in the **good** state is $a_{11} = 0.953$. This provides a measure of how good a bearing is: the higher this value is, the longer the bearing will remain in **good** condition. We know that a more severe fault has a bigger RMS value. Remember that the emission probabilities are assumed to be Gaussian and the observations are RMS values where vector $\boldsymbol{\mu}_1$ denotes the average RMS value for each state. Then we conclude that the **bad** state corresponds to the third entry, since it has the highest RMS value. If we check a_{33} or the probability of the bearing remaining in the **bad** state, we find that its value is almost one ($a_{33} = 0.99$), which is reasonable since the bearing will remain in this state once it has failed. We conclude that the **good** state corresponds to the first entries of the learned parameters, whereas the **fair** state corresponds to the second entries and the **bad** state corresponds to the third entries. Note that states will not generally be as clearly ordered as in this case; a good interpretation and a clear physical reading of the learned parameters are key factors in decoding the learned parameters.

Eq. 4.12 shows the learned model parameters for operating condition 2.

$$\mathbf{A}_2 = \begin{pmatrix} 0.994 & 0.005 & 0.001 \\ 0.009 & 0.991 & 0.000 \\ 0.008 & 0.000 & 0.992 \end{pmatrix}$$

$$\boldsymbol{\pi}_2^T = \begin{pmatrix} 0 & 0 & 1 \end{pmatrix} \tag{4.12}$$

$$\boldsymbol{\mu}_2^T = \begin{pmatrix} 1.018 & 1.553 & 0.508 \end{pmatrix}$$

$$(\boldsymbol{\sigma}_2^2)^T = \begin{pmatrix} 0.011 & 0.157 & 0.006 \end{pmatrix}.$$

We will decode the hidden states. The third entry of $\boldsymbol{\pi}_2$ has probability one and is recognized as the **good** state. We find that the highest RMS value in the $\boldsymbol{\mu}_2$ vector corresponds to the second entry; hence it is recognized as the **bad** state. We conclude, then, that the third entries represent the **good** state, the first entries denote the **fair** state and the second entries correspond to the **bad** state.

Eq. 4.13 shows the learned parameters for the operating condition 3.

$$\mathbf{A}_3 = \begin{pmatrix} 0.996 & 0.001 & 0.003 \\ 0.000 & 0.962 & 0.038 \\ 0.029 & 0.009 & 0.962 \end{pmatrix}$$

$$\boldsymbol{\pi}_3^T = \begin{pmatrix} 0.5 & 0.0 & 0.5 \end{pmatrix}$$

$$\boldsymbol{\mu}_3^T = \begin{pmatrix} 0.422 & 1.516 & 0.549 \end{pmatrix}$$

$$(\boldsymbol{\sigma}_3^2)^T = \begin{pmatrix} 0.001 & 0.506 & 0.002 \end{pmatrix}. \tag{4.13}$$

We would expect that the bearing state is always **good** at the start time. However, looking at vector $\boldsymbol{\pi}_3$, there is no entry with probability one. Therefore, with this criterion, none of the states can be classified as **good** state. Let us check vector $\boldsymbol{\mu}_3$ to determine the **good** state. We pick the entry with the smallest RMS value as the **good** state and the entry with the highest value as the **bad** state. Since the first entry has the smallest value, it is recognized as the **good** state. On the other hand, the second entry has the highest value and is therefore decoded as the **bad** state, with the third entry being the `fair` state.

Note that this codification is necessary for RUL estimation since we need an ordered set of states, indicating, for each pair of states, which represents a better state for the bearing.

4.5 Results and Discussion

This section contains the RUL estimation results, comparing the HMM outcomes with actual RUL values. For each operating condition, one testing dataset was selected for illustrative purposes. Datasets 6, 11 and 17 have been selected for operating conditions 1, 2 and 3, respectively.

4.5.1 RUL Results

Fig. 4.5 shows the RUL results for the operating condition test datasets. The blue line represents the actual RUL value, whereas the yellow line denotes the RUL prediction. The closer the yellow to the blue line, the better the prognosis. The relative error of RUL estimations for each test dataset is shown in Table 4.3. This relative error is computed as the absolute difference of actual and estimated RUL values divided by the actual RUL value. The relative error has been computed using a Hann window:

$$\text{RUL relative error} = \frac{1}{T} \sum_{t=1}^{T} w(t) \frac{|\text{RUL}(t) - \widehat{\text{RUL}}(t)|}{\text{RUL}(t)}, \tag{4.14}$$

TABLE 4.3

Relative error for each test dataset

Dataset	RUL relative error
6	10.67
11	1.72
17	362.74

where $w(t) = \sin(\frac{\pi t}{T})$, and T satisfies $\text{RUL}(T) = 0$. The use of the Hann window avoids overpenalizing the relative error when the $\text{RUL}(t)$ is close to 0.

Fig. 4.5(a) shows the results for operating condition 1, where the estimated RUL value slightly overestimates the actual RUL value. As shown in Table 4.3, the relative error is 10.67%.

Fig. 4.5(b) shows the results for operating condition 2, where predicted and actual RUL values are very close throughout the bearing life. This planning strategy would not cost almost any money or time as the relative error is very low.

For operating condition 3, its RUL prediction is shown in Fig. 4.5(c). In this case, the estimated RUL value is highly overestimated, especially from $t = 0$ s to $t = 700$ s. At $t = 700$ s, the estimated RUL values suddenly decrease and get closer to the actual RUL values up to the end. The actual RUL values never lie within the confidence interval, so this situation is undesirable, producing a relative error higher than 100%, as shown in Table 4.3. Notice that a relative error higher than 100% can only be obtained if the prediction is overestimated.

4.5.2 Interpretation of the Degradation Model

The degradation model implemented here expects the ball bearing to evolve towards a higher failure state. The bearing is not expected to return to a previous state. Therefore, we only add the expected mean times $\mathbb{E}[D_i]$ of forward states and the expected remaining time in the current state (Eq. 4.6). This condition is equivalent to saying that the transition matrix $\mathbf{A}$ is upper triangular, as in Eq. 4.15 with a probability of $\sum_{j=1}^{h} a_{ij} = 1, \forall i = 1, \ldots, h$ and $a_{ij} = 0$ if $i < j$. The assumption that the transition matrix $\mathbf{A}$ is upper triangular (Eq. 4.15) is an optimistic view. It can be verified that in Eq. 4.11 – Eq. 4.13, this assumption does not hold and can be the main reason of the poor performance in operating condition 3.

$$\mathbf{A} = \begin{pmatrix} a_{11} & a_{12} & a_{13} & \ldots & a_{1h} \\ 0 & a_{22} & a_{23} & \ldots & a_{2h} \\ 0 & 0 & a_{33} & \ldots & a_{3h} \\ \ldots & \ldots & \ldots & \ldots & \ldots \\ 0 & 0 & 0 & \ldots & a_{hh} \end{pmatrix}. \tag{4.15}$$

On the other hand, a large number of training datasets is required to get a better estimation of the transition matrix and the parameters $\hat{\mu}_{D_i}$ from Eq. 4.9 and $\hat{\sigma}^2_{D_i}$ from Eq. 4.10. In this case, we only had two training datasets for each operating condition and it does not seem enough to obtain an accurate estimation in some cases. However, we have found that RUL prediction can be accurate and help with prognosis.

4.6 Conclusions and Future Research

4.6.1 Conclusions

HMMs are useful for understanding latent variables like the health states of a bearing. Nevertheless, large training datasets are needed to accurately estimate all the parameters of the HMMs. On the other hand, a large number of datasets leads to computational problems (limited memory for parameter learning of hidden state estimation). The parameters of the trained model must be interpreted in order to gain a better understanding of the bearing health states. The Viterbi algorithm is an important method for estimating the states of a bearing. The estimation of these hidden states is a key issue to RUL estimation. RUL models also make assumptions that may not hold in the real world. In spite of these drawbacks, accurate predictions can be achieved.

The feature extraction is crucial for parameter estimation. We must first ensure that the physical phenomenon has been correctly sampled. Filters can be used, if needed, to attenuate noise or highlight certain frequencies. Once we have a significant signal, features can be extracted. For this case study, we have used the RMS value since the literature shows evidence of the direct proportional relationship between RMS values and fault evolution. However, we could have used other statistical measures like the kurtosis, variance, or multidimensional observations with all these features; nevertheless, we must be capable of interpreting the estimated parameters and deduce the corresponding hidden states.

4.6.2 Future Research

The evolution of any crack in a bearing depends on its previous states. However, the HMM approach considers observations to be only dependent on the previous observation, which is not enough in some scenarios. Therefore, new approaches are needed. Chen et al. (2018) use an autocorrelated HMM to predict the RUL of a system; they assume there is a dependency between observations. Taking up this idea of correlation with past states in HMM, Petropoulos et al. (2017) propose a new HMM formulation called variable dependence jump HMM. Likewise Liu et al. (2015) develop a continuous-time hidden Markov model (CT-HMM). A CT-HMM is an HMM in which both the hidden state transitions and the observations can occur at arbitrary continuous times. This is a reasonable assumption in the case of the health state of a bearing. Moving away from HMMs, Cartella et al. (2015) use hidden semi-Markov models, where the time duration of the hidden states is relevant for the model and can modify the transition matrix **A**. As a result, they modify the forward-backward and Viterbi algorithms to take into account these state durations. On the other hand, a bearing may fail due to different failure modes, and each failure mode causes a different degradation process. Le et al. (2015) develop a multibranch hidden semi-Markov model in which each branch contains a HMM that represents a failure mode.

Clearly, the research trend in this field is towards weakened Markovian assumptions with the modification of the EM, Viterbi and backward-forward algorithms. The idea is to model more general and realistic situations where the pure Markovian property may lead to inconsistencies. Another important issue is to determine the failure mode online in order to get a more precise model describing degradation, where it would be useful to mix filtering (kurtogram for example) methods for diagnosis with prognosis methods.

For this case study we have only used the RMS values to learn the model parameters. Since only one feature has been used to train the HMMs, model parameters are not difficult to interpret and the model configuration is clear; however, if more time or frequency features (which can be extracted as shown in Fig. 4.6) are used, the model and its parameters can be harder to understand and interpret. Nevertheless, more insights might be obtained, leading to more accurate and informative models.

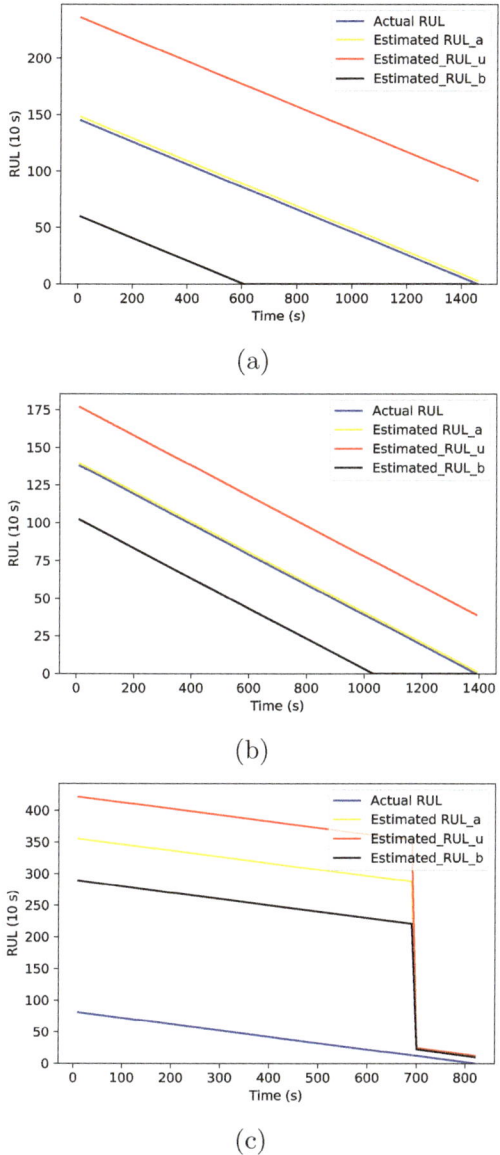

FIGURE 4.5
RUL estimations for the three test datasets selected, one per operating condition. (a) Operating condition 1. (b) Operating condition 2. (c) Operating condition 3. The blue line represents the true RUL value for each timepoint in time and the yellow line is the expected RUL value predicted from the learned model. The red and black lines stand for the upper and lower bounds of the RUL confidence interval, respectively.

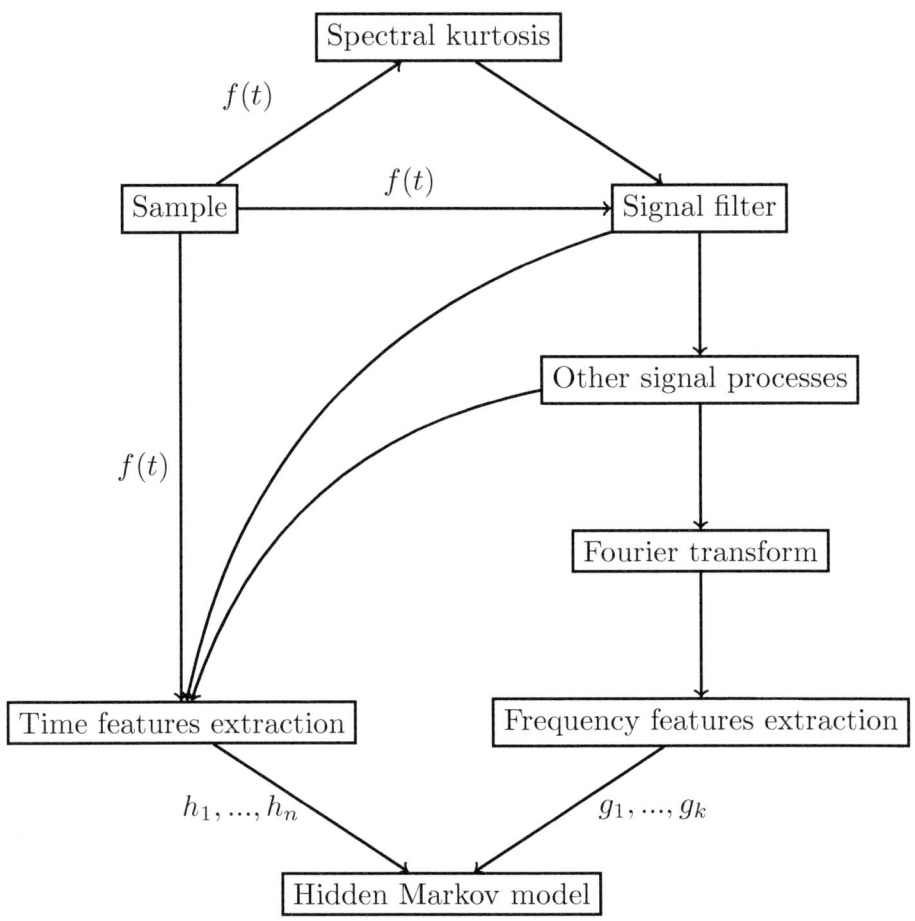

FIGURE 4.6
A diagram of an extended modeling procedure including some frequency features. The idea is to use not only time features as RMS to train a HMM, but also features from the signal spectrum. In the above diagram, the output from spectral kurtosis is taken into account and more sophisticated signal processing techniques can be used to remove the noise from the signal. Once the signal has been processed, $g_1, \ldots, g_k$ features are extracted from the spectrum. For example, the amplitude of the frequencies from the BPFO, BPFI, FTF, BSF and their harmonics can be used as features. Also, the HMM can be replaced with hidden semi-Markov models or autoregressive HMMs.

5

Machine-Level Case Study: Fingerprint of Industrial Motors

5.1   Introduction

Nowadays, general-purpose performance models for products like pumps, servomotors or spindles are developed based on theory, experience or under laboratory conditions because there is no way of knowing exactly where they will be installed and which will be their specific operating conditions. Besides, these types of products are developed to work under a wide range of operating conditions where performance is defined as nominal behavior.

At machine level, the fourth industrial revolution provides for the use of data from different manufacturing assets to gather useful knowledge. This knowledge can be used to compare the performance of similar parts, e.g., the effect of a specific boundary condition on throughput time or the effect of operating conditions on **degradation**. Additionally, this feature-based knowledge can be extrapolated from machines to other levels, like machine components at the bottom level and manufacturing plants at the top level.

Lee et al. (2014) explained that there are similarities between machines performing the same tasks at the same maintenance level, where health conditions and performance may be similar, leading to a potentially useful pattern.

Therefore, Industrial Internet of Things (IIoT) technologies are capable of moving away from theory-based or laboratory models to real operating data-based models. The insights gained from this approach could be useful for comparing information on anything from machine performance to maintenance, thus having a direct positive impact on overall plant utilization resulting in greater productivity.

To illustrate this conceptualization, the case study reported here focuses on machine components, specifically, machine tool axis servomotors. The function of this component is to drive the machine tool. Consequently, it suffers high levels of jerk related to the positioning control systems. Depending on its usage, this situation leads to high levels of stress that could produce premature degradation of the internal components. Additionally, servomotors are rotating machinery, as a result of which extrapolation to other rotation-based components, e.g., spindles or pumps, is straightforward.

5.2 Performance of Industrial Motors as a Fingerprint

5.2.1 Improving Reliability Models with Fingerprints

One of the main requirements of a machine component is that it should be able to withstand what are known as service conditions. Service conditions are normally defined, described and quantified during the early design phases. Withstandability is an inherent characteristic called strength that depends on the properties (mechanical, chemical, etc.) of the chosen material. On the other hand, service conditions are a collection of loads (tension, compression, shear, bending, torsion) that affect machine component performance (Shigley and Mischke, 1956).

However, there are uncertainties about both the strength of a material, whose chemical composition, production and anisotropy may vary, and the specific service conditions. This could compromise machine component performance over time, affecting what is known as **reliability**. Formally, reliability is the probability of a machine component performing its intended function for a specified period of time without failure.

Reliability is one example of a statistical model of the pattern of variation (Shigley et al., 2004) for a component. This pattern is the stable state related to the component. However, systematic and random effects will be mixed if evidence is gathered by measurement. Therefore, statistics-based models will separate out such effects and produce a clear approximation of the pattern, equivalent to reliability.

To model component reliability, evidence of behavior has to be gathered. Traditionally, destructive testing has been used to measure material strength under service conditions. However, testing is conducted under controlled conditions. This could bypass specific operating conditions and have serious effects on performance. For example, servomotors are selected from catalogs based on expected conditions generally sourced from information gathered during the design phase, when nominal and maximum conditions are defined. At this stage, it is impossible to precisely estimate real operating conditions under random circumstances. Hence, the servomotor may have to operate outside the nominal region described in commercial catalogs. If operating conditions are outside nominal values for long periods of time, premature degradation might occur, reducing machine utilization.

Destructive testing is necessary to model component reliability. However, it is expensive and sometimes unfeasible (e.g., nuclear plants or aerospace equipment). Therefore, engineers normally extrapolate reliability models defining a group of components. Components with the same specific material and assembly tolerances are defined as a group of identical components. With regard to the selected servomotor example, this means that servomotors with the same catalog reference are identical.

Using the concept of real operating **data-based models** developed under the fourth industrial revolution paradigm and described in Section 1.1, it is possible to fit a theoretical model using real operating data collected from advanced sensors. This yields the pattern of variation model for a component or asset, measuring real values for materials and operating conditions. This pattern will be useful in the design phase (servomotor selection) or during asset quality control manufacturing (mean performance around a nominal value).

As a design phase example, a servomotor with a nominal torque of 27 N·m at 100 ^{o}C is used to move the X-axis of a milling machine. Fig. 5.1 plots the mean torque and temperature measured during real operation. Because milling processes use the X-axis depending on the needs of the work product, operating conditions will not necessarily be at their nominal value. In this case, the mean torque and temperature are always far below the nominal value, showing that a smaller and cheaper motor would be a better choice. Additionally, it illustrates that operating conditions are stable over time. This makes it harder to detect specific behavior useful for selecting the lowest cost servomotor unlikely to experience premature degradation.

Regarding quality control, it is important to know how reliable a specific component is prior to installation, i.e., servomotor quality has to be controlled before machine assembly. This means that it is not feasible to get performance values that are fine-tuned to the behavior of each component under production conditions. Hence, it is extremely useful to have a pattern of variation model as a benchmark for efficiently checking performances.

Throughout this case study, the pattern of variation is defined as an asset fingerprint, enabling self-comparison as outlined by Lee et al. (2015), namely, that asset performance is comparable with the asset fingerprint. This fingerprint approach is described as a characteristic-wise partition of a set into smaller subsets, using clustering techniques. Clusters are defined according to the unsupervised association methods used by the clustering algorithms detailed in Section 2.3.

There are accepted manufacturing tolerances due to component anisotropies leading to normal performance deviations, i.e., tolerances around nominal behavior. If the fingerprint is built using data from only one component, there will be a higher rejection rate, leading to good components being scrapped. Therefore, a more general fingerprint has to be built using data from many components with the same reference and application in order to take into account a larger number of normal performance deviations.

This generalization process is called consensual component fingerprint and is illustrated in Fig. 5.2. Therefore, component **fingerprints** can be joined to create a cluster, which consensually takes into account the shape of the natural groups from each element.

5.2.2   Industrial Internet Consortium Testbed

As previously mentioned, this case study focuses on rotative machinery, which is actually quite common across the manufacturing industry. Specifically, we

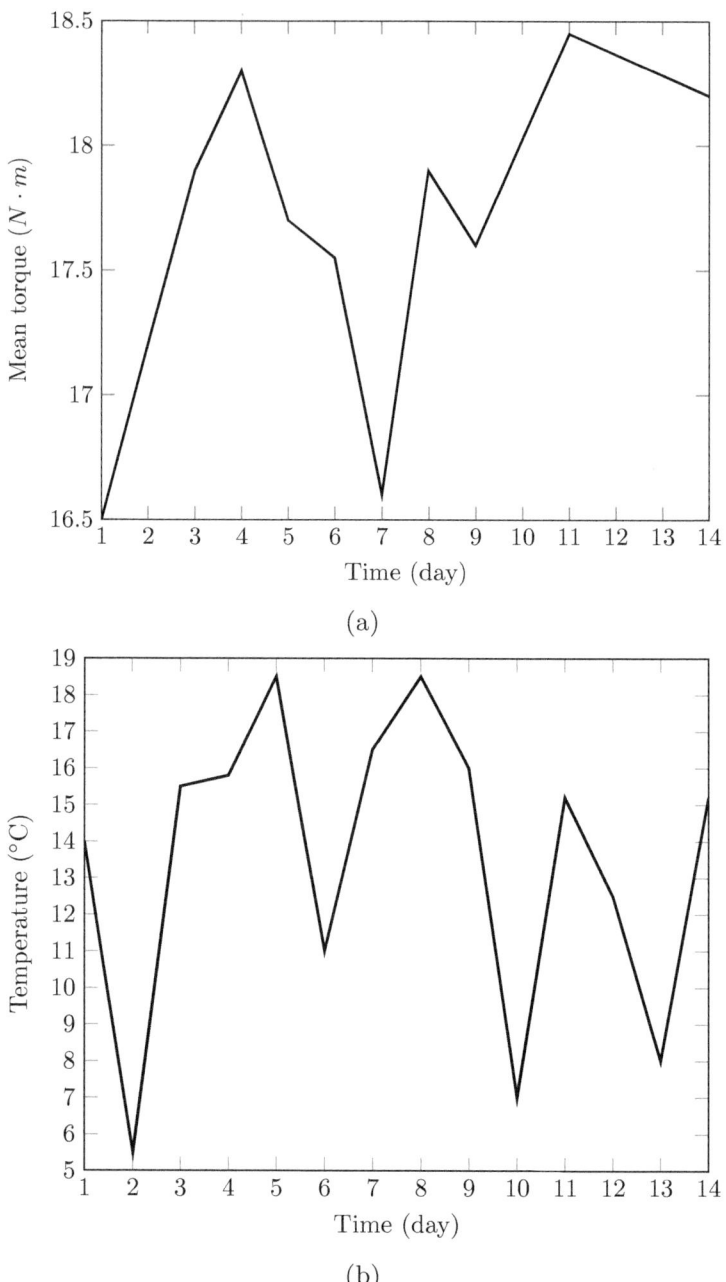

FIGURE 5.1
Servomotor values measured during real operation with nominal value $27\ \mathrm{N\cdot m}$ at $100°C$. (a) Servomotor mean torque. (b) Servomotor mean temperature.

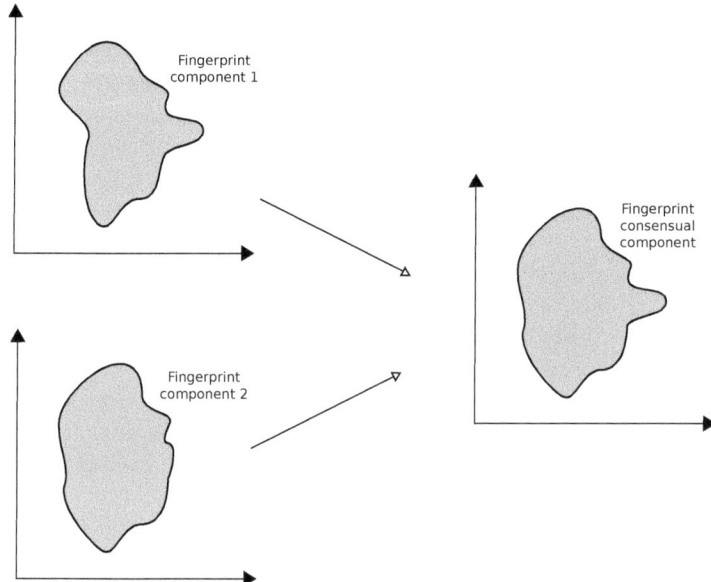

FIGURE 5.2
Generalized component performance fingerprint approach.

study servomotors used for positioning the machine tool axis. Nevertheless, the resulting methodology is easily extrapolated to other machine systems, like spindles or motors. This is possible because the shaft and bearings are the main mechanical parts subject to degradation inside rotative machinery (Fig. 5.3).

A common issue related to servomotors is their performance when brand new. It is important to know their starting conditions to infer if they are reliable enough to be installed. For this reason, as described by Siddique et al. (2005), the performance of the internal rotating components of electrical motors is studied under laboratory conditions to provide a clear picture,

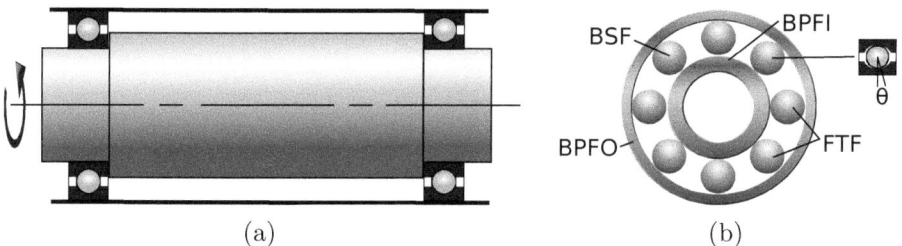

FIGURE 5.3
(a) Shaft and bearing assembly. (b) Bearing composition.

without contextual interference, of the integrity of ball screws, guides, cable holders, etc.

Usually, deviations in brand new servomotor behavior are caused by internal ball bearings. Bearings are the weakest servomotor components and are selected using catalogs that take expected nominal operation as the selection key. However, such catalogs are a collection of bearing behavior results from destructive testing. Unfortunately, bearings may have non-linear behaviors that are not completely modeled by lab testing.

Traditionally, uncertainties produced by non-linear behaviors are mitigated using a design factor ($\bar{n}_d$) during selection. The main effect of $\bar{n}_d$ is to move away from the boundary values, that is, if the component behavior under specific conditions is well known, then $\bar{n}_d = 1$, else $\bar{n}_d > 1$. Generally, this safety factor is selected based on laboratory and experience-based know-how. Bearing manufacturers have extensive know-how, but external factors caused by other parts within the assembly may affect their performance, causing brand new elements to behave erratically.

In this case study, a fingerprint will be developed using new servomotors in order to get a benchmark to compare servomotors with the same reference before installation. With the aim of isolating unwanted external factors, testing will be done under no-load conditions, measuring four variables: shaft angular speed, power consumption, temperature and vibration. These variables are normally used to analyze rotative machinery performance within the industry and are directly related to bearings and shaft strength. Therefore, their values can give the following information:

- Shaft angular speed, Ω, i.e., shaft revolutions per minute. Shaft angular speed is the variable controlled by the servomotor driver and numerical control unit (NCU), and is used as a reference for testing.

- Power consumption, P, is capable of showing up internal anomalies when there is a strong variability in its value under stable conditions. For example, if there is a part, like a faulty bearing, interfering with rotation, the servomotor will need more power to maintain its rotating speed.

- Temperature, T, like power consumption, captures internal anomalies. Temperature will be affected if behavior is out of the ordinary. For example, a fault in a bearing has a negative effect on its friction coefficient, leading to an increase in the energy dissipated in the form of heat detected by a thermocouple.

- Vibration is one of the traditional indicators used to detect internal performance because it is capable of showing up faulty behaviors in advance. However, the interpretation of vibration is not straightforward, and more expertise is required to understand its behavior in a faulty component.

Nevertheless, we study only vibration values in shaft and bearings in this particular case study. For this purpose, the vibration variable is broken down as follows:

- Vibration related with shaft: the servomotor rotating frequency has to be monitored in order to determine the value of shaft vibration. For example, if the servomotor is running at 3,000 rpm, the rotating frequency (F_{shaft}) will be $3,000 \text{ rpm} \times \frac{1 \min}{60 \text{ s}} = 50$ Hz. Therefore, the vibration value will be the peak or RMS value at 50 Hz (A_{shaft}), which is called the monitoring frequency. A change in the vibration amplitude value at this frequency may indicate anomalies related to shaft balance or buckling.

- Vibration related with the bearing: the vibration values of a bearing are broken down according to four different monitoring frequencies because it is an assembled mechanical component: fundamental train frequency or FTF (Eq. 5.1), ball pass frequency of inner ring or BPFI (Eq. 5.2), ball pass frequency of outer ring or BPFO (Eq. 5.3) and ball spin frequency or BSF (Eq. 5.4), where Ω is shaft rpm, Bd is the ball or roller diameter, Nb is the number of balls or rollers, Pd is the pitch diameter and θ is the contact angle to the rolling path (outer or inner ring) as illustrated in Fig. 5.3. Therefore, peak or RMS values at these frequencies stand for the vibration of each bearing part. Hence, it is possible during data analysis to ascertain which part of the bearing is not working properly.

$$FTF = \frac{1}{2} \frac{\Omega}{60} \left(1 - \frac{Bd}{Pd} \cos \theta \right), \tag{5.1}$$

$$BPFI = \frac{Nb}{2} \frac{\Omega}{60} \left(1 + \frac{Bd}{Pd} \cos \theta \right), \tag{5.2}$$

$$BPFO = \frac{Nb}{2} \frac{\Omega}{60} \left(1 - \frac{Bd}{Pd} \cos \theta \right), \tag{5.3}$$

$$BSF = \frac{Pd}{2Bd} \frac{\Omega}{60} \left[1 - \left(\frac{Bd}{Pd} \right)^2 \cos \theta \right]. \tag{5.4}$$

We use an experimental servomotor testbed to demonstrate the fingerprint approach. Fig. 5.4 shows the testbed infrastructure that is able to reproduce the real behavior of a machine and all its subsystems from data acquisition to analysis[1].

In this case, it has been configured to get no-load variables under different rotating speed scenarios. The servomotors used for testing are three SIEMENS 1FK7042-2AF71, with the characteristics described in Table 5.1.

These servomotors are equipped with two ref. 6204 bearings with the characteristics described in Table 5.2.

---

[1]http://www.iiconsortium.org/smart-factory-machine-learning.htm

(a)   (b)

FIGURE 5.4
(a) Industrial Internet Consortium testbed. (b) Data acquisition system using a cyber-physical system.

TABLE 5.1
Servomotor specifications[2]

Specification	Value
Rated speed	3,000 rpm
Static torque	$3.0 \text{ N} \cdot \text{m}$
Stall current	2.2 A
Rated torque	$2.6 \text{ N} \cdot \text{m}$
Rated current	2.0 A
Rotor moment of inertia	$2.9 \text{ kg} \cdot \text{m}^2$

TABLE 5.2
Ball bearing ref. 6204 specifications with $Bd = 0.312$ mm, $Nb = 8$ balls, $Pd = 1.358$ mm and $\theta = 0^o$

Vibration type	Value (Hz)
FTF	0.39 rpm/60
$BPFI$	4.92 rpm/60
$BPFO$	3.08 rpm/60
BSF	2.06 rpm/60

---

[2]Data from SIEMENS SIMOTICS S-1FK7 servomotor catalog.

TABLE 5.3

NC-code program for testbed servomotors

NC-Code
INI
G01 X5000 Y5000 Z5000 F83120
G01 X0 Y0 Z0
GOTO INI
M30

The accelerometers used to collect the bearing and shaft vibration signal have a nominal sensitivity of 100 mV/g and a frequency range of 0.2 Hz to 10,000 Hz in ± 3 dB. Additionally, power and temperature values are gathered directly from the NCU, which is a SIEMENS SINUMERIK 840D. This NCU stores values from variable memory spaces in specific databases where they are collected by the acquisition system.

5.2.3 Testbed Dataset Description

We programmed a specific NCU cycle to move the servomotors under the same conditions in order to get a dataset with enough information on each servomotor. Therefore, a NC-Code program (shown in Table 5.3) was developed to move the servomotors to a specified position and back to their original position at maximum speed. Specifically, three servomotors will be moved to position 5.000 mm at a feed-rate (F) of 83.120 $\frac{mm}{min}$, equivalent to 2.400 rpm, and then back to position 0 mm, restarting the cycle. This cycle illustrates the behavior of each servomotor operating at near maximum speed during a clockwise and counterclockwise rotation.

The dataset acquired from the testbed is taken from the NCU using a cyber-physical system (CPS) shown in Fig. 5.4(b). Its job is to gather the rotating speed, power and temperature values and send them to a remote database.

Additionally, the CPS acquires signals from accelerometers located in each servomotor and the internal FPGA calculates the fast Fourier transform[3] (FFT) of the signal. Having defined the shaft and bearing monitoring frequencies in terms of servomotor rpm, the CPS uses the FFT to calculate the acceleration amplitude of each part (see Fig. 5.5). These values are also sent to the remote database and synchronized with the NCU values.

Since variables behave differently, acquisition time has been set at the slowest variable of 480 ms in order to simplify the dataset. This simplification should help to avoid pre-processing or sensor fusion steps before carrying out the data analysis.

---

[3]A fast Fourier transform is an algorithm that samples a signal over a period of time (or space) and divides it into its frequency components.

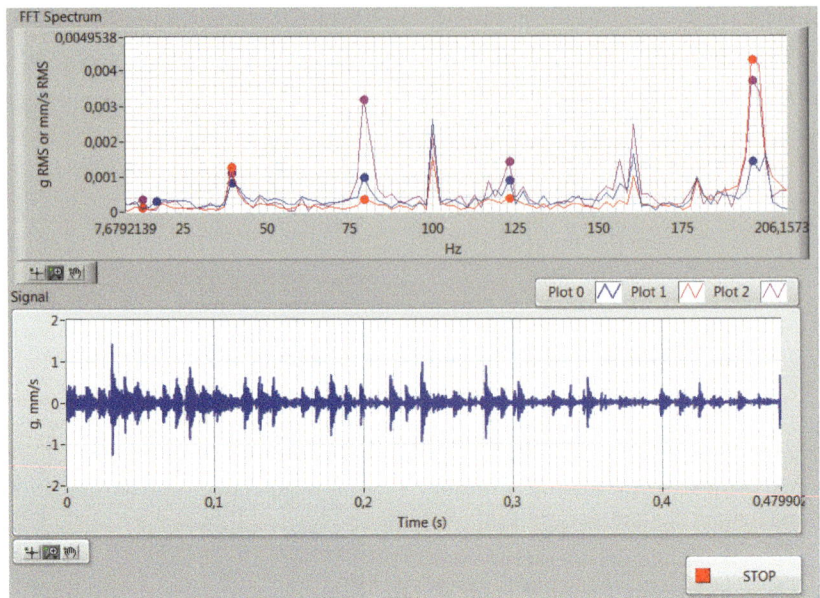

FIGURE 5.5
Accelerometer dashboard: time-based signal and fast Fourier transform.

For this case study, we built a dataset covering one week's operation to get a representative number of instances. The size is 1,462,585 instances by a total of 39 variables, 13 per servomotor:

- Angular speed, Ω.

- Power, P.

- Torque, τ.

- Vibration amplitude: A_{shaft}, A_{FTF}, A_{BPFI}, A_{BPFO}, A_{BSF}.

- Vibration frequencies: F_{shaft}, FTF, $BPFI$, $BPFO$, BSF.

5.3   Clustering Algorithms for Fingerprint Development

We use unsupervised learning (Section 2.3) in order to find the servomotor fingerprints as defined in Section 5.1, as there is no class to be predicted. Instead instances are divided into natural groups (Xu and Tian, 2015), which will be equivalent to a servomotor pattern of variation. We applied and compared the five different clustering methods listed in Table 5.4 and explained in Section 2.3. They are briefly explained below.

TABLE 5.4
Clustering methods and algorithms used in this case study

Clustering methods	Algorithm
Hierarchical	Agglomerative
Partitional	K-means
Spectral clustering	Shi and Malik (SM)
Affinity propagation	Affinity Propagation (AP)
Probabilistic	Gaussian mixture model (GMM)

5.3.1 Agglomerative Hierarchical Clustering

As discussed in Section 2.3.1, agglomerative, bottom-up or ascending hierarchical clustering assumes that each instance is a cluster, then merges pairs of clusters as it moves up the hierarchy.

The parameters used by agglomerative hierarchical clustering are type of linkage method, number of clusters K, connectivity matrix and distance metric.

- Linkage method: the linkage criterion is the distance between two clusters used by the algorithm in order to find the optimum merging. We use Ward's method which computes the dissimilarity between two clusters, Cl_i and Cl_j, as the difference between the summed square in their joint cluster and the addition of the summed square distances to the centroid within these two clusters.

- Number of clusters K: selected according to the experts' opinion.

- Connectivity matrix and distance metric for computing the linkage. According to Ward's method, the distance is Euclidean.

5.3.2 K-means Clustering

K-means (Section 2.3.2) is an algorithm that partitions a set of n-dimensional points $\mathcal{D} = \{\mathbf{x}^1, \ldots, \mathbf{x}^N\}$ into K clusters $Cl_1, \ldots, Cl_K$ based on the minimization of the square-error-criterion.

The parameters used for the K-means algorithm are number of clusters K, cluster initialization and distance. Therefore,

- Number of clusters K: the major challenge is to estimate the optimum number of clusters, as there is no perfect mathematical criterion for selecting K (Tibshirani et al., 2001). Therefore, the number of clusters is, in this case, selected based on expert opinions with meaningful clustering results. However, for the sake of completeness, we analyze results with three different K values: 3, 5 and 7.

- Cluster initialization: as K-means may converge to local minima, the algorithm is sensitive to initialization. The most common strategy for cluster initialization is to choose K instances at random and then use the instance with the minimum squared error. However, there is no guarantee that it will not get trapped in local optima, and speed might be compromised.

  In this case, a smart variant of this initialization strategy called K-means++ (Arthur and Vassilvitskii, 2007) is used to speed up convergence. The main idea of this initialization algorithm is to pick one center Cl_1, chosen uniformly from $\mathcal{D}$, weigh each instance based on the squared distance to the centroid and sequentially select $K - 1$ new centroids based on the largest weight value to the fixed cluster centers. This strategy ensures that centroids are well spread over the data space, reducing errors due to local optima and decreasing additional calculations for partitioning purposes.

- Distance: we chose the Euclidean distance. This means that the K-means algorithm will find spherical or ball-shaped clusters in data (Jain, 2010).

5.3.3   Spectral Clustering

The objective of spectral clustering (von Luxburg, 2007) is to find a partition of a similarity graph defined by $G = (V, E)$ where the edges between different groups have very low weights and the edges within a group have very high weights. Shi and Malik (SM) algorithm is selected in this use case (Shi and Malik, 2000). This algorithm is referred to as a bipartitioning algorithm because it splits points into two groups until K partitions are formed.

The parameters of the SM algorithm are similarity graph (affinity matrix) and number of clusters K.

- Similarity graph, which is built using the pairwise similarities or pairwise distances from instances in $\mathcal{D}$. In Section 2.3.3, three different similarity graphs have been described: ϵ-neighborhood graph, k-nearest neighbor graph, and the fully connected graph. In this case study, the k-nearest neighbor graph has been used.

- Number of clusters K, chosen as described for the K-means algorithm.

5.3.4   Affinity Propagation

The main goal of affinity propagation (AP) (Frey and Dueck, 2007) is to find a subset of representative data instances. In order to identify such exemplars, data similarity is measured as described in Section 2.3.4. Basically, the affinity between two points is checked using two messages:

- Responsibility $r(\mathbf{x}^i, \mathbf{x}^k)$, which takes into account the accumulated evidence of how well suited $\mathbf{x}^k$ is to serve as the exemplar for $\mathbf{x}^i$ with respect to other possible exemplars.

- Availability $a(\mathbf{x}^i, \mathbf{x}^k)$, which takes into account the accumulated evidence of how appropriate it would be for $\mathbf{x}^i$ to pick $\mathbf{x}^k$ as its exemplar.

The main parameters for the AP algorithm are preference and damping.

- Preference, called $s(\mathbf{x}^i, \mathbf{x}^i)$, is the a priori suitability of a point $\mathbf{x}^i$ to serve as an exemplar. Therefore, the preference controls the number of exemplars (clusters) to be found. A high preference value may produce a large number of exemplars, whereas low values may yield a small number of exemplars. Preferences must be set to a common value, usually, to the minimum or median of input similarities.

- Damping is the factor $\lambda \in (0, 1)$ that limits overshooting during the computation of responsibility and availability, i.e., messages. Therefore, high damping produces smaller changes in the messages, the processing time until convergence may increase. In contrast, low damping may cause solution overshooting, thus blocking convergence.

5.3.5 Gaussian Mixture Model Clustering

Gaussian mixture model (GMM) (McLachlan and Peel, 2004) clustering uses the probability distribution as a measure of similarity between uncertain objects, e.g., objects with the same mean but different variance. As discussed in Section 2.3.5, the GMM algorithm needs to search for an applicable Gaussian mixture model m, whose components have the same covariance matrix (Biernacki et al., 2000).

The parameters of the GMM algorithm are as follows:

- Covariance type, which is the matrix model to be found. It can be full, where each component has its own covariance matrix; tied, where all components share the same covariance matrix; diagonal, where each component has its own diagonal matrix; or spherical, where each component has its own single variance.

- Initialization: like K-means, the GMM algorithm is sensitive to initialization and may converge to local minima yielding different results. Therefore, we use two types of initialization:

  - Random, where the instance with least minimum squared error after use is taken.
  - K-means, where the K-means algorithm is used to get initial components.

- Number of components, chosen as described for the K-means algorithms.

5.3.6 Implementation Details

We used the `scikit-learn` library in order to implement each of the clustering algorithms (Pedregosa et al., 2011). As the main purpose of this chapter is to illustrate how clustering algorithms find the asset fingerprint (see Section 5.1), algorithm efficiency is not a primary concern. Additionally, experiments were conducted using a subset of 12,000 data instances randomly extracted from the original dataset and 36 variables, leaving out the angular speed variables for the three servomotors, Ω from the variables listed in Section 5.2.3, as it is constant at 2,400 rpm. This should improve result visualization.

The parameters used in each algorithm are described below:

- Hierarchical agglomerative clustering: Ward's was the selected linkage criterion and the Euclidean distance was selected as the distance metric.

- K-means: we employed the `scikit-learn` default parameters using K-means++ for cluster initialization and the Euclidean distance.

- Spectral clustering: we also calculated the affinity matrix using the `kneighbors_graph` function. We used the arpack eigenvalue decomposition strategy, designed to solve large-scale eigenvalue problems more efficiently.

- Affinity propagation: the damping value (λ) was set to 0.75. The preference value for this case study was set to five times the minimum input similarity to find an appropriate number of clusters. Input similarities were precalculated using the `euclidean_distances` function.

- Gaussian mixture model: the covariance type was set to full, and for the initialization we use K-means.

In order to check the behavior of the algorithms when the number of clusters changes, the algorithms were executed with the value K set as 3, 5, and 7. This selection of K values is not applicable for the affinity propagation algorithm as explained in Section 5.3.4.

To visually inspect the clustering behavior of the 36 variables in a 2-D space and effectively analyze the effect of K, we ran multidimensional scaling (Section 2.2.1.3).

5.4 Results and Discussion

As shown in Fig. 5.6 – 5.8, the 2D representation of the 36 servomotor variables is highly concentrated in a very definite region, there being hardly any outliers. Intuitively, this result is important for validation, because it clearly denotes the behavior of high-quality brand new servomotors, based on which a pattern can be built.

TABLE 5.5

X-axis servomotor cluster centroids

Cluster	P (W)	T (°C)	$A_{FTF}(g)$	$A_{\text{shaft}}(g)$	$A_{BSF}(g)$	$A_{BPFO}(g)$	$A_{BPFI}(g)$
0	4.5	36.3	0.0003	0.0014	0.0009	0.0004	0.0005
1	23.3	35.6	0.0003	0.0014	0.0009	0.0005	0.0005
2	20.3	38.0	0.0004	0.0012	0.0009	0.0004	0.0005

Point clouds shown in Fig 5.6 – 5.8 may be referred to as the servomotor MDS-fingerprint, which represents how good their test cycle performance is with respect to each of their variables. Larger point distances to the cluster would denote anomalous servomotors. The distance threshold must be defined after sufficient testing with more servomotors that have the same reference. Nevertheless, this approach is outside the scope of this chapter.

After running the five clustering algorithms, we found that the cluster shapes are similar regardless of the algorithm. Within the denser data region in particular, there are three predominant clusters with a definite shape and distribution showing three different servomotor behaviors.

From the engineering point of view, these three behaviors could be directly related to the servomotor states during operation: idle, acceleration/deceleration and constant speed. Therefore, these three behaviors are defined as servomotor clusters.

However, the differences between centroids are more noticeable even if they are in the same area. K-means and agglomerative algorithms show similarities for some K values. The spectral clustering and GMM centroid positions for $K = 3$ are similar too. Nevertheless, centroids are concentrated in the middle of the instance cloud.

For affinity propagation, the algorithm automatically detects nine different clusters using the parameters described in Section 5.3.6. Shapes and centroid positions are similar, but this algorithm is highly parameter sensitive, where small changes to parameters may cause radically different results, especially, with respect to preference.

We selected $K = 3$ and the agglomerative algorithm to illustrate the analysis of the clustering results in order to study the behavior of each servomotor. Additionally, power consumption and shaft vibration were the variables selected for this purpose. Both variables provided interesting information about motor performance. However, other combinations could be selected depending on needs.

Results are shown in Fig. 5.9, where red (Cluster 0), green (Cluster 1) and blue (Cluster 2) clusters stand for different levels of power, validating the three servomotor clusters detected using the MDS.

For further analysis, centroid coordinates are shown in Tables 5.5 – 5.7. Analyzing each of the three clusters, we find that:

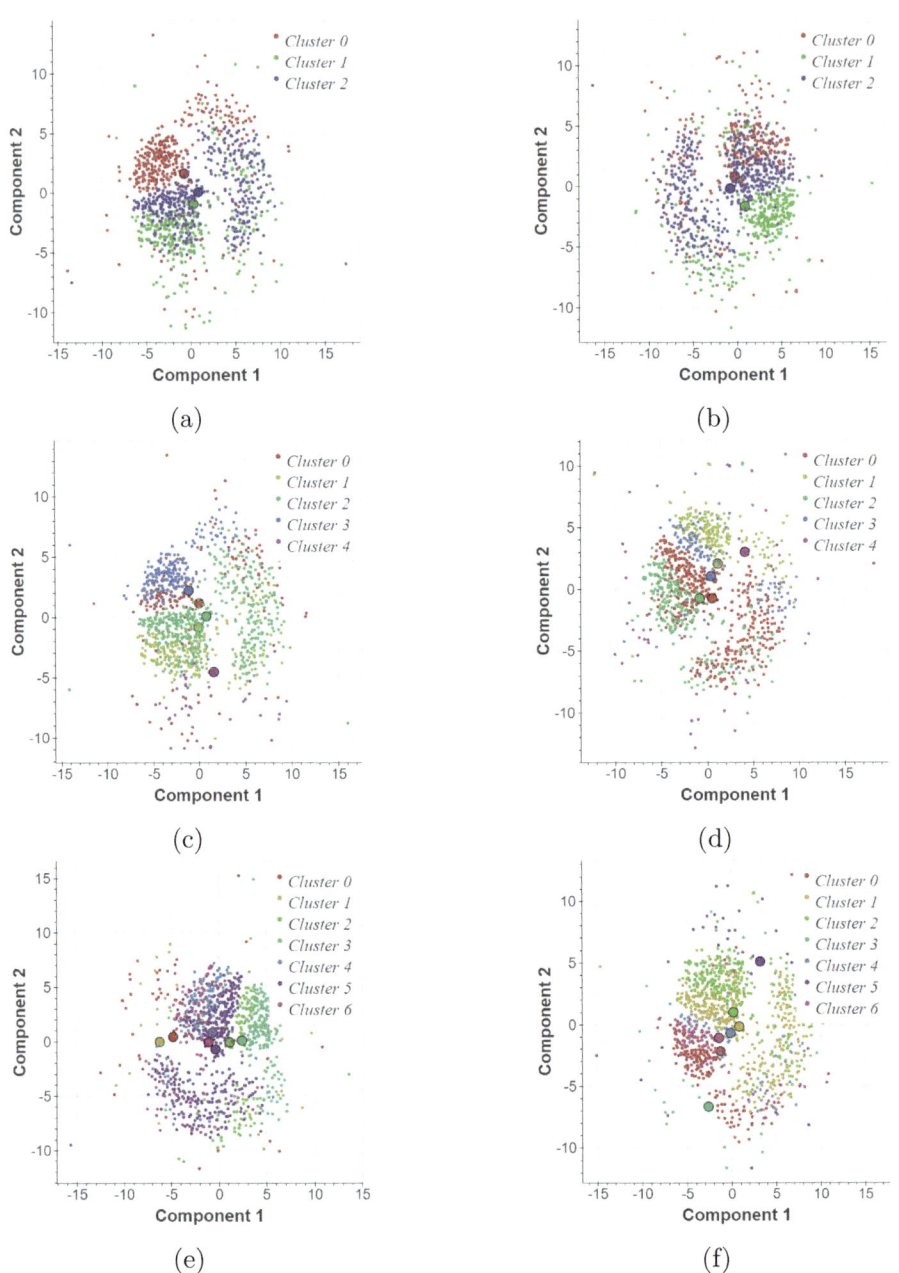

FIGURE 5.6
MDS for agglomerative hierarchical and K-means algorithm with different values of K. (a) Agglomerative with $K = 3$. (b) K-means with $K = 3$. (c) Agglomerative with $K = 5$. (d) K-means with $K = 5$. (e) Agglomerative with $K = 7$. (f) K-means with $K = 7$.

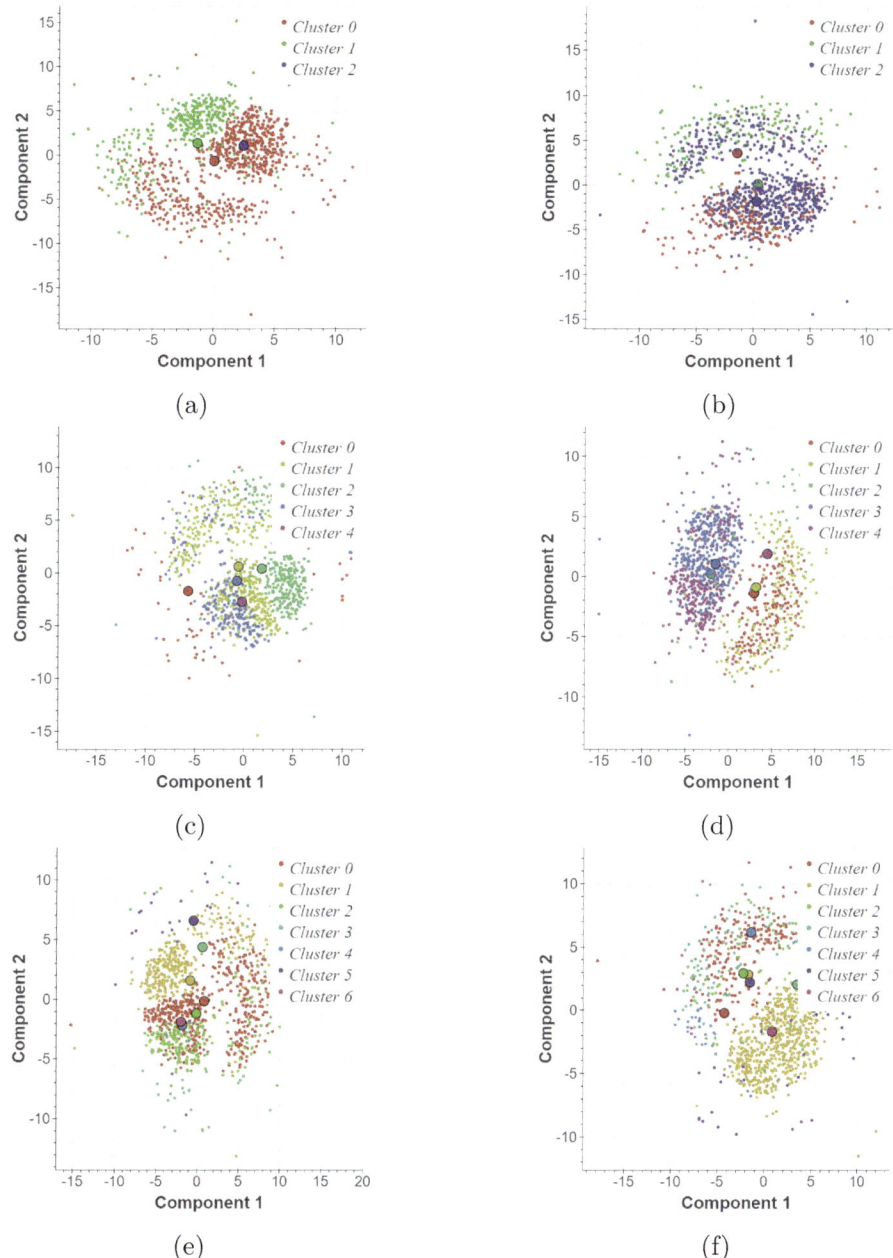

FIGURE 5.7
MDS for spectral clustering and GMM algorithm with different values of K.
(a) Spectral clustering with $K = 3$. (b) GMM with $K = 3$. (c) Spectral
clustering with $K = 5$. (d) GMM with $K = 5$. (e) Spectral clustering with
$K = 7$. (f) GMM with $K = 7$.

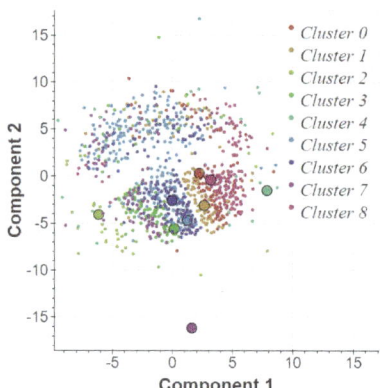

FIGURE 5.8
MDS for affinity propagation algorithm.

TABLE 5.6
Y-axis servomotor cluster centroids

Cluster	P (W)	T (°C)	$A_{FTF}(g)$	$A_{\text{shaft}}(g)$	$A_{BSF}(g)$	$A_{BPFO}(g)$	$A_{BPFI}(g)$
0	5.41	36.6	0.0002	0.0022	0.0052	0.0004	0.0030
1	32.8	38.6	0.0002	0.0023	0.0050	0.0004	0.0029
2	21.1	36.9	0.0002	0.0018	0.0045	0.0003	0.0026

TABLE 5.7
Z-axis servomotor cluster centroids

Cluster	P (W)	T (°C)	$A_{FTF}(g)$	$A_{\text{shaft}}(g)$	$A_{BSF}(g)$	$A_{BPFO}(g)$	$A_{BPFI}(g)$
0	4.6	33.4	0.0002	0.0022	0.0058	0.0008	0.0023
1	24.1	32.8	0.0002	0.0023	0.0057	0.0008	0.0022
2	21.6	34.7	0.0002	0.0018	0.0050	0.0007	0.0020

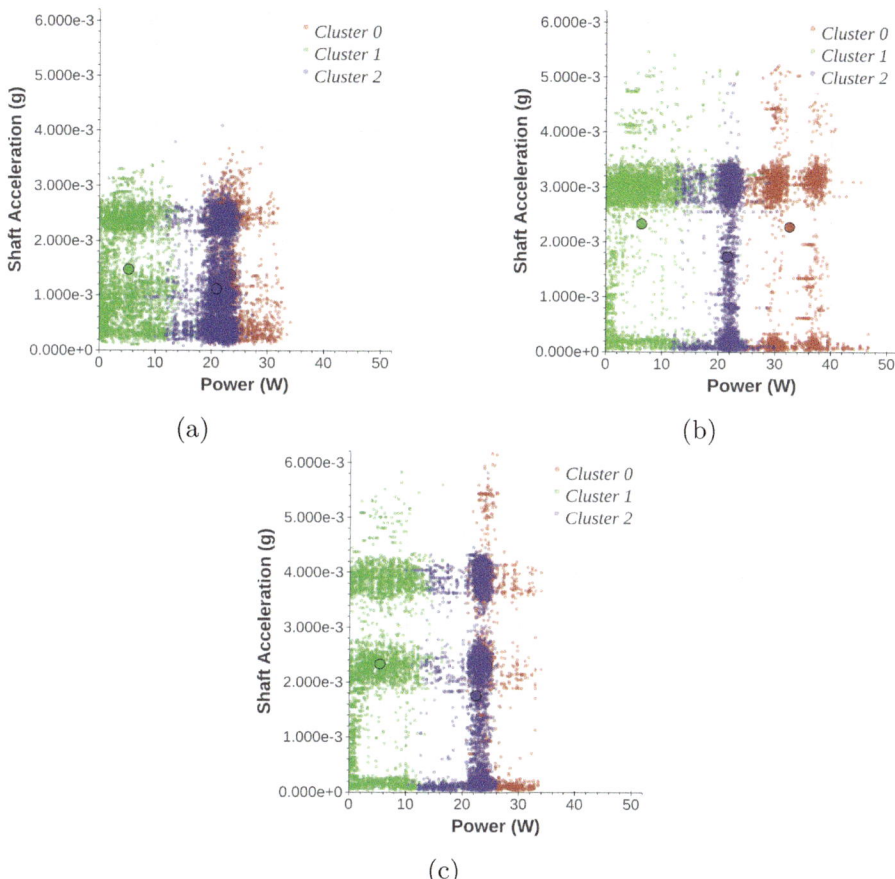

(a)

(b)

(c)

FIGURE 5.9
Power vs. shaft vibration. (a) X-axis servomotor. (b) Y-axis servomotor. (c) Z-axis servomotor.

- Cluster 0 represents low levels of power, ranging from 0 to 10 W with a centroid between 4.4 and 5.4 W. This means that this cluster is related to the idle class, where the motors are stopped and power consumption is at the minimum. Power is not 0 W as expected because servomotors need power to stay in the same position. The values of vibration are sparser for the X-axis servomotor than for the other servomotors. Stronger shaft vibration is found in Y and Z servos with centroids at 22 mg.

- Cluster 1 represents high levels of power, and it is prominent in the Y-axis servomotor. Therefore, this cluster is related to the constant speed class, as it needs maximum power to perform the operation. The starting point is near 25 W. The maximum for the Y-axis servomotor is 48 W, meaning that this servomotor needs more power to perform the same operation. Centroids for power are completely different, namely, 33 W for the Y-axis and 23 W – 24 W for the X- and Z-axis servomotors. However, shaft vibration is the same for the Y-axis and Z-axis servos.

- Cluster 2 instances are around 20 W, at which point this cluster is clearly distinct. From 10 W to 15 W, values are confused with Cluster 0. This cluster is related to the acceleration/deceleration class, having mid-range power with some sporadic peaks that are necessary to switch from the idle state and overcome the inertia of the servomotor internal parts. Centroids are similar, although there are differences in vibration values for the X-axis servomotor. Vibration is only sparse when power is around 20 W.

Therefore, the cluster shapes and centroids are able to leverage new information about the system under analysis, that is, cluster shapes represent the fingerprint of the servomotor in a specific state: idle, constant speed and acceleration/deceleration, and centroids denote the mean operating values within the cluster. Any differences in terms of shape and centroid could be defined as an anomaly requiring inspection to define the root cause.

As explained by Diaz-Rozo et al. (2017), the shapes and centroids could represent knowledge discovery in terms of the internal behavior of the parts. In this case, the GMM algorithm was the most significant in terms of new knowledge as spindles were analyzed during metal cutting. However, for this use case aimed at analyzing the fingerprints of each servomotor, algorithms like K-means or hierarchical agglomerative clustering provide an expert with sufficient information.

For example, a comparison between servomotor fingerprints can yield information about the X-axis servomotor behavior, which has less vibration and consumes less power than the others. Shaft vibration can provide information about shaft unbalance or buckling. However, an increase in power consumption on top of shaft vibration could be a sign of a shaft and ball bearing misalignment for the Y- and Z-axis servomotors. Such a misalignment is not critical in this case, as the servomotors have the required nominal performance. However, this difference could be critical when the servomotor reaches 80% of its useful life, as the misalignment could evolve into an premature degradation.

5.5 Conclusions and Future Research

5.5.1 Conclusions

As described in the experimental results of this case study, clustering techniques are useful for detecting behavior patterns or fingerprints at machine level. In this case, we analyzed three brand new servomotors with the same reference, showing that, even if they are theoretically identical, there are important differences between the servos and that these differences will grow during operation due to degradation.

Finding patterns that can help to develop a general fingerprint of the part would be useful for benchmarking the component status prior to installation. We studied servomotors, but this procedure could be applied to analyze more critical parts, for example, machining spindles, pumps and many other components.

This case study found that the agglomerative hierarchical algorithm was the most efficient algorithm, and this algorithm provided more interpretable results from the engineering point of view. However, there are other potential options, like K-means (the fastest algorithm in terms of processing time) or Gaussian mixture models that could possibly yield robust results.

5.5.2 Future Research

Clustering algorithms are highly applicable in this type of analysis requiring the use of a fingerprint behavior pattern as a benchmark, because they are not hard to implement. However, they require extensive testing beforehand for the purpose of algorithm tuning. Additionally, some algorithms are parameter sensitive, and it is important to gain thorough knowledge of their role.

Besides, clustering algorithms need predefined configuration parameters, for example, number of clusters. In this case, knowledge of component behavior (e.g., idle, acceleration/deceleration, constant speed) has to be gathered from experience. Therefore, clustering algorithm exploration capabilities like unsupervised learning have to be supplemented by expert opinions to ensure useful knowledge discovery.

6

Production-Level Case Study: Automated Visual Inspection of a Laser Process

6.1 Introduction

One of the main opportunities that machine learning offers to the smart factories of the future is the possibility of analyzing large amounts of data output by manufacturing activities while they are underway. The outcome of this analysis will be to identify patterns enabling the detection of unwanted situations and anomalies in industrial processes. The aim is to improve production quality by automatically pinpointing possibly defective manufactured products for their immediate set aside and revision as soon as they have been produced and before the end of the manufacturing process. This is known as **in-process** quality control.

Although visual inspection and quality control were traditionally performed by human experts, **automated visual inspection** (**AVI**) systems are being studied and used more and more often in manufacturing processes in order to enhance automation (Golnabi and Asadpour, 2007). Malamas et al. (2003) noted that, even though they are better than machines at visual inspection and quality control in many situations, human experts are slower, get tired, are inconsistent, are unable to simultaneously account for a lot of variables, and are hard to find, train and maintain. Additionally, there are very demanding situations in manufacturing caused by fast or repetitive analysis requirements or hazardous environments where computer vision may effectively replace human inspection.

In typical industrial AVI systems like the one shown in Fig. 6.1, a fixed camera (or several cameras) with sufficient illumination captures images of a scene under inspection. These raw images are then preprocessed to remove noise, background or unwanted reflections. At this point, a set of features containing key information, such as the size, position or contour of objects, or specific measurements of certain regions, are extracted from the preprocessed images. These features are known in advance, and the position of the camera and the illumination of the scene are arranged in order to optimize their perception. Machine learning techniques are then applied in order to analyze the extracted features and make decisions that are communicated to the manufacturing process control systems for their execution. The feature extraction and analysis

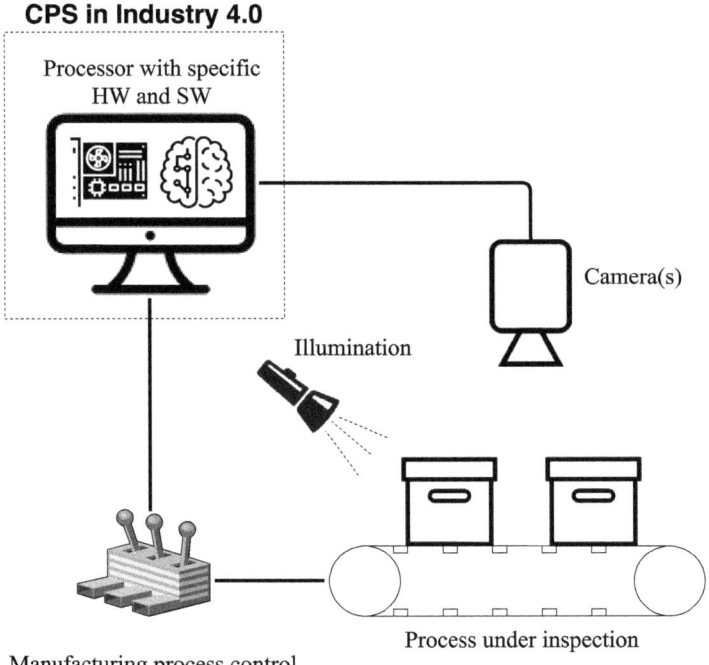

FIGURE 6.1
Typical industrial AVI system.

tasks are performed with software (SW) built ad-hoc for specific applications because no industrial machine vision system is capable of performing all analysis tasks in every application field (Malamas et al., 2003). The software is also programmed in application-specific hardware (HW), such as digital signal processors, application-specific integrated circuits, or FPGAs, capable of operating in highly time constrained and computationally intensive processes. In smart factories, these specialized processors will be the heart of the CPS.

In this case study, we report an AVI system for the in-process quality control of the laser **surface heat treatment** of steel cylinders[1]. Several works have highlighted how inspection methods can be based on the output of the monitoring of laser processes with high-speed thermal cameras, since the recorded emissions provide information about the stability and dynamics of the process (Alippi et al., 2001; Jäger et al., 2008; Atienza et al., 2016; Ogbechie et al., 2017). Thus, any anomalous sequences that are recorded are related to defects during the laser surface heating process.

In the construction of the AVI system, however, we found that the only available examples were from correctly processed cylinders. This scenario is very common in manufacturing inspection applications because significant aberrations rarely occur in efficient industrial processes (Timusk et al., 2008). This makes it difficult to train automated systems that rely on statistical learning because they require datasets with examples of faulty situations, balanced, whenever possible, against examples of normal conditions (Jäger et al., 2008; Surace and Worden, 2010). When errors have not been reported during the training stage, the classification task of discerning between normal and anomalous products can be performed using **one-class classification**. One-class classification is an anomaly detection technique used in machine learning to solve binary classification problems when all the labeled examples belong to one of the classes (Chandola et al., 2009).

Additionally, a requirement that is in growing demand in real-life problems is to have interpretable machine learning models. Here, good model accuracy is not enough: the model and its operation have to be understandable and the outcomes and the patterns learned by the machine to yield those outcomes have to have an explanation. With this meaningful model, decision makers will have a reliable tool for making their choices. In summary, following the color-coded levels of interpretability proposed by Sjöberg et al. (1995), we should steer clear of blackbox models (Section 2.1) and look for more transparent, so-called **gray-box**, models capable of providing an interpretation of what the machine has automatically learned from data. At the other end of the scale, we have **white-box** models that are based purely on prior theoretical knowledge (like a system of differential equations). They are useful only in very controlled and constrained scenarios.

In order to meet the interpretability requirement, we also aim in this case study to test if the automatically learned model is capable of capturing the

---

[1]An exhaustive description of the laser process is given in Gabilondo et al. (2015).

physical characteristics and spatio-temporal patterns of the laser process under normal conditions. This particular approach to interpretability is consistent with the decomposability level of transparency introduced by Lipton (2016), where each part of the model should have an intuitive explanation. Note that this means that the model inputs should also be individually interpretable, ruling out the use of highly engineered or anonymous features. This is a common drawback of gray-box models since they empower model introspection often at the expense of prediction accuracy.

The chapter is organized as follows. Section 6.2 introduces the laser surface heat treatment process and explains the methods used to acquire the image sequences. Section 6.3 describes the machine learning strategy applied to build the AVI system capable of analyzing these image sequences and automatically performing in-process quality control. The performance assessment of the AVI system is reported and discussed in Section 6.4. This section also thoroughly describes the spatio-temporal relationships of the laser process deduced from the machine learning model. Finally, Section 6.5 summarizes the main conclusions and future directions.

6.2   Laser Surface Heat Treatment

A common requirement in industry is to modify the surface mechanical properties of steel workpieces to meet production process or final application requirements. These modifications are achieved through heat treatments that are based on applying heating and cooling cycles to the steel workpieces. There are two different types of heat treatments depending on how fast these cycles are enacted: annealing and hardening. Annealing is characterized by a slow cooling rate of the material resulting in a softer material. In contrast, hardening applies a fast cooling rate that produces martensite formation, strengthening the material, but making it brittler. The time-temperature-transformation curve (**TTT curve**) illustrated in Fig. 6.2 shows a possible cooling trajectory of a hardening heat treatment. First of all, the steel has to be heated to a temperature that is high enough (approximately 800°C) to convert it into the austenite phase. Then the material is quenched by cooling it fast enough to avoid the nose of the TTT curve, passing from the austenite to the martensite phase.

A certain amount of energy has to be applied to the material in order to reach the required temperature in the austenitizing step. This is normally carried out in gas or electric furnaces. However, if the heat treatment has to be applied selectively, e.g., only to the surface of the steel workpiece, some other energy sources can be used: flame, induction, high-frequency resistance, electron beam or laser beam. Electron and laser beams are capable of heating small and localized areas. The main difference between the two technologies is

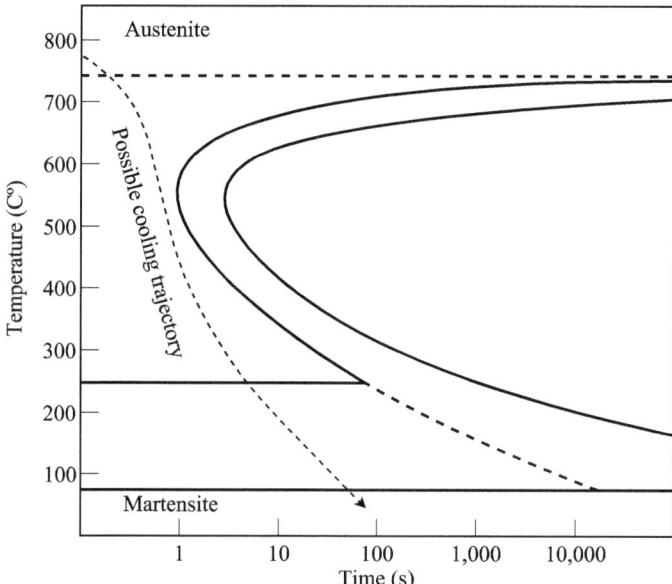

FIGURE 6.2
TTT curve with a possible cooling trajectory of a hardening process.

the cost. On the one hand, electron beam needs an inert gas atmosphere with a relatively small process chamber and expensive peripheral equipment. On the other hand, laser beam is able to work without any special atmospheric requirement, and is a very promising technology for industrial applications.

Even though the dynamics of thermal processes are relatively slow, electron and laser beam are high-density energy sources that induce fast heating-cooling cycles. For this reason, high-speed thermal cameras that record the generated radiation are the key technology used to monitor these processes. Thus, as a result of the combination of fast cycles, requiring data collection in short sampling times and thermal cameras that provide multidimensional data, an AVI system for a beam-based heat treatment will have to analyze large amounts of information. This increases the computational power required by the system and jeopardizes its capability of providing on-time feedback. CPSs are able to handle this situation because of their embedded processing capabilities (Baheti and Gill, 2011).

6.2.1   Image Acquisition

The case study dataset was gathered during a real experiment carried out by (Diaz et al., 2016) on January 2016, recording the laser surface heat treatment of 32 steel cylinders. Fig. 6.3 illustrates the experiment in which a steel cylinder rotated on its own axis while its surface was hit by a laser beam. This produced a **heat-affected zone** (HAZ) on the surface of the cylinder that was monitored by a fixed thermal camera. The camera used in the experiment was a high-speed thermal camera with a recording rate of 1,000 frames per second and a region of interest of 32 × 32 pixels, each of which could have 1,024 different colors (10 bits per pixel) proportional to the temperature reading. The field of view of the images was approximately 350 mm^2, while the area of the laser beam spot was 3 mm^2. This moved along the cylinder width, producing a 200 mm^2 HAZ. One full rotation of the surface of each cylinder took 21.5 seconds. Therefore, sequences of 21,500 frames were output for each processed cylinder.

A sample image of the HAZ produced during the normal process is shown in Fig. 6.4(a), where the laser spot is noticeable at the top right of the image (green circle). The spot was programmed to move along the steel surface according to a pattern, as represented in Fig. 6.4(b). This pattern was repeated at a frequency of 100 Hz. Therefore, the camera captured approximately 10 frames per cycle.

Nevertheless, sequence analysis was subject to other difficulties because the process was not stationary. On the one hand, there was a two-second (2,000-frame) thermal transient at the beginning of the process until the HAZ reached a high enough temperature because the cylinders were initially at room temperature (see Fig. 6.4(c)). On the other hand, the spot pattern was modified for approximately four seconds (4,000 frames) in order to avoid an obstacle on the surface of the steel cylinders. The pattern variants are shown in Fig. 6.5.

During the experiment, no anomalies were detected in the 32 processed cylinders, and they were considered normal. This is very common in mass-production industries, where machines are expected to manufacture thousands of error-free workpieces every day without stopping. For this reason, experts decided to simulate two different defects in the 32 normal sequences in order to assess the response of the AVI system to anomalies[2]:

- Defect in the laser power supply unit (negative offset): The laser scanner control was in charge of adjusting the energy that the beam deposited on the HAZ. A failure in the power supply unit could prevent a high enough temperature from being reached to correctly treat the surface of the steel cylinders. This was simulated by introducing a negative offset on the pixel values. The value of the negative offset was set first to 3.5% and then to 4% of the pixel value range (36 and 41 units, respectively).

- Camera sensor wear (noise): The camera was operating in dirty conditions due to heat, sparks and smoke that gradually stained or deteriorated the sensors, producing noise. This situation was simulated by adding Gaussian noise centered on the real pixel values. The standard deviation of this noise was set to 2.5% of the pixel value range (26 units).

---

[2]The percentages selected for simulating defects in the correctly processed steel cylinders are justified in Section 6.4.1.

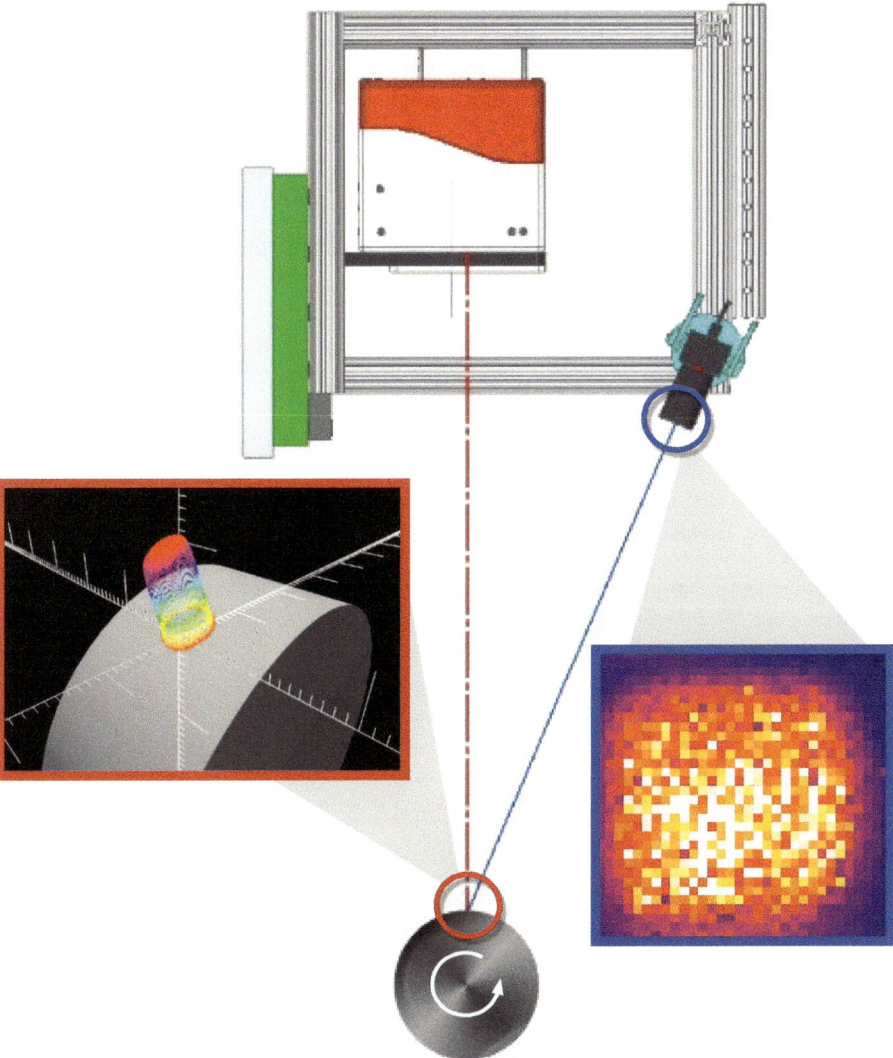

FIGURE 6.3
The diagram shows the physical arrangement of the different elements used to carry out and monitor the laser surface heat treatment of the steel cylinders (Diaz et al., 2016). The laser beam (dashed-red line) hits the surface of the rotating steel cylinder. The area of the laser beam spot was smaller than the width of the cylinder. Therefore, it moved very fast according to a predefined pattern in order to heat the whole surface of the cylinder. This movement produced a heat-affected zone (HAZ) that was recorded by a fixed high-speed thermal camera (blue continuous line).

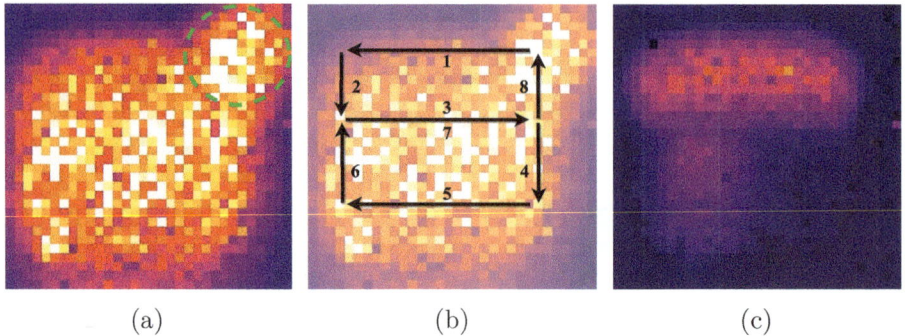

(a)   (b)   (c)

FIGURE 6.4
(a) An illustrative frame taken from the HAZ by the high-speed thermal camera during the laser process. (b) The pattern that the spot traced to produce the HAZ in normal conditions as defined by Gabilondo et al. (2015) in the U.S. patent property of Etxe-Tar, S.A. The numbers indicate the order in which the different segments of the pattern were formed. (c) Thermal transient in the HAZ at the beginning of the process.

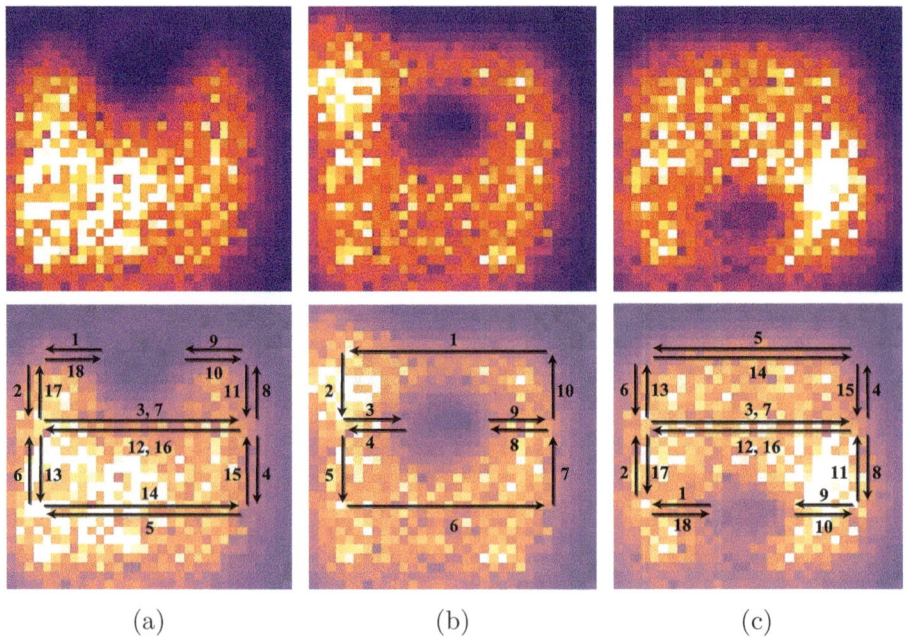

(a)   (b)   (c)

FIGURE 6.5
During the heat treatment, the spot was programmed to avoid an obstacle on the surface of the cylinders. There were three different variants of the spot movement pattern depending on the position of the obstacle, namely, when it was at the top (a), in the middle (b) or at the bottom (c) of the HAZ.

6.2.2   Response Time Requirement

Experts defined the in-process response time required for this application as three seconds, since this was the minimum time required by the production process to be prepared for the next manufacturing step.

6.3   Anomaly Detection-Based AVI System

Anomaly detection is the branch of machine learning in charge of solving the problem of finding patterns in data that do not correspond with an expected **normal behavior**. Chandola et al. (2009) remarked that these patterns are commonly named differently depending on the application domain. Some examples are outliers, discordant observations, exceptions, aberrations, surprises, peculiarities or contaminations. Anomaly detection is very similar to **novelty detection** and both are often used indistinctly. But, even if the techniques used are common in both tasks, they have a subtle difference: the patterns discovered in novelty detection do not have to be related necessarily with a negative situation in the system, but an evolution of its normal behavior (Pimentel et al., 2014).

Anomaly detection problems are characterized by having **unbalanced** training datasets where the normal behavior is well sampled while anomalies are severely under-sampled (being rare or even non-existent). The classification problems that arise are illustrated in Fig. 6.6 with a two-dimensional dataset in the feature space. Fig. 6.6(a) shows a multiclass classification problem where the three normal behaviors are represented with the following class labels $(C = c_1, C = c_2, C = c_3)$. Meanwhile, Fig. 6.6(b) shows a one-class classification problem where the normal behavior is represented with only one label $(C = c_1)$. The objective of both problems is to distinguish anomalies $(\mathbf{a}_i)$ from the normal behavior. However, in multiclass problems it is necessary to determine the type of normal behavior of an observation, while one-class classification is a binary classification problem. In any case, the classification task implies using the training observations for finding a boundary that separates the different classes in the best possible way within the space of the features that characterize the system. Then, the model learned is used for classifying test instances within one of the possible classes.

Pimentel et al. (2014) pointed out that one-class classification scenarios are frequent in critical applications, such as fault detection in space crafts, fraud detection of credit cards, intrusion in computer networks, healthcare diseases, etc. In these situations, it is highly expensive and difficult to get samples from the failures of the systems (He and Garcia, 2009). So, the classification framework is based on learning a **model of normality** from the available normal training data. This model is then used for assigning an **anomaly**

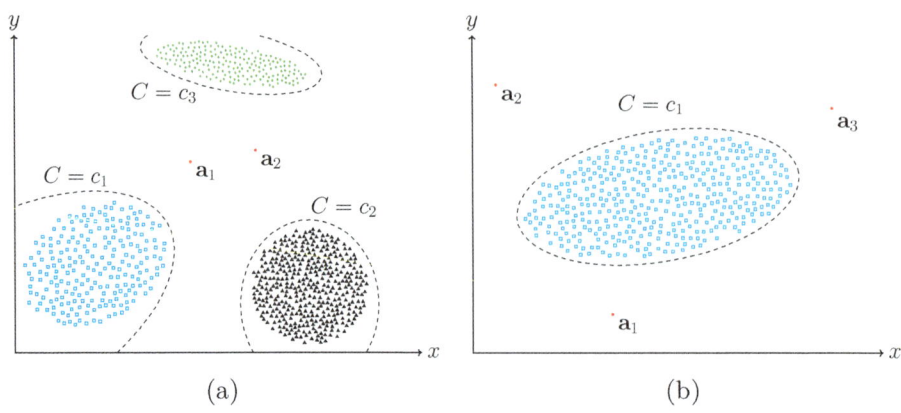

FIGURE 6.6

Example of anomalies ($\mathbf{a}_i$) and normal instances grouped by its corresponding class labels ($C = c_i$) in a two-dimensional dataset. We can distinguish the multiclass classification (a) and the one-class classification (b) scenarios.

score to new unseen test data, where a large anomaly score means a higher degree of "anomaly" with respect to the normality model. Finally, an **anomaly threshold** has to be defined for establishing the decision boundary, such that new examples are classified as "anomalous" if its anomaly score is higher than the anomaly threshold, or "normal" otherwise.

6.3.1 Anomaly Detection Algorithms in Image Processing

Anomaly detection is useful in image processing when we are interested in finding any changes in an image sequence along a period of time or noticing areas of a static image which seem to be anomalous. Chandola et al. (2009) noted that in this situation anomalies are usually produced by motion or insertion of foreign objects or instrumentation errors, requiring to consider both the spatial and temporal characteristics of the images. However, one of the main issues when dealing with images is that they are normally a large size input, since images are made of a big number of pixels. From each pixel several continuous attributes such as color, lightness and texture can be extracted.

According to Pimentel et al. (2014) extracting novel data from video streams is becoming more and more important because of the current availability of large amounts of data, and because of the lack of automated methods for extracting important details from such media. In this section we review the main machine learning techniques used for building anomaly detection systems within image processing applications. They can be divided into four different groups, namely, probabilistic, distance-based, reconstruction-based and domain-based anomaly detection techniques (Pimentel et al., 2014).

6.3.1.1 Probabilistic Anomaly Detection

Probabilistic anomaly detection is based on building a statistical model that represents the underlying probability density function of data in normal conditions. Thus, anomalies are identified in terms of their low probability of being generated by the normality model. This requires to define a threshold, that is often a difficult task.

We can distinguish two different types of probabilistic anomaly detection, namely, parametric and non-parametric approaches. The former assume that the probabilistic distribution of the normal data is generated by a known underlying parametric distribution. Furthermore, after having the normality model, only a small amount of information has to be kept instead of requiring the storage of the complete training dataset. This assumption could produce a very important bias when the presupposed model does not actually fit the data. In contrast, non-parametric approaches are more flexible since they do not make any assumption about the probabilistic distribution of the data, but estimate it directly. However, in both cases the models tend to grow in size for accommodating the complexity of the data, requiring large training datasets for estimating the free parameters.

Parametric approaches

State-space models are often used for carrying out anomaly detection when dealing with time-series data, being hidden Markov models (HMMs) (see Section 2.6.3) one of the most common approaches. Anomaly detection with HMMs has been normally performed by establishing a threshold to the likelihood of an observation sequence giving the normality model (Yeung and Ding, 2003), or by defining explicitly an "anomalous" state in the HMM (Smyth, 1994). For example, in Jäger et al. (2008) HMMs were used for detecting unusual events in image sequences recorded from an industrial laser welding process.

Non-parametric approaches

The most used non-parametric technique in anomaly detection is **kernel density estimators (KDEs)** that build the probability density function of the normal behavior of a system by placing (typically Gaussian) kernels on each data point and aggregating them. For example, in Atienza et al. (2016) KDEs were used for detecting anomalies in a laser surface heat treatment recorded with a high-speed thermal camera by tracking the movement of the laser beam spot.

6.3.1.2 Distance-Based Anomaly Detection

Distance-based methods assume that normal data are grouped compactly in particular spatial regions of the space of features, while anomalous cases appear far from these groups. Under this premise, anomaly detection relies on the definition of a distance metric capable of assessing correctly how similar test instances and normal groups are. We can distinguish two different types of distance-based anomaly detection approaches, namely, nearest neighbors (Section 2.4.3) and clustering (Section 2.3) approaches.

Nearest neighbors approaches

The most used technique is k-nearest neighbors (k-NN) that calculates the distance (normally Euclidean) of a data point to its k-nearest neighbors. This should be small if the point was to be considered as "normal" and high otherwise (Zhang and Wang, 2006). However, the k-nearest neighbors have to be found first, requiring to store the complete training dataset. Additionally, in high-dimensional problems it is complex to compute the distance metric between a point and its neighbors considering all the space of features, so heuristic functions should be employed for considering only a reduced subspace. Additionally, the selection of the parameter k and the anomaly threshold are also critical in this kind of approach. More concretely, for establishing the anomaly threshold in problems where the data points are distributed heterogeneously in the space of attributes it is necessary to use density-based schemes, such as local outlier factor (LOF) algorithm (Breunig et al., 2000), that take into account the data local properties. LOF was used in Pokrajac et al. (2007) for finding unusual trajectories in surveillance videos.

Clustering approaches

Clustering algorithms characterize the normal behavior of a system with a reduced number of prototype points in the space of attributes. Then, the distance of a test instance to its nearest prototype helps to discriminate if it is a "normal" or an "anomalous" point. The different clustering-based algorithms differ in how they define these prototypes, being K-means the most used algorithm for data streams. An advantage of clustering-based algorithms is that they only require to store the information of the prototype points rather than the complete training dataset. Additionally, they allow to build incremental models where new data points could constitute a new cluster or can change the properties of existing prototypes. However, as in nearest neighbors approaches, clustering algorithms suffer with high-dimensional data and their performance highly depends on the proper selection of the number of clusters. In Zeng et al. (2008) a clustering-based algorithm was used in order to extract key-frames from news, entertainment, home and sports videos.

6.3.1.3 Reconstruction-Based Anomaly Detection

Reconstruction techniques are capable of modeling in a flexible and autonomous way a regression model from the training dataset. From the point of view of anomaly detection, reconstruction-based approaches learn the normality model from input data and use it later on for contrasting it against new test instances in order to identify outliers, which show a large reconstruction error, i.e, there is a wide distance between the test instance and the output generated by the model. It is important to note that reconstruction-based techniques rely on several parameters that define the structure of the model and need to be very carefully optimized, since solutions are very sensitive to them.

Artificial neural networks (Section 2.4.6) are the most used reconstruction-based models and they have been successfully applied to numerous anomaly detection applications (Markou and Singh, 2003). For example, in Markou and Singh (2006) a novelty detection method based on artificial neural networks was used for analyzing image sequences. Additionally, authors like Newman and Jain (1995) or Malamas et al. (2003) have noticed that artificial neural networks are very appropriate for AVI applications. A recent example can be found in Sun et al. (2016) where artificial neural networks were employed for inspecting automatically thermal fuse images.

6.3.1.4 Domain-Based Anomaly Detection

Domain-based methods create a boundary around the normal training data, building a normal domain. One of the key peculiarities of these kinds of approaches is that they are known to be "insensitive" to the specific sampling and density of the target class (Pimentel et al., 2014). Then, for classifying a new test instance they only consider its location with respect to the normal domain. An advantage of domain-based models is that they only require to store the training data in charge of defining the boundary region. However, it is complicated to select the adequate parameters that define the size of this boundary region.

The most popular domain-based methods for anomaly detection are the ones based on support vector machines (SVMs) (see Section 2.4.7) (Cortes and Vapnik, 1995), namely, one-class SVMs (Schölkopf et al., 2000) and support vector data description (Tax and Duin, 1999). For example Diehl and Hampshire (2002) proposed a classification framework based on SVMs for aiding users to detect anomalies in the behavior of people or cars from surveillance videos. Additionally, authors like Huang and Pan (2015) have noticed that SVMs provide very good results in AVI applications for the semiconductor industry. Xie et al. (2014) proposed an optical inspection technique that used SVMs for detecting and identifying common defects in noisy images from printed circuit boards and semiconductor wafers.

6.3.2 Proposed Methodology

The AVI system proposed was composed of a classification framework for analyzing the recorded image sequences of the laser surface heat treatment of steel cylinders and deciding in an in-process manner whether or not new unseen sequences were correctly processed. However, as already mentioned, only examples of error-free sequences were available during the training phase.

In this situation, one-class classification can be used. This consists of modeling the normal behavior of the process from the available normal sequences and then identifying whether new unseen sequences differ significantly from the learned normal condition.

Fig. 6.7 illustrates a schematic flowchart of the proposed anomaly detection-based AVI system. The first step was to preprocess the image sequences to extract a reduced number of features in order to accurately represent the normal behavior of the stochastic process. This dimension reduction step is crucial in computer vision since images are high-dimensional data. However, this feature subset selection (Section 2.4.2) must respect the variable interpretability so as to maintain model transparency. This is why we ruled out highly engineered feature extraction techniques commonly used in computer vision, such as PCA (Section 2.2.1.3). The details of how the feature subset selection was implemented are reported in Section 6.3.2.1.

The features extracted from the training sequences were used to represent the normal behavior of the process. We have seen in Section 6.3.1 the most extended techniques in the literature used for learning the normal behavior of temporal systems. HMMs are according to Barber and Cemgil (2010), the most used probabilistic graphical models for modeling time series. However, HMMs use hidden variables that are not physically meaningful. Therefore, we proposed the use of dynamic Bayesian networks (DBNs), see Section 2.6.2 (Dean and Kanazawa, 1989). DBNs are a generalization of HMMs and the natural temporal extension of Bayesian networks (BNs), which are known to provide an interpretable representation of uncertain knowledge (Friedman et al., 2000; Koller and Friedman, 2009). In fact, DBNs have already been proved to successfully describe the spatio-temporal relationships of monitored stochastic systems in different domains without the use of hidden variables, e.g., in neuroscience for learning the temporal connections of brain regions (Rajapakse and Zhou, 2007), in bioinformatics for inferring the interactions of DNA microarrays (Husmeier, 2003), or in engineering for detecting faults in autonomous spacecraft (Codetta-Raiteri and Portinale, 2015). More details about DBN implementation are given in Section 6.3.2.2.

After learning the normality model, we detected image sequences with anomalies in terms of how far removed they were from normal sequences, measured, in anomaly detection with the anomaly score. Pimentel et al. (2014) noted that a common choice for this score in probabilistic methods is the log-likelihood $\log \mathcal{L}(\mathbf{o}|M)$ of an observation $\mathbf{o}$ (in this case an image sequence) with respect to the normality model M. The likelihood $\mathcal{L}(\mathbf{o}|M)$ represents the probability of observing $\mathbf{o}$ given M, and the logarithm scale transformation is used to deal with very small probabilities. In summary, the log-likelihood is a negative value that tends to zero for very probable examples and to minus infinity for very unlikely examples. Therefore, we used the negative of the log-likelihood as the anomaly score:

$$\mathrm{AS}(\mathbf{o}) = -\log \mathcal{L}(\mathbf{o}|M) = -\log p(\mathbf{o}|M). \tag{6.1}$$

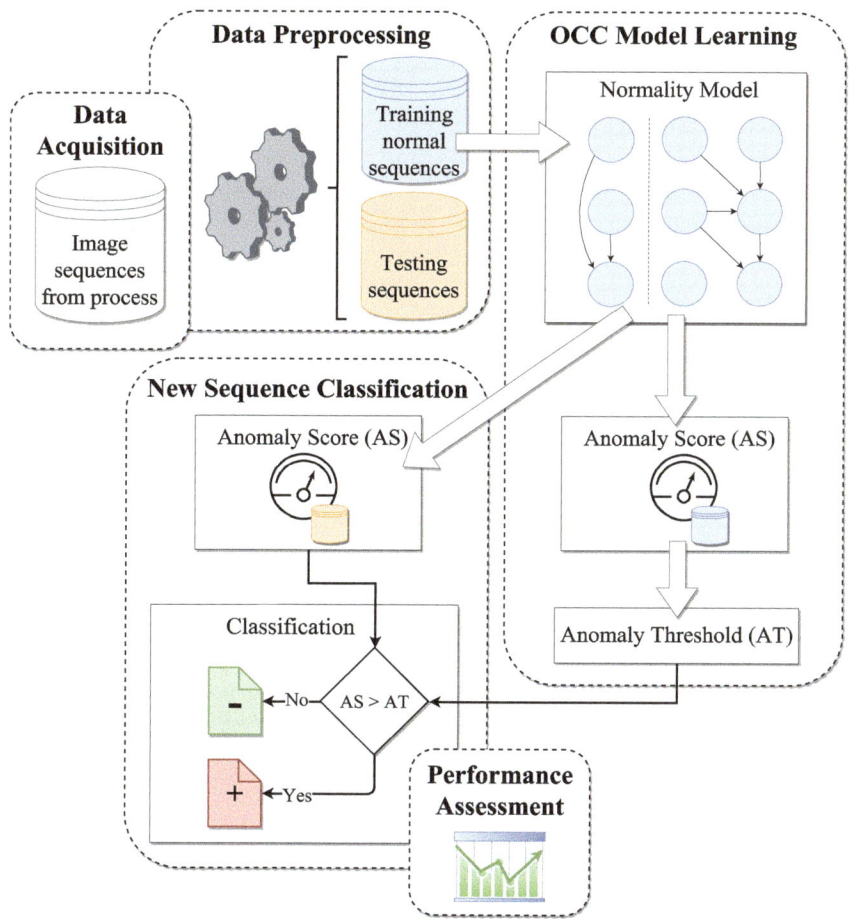

FIGURE 6.7

Schematic flowchart of the AVI system. In this one-class classification scenario, the data acquired from the laser process corresponded to its normal behavior only. Thus, we added simulated defects to the dataset. Then the dataset was preprocessed to extract meaningful features from the images and divided into training and test sets. Only normal sequences were available in the training set, whereas the test set included both normal and anomalous sequences. The preprocessed training normal image sequences were used to learn the normality model with DBNs. Then, their anomaly score (AS) was calculated and used to establish the anomaly threshold (AT) by selecting the least normal example. Afterwards, the AVI system classified a new test sequence by calculating its anomaly score and comparing it with the anomaly threshold: if the anomaly score was greater than the anomaly threshold, the sequence was classified as anomalous (positive class), otherwise it was classified as normal (negative class). Finally, the performance of the AVI system was assessed for both normal and anomalous sequences based on its classification accuracy.

We then had to establish the anomaly threshold in order to discriminate whether or not a sequence was far from normality. Taking up the proposal of other authors (Yeung and Ding, 2003; Bishop, 1994; Zorriassatine et al., 2005), we established the anomaly threshold by calculating the anomaly scores of the normal sequences in the training set and selecting the least normal sequence, i.e., the one with the biggest anomaly score. Consequently, the anomaly scores of new sequences greater than the anomaly threshold were considered to be too far removed from the normal behavior of the system and classified as anomalous (positive class); otherwise, they were classified as normal (negative class).

Finally, the performance of the AVI system was assessed using both the originally acquired normal sequences and the simulated anomalous sequences. The proposed method is explained in detail in Section 6.3.2.3.

6.3.2.1   Feature Extraction

A frame of the recorded videos taken at time t is composed of m pixels (1,024 in this case) that can be represented as a feature vector $\mathbf{R}[t] = (R_1[t], ..., R_m[t])$. Thus, the frames in a video form a multivariate time series $\{\mathbf{R}[1], ..., \mathbf{R}[T]\}$, where 1 and T are the initial and final (21,500 in this case) times observed, respectively. Modeling the time series of each pixel is a high-dimensional process since m is normally very large in computer vision problems. Considering that we needed an in-process response from the AVI system, it would have been too time consuming and computationally prohibitive to model the problem in this manner. Therefore, the number of features was reduced using feature subset selection techniques.

The proposed strategy is illustrated in Fig. 6.8 and was based on the spatial correlations among pixels. First, highly correlated pixels were grouped into k clusters, i.e., regions of the HAZ with similar behavior. For simplicity's sake, the regions were assumed to be the same for all the frames of the video sequences. Then the new feature vector of a frame at time t, $\mathbf{Q}[t]$, was output by extracting s statistical measures from the pixel values of each cluster. In doing so, the dimension of the feature vector $\mathbf{Q}[t] = (Q_1[t], ..., Q_{k \cdot s}[t])$ was drastically reduced, since the total number of extracted variables, $k \cdot s$, was lower than when we initially considered all m pixels.

We employed the 32 available image sequences and agglomerative hierarchical clustering algorithm (Section 2.3) with Ward's method and Euclidian distance (Xu and Tian, 2015) to segment the frame into regions. Apart from the pixel color information in the frames, the algorithm also had access to another piece of information: the neighbors of each pixel within the frame space summarized in a connectivity matrix. The role of this matrix was to maintain the spatial relationships between pixels to prevent the inclusion of unconnected pixels in the same cluster. In order to select the number c of clusters, experts defined a qualitative threshold criterion in terms of the maximum number of clusters in the frame that did not include any **artifacts**. Artifacts

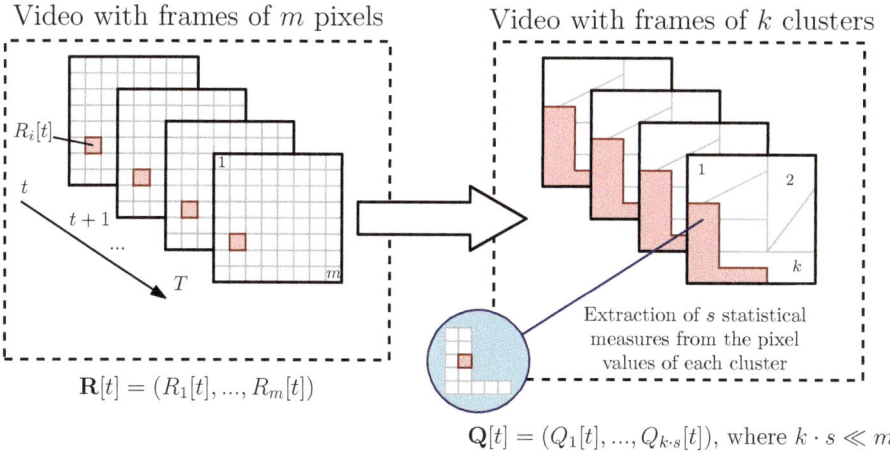

Video with frames of m pixels   Video with frames of k clusters

$$\mathbf{R}[t] = (R_1[t], ..., R_m[t])$$

Extraction of s statistical measures from the pixel values of each cluster

$$\mathbf{Q}[t] = (Q_1[t], ..., Q_{k \cdot s}[t]), \text{ where } k \cdot s \ll m$$

FIGURE 6.8
Dimensionality reduction of the feature vector $\mathbf{R}[t]$ to $\mathbf{Q}[t]$ based on segmenting the frames into k different regions and extracting s statistical measures from their pixel values.

were considered as pixel clusters without a physical explanation, i.e., very small regions or spread in unconnected areas. The hierarchical agglomerative clustering identified 14 artifact-free clusters within the images, i.e., the frame was divided into 14 disjoint regions. The resulting segmented frame is shown in Fig. 6.9(a). The regions adjacent to the edges of the image (clusters 1, 2, 11, 13 and 14) were discarded because they were considered to be background: their variability was low and they did not exhibit significant activity during the process. Thus, the remaining nine clusters ($k = 9$) corresponded to the segmentation of the HAZ.

Four meaningful statistical measures ($s = 4$) were extracted from the pixel values of each cluster: the median that gave an idea of the general temperature in the region without being affected by outliers, the standard deviation that represented the degree of homogeneity of the temperature in the region, and the maximum and minimum values that reflected the extreme temperatures in the region.

All these features represented a color proportional to the temperature. The number of possible colors (discrete values), $\text{Val}(R_i)$, for each pixel R_i is often greater than the number of categories that discrete statistical models can deal with. Therefore, the colors had to be integrated into a reduced number of bins for their analysis. More specifically, the $\text{Val}(R_i)$ of the camera used in this case study was 1,024, i.e., the pixels were able to take 1,024 different colors proportional to the surface temperature of the HAZ. Experts decided to group the 1,024 possible colors for each of the four extracted statistical measures into 10 bins ($\text{Val}(Q_i) = 10$). To build the 10 bins, we used, as a first and simple

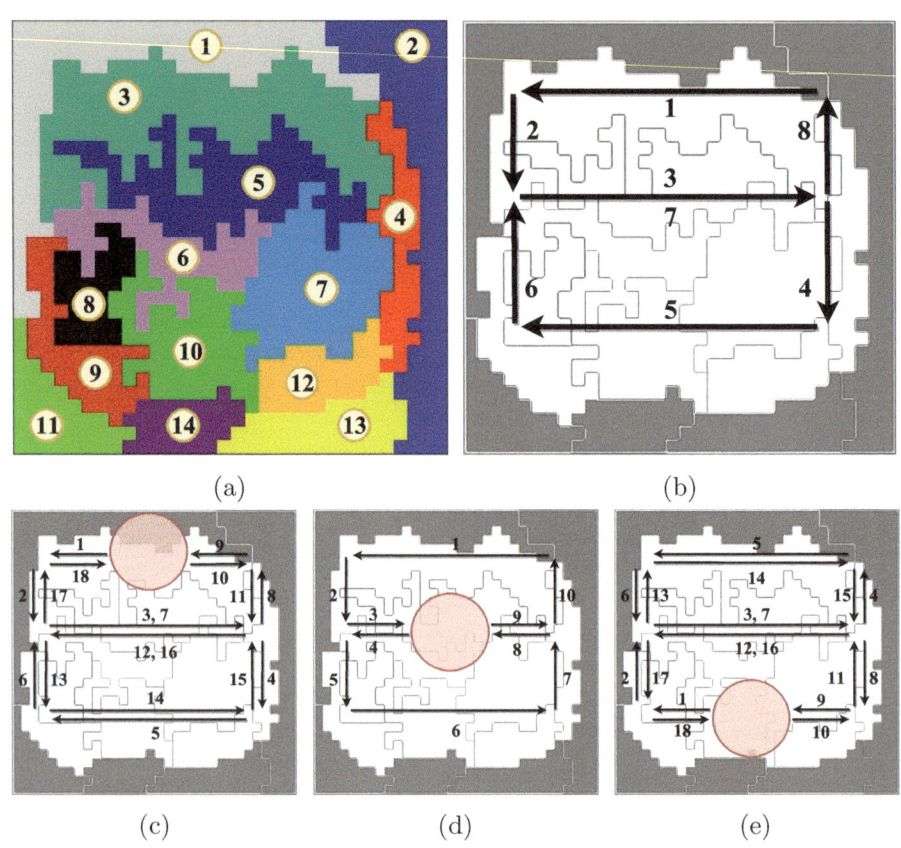

(a)   (b)

(c)   (d)   (e)

FIGURE 6.9

(a) The 14 regions into which the frame was segmented. The regions adjacent to the edges were considered to be background. (b) The movement pattern of the spot through the regions under normal conditions. However, this pattern was changed during the obstacle avoidance stage according to the position of the obstacle, namely at the top (c), in the middle (d) and at the bottom (e) of the HAZ.

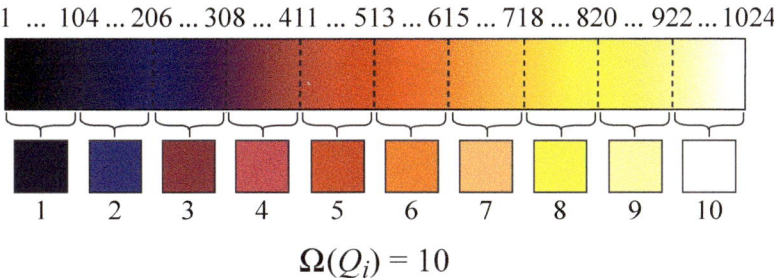

$$\Omega(Q_i) = 10$$

FIGURE 6.10
Equal-width interval binning discretization was used to reduce the initial number of possible discrete pixel values (colors) (1,024) to only 10 by assigning the same label to all values within an interval, all with the same width (102 colors).

approximation, the equal-width interval binning discretization (Section 2.2.1.5) method (Catlett, 1991), where each bin grouped approximately 102 colors. The method is illustrated in Fig. 6.10.

Using these techniques, the dimension of the feature vector $\mathbf{R}[t]$ was reduced from $m = 1,024$ variables to $k \cdot s = 36$ variables, and their values were in the discrete range $\{1,...,10\}$. The AVI system used by the time series of this new feature vector $\{\mathbf{Q}[1], ..., \mathbf{Q}[T]\}$, where $T = 21,500$, to analyze and classify the processed cylinders.

6.3.2.2 Dynamic Bayesian Networks Implementation

In this case study, the normality model was learned with both the DHC and DMMHC algorithms, already introduced in Section 2.6.2, in order to compare their performance. They were implemented by extending both the hill-climbing and MMHC algorithms in the `bnlearn` R package (Scutari, 2010) (Section 2.8) to the temporal domain. The BIC score (Section 2.5.3.2) was used to learn the structure of the prior and transition networks. Bayesian parameter estimation (Section 2.2.2.1) was used to learn the CPTs (Section 2.5.1) of each variable, since it yielded similar results to the MLE technique and avoided having zero probabilities for the unobserved configurations in the dataset.

However, additional constraints were placed on the arcs in order to output coherent relationships between the features extracted from the different regions into which the HAZ was segmented (see Fig. 6.11). First, only arcs between variables of the same type (e.g., medians with medians) were allowed if the variables belonged to different clusters. If these arcs connected variables in

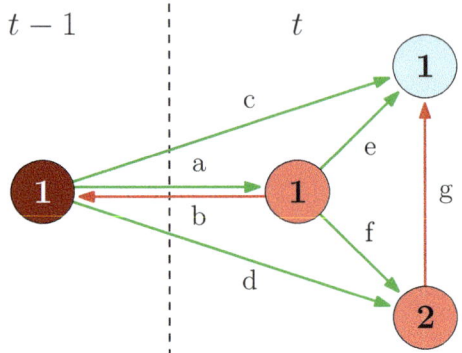

FIGURE 6.11
Constraints were placed on the arcs between variables in the implementation
of the DBN algorithms. Variables are represented by a number and a color.
Variables labeled with the same number belonged to the same region and
variables labeled with the same color belonged to the same feature extracted
from the regions. These variables could be observed in the past $(t-1)$ (darker
color) or in the present frame (t) (lighter color). Additionally, permitted arcs
are colored green, whereas banned arcs are colored red. Since time naturally
flows from past to present, arcs in the opposite direction were prohibited (b).
For this particular application, the arcs connecting different types of variables
from different regions (g) were also prohibited. All other arcs, namely
persistent (a), temporal intra-region (c), temporal inter-region (d),
instantaneous intra-region (e) and instantaneous inter-region (f) arcs, were
permitted.

the same time slice, they were called **instantaneous inter-region arcs** (f),
whereas if they connected variables in different time slices, they were called
temporal inter-region arcs (d). Second, any arcs connecting variables from
the same region were permitted (e.g., medians with minimums). If these arcs
connected variables in the same time slice, they were called **instantaneous
intra-region arcs** (e), whereas if they connected variables in different time
slices, they were divided into arcs connecting the same variable type, called
persistent arcs (a), and arcs connecting different variable types, called **temporal intra-region arcs** (c). Also, the number of possible parents of each
variable was limited to two in order to reduce complexity and enhance the
interpretability of the resulting model.

Finally, we also made the required assumptions set out above in order
to study the causal relations appearing in the normality model learned with
DBNs.

6.3.2.3   Performance Assessment

To assess AVI system performance with regard to the detection of sequences with anomalies without triggering false alarms, we used the 32 available sequences of normal images and the 64 sequences with simulated anomalies (32 sequences with negative offset anomaly and another 32 sequences with noise anomaly).

As in any classification problem, we built a confusion matrix comparing the output of the classification against the real labels of the sequences. In this case, we had a binary classification problem with the negative class (N) for normal sequences and the positive class (P) for sequences with anomalies. We extracted two figures of merit from the confusion matrix to assess the performance of the AVI system:

$$\text{sensitivity} = \frac{TP}{TP + FN} , \qquad \text{specificity} = \frac{TN}{FP + TN} , \qquad (6.2)$$

where the correctly classified sequences were the true positives (TP) and true negatives (TN), and the misclassified sequences were the false negatives (FN) and false positives (FP). Specificity accounted for the percentage of normal sequences that the AVI system was able to classify correctly. In contrast, sensitivity (one for each type of defect simulated based on the normal image sequences) accounted for the percentage of sequences with anomalies that the AVI system was able to detect correctly.

To calculate sensitivities, we learned the normality model with the 32 normal sequences, whereas the sequences with simulated anomalies were used for testing. For specificity, on the other hand, there would have been a risk, due to the small sample size available, of a higher variability in the results if we had used disjoint datasets to train and test the system response during the classification of normal sequences. Hence, a k-fold cross-validation method was set up to estimate the specificity of the AVI system, where experts set the parameter k to 8.

6.4   Results and Discussion

6.4.1   Performance of the AVI System

Experts wanted to ascertain which was the smallest perturbation in the data gathered from the normal process used for learning in the AVI system that at least one of the DBN algorithms was capable of detecting as anomalous in at least 80% of the cases. The smallest percentages of the standard deviation of the Gaussian noise and the negative offset that met this requirement were 2.5% and 3.5%, respectively. Experts found these results to be satisfactory. Additionally, it is reasonable to expect that if these percentages had been

TABLE 6.1
Specificity (normal) and sensitivities (noise and negative offset) of the AVI system when learning the normality model with the DHC and DMMHC algorithms

DBN algorithm	Normal	Noise (2.5%)	Negative offset (3.5%)	Negative offset (4%)
DHC	93.8%	100%	78.1%	100%
DMMHC	90.6%	62.5%	81.3%	100%

bigger, the anomalies would have been more noticeable and have been more readily detected by the AVI system, thereby increasing sensitivity. This was demonstrated by increasing the negative offset anomaly to 4%. Table 6.1 reports the specificity and sensitivities achieved by the AVI systems learned with each of the proposed DBN algorithms when applied to normal and anomalous image sequences.

DHC correctly classified 93.8% of the normal sequences, while DMMHC achieved just over 90%. Hence, the response of the classification system when classifying normal sequences was slightly better with DHC. DHC also out-performed DMMHC when detecting anomalies produced by Gaussian noise (with a more notable difference in this case), since sensitivity was 100% for DHC and only 62.5% for DMMHC. However, this tendency was reversed for the detection of anomalies produced by negative offset. Even though both algorithms detected 100% of anomalous sequences with a negative offset of 4%, DMMHC worked better at lower disturbances, achieving a sensitivity of 81.3% for a negative offset of 3.5%, while DHC scored only 78.1%.

It is vital in industrial applications to detect most of the sequences with errors (high sensitivity) without triggering false alarms (high specificity). A high sensitivity ensures the early detection of errors, identifying defective workpieces to prevent them from being further processed; whereas, a high specificity avoids having to close down the production line unnecessarily, improving line availability. This is especially critical for plant managers because they lose faith in the monitoring system if too many false positives are detected and end up turning it off to avoid downtimes. Specificity or sensitivity could be more or less important depending on the specific application. In this particular laser application, the aim was to reach a trade-off between both measures. Thus, the best option was to use the DHC algorithm to learn the AVI system normality model. This ensured the highest specificity with sensitivities better than 78% for the different types of anomalies.

The AVI system was implemented on a PC with an Intel Core i7 processor and 16GB of RAM. Here, the proposed methodology met the in-process classification requirement of taking less than three seconds to classify a new

TABLE 6.2

Mean time and standard deviation (in seconds) taken by the AVI system learned with the DHC and DMMHC algorithms to classify a new sequence on a PC with an Intel Core i7 processor and 16GB of RAM (the results reported after repeating the process 1,000 times)

DBN algorithm	Mean time	Standard deviation
DHC	2.034	0.021
DMMHC	2.020	0.017

sequence with both the DHC and DMMHC algorithms. As Table 6.2 shows, both were able to classify new sequences in approximately two seconds[3].

Finally, note that the widespread lack of examples with errors is not the only reason why the applied anomaly detection approach is appropriate in manufacturing. In fact, there is such a wide range of things that could go wrong in such an uncertain world as industrial practice that it would be unmanageable to try to learn a model for each possibility. The "generalizability" required for quality control activities is achieved in anomaly detection by modeling the normality of the process and then detecting situations that deviate from the norm.

6.4.2 Interpretation of the Normality Model

We have seen that the normality model that performed best and most closely represented the dynamic behavior of the normal laser process was the one learned with the DHC algorithm. We are now interested in seeing what spatio-temporal properties of the thermal process this DBN is able to learn directly from data. To be precise, we want to find out if it is able to represent the movement pattern of the spot during the normal behavior of the process across the different regions of the HAZ. To do this, we first analyzed the structure of the DBN, and then, its parameters. For this purpose, we did not have to study the relationships appearing at the beginning of the laser process represented by the prior network because the first frame always belonged to the transient stage where the surface of the steel cylinder was at room temperature. Therefore, we focused on analyzing only the transition network.

6.4.2.1 Relationships in the Dynamic Bayesian Network Structure

Fig. 6.12 shows the structure of the transition network learned with the DHC algorithm. Node labels correspond to the region number as specified in Fig. 6.9. Node colors represent the type of variable (median (med), standard deviation (sd), minimum (min) and maximum (max)). Darker nodes in the left column

---

[3]Considering that the preprocessing step was carried out during image acquisition, which is a common approach.

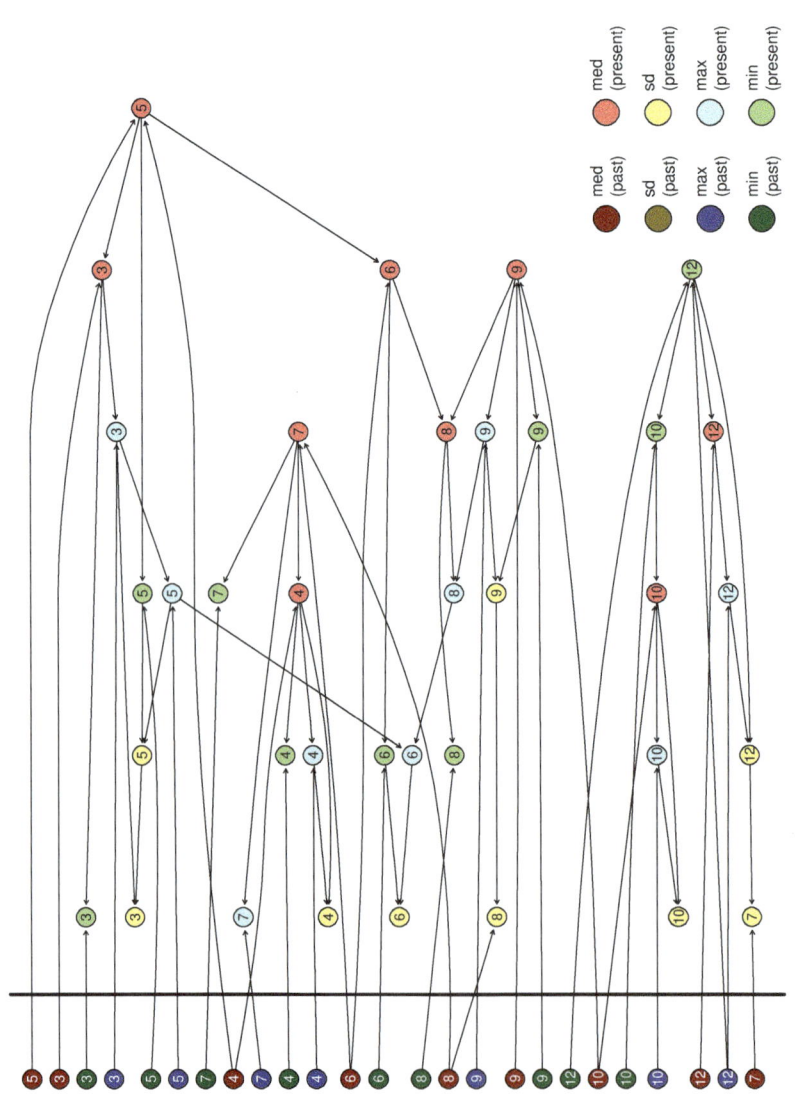

FIGURE 6.12
Transition network learned with the DHC algorithm. A vertical line separates the past and the present frames.

represent the state of the variables in the past frame, whereas the lighter colored nodes represent the state of the variables in the present frame. Only 61 out of the 72 arcs are represented because nine variables in the past frame were independent, i.e., had no incoming or outgoing arcs. Table 6.3 lists the number of arcs appearing in the network, broken down by the type of relationship they produced. Note that all the variables had two parents. This was the maximum number allowed in order to reduce the complexity of the model.

Some conclusions of the process can be drawn from the information on the transition network. The median, maximum and minimum were persistent variables in 85.2% of the cases. This was compatible with the inertia property of thermal processes where the temperature of a region tends to be stable unless affected by an external source. This finding was particularly important for the median of the regions because we wanted the temperature of the HAZ to be stable at a high enough value to reach the austenite phase. However, the medians of regions 7 and 8 were not persistent and had an incoming arc from the medians in the past frame of regions 6 and 8, and in the present frame of region 9, respectively. This meant that the median temperature of adjacent regions had a greater impact in these cases.

On the other hand, the standard deviation was never persistent and usually depended on the values in the present frame of the other variables in its region, namely the maximum and minimum or the minimum and median. Another possibility (regions 3, 7 and 8) was that the standard deviation was instantaneously influenced by that of an adjacent region (regions 5, 12 and 9, respectively), meaning that knowledge of the degree of disorder in the first region sufficed to infer the degree of disorder in the second region.

Moreover, the common structure within regions was for the median to be the parent of both minimum and maximum. Then, the median again or the minimum or maximum was usually the parent of the standard deviation. The direction of these arcs was aligned with what we might expect from a thermal point of view, since the maximum and minimum values are usually proportional to the average heat in a region (represented here by the median). Additionally, a discrepancy in the trend alignment of at least two of the above variables could signify a high heterogeneity in the temperature of the region, increasing the standard deviation. In this way, we concluded that the relationships captured by the DBN structure seemed reasonable.

Another interesting fact was that the median appeared to be the most influential variable, since it was normally the ancestor of the other variables of the region in the present frame. This conclusion was tested using **network centralities** that assign a score to nodes in a network based on their structural properties (Zaman, 2011). They have proved to be very powerful tools for analyzing **complex networks** with thousands of nodes and arcs, like tools used to model web searches in the Internet (Page et al., 1999), or social networks (Bar-Yossef and Mashiach, 2008; Zaman, 2011). In this particular case, we wanted to determine which transition network nodes were the most influential in terms of their capability of reaching more network nodes. The

TABLE 6.3
Number (in parentheses) of network arcs learned with the DHC algorithm
according to the type of direct relationship. They are broken down by type of
variable when an arc connected two variables of the same type, which is the
case only for persistent and inter-region arcs. For instance, the arc from
med_4_past to *med_5_present* is a non-persistent temporal arc that connects
two regions (inter-region) through the medians

Total (72)	Instantaneous (42)	Intra-region (29)		
		Inter-region (13)	med (5)	
			sd (3)	
			max (4)	
			min (1)	
	Temporal (30)	Persistent (23)	med (7)	
			sd (0)	
			max (7)	
			min (9)	
		Not persistent (7)	Intra-region (3)	
			Inter-region (4)	med (4)
				sd (0)
				max (0)
				min (0)

most important node properties for answering this question appeared to be the number of outgoing arcs and the number of directed paths to other nodes. Based on these structural features, the following network centralities were used to rank the variables (see Table 6.4):

- **Outdegree**. This is the simplest score and is based on counting the number of arcs pointing out from a node. In the case of BNs, the outdegree corresponds to the number of children of a variable and indicates how many variables are directly influenced by the node. The drawback of this score is that it only captures the local structural properties of a single node and does not provide information on the global network structure.

- **Outgoing closeness**. Closeness captures how close a node is to all other nodes in the network (Sabidussi, 1966). Large outgoing closeness means that a node is connected to most of the nodes by an outgoing directed path, and that this path is short. Hence, the outgoing closeness of a node is defined as the inverse of the sum of distances of the shortest paths from the node to the other nodes. For this case study, the distance between all adjacent nodes was set to one. Additionally, if a node did not have a direct path to another one, the distance was the total number of arcs (72 in this case). Note that we used the normalized outgoing closeness that is calculated by multiplying the total number of nodes by the outgoing closeness.

- **Betweenness**. This score measures the extent to which the removal of a node would affect network connectivity (Freeman, 1977). The betweenness of a node is defined as the number of shortest paths that pass through a node. Hence, a high betweenness means that most of the paths are influenced by this node. In contrast to the other scores examined, betweenness attaches no importance to source or leaf nodes because no paths pass through them.

- **Reverse PageRank**. Eigenvector centrality attaches importance not only to the number of nodes that can be reached by a node, but also to how important the contacted nodes are. For example, a node connected to many unimportant nodes may be less important than a node with fewer neighbors that are, however, of more importance. Different eigenvector centrality methods are distinguished principally by the way they define how important nodes are. For PageRank (Page et al., 1999), a large number of outgoing arcs in a node is a sign of lower worth, and thus the importance of a node is defined as the inverse of its outdegree. In contrast, Reverse PageRank penalizes the in-going arcs, since it works like PageRank but with the arcs in the graph previously reversed. Gleich (2015) noted that, intuitively speaking, Reverse PageRank models somebody that follows incoming links instead of outgoing links. In other words, a high Reverse PageRank suggests nodes that can reach many others in the graph. Therefore, as other authors have pointed out (Bar-Yossef and Mashiach, 2008), Reverse PageRank is a good heuristic for finding influential nodes in networks, i.e., nodes that can spread their influence widely.

TABLE 6.4

Ranking of the most influential variables in the transition network according to outdegree, outgoing closeness, betweenness and Reverse PageRank network centrality measures. The medians in both the past and present frames are in bold

	Outdegree		Closeness (out)		Betweenness		Reverse PageRank	
Ranking	Node	Score	Node	Score	Node	Score	Node	Score
1	**med_4_present**	3	**med_4_past**	0.018694	**med_5_present**	28	**med_5_present**	0.030161
2	**med_5_present**	3	**med_5_past**	0.017406	**med_6_present**	22.5	**med_4_past**	0.029133
3	**med_7_present**	3	**med_5_present**	0.017166	max_3_present	21	**med_9_present**	0.028343
4	**med_9_present**	3	**med_6_past**	0.017158	**med_8_present**	21	**med_10_past**	0.026918
5	min_12_present	3	**med_10_past**	0.016865	**med_3_present**	19	**med_6_past**	0.026287
6	**med_4_past**	2	**med_9_past**	0.016060	**med_9_present**	18	min_12_present	0.024846
7	**med_6_past**	2	**med_9_present**	0.015838	max_5_present	17.5	max_12_past	0.023990
8	**med_8_past**	2	max_12_past	0.015827	max_8_present	15.5	**med_7_present**	0.023100
9	**med_10_past**	2	min_12_past	0.015820	min_12_present	14	**med_8_past**	0.021193
10	max_12_past	2	min_12_present	0.015601	max_6_present	13	**med_5_past**	0.020801
11	**med_3_present**	2	**med_8_past**	0.015594	max_9_present	12.5	**med_9_past**	0.020029
12	max_3_present	2	**med_3_past**	0.015570	**med_4_present**	12	**med_6_present**	0.019968
13	max_5_present	2	**med_3_present**	0.015355	**med_7_present**	12	**med_4_present**	0.019603
14	**med_6_present**	2	**med_7_present**	0.015142	**med_10_present**	12	**med_3_present**	0.019399
15	**med_8_present**	2	**med_6_present**	0.015135	min_10_present	12	max_3_present	0.018878
16	max_9_present	2	max_3_past	0.015122	sd_9_present	7	min_12_past	0.018543
17	**med_10_present**	2	max_9_past	0.015122	min_5_present	6.5	max_9_present	0.018265
18	**med_3_past**	1	max_3_present	0.014913	min_6_present	6	max_5_present	0.017652
19	max_3_past	1	max_9_present	0.014913	sd_12_present	6	**med_8_present**	0.016823
20	min_3_past	1	max_5_past	0.014907	sd_5_present	5.5	**med_3_past**	0.016227
21	max_4_past	1	max_5_present	0.014700	min_9_present	5	**med_10_present**	0.016210
22	min_4_past	1	**med_8_present**	0.014697	**med_12_present**	5	max_3_past	0.016006
23	**med_5_past**	1	min_10_past	0.014691	max_12_present	5	max_9_past	0.015746
24	max_5_past	1	**med_12_past**	0.014688	max_4_present	1	max_5_past	0.015485
25	min_5_past	1	**med_4_present**	0.014493	max_10_present	1	min_10_present	0.014872
26	min_6_past	1	min_10_present	0.014487	**med_3_past**	0	min_10_past	0.014304
27	**med_7_past**	1	min_5_past	0.014484	max_3_past	0	**med_12_past**	0.013691
28	max_7_past	1	min_9_past	0.014484	min_3_past	0	min_5_past	0.013430
29	min_7_past	1	**med_12_present**	0.014484	**med_4_past**	0	min_9_past	0.013430
30	min_8_past	1	**med_10_present**	0.014286	max_4_past	0	**med_12_present**	0.013430
31	**med_9_past**	1	max_4_past	0.014283	min_4_past	0	max_4_past	0.012818
32	max_9_past	1	min_6_past	0.014283	**med_5_past**	0	min_6_past	0.012818
33	min_9_past	1	max_10_past	0.014283	max_5_past	0	max_10_past	0.012818
34	max_10_past	1	min_5_present	0.014283	min_5_past	0	min_5_present	0.012818
35	min_10_past	1	max_8_present	0.014283	**med_6_past**	0	max_8_present	0.012818
36	**med_12_past**	1	min_9_present	0.014283	min_6_past	0	min_9_present	0.012818
37	min_12_past	1	max_12_present	0.014283	**med_7_past**	0	max_12_present	0.012818
38	max_4_present	1	min_3_past	0.014085	max_7_past	0	min_3_past	0.011376
39	sd_5_present	1	min_4_past	0.014085	min_7_past	0	min_4_past	0.011376
40	min_5_present	1	**med_7_past**	0.014085	**med_8_past**	0	**med_7_past**	0.011376
41	max_6_present	1	max_7_past	0.014085	min_8_past	0	max_7_past	0.011376
42	min_6_present	1	min_7_past	0.014085	**med_9_past**	0	min_7_past	0.011376
43	max_8_present	1	max_8_past	0.014085	max_9_past	0	min_8_past	0.011376
44	sd_9_present	1	max_4_present	0.014085	min_9_past	0	max_4_present	0.011376
45	min_9_present	1	sd_5_present	0.014085	**med_10_past**	0	sd_5_present	0.011376
46	max_10_present	1	max_6_present	0.014085	max_10_past	0	max_6_present	0.011376
47	min_10_present	1	min_6_present	0.014085	min_10_past	0	min_6_present	0.011376
48	**med_12_present**	1	sd_9_present	0.014085	**med_12_past**	0	sd_9_present	0.011376
49	sd_12_present	1	max_10_present	0.014085	max_12_past	0	max_10_present	0.011376
50	max_12_present	1	sd_12_present	0.014085	min_12_past	0	sd_12_present	0.011376
51	sd_3_present	0	sd_3_present	0.013889	sd_3_present	0	sd_3_present	0.007983
52	min_3_present	0	min_3_present	0.013889	min_3_present	0	min_3_present	0.007983
53	sd_4_present	0	sd_4_present	0.013889	sd_4_present	0	sd_4_present	0.007983
54	min_4_present	0	min_4_present	0.013889	min_4_present	0	min_4_present	0.007983
55	sd_6_present	0	sd_6_present	0.013889	sd_6_present	0	sd_6_present	0.007983
56	sd_7_present	0	sd_7_present	0.013889	sd_7_present	0	sd_7_present	0.007983
57	max_7_present	0	max_7_present	0.013889	max_7_present	0	max_7_present	0.007983
58	min_7_present	0	min_7_present	0.013889	min_7_present	0	min_7_present	0.007983
59	sd_8_present	0	sd_8_present	0.013889	sd_8_present	0	sd_8_present	0.007983
60	min_8_present	0	min_8_present	0.013889	min_8_present	0	min_8_present	0.007983
61	sd_10_present	0	sd_10_present	0.013889	sd_10_present	0	sd_10_present	0.007983

The results in Table 6.4 indicate that network centrality measures generally identified the median as the most influential type of variable, since it occupied the top positions of the ranking in all cases. To be more precise, if we focus on Reverse PageRank, we find that, except for region 12 (where the minimum was the most influential variable), the median of a region, in both the present and past frames, was more influential than any other type of variable. In fact, of the top 14 positions, 12 corresponded to the medians of seven different regions.

It is also interesting to see that outgoing closeness yielded similar results to the findings reported for Reverse PageRank. This is because both took into account the number of nodes reachable from each node. Outdegree, on the other hand, was only able to analyze the structure locally. For example, the most influential node for outdegree was the median of region 4 in the present frame (*med_4_present*) with three outgoing arcs. Looking at the network in Fig. 6.12, however, those arcs were not so influential because they pointed to leaf nodes. Reverse PageRank was able to take this into account and ranked *med_4_present* in the 13th position. Looking at betweenness, we find that all the nodes (including leaf nodes) in the past frame were scored zero since, because of the non-symmetry of temporality, they had to be parent nodes. For this problem, however, it was also important to measure their influence. This shows how critical it is to select the correct network centrality measure in order to get useful conclusions.

Markov Blanket

Intuitively, we expected closer regions to have a thermodynamic influence on each other and to be independent of distant regions. The DBN structure can answer these questions through the query: Does a given variable belong to the Markov blanket (Section 2.4.9) of another variable?

Translating this concept to our application, we wanted to identify the minimal number of regions that knowing their state in the past or present frame shielded the state in the present frame of a specific target region from the influence of the states of the other regions (i.e., made them independent). Since each target region was composed of a set of four variables, we defined the Markov blanket of a target region as the union of the Markov blankets of their variables. Then, even if only one variable from a different region in the past or present frame was in the Markov blanket of the target region, we identified that region as part of the Markov blanket of the target region.

Fig. 6.13 shows, for each target region (in yellow), which other regions (in blue) shielded them from the rest (in white). We find that the regions were locally dependent on other adjacent or fairly close regions (such as regions 7 and 8 in Fig. 6.13(e)). At first glance, we could guess at the trail of the spot. For example, when it hits several regions at the same time, like regions 6 and 9 with respect to region 8 in Fig. 6.13(f); or when it moves across regions, like region 10 with respect to region 9 in Fig. 6.13(g), or regions 6 and 8 with respect to region 7 in Fig. 6.13(e).

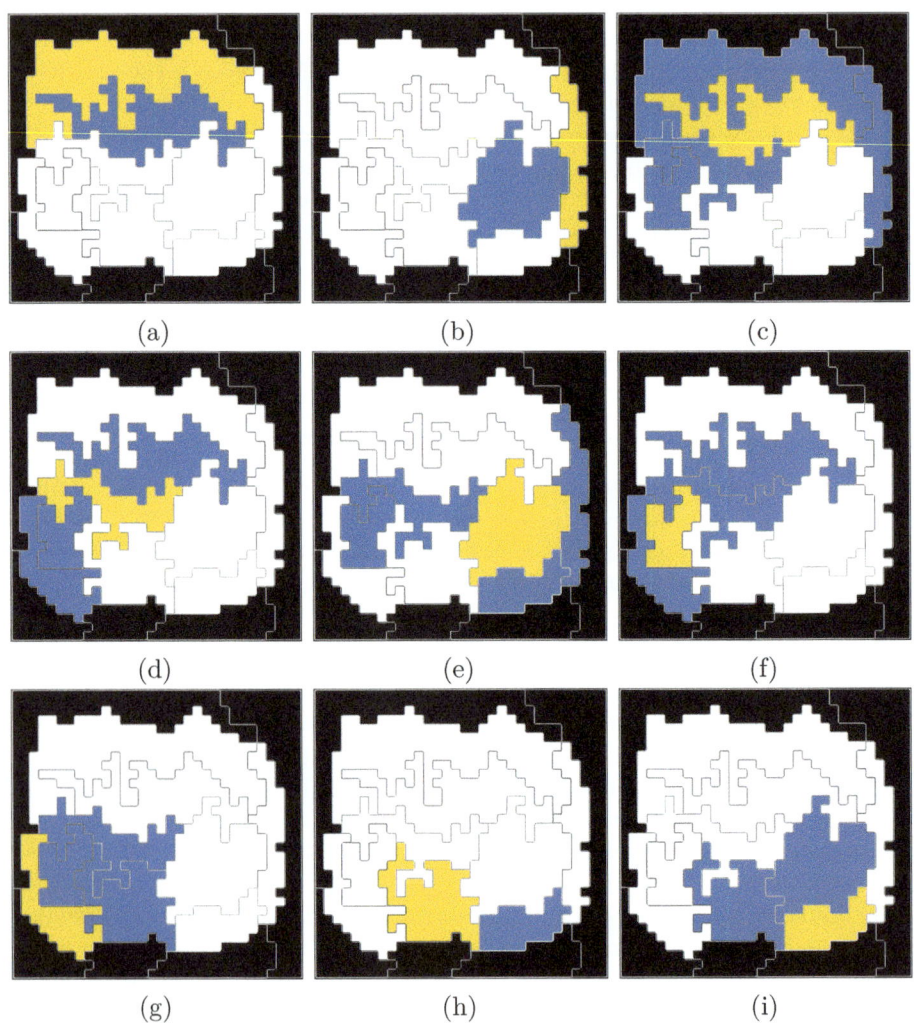

FIGURE 6.13
Illustration of the regions with variables within the Markov blanket (in blue) of the variables of the target region (in yellow). Knowledge of the state of these regions shielded the target region from the influence of other regions (in white). As expected, both the regions and their Markov blanket regions were close. Markov blanket of (a) region 3, (b) region 4, (c) region 5, (d) region 6, (e) region 7, (f) region 8, (g) region 9, (h) region 10 and (i) region 12.

Causal Influence

By taking a closer look at the direction of inter-region arcs, we were able to establish some direct causal influences between regions. More precisely, we wanted to find out which regions had a direct effect on each region. We defined a region to be the cause of a target region in the present frame if at least one of its variables in the past or present frame was the parent in the transition network of a variable of the target region. Fig. 6.14 shows the parent regions (green) for each of the regions in the present state (yellow). We made a distinction between two types of parental relationships: relationships produced by instantaneous arcs only (light green) and relationships produced by temporal arcs only (dark green). In no case did the same region have a mixture of these two types of relationships over the target region. Note that the results for direct causal influence were consistent with a particular case of the results for Markov blankets, since the focus is on the parents of a target region from a different region. By definition, they also belong to the Markov blanket of the target region.

We first analyzed the regions that instantaneously influenced (colored in light green) the state of other regions. They were regions adjacent to the one that they were influencing, and the images recorded during the process showed that they were all consistent with situations where the spot was hitting both regions at the same time. For this reason, it was possible to somehow infer the state of the target region from the known state of its neighbor. There were even some cases where, because of their width, the spot hit the same regions in consecutive frames, and they became very related. In such situations, some of the variables of a region were children of the other region or vice versa, resulting in regions that were simultaneously children and parents of a different region. This applied to regions 3 and 5, and 6 and 8 and could be an indication that the DBN detected these highly related regions as artifacts produced when segmenting the HAZ. Therefore, they could potentially have been merged into a single region.

We then analyzed the regions that had a temporal influence over another region, i.e., the state in the past of these regions was conditioning the present state of their child regions. This was the case of region 4 with respect to region 5 (Fig. 6.14(c)), regions 8 and 6 with respect to region 7 (Fig. 6.14(e)), and region 10 with respect to region 9 (Fig. 6.14(g)). In all cases, we found that the connected regions were situated along the same horizontal line. In fact, they were related to the horizontal movement of the spot when tracing the middle and bottom sections of the pattern under normal conditions (segments 3 and 7, and 5 in Fig. 6.9(b), respectively). The type of variable that was capable of capturing these temporal inter-region connections was the median.

From these results, we can conclude that the DBN was able to learn that the separate temporal characterization of each region was not enough to represent the thermal properties of the process because there were also spatio-temporal

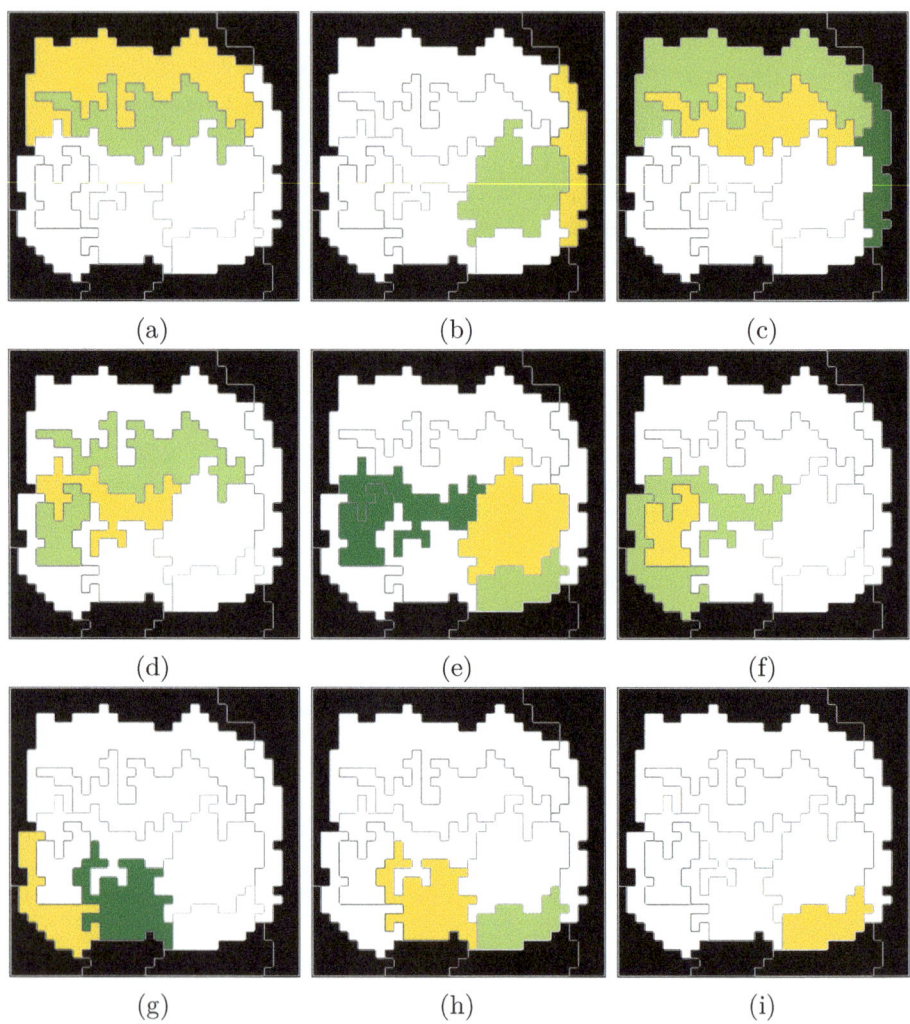

FIGURE 6.14

Illustration of the regions with variables that were parents (in green) of at least one variable of the target region (in yellow). There were two types of parent regions: regions that produced instantaneous influences only (light green) and regions that produced temporal influences only (dark green). In no case did the same region have a mixture of these two types of relationships over the target region. The spot movement patterns during the process were captured by the direct temporal causal influences. Causal effect in (a) region 3, (b) region 4, (c) region 5, (d) region 6, (e) region 7, (f) region 8, (g) region 9, (h) region 10 and (i) region 12.

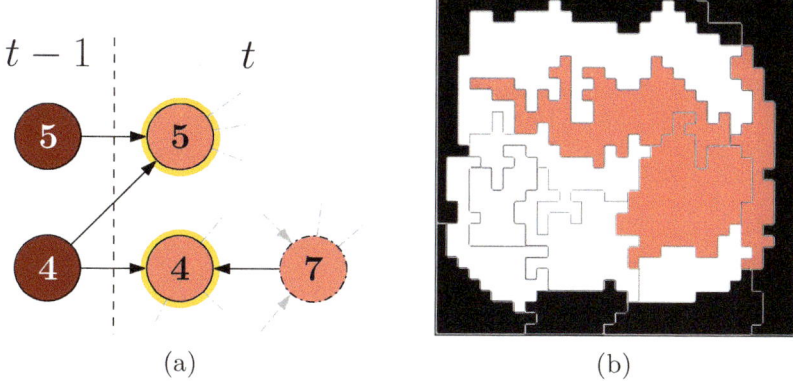

FIGURE 6.15
(a) Subgraph of the transition network in Fig. 6.12 representing the nodes whose parameters were analyzed (*med_5_present* and *med_4_present*) and their parent nodes. (b) The regions of the HAZ involved in the subgraph.

relationships among neighboring regions produced by the movement of the spot. These relationships were represented in the DBN by inter-region arcs.

6.4.2.2 Relationships in the Dynamic Bayesian Network Parameters

In this section, we study the causal influences learned by the DBN further by analyzing their parameters. The aim is to understand the impact that the different states of the parent variables were having on the children variables of the DBN based on two thoroughly explained examples, thereby representing the thermal effects of the movement of the spot in the HAZ. To be precise, we analyzed the parameters in the present frame of the two most influential variables according to Reverse PageRank centrality (see Table 6.4): the medians of regions 4 and 5. These variables were directly related in the transition network through a temporal inter-region arc (see Fig. 6.15(a)) from region 4 to region 5. By studying their parameters, we were able to gain insight into the spatio-temporal behavior of the laser process when the spot moved along the intermediate and right areas of the HAZ as highlighted in Fig. 6.15(b).

Note that the literature has, to the best of our knowledge, commonly obviated this kind of parameter analysis, presumably because of the exponential explosion of variable parameters with the number of its parents. In this case study, the analysis was approachable because the number of parents was limited to only two per variable. In fact, we found that all the variables in the present frame had two parents. Thus, their parameters, θ_X, answered the question: Given that the parents $\mathbf{Pa}(X) = \{Y, Z\}$ of variable X took the specific state pa_X^j, what is the probability of a specific state $X = x_k$? As explained in Section 2.5.1, the CPTs of categorical variables are commonly rep-

TABLE 6.5

Compilation of the range of hottest states observed in the present frame for the medians of the different analyzed regions

Region	4	5	7
States range	3-6	7-10	6-9

resented in conditional probability tables (CPTs). Fig. 6.16 shows an example particularized for the case where the domain of X is $\{x_1, x_2, x_3\}$, while the domains of the parent variables Y and Z are $\{y_1, y_2, y_3, y_4\}$ and $\{z_1, z_2, z_3, z_4, z_5\}$, respectively.

Here, each element θ_{Xjk} of the CPT corresponds to $p(X = x_k|\mathbf{Pa}(X) = \mathbf{pa}_X^j)$, meeting the condition that $\sum_k p(X = x_k|\mathbf{Pa}(X) = \mathbf{pa}_X^j) = 1$, where $k = 1, 2, 3$ (Fig. 6.16 shows an example for $Y = y_2$ and $Z = z_3$). Since we are modeling three variables, we can represent the CPT graphically in 3D, where, for each state $X = x_k$, we have a matrix with the probability of that state conditioned upon the different states of Y and Z. These matrices can be illustrated as a heat map with a different color for each probability value according to a color gradient (see Fig. 6.17 for an example).

We applied the above technique in order to graphically analyze the medians in the present frame of regions 4 and 5. Since both were persistent, the states of the variable in the past frame were located in the rows of the matrices (as Y), while the states of the other parent variable were placed in the columns of the matrices (as Z).

However, we were not interested in analyzing all the states of the medians because there were regions very close to the background that did not reach the maximum temperature during the process. Therefore, we knew in advance that the higher states of their median were going to be very unlikely, and, as a consequence, they would have low probabilities. Additionally, looking back at Fig. 6.4(c), the workpiece was at room temperature at the beginning of the process, so there was a two-second heat transient in the HAZ before reaching the desired stable working condition. This unwanted phenomenon was learned by the DBN and represented in the parameters of the lower states of the medians. Therefore, we considered for the analysis only the four highest consecutive states (40% of the range of the possible pixel colors that amounted to approximately 410 different values) in the present frame for which the heat map visibly showed that there was a significant probability. Table 6.5 shows for each of the analyzed regions the ranges of states considered for the median. Region 4 and, less markedly, region 7 did not reach the maximum state because they were in contact or near the background.

Fig. 6.17 shows the CPT of *med_4_present* (Fig. 6.17(a)) and *med_5_present* (Fig. 6.17(b)) for the considered states specified in Table 6.5. The color gradient for the different probabilities went from white (with prob-

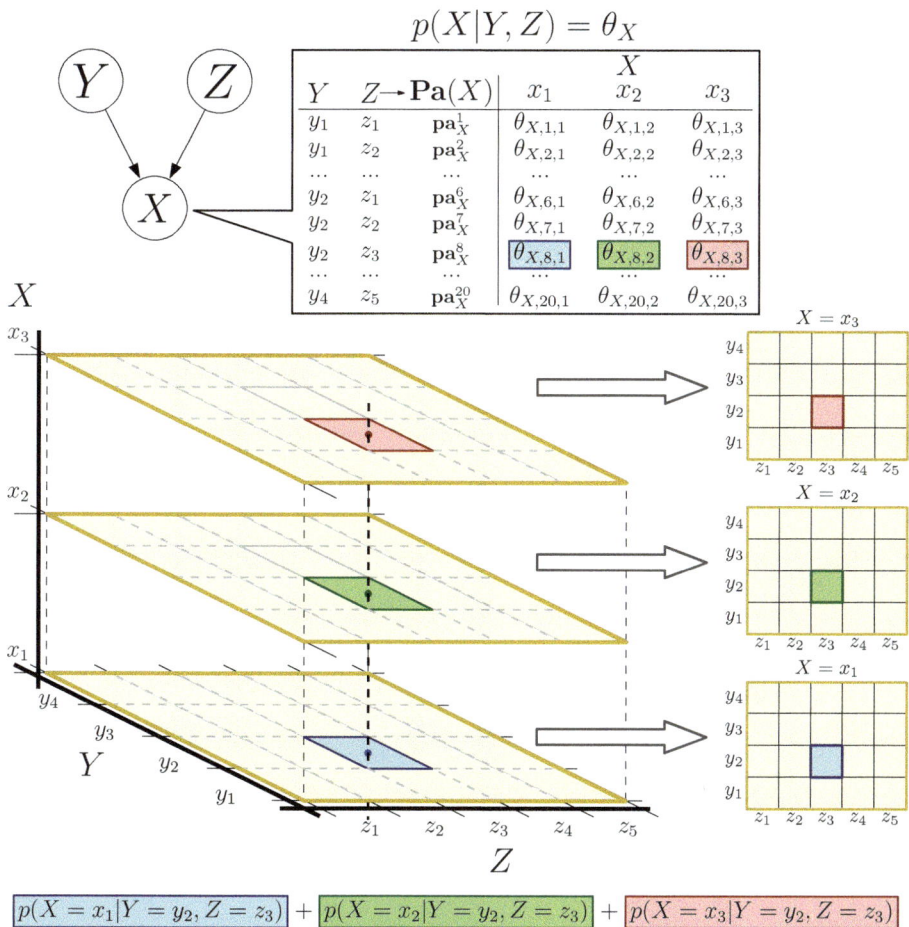

FIGURE 6.16
CPT of variable X that has two parents, $\mathbf{Pa}(X) = \{Y, Z\}$. Here, the CPT can be represented three-dimensionally, where, for each state $X = x_k$, there is a matrix with the probability of that state conditioned upon the different combinations of states of Y and Z ($\mathbf{pa}_X^j$).

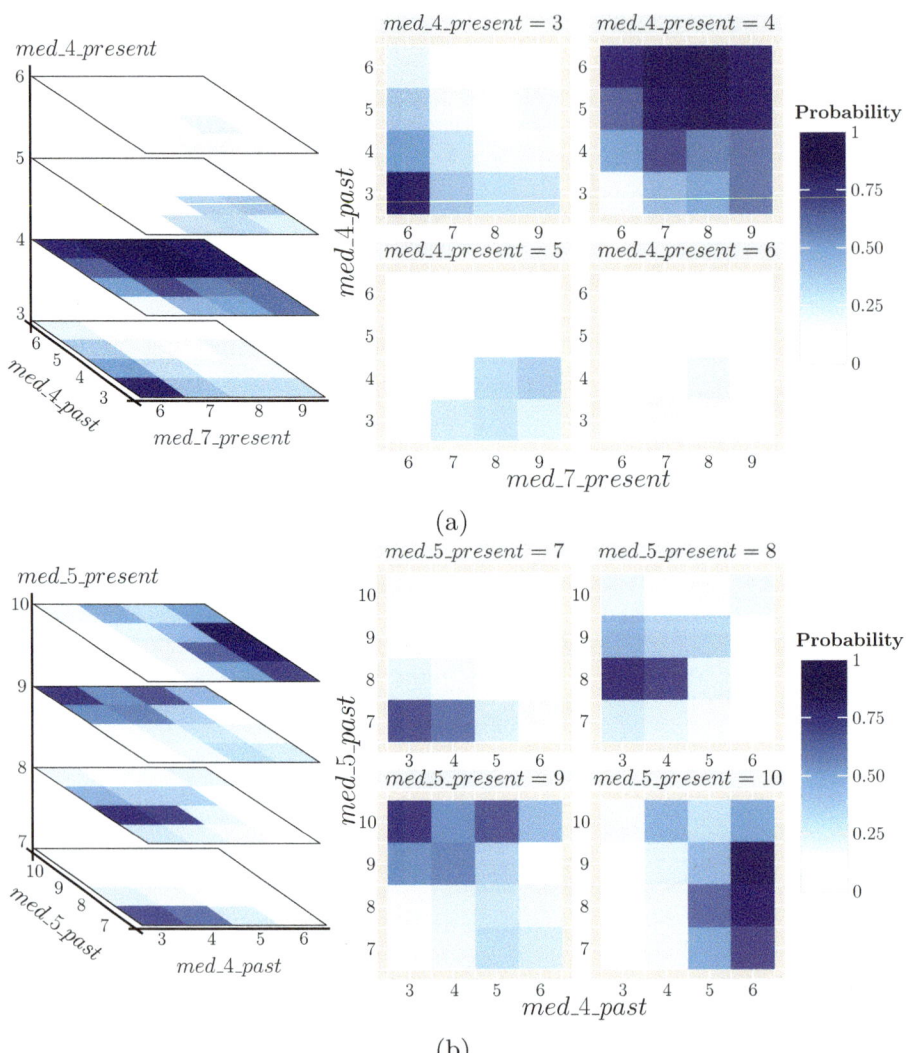

FIGURE 6.17

CPTs of the median in the present frame of regions 4 (a) and 5 (b). The CPTs were reduced to the states specified in Table 6.5. Each matrix corresponds to the probabilities (represented by a color gradient) of a fixed state of the child variable for the different states of the parent variables. Since the analyzed variables were persistent, their states in the past frame were always situated in the rows of the matrices. The matrices were sorted according to the state of the analyzed variable in ascending order from left to right and top to bottom.

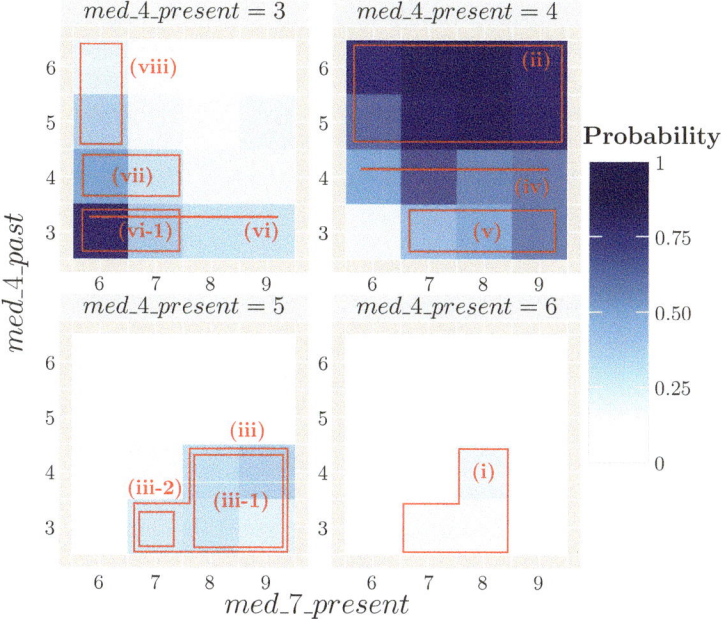

FIGURE 6.18
Annotated version of the CPT of the median in the present frame of region 4
(*med_4_present*) illustrated in Fig. 6.17(a).

ability zero) to dark blue (with probability one). These reduced CPTs were
analyzed to check whether the movement pattern of the spot was represented
in the causal relations and whether the behavior of the different regions was
stable when they were not hit by the spot.

CPT of the median of region 4 in the present frame

Fig. 6.18 shows the annotated version of the CPT of *med_4_present* shown
in Fig. 6.17(a). The indexes in parentheses and in Roman and Arabic numerals
are used in the following to help the reader find the information in the different
matrices.

The maximum median value of region 4 (state 6) was the lowest of all
the regions because it was in contact with the background on the right side
of the HAZ, and the spot only hit it partially when it finished segments 3
and 7 under normal conditions and, even more slightly, when it moved along
segments 4 and 8 (see Fig. 6.9(b)). This maximum state was reached when
the median of the region had previously been cold (states 3 or 4) and region
7 was hot, but not maximum, at that same time (median in states 7 or 8)
(annotation i). This was compatible with the deduction that the maximum
state was reached when the spot was finishing segments 3 or 7, lightly hitting

region 7, which was located beside region 4. This maximum temperature was not stable because it had a very high probability of decreasing rapidly to state 4 in the next frame (annotation ii). This was, presumably, because of its proximity to the background. Likewise, state 5, which was the next hottest state, was reached only from lower temperatures, but this time, with more disparate values of the median of region 7 (annotation iii). On the one hand, when the median was very hot (states 8 and 9) (annotation iii-1), this might mean that the spot was at segment 4 and starting on segment 5. On the other hand, when the medians of both region 4 and region 7 were colder (states 3 and 7, respectively) (annotation iii-2), this could be indicative of the spot being at the end of segment 7 and starting on segment 8.

The most stable median temperature of region 4 corresponded to state 4 because it was where the median decreased after exposure to the spot (annotation ii). This was a highly persistent state, and had a high probability of continuing into the next frame (annotation iv). It could be reached from state 3 provided the state of region 7 was not the absolute minimum (annotation v). State 3 was also highly stable (annotation vi), having a higher probability of being persistent at low values of the median of region 7 (annotation vi-1). It could plausibly be reached from state 4 if the state of region 7 was cold (states 6 and 7) (annotation vii), meaning that the spot was distant from both regions. However, it was striking that it could be reached from the hottest states (states 5 and 6) in the past frame with region 7 in a very cold state (state 6) in the present frame (annotation viii) because it meant a sudden drop in temperature in both regions. This could be an example of what occurred during the unstable initial heating transient, where a region rapidly cooled down after the spot stopped hitting it, causing a big temperature dip.

CPT of the median of region 5 in the present frame

As for the previous case, Fig. 6.19 shows the annotated version of the CPT of *med_5_present* illustrated in Fig. 6.17(b). Again, the indexes in parentheses and in Roman and Arabic numerals are used in the following to help the reader find the information in the different matrices. Additionally, capital letters are also used.

By analyzing the CPT of this inter-region temporal relationship, we expected to see the movement of the spot when it was over regions 4 and 5 corresponding, in normal conditions, to the end of segments 3 and 7, along segments 4 and 8, and the beginning of segment 1 (see Fig. 6.9(b)).

Whenever the state of the median of region 4 was stable (states 3 and 4 situated in the first two columns of each matrix and marked with "S"), indicating that the spot was not over this region, we found that the median in region 5 was generally very persistent when its state was not maximum (annotation i). This was compatible with the localization of the region in the center of the HAZ and its horizontally extended shape, having a stable temperature during the process when it was not hit by the spot. This was

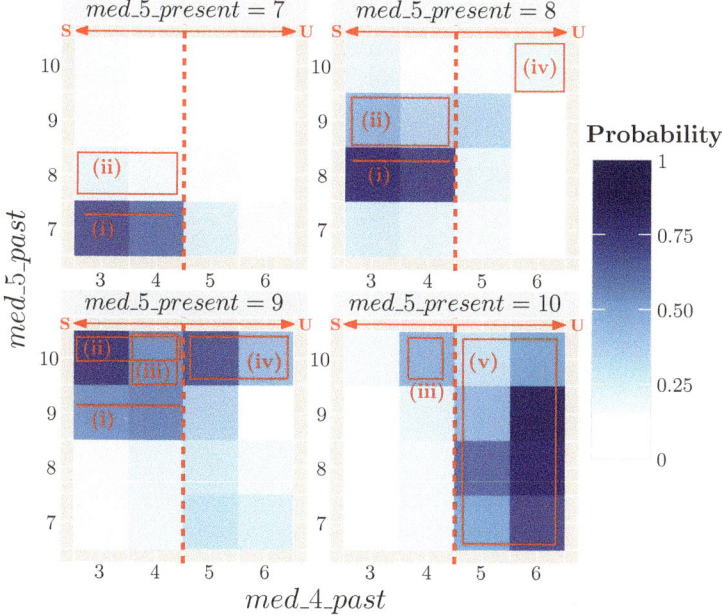

FIGURE 6.19
Annotated version of the CPT of the median in the present frame of region 5
(*med_5_present*) illustrated in Fig. 6.17(b).

corroborated by the fact that it was likely for states 7, 8 and 9 to be reached
through a gradual decrease of the median from one state to the next without
big jumps (annotation ii). Looking more closely at the time when the maximum
value of the median in region 5 was reached and the median of region 4 was
stable at state 4 (indicating that the spot was hitting only region 5), we found
that the tendency of region 5 was to decrease its median to state 9 or remain
in this maximum state (annotation iii). This was compatible with the time
when the spot was moving along segments 1, 3 and 7 of the pattern in normal
conditions, since the spot remained above region 5 for several frames.

When the spot was over region 4, which was unstable (states 5 and 6
situated in the last two columns of each matrix and marked with "U"), we saw
that there were probabilities that, after reaching the maximum state, region 5
cooled down to states 9 or 8 (annotation iv). This was compatible with the
movement of the spot to the right during segment 3 and the beginning of
segment 4, since after both had been hit by the spot it moved away. However,
it was surprising that, for high values of the median in region 4 in the previous
frame, there was a high probability of the maximum median in region 5 being
reached (or maintained) irrespective of its past temperature (annotation v).
This revealed something that was out of the question in normal conditions,
namely, the right to left movement of the spot from region 4 to region 5.

Frame 19515

Frame 19516

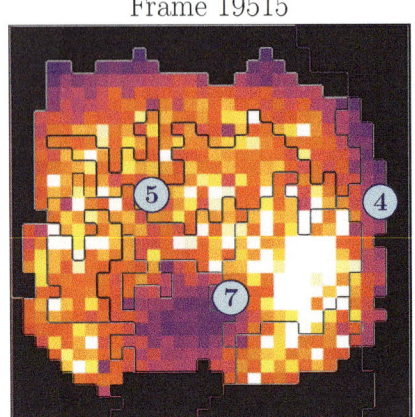
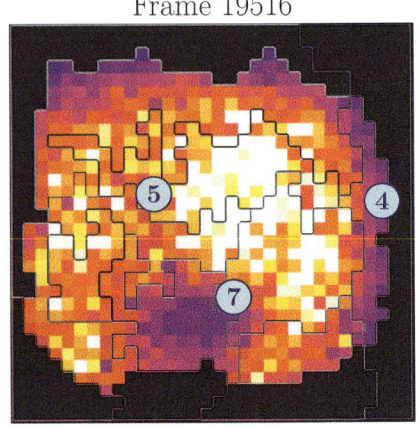

FIGURE 6.20
Two consecutive frames recorded from the laser process, showing how the normal movement pattern of the spot changed to avoid an obstacle at the bottom of the HAZ, going from regions 4 and 7 to region 5. To be exact, the spot was covering segment 11 in frame 19515 and segment 12 in frame 19516, according to the movement pattern illustrated in Fig. 6.9(e).

Nevertheless, this was feasible during the frames where the spot was avoiding an obstacle at the top or bottom of the HAZ (see Fig. 6.9(c) and Fig. 6.9(e), respectively). There, the direction of the horizontal segment of the pattern was inverted, moving from region 4 to region 5 (see Fig. 6.20 for an example). Experts noted that this phenomenon was particularly pronounced when the obstacle was at the bottom of the HAZ because the spot hit region 4 for longer, allowing it to reach higher temperatures. In fact, there was evidence of the median of region 4 reaching states 7 and 8 in this situation, but this was so unlikely that they were not visible in the CPT heat maps. This was a clear example of the major effect that the obstacle avoidance step of the normal laser process had on the CPT even if it occurred during a small fraction of the process.

6.5   Conclusions and Future Research

6.5.1   Conclusions

This case study reported an in-process AVI system learned from a number of error-free sequences through DBN and one-class classification techniques for the detection of anomalies in real image sequences from the laser surface heat treatment of steel workpieces. The implementation of this AVI system in a production line will provide on-time feedback about the quality of the process and minimize product failures and waste. To be precise, wrongly processed workpieces will be immediately marked and removed from the production line for later manual inspection.

The normal behavior of the process was learned using DBNs that provided an interpretable representation of the dynamics of the laser process. We saw how the structure of the DBN embodied conditional dependence and independence relationships among the features of the system that were exploited in order to understand how they interacted locally. These interactions were seen, under restrictive assumptions, as local causal influences that were reflected in the parameters of the DBN. We used all this information to verify that the machine was accurately learning the inherent patterns of the laser process.

Furthermore, DBNs, as shown above, could also be helpful for discovering new knowledge by finding relationships that were previously unknown, allowing experts to gain insight into the thermodynamic-spatial behavior that occurred in the HAZ where the laser spot was moving.

Additionally, thanks to their transparency, we could have detected wrong or illogical relationships in the DBN produced, for example, by noise in the measurements. In these situations, DBNs can be "repaired" by deleting or adding arcs in the structure, or modifying some parameters. This possibility of adding expert prior knowledge to the machine learning model is a valuable capability of BNs that is missing in blackbox models like artificial neural networks.

All the above points highlight that DBNs are a promising tool for the in-depth analysis of dynamic processes, which are very common in manufacturing environments.

6.5.2 Future Research

We observed that the spatio-temporal relationships automatically learned with DBNs were consistent with the properties of the laser process in normal conditions, namely, the direction of the movement of the spot and the stability of the temperature. However, we also found that the non-stationarity of the normal process produced by the initial heating of the HAZ and the obstacle avoidance step affected the results. In order to avoid this, we can learn a DBN for each of the different stationary stages of the process and decide which one is more suitable depending on the conditions of the process. A different approach would be to use a model that can deal directly with non-stationary data like the DBN approach proposed by Robinson and Hartemink (2010).

The first-order Markov assumption may not be sufficient in some applications, requiring us to look further into the past. This is the case, for example, of processes monitored on small time scales. k-TBNs are a possible option in this case (Hulst, 2006).

Finally, one-class classification is appropriate in situations where there are few examples with errors. Nevertheless, it is true that malfunctions provide very valuable information. Therefore, authors like Jäger et al. (2008) proposed the use of incremental models within the anomaly detection approach. Incremental models are capable of integrating examples of verified errors in the framework to improve their future detection. The next logical step after identifying several different causes of errors is to use these for the purpose of diagnosis, i.e., identifying which of the already known causes was behind a new failure (multiclass classification) or even detecting that the new failure was caused by something not yet recorded (novelty detection). These are key capabilities within the Industry 4.0 and Industrial Internet of Things paradigms because CPSs are expected to be self-adaptive, i.e., be capable of automatically updating any obsolete models from the continuous flow of information.

7

Distribution-Level Case Study: Forecasting of Air Freight Delays

7.1 Introduction

Not all the industrial processes required to create a final product can usually be enacted in the same physical place. In fact, a hierarchy of industries (often called **supply chain**) can be built for most industrial outputs. For example, different industries, ranging from iron ore mining that extracts the raw materials to car assembly, through many intermediate processing industries, such as the metallurgy or machine tool industries, are necessary to produce a car. As a result, the distribution of goods has a major impact on the correct operation of a factory or group of factories by transporting materials, workpieces and final goods.

The distribution of goods is usually called **logistics**. The Council of Supply Chain Management Professionals (CSCMP) defines logistics as:

Logistics

The process of planning, implementing, and controlling procedures for the efficient and effective transportation and storage of goods including services, and related information from the point of origin to the point of consumption for the purpose of conforming to customer requirements. This definition includes inbound, outbound, internal, and external movements.

The CSCMP definition of logistics covers three different activities: planning, implementation and control. Planning procedures usually create a delivery plan before actual transportation. The delivery plan includes the route definition and resource allocation (e.g., means of transportation and human resources) to meet customer requirements. Planning also involves other types of activities such as the design of contingency plans, defining a protocol to deal with unwanted situations before they occur. The logistics planning of a transport company can be rather complex because resources are limited and their use should be optimized to improve profitability and customer service quality. There is sometimes also some uncertainty about the volume of cargo to be transported in the short and medium term. Thus, good supply chain planning is essential to meet the agreed freight delivery deadlines. Logistic procedures are implemented by taking the necessary actions to complete the shipment. This involves the actual transportation, as well as customer order management or material handling. Unexpected situations, such as bad weather conditions, mechanical breakdowns, traffic jams, thefts, etc., can occur during implementation. A possible response to such situations is the application of a contingency plan, possibly involving shipment replanning to meet customer requirements. Control procedures consist of comparing planned and actual outcomes. Control procedures are potentially more successful if they are applied in real time in order to detect any deviation from the plan as soon as possible.

According to the CSCMP definition, the purpose of logistics is to meet customer requirements. These requirements usually consist of on-time and in-full delivery of largely defect-free products. Note that the necessary condition is usually that an order is shipped on time rather than shipped as soon as possible. This is an important distinction because, if resources are short, it may be a better strategy not to send a shipment as soon as the customer order arrives.

Machine learning can be helpful in the distribution industry to deal with some of these problems: demand prediction for each stakeholder in the supply chain (Carbonneau et al., 2008) or advance delay forecasting (Metzger et al., 2015; Ciccio et al., 2016).

In this case study, several classifiers (Section 2.4) are applied to forecast air freight delays using real Cargo 2000 data. To ensure a fair classifier comparison, we apply multiple hypothesis testing (Demšar, 2006; García and Herrera, 2008). As an additional exercise, we try to learn more about the analyzed air freight processes by interpreting some of the most transparent models, such as classification trees, rule induction or Bayesian classifiers.

This case study contains different shipments possibly composed of several transport lines that need to be collapsed. As multiple transport lines have to be synchronized, this is considered to be a non-trivial logistics problem illustrating how machine learning can be of use in the distribution industry.

This chapter is organized as follows. Section 7.2 explains the air freight delivery process and how the data should be preprocessed. Section 7.3 introduces the machine learning algorithm parameters that can influence classifier performance. A quantitative and qualitative comparison between all classifiers is performed in Section 7.4 after classifier parameter selection. This section also reports the results of online classification. Finally, Section 7.5 summarizes the main conclusions and future research directions.

7.2 Air Freight Process

This section describes the air freight dataset used in this case study. The dataset was introduced by Metzger et al. (2015), who compared machine learning, constraint satisfaction and quality of service aggregation techniques to forecast air freight delays. The dataset is composed of real data recorded by the Cargo 2000 group (renamed Cargo iQ as of 2016), an International Air Transport Association (IATA) initiative. Its aim is to deliver a new quality management system for the air cargo industry.

Each delivery in the Cargo 2000 system receives a master operating plan[1]. Shipment planning involves computing the delivery route across different airports and an estimated time for completion of each transport service of which a shipment is composed. The agents involved in the shipment share predefined agreed XML Cargo 2000 messages in real-time when a new transport service has been completed. If shipment process delays are predicted, a shipment can be rescheduled to avoid delays. This could improve the customer service quality.

The dataset used in this case study was made available[2] by Metzger et al. (2015). Fig. 7.1 shows the UML 2.0 activity diagram of each business process in the dataset. It pictures the structure for a freight forwarding company, consolidating up to three smaller shipments from suppliers which are then shipped together to customers in order to benefit from better freight rates or increased cargo security (Metzger et al., 2015). Thus, each business process is composed of up to four transport legs with at most three inbound transport legs and a single mandatory outbound transport leg from the place where the freight is consolidated.

Each transport leg involves the execution of different kinds of transport services, corresponding to different Cargo 2000 messages:

1. **RCS** (Freight reception): freight is received by airline. It is delivered and checked in at departure warehouse.

2. **DEP** (Freight departure): goods are delivered to aircraft and, once confirmed on board, aircraft departs.

3. **RCF** (Freight arrival): freight is transported by air and arrives at destination airport. Upon arrival, freight is checked in and stored at arrival warehouse.

4. **DLV** (Freight delivery): freight is delivered from destination airport warehouse to customer.

As shown in Fig. 7.1, there is a loop (denoted by a segment) from RCF to DEP, which is used to model stopover airports. Each transport leg can contain

---

[1]http://www.iata.org/whatwedo/cargo/cargoiq/Pages/master-operating-plan.aspx
[2]http://www.s-cube-network.eu/c2k

up to four trips, although the dataset does not contain any transport leg with more than three trips.

The dataset contains 3,942 actual business processes, comprising 7,932 transport legs and 56,082 transport services. The information available in the dataset is

- The number of transport legs.

- For each transport leg, the number of trips.

- For each transport trip, an anonymous code for the origin and destination airports.

- For each transport service, its respective planned and actual times.

- Unique identifiers for each business process and transport leg.

In total, there are 98 variables in the dataset. The dataset does, of course, include all actual times because the business processes have finished. However, actual times are shared in real time with the Cargo 2000 system as the business process progresses. In this case study, we simulate this behavior to gain insight into how machine learning method performance improves when new information about actual times becomes available.

Table 7.1 shows the number of transport services of each type and the rate of violations of the planned times. Note that 26.6% of the business processes did not finish on time. The majority of delayed transport services are of the DEP type. DEP transport services are the most unpredictable, perhaps because external factors, such as meteorological conditions or airport traffic congestion, may have a bearing on departure from the airport. It is important to note that, although 84% of DEP transport services are delayed, the rate of delayed business processes is relatively lower on mainly two grounds:

- Time loss during the DEP process can be recovered across the remaining transport services.

- A delay in an inbound transport leg because of a DEP process delay will not delay the entire business process provided the delayed transport leg finishes before the longer inbound transport leg. The outbound transport leg starts when the last inbound transport leg has been consolidated at the hub.

7.2.1 Data Preprocessing

The number of transport legs, and the number of trips for each transport leg, may vary across different business processes. We cannot make any assumptions about the structure of the business process in advance. The non-existent transport services for the missing trips and missing transport legs are marked

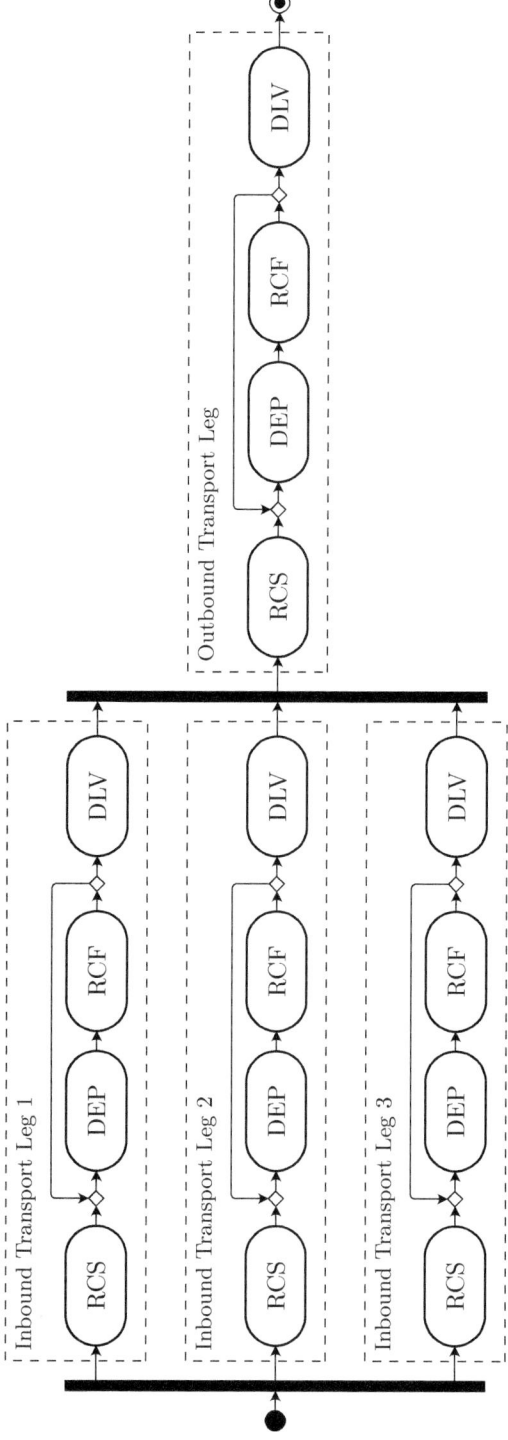

FIGURE 7.1

UML 2.0 diagram of the business process involving up to three shipments that are consolidated before being sent to the customer (Metzger et al., 2015).

TABLE 7.1

Number of transport services grouped by type and their respective actual rate of violation of planned times (Metzger et al., 2015)

	Dataset instances	Actual rate of violation (%)
Transport service:	Σ 56,082	
RCS (Freight reception)	11,874	5.8
DEP (Freight departure)	16,167	84.0
RCF (Freight arrival)	16,167	19.5
DLV (Freight delivery)	11,874	24.0
Business Process	3,942	26.6

as missing values. There is no way of automatically imputing missing values (Section 2.2.1), because it does not make sense to assign planned and actual times for non-existent transport legs and trips.

Table 7.2 shows two example instances of the dataset. The outbound transport leg is analogous to the inbound transport legs and is not shown here. The variable nr is a unique identifier for each business process, and the distinction between planned and actual times is represented by the suffix $\_p$ and $\_e$, respectively. There are three different dep_x and rcf_x variables for each transport leg because three is the maximum number of stopovers in the dataset. In addition, $*\_place$ variables contain an anonymized IATA code representing each departure/reception airport (Section 7.2.1.3) for each freight trip. NA values represent missing data. As shown, there is a different number of missing values because the number of transport legs and the number of trips in each transport leg vary. Instance 1 is composed of two legs with one trip in Transport leg 1 and two trips in Transport leg 2. On the other hand, Instance 2 includes only one trip in Transport leg 1. Therefore, Instance 2 has a higher number of missing values. The class variable (denoted as Delay), can be calculated from the service execution times. The planned/actual time of a given business process is the planned/actual time of the longest inbound transport leg, plus the planned/actual time of the outbound transport leg.

There are four main issues that should be handled in the preprocessing step:

1. How to deal with the missing values for the planned/actual times (Section 7.2.1.1).

2. How to clarify the meaning of each variable (Section 7.2.1.2).

3. How to use the airport code variables, whose cardinality is far too large, appropriately (Section 7.2.1.3).

4. How to improve the commensurability of service execution times (Section 7.2.1.4).

7.2.1.1 Simplification of Planned/Actual Times

Missing values (Section 2.2.1) can be hard to deal with. There are three main solutions: imputation, complete-case analysis and embedded classifier support for missing values (usually involving data imputation during classifier training, e.g., classification trees). In this case study, automatic imputation is not possible because it does not make sense to generate time values for non-existent deliveries; neither is the complete-case analysis of instances with missing values feasible, because all the instances have some missing data. Multiple classifiers will be applied to the Cargo 2000 dataset, and we cannot be sure that every classifier is capable of dealing with missing values. The proposed solution is to apply manual imputation to homogenize the dataset such that the structure of the business process (i.e., the number of transport legs and the number of trips in each transport leg) changes as little as possible.

The non-existent transport legs and trips are marked as missing values in the dataset. Some classifiers cannot be applied to datasets with missing data values. As each time variable could possibly have a non-missing value in any instance, we pretend that each existent transport leg contains three trips. However, the imputed value for the missing value should not change the structure of the business process. For this reason, a zero value is imputed to the planned/actual time for the non-existing trips of each existing transport leg:

$$
\begin{aligned}
ij\_dep\_k\_p &= 0 \\
ij\_rcf\_k\_p &= 0 \\
ij\_dep\_k\_e &= 0 \\
ij\_rcf\_k\_e &= 0,
\end{aligned}
\quad , \forall\, j, k \mid ij\_hops \neq \text{NA},\, k > ij\_hops \qquad (7.1)
$$

where $ij\_dep\_k\_p$ and $ij\_rcf\_k\_p$ are the planned times for the k-th trip of the j-th inbound transport leg of the DEP and RCF services. Respectively, actual times are represented similarly with the suffix $\_e$. The number of trips for the j-th transport leg is denoted as ij_hops. Eq. 7.1 checks for a transport leg with the condition $ij\_hops \neq \text{NA}$. Moreover, it applies the imputation for the non-existing trips with the condition $k > ij\_hops$. The same preprocessing should be applied to the outbound leg.

A zero value does not change the duration of any transport leg or the business process. Also, as the actual time is equal to the planned time, the transformation does not add any delayed transport services.

This imputation does not solve the problem of how to deal with the non-existent transport legs, as all transport service times on those transport legs are marked as missing. The solution to this problem is proposed in Section 7.2.1.3.

This is not the only possible transformation of the time data that solves the problem of missing data in the non-existing trips. For example, we could sum all DEP and RCF variables to create a super collapsed transport service that includes all the planned and actual times of every departure and arrival:

TABLE 7.2
Inbound transport leg data for two business processes. Two instances are
shown as examples of the changing number of missing data. The table has
been divided into two parts because of the high data dimensionality. The
columns on both sides of the table contain information on a different instance

	Inst. 1	Inst. 2		Inst. 1	Inst. 2
nr	1	2	*i1_hops*	1	1
i2_hops	2	NA	*i3_hops*	NA	NA
i1_rcs_p	844	4380	*i1_rcs_e*	584	4119
i1_dep_1_p	90	90	*i1_dep_1_e*	297	280
i1_rcf_1_p	1935	905	*i1_rcf_1_e*	1415	547
i1_dep_2_p	NA	NA	*i1_dep_2_e*	NA	NA
i1_rcf_2_p	NA	NA	*i1_rcf_2_e*	NA	NA
i1_dep_3_p	NA	NA	*i1_dep_3_e*	NA	NA
i1_rcf_3_p	NA	NA	*i1_rcf_3_e*	NA	NA
i1_dlv_p	3780	3780	*i1_dlv_e*	5790	321
i1_dep_1_place	700	456	*i1_rcf_1_place*	431	700
i1_dep_2_place	NA	NA	*i1_rcf_2_place*	NA	NA
i1_dep_3_place	NA	NA	*i1_rcf_3_place*	NA	NA
i2_rcs_p	2964	NA	*i2_rcs_e*	2888	NA
i2_dep_1_p	180	NA	*i2_dep_1_e*	239	NA
i2_rcf_1_p	970	NA	*i2_rcf_1_e*	756	NA
i2_dep_2_p	160	NA	*i2_dep_2_e*	331	NA
i2_rcf_2_p	1080	NA	*i2_rcf_2_e*	1142	NA
i2_dep_3_p	NA	NA	*i2_dep_3_e*	NA	NA
i2_rcf_3_p	NA	NA	*i2_rcf_3_e*	NA	NA
i2_dlv_p	7020	NA	*i2_dlv_e*	6628	NA
i2_dep_1_place	257	NA	*i2_rcf_1_place*	149	NA
i2_dep_2_place	149	NA	*i2_rcf_2_place*	431	NA
i2_dep_3_place	NA	NA	*i2_rcf_3_place*	NA	NA
i3_rcs_p	NA	NA	*i3_rcs_e*	NA	NA
i3_dep_1_p	NA	NA	*i3_dep_1_e*	NA	NA
i3_rcf_1_p	NA	NA	*i3_rcf_1_e*	NA	NA
i3_dep_2_p	NA	NA	*i3_dep_2_e*	NA	NA
i3_rcf_2_p	NA	NA	*i3_rcf_2_e*	NA	NA
i3_dep_3_p	NA	NA	*i3_dep_3_e*	NA	NA
i3_rcf_3_p	NA	NA	*i3_rcf_3_e*	NA	NA
i3_dlv_p	NA	NA	*i3_dlv_e*	NA	NA
i3_dep_1_place	NA	NA	*i3_rcf_1_place*	NA	NA
i3_dep_2_place	NA	NA	*i3_rcf_2_place*	NA	NA
i3_dep_3_place	NA	NA	*i3_rcf_3_place*	NA	NA
Delay	False	False			

$$\text{collapsed}_j\_p = \sum_{k=1}^{ij\_hops} (ij\_dep\_k\_p + ij\_rcf\_k\_p)$$

$$\text{collapsed}_j\_e = \sum_{k=1}^{ij\_hops} (ij\_dep\_k\_e + ij\_rcf\_k\_e).$$

Again, missing data are not considered, although the classifier could, thanks to the auxiliary variables ij_hops, still ascertain the number of trips in each transport leg. Furthermore, this transformation generates a smaller set of variables for the classifier. Nevertheless, we did not use this data representation in this case study because it does not report updates about the status of the business process until all the stopover flights have finished. As we are looking for a finer-grained analysis of the delivery process, the separation of DEP and RCF is a better option.

7.2.1.2 Transport Leg Reordering

In the Cargo 2000 dataset, there are many variables with a similar meaning such as the planned/actual times for the inbound transport services. These variables would be treated as more or less equivalent by the classifier because none of the inbound transport legs are more important or discriminant than the others. Classifier interpretability and discriminant power could be improved if each transport leg were given a different meaning.

Section 7.2 mentioned that the freight is consolidated at a specified airport. All the inbound transport legs have to finish before the outbound transport leg of the business process can start. This suggests that the longest of the three inbound transport legs will be especially important. This leg will be denoted as bottleneck transport leg. Without any data preprocessing, the bottleneck transport leg could be any of the three inbound transport legs. We reorder the transport legs by time. According to this data transformation, leg $i1$ will always be the bottleneck and $i3$ will be the shortest transport leg. Note that this reordering does not change the structure of the business process (the number of transport legs or trips). Nevertheless, it clarifies the meaning of the variables of each transport leg. For example, it would be reasonable for a classifier to attach more importance to the $i1$ transport leg because a delay in the bottleneck potentially has a greater effect on the business process.

An unresolved data preprocessing issue is how to deal with non-existent transport legs. After reordering, the variables corresponding to the bottleneck transport leg are easily located. We consider these to be the most important variables, because there is no margin for a delay in that transport leg. Therefore, these are the only variables that will be fed to the classifiers. This simplifies the problem as shown in the UML diagram in Fig 7.2. Using this representation, and the transformation described in Section 7.2.1.1, we can avoid all the missing values.

As the business process progresses, more actual times become available. These actual times can be used to recompute the reordering of the legs, taking into account the new information. The following rule will be used: when available, it is preferable to use actual times over the respective planned times. When the actual times are considered to compute the bottleneck leg, it could change across the development of the business process. This can be useful if the non-bottleneck transport legs do not have a very wide margin and a small delay could change the bottleneck transport leg. The online classification simulation is presented in Section 7.4.2.2.

7.2.1.3 Airport Simplification

The values of the airport code variable range from 100 to 816 and are a unique identifier for each airport. The IATA codes in the original dataset were masked on the grounds of confidentiality. As shown in Table 7.2, the departure/reception airports (tagged as *leg_dep_nhop_place* and *leg_rcf_nhop_place*, respectively) are recorded in the original dataset. Note that the code in *leg_rcf_1_place* is always the same as *leg_dep_2_place*, and also, the code in *leg_rcf_2_place* is always the same as *leg_dep_3_place*. In other words, the departure airport for one trip will be the reception airport for the previous trip. This is an undesirable value repetition, and the number of airport variables can be reduced to at most four for each transport leg accounting for exactly the same information. To be precise, we could use the following variables: *leg_dep_1_place*, *leg_rcf_1_place*, *leg_rcf_2_place*, *leg_rcf_3_place*. This finding reduces dataset dimensionality by avoiding information redundancy.

Also, the variables encoding the airports can be quite tricky to handle because of their high cardinality (717 different possible values). Nevertheless, if we count all the unique values for each *_place* column, we find that the original dataset contains only 237 unique airports. This number of different values is still too large for these variables to be easily processed. Suppose, for example, that we create a naive Bayes model (Section 2.4.9) without any previous preprocessing of the *_place* variables. The result for the node *i1_dep_1_place* is shown in Fig. 7.3. Looking at the conditional probability table (CPT) of node *i1_dep_1_place*, we note that there are 142 different unique values of this variable. The probability in most of the rows is very low (even 0). Even if we could remove the zero probabilities using Laplace estimation (see Section 2.2.2.1), the resulting model would be very difficult to apply in a real situation due to a lack of generality. For example, what would happen if a business process with an unknown airport had to be classified? The classifier would not be able to output a response for the unknown airport because there is no entry in the CPT for the variable.

We propose an alternative that can reduce the cardinality of the *_place* variables and is more general than the original dataset encoding. Thus, we need to group the airports together using a known criterion to reduce airport

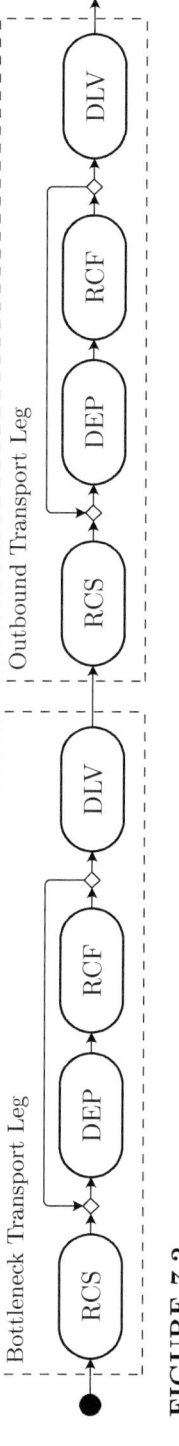

FIGURE 7.2
UML 2.0 diagram of the business process taking into account the bottleneck transport leg only.

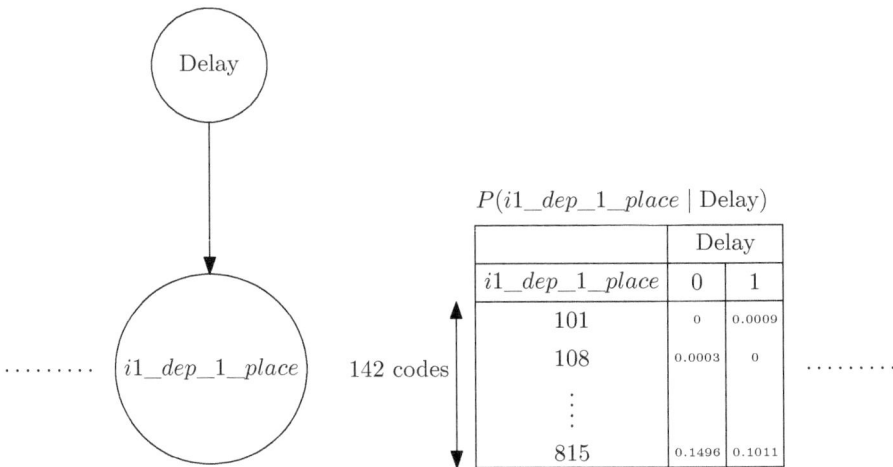

FIGURE 7.3
Example of a CPT in a naive Bayes classifier for a variable with high cardinality.

cardinality. As the original IATA codes have been masked, we cannot use information about the airports. The only known information is the number of times each airport has been used in the Cargo 2000 dataset. We assume that the frequency of use of each airport is representative of its real traffic, and this level of traffic can have an impact on service times. For example, there are more likely to be landing and take-off delays at a congested than at a low traffic airport.

Therefore, we create four possible airport labels: low traffic (L), medium traffic (M), high traffic (H) and also a non-existing tag (NA) for the non-existent flights (less than three trips in a transport leg). Airport usage has been computed counting the number of take-off and landing (DEP and RCF) services for each anonymized IATA airport code. The least used airports that account for at most the 33% of total airport uses will be tagged as L. The least used airports that have not been tagged and also account for at most the 33% of total airport uses will be tagged as M. The rest of the non-tagged airports are tagged as H. We opted for equal-frequency discretization (Section 2.2.1) because it provides a fair division of the airports. None of the tags is overrepresented in the dataset (each airport label contains about the same frequency), whereas it still provides a division following the criterion that we defined for airport use. Fig. 7.4 shows the cumulative sum of airport uses. Also, the 33% and 66% thresholds of the total sum of airport uses are represented as blue/orange horizontal lines, respectively. The label of each airport is color coded: blue for low traffic airports, orange for medium traffic airports and red for high traffic airports. We find that there is a clear imbalance in the number of airports for

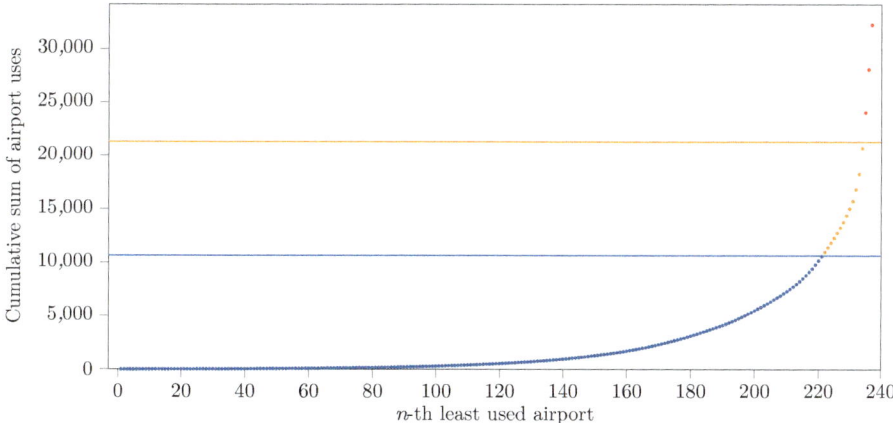

FIGURE 7.4
Cumulative sum of the number of uses for each airport sorted in ascending order. The n-th airport on the x-axis corresponds to the n-th least used airport. Low/medium/high traffic airports are color coded blue/orange/red, respectively. The blue and orange horizontal lines are the cumulative maximum values for an airport to be tagged as low/medium traffic airport, respectively.

each label: there are 221 low traffic airports, 13 medium traffic airports and three high traffic airports.

This transformation of the airport information makes the job of the classifier easier because the cardinality of each _place variable is reduced to four. Also, if an instance with a new airport (not in the dataset) is to be classified, the airport will be tagged as L and the instance can be classified. Furthermore, the tag of each airport and the number of uses can be updated as new data come in. Therefore, new information can update our knowledge about each airport and improve our classification.

7.2.1.4 Normalizing the Length of Each Business Process

Each service execution (RCS, DEP, RCF, DLV) can take a different length of time for each flight or set of flights. This could occur for various reasons: for example, the distance covered or the weight/volume of the different freights could vary enormously for different business processes. In the first case, a larger distance will be correlated with a longer RCF time. A heavier weight/volume, on the other hand, could make the other service processes harder to manage. For this reason, an absolute time value is not really meaningful for detecting delays in the service executions and, thus, across the whole business process. A time relative to the business process duration could be more significant.

Imagine that we ordered a national delivery in a European country. We know that a given trip in the shipment took 300 minutes and that the whole business process was delayed. Is the value of 300 minutes really meaningful for predicting a delay in a subsequent shipment? This could be well below delay expectations for a long-haul international shipment. As we do not know where each airport is located in the Cargo 2000 dataset, we cannot take into account the distance to correct the absolute times. Suppose, instead, that we used relative times in the above example. Then, we would say that the national shipment trip took 80% of the total planned business process time. If we find a long-haul international shipment where a given trip accounted for 80% of the business process time, this international shipment could reasonably be classified as a possible delay because this is not a usual feature of non-delayed national or international business processes.

Of course, this correction is not perfect and can underrate/overrate the expected time for short-/long-haul flights or light/heavy freights because a particular service execution may take more or less time for flights with different characteristics. Nevertheless, relative times are more commensurable than absolute times and are always in the same $[0, 1]$ range.

7.3 Supervised Classification Algorithms for Forecasting Delays

We apply the most common state-of-the-art classifiers to Cargo 2000 datasets preprocessed as described in Section 7.2.1. These classifiers are explained in depth in Section 2.4. In this chapter, we briefly remind their behavior to explain their parameters.

The classifiers are implemented in the WEKA (Section 2.7) software package (version 3.8.1) (Hall et al., 2009). WEKA is one of the most used frameworks in the machine learning community because it is easy to use and offers a wide range of options. In addition to supervised classification, WEKA can also perform other types of tasks such as clustering, variable association discovery, feature subset selection or data visualization. This chapter focuses on supervised classification tasks. The description of the classifier parameters will be driven mainly by the WEKA implementation.

7.3.1 k-Nearest Neighbors

k-nearest neighbors (Cover and Hart, 1967), often shortened to k-NN, assume that similar instances have similar classifications. The instances that are most alike are the nearest instances in the feature space. The algorithm's principal computational cost is to compute the k-nearest neighbors that will (usually) vote for the class label of the instance. Section 2.4.3 provides further details.

The following parameters of the k-NN algorithm can be tuned in WEKA:

- k value: the number of nearest neighbors considered by the algorithm.

- Search algorithm: the manner in which the algorithm should find the nearest neighbors. The most usual alternatives are linear search, k-d trees, ball trees.

- Distance function: the distance in the feature space. It can be calculated using different functions. The most common functions are Euclidean, Manhattan and Minkowski distances (Section 2.3).

- Weighting scheme: system for indicating how great a role the nearest instances play in determining the class label. There are some options in the weighting scheme: no weighting, inverse of distance and $1 -$ distance.

7.3.2 Classification Trees

Classification trees create a tree or hierarchy to represent a disjunction of constraint conjunctions on the variable values. The tree nodes contain a specific test for some variable. Each branch of a node corresponds to each possible node test outcome. A class label is assigned, instead of a variable test, to the tree leaves. A test instance has to traverse the tree from the root to a leaf, always advancing through the branches that pass the corresponding tests. We use the C4.5 algorithm (Quinlan, 1993) to build a classification tree. Further details about classification trees are given in Section 2.4.4. Several changes can be made to the way the algorithm builds and prunes the tree:

- Construction changes:

  - Minimum number of instances per leaf: this parameter avoids leaves that do no have enough instances, as this can be a cause of overfitting. Any partition that produces a leaf with too few instances is avoided.
  - Binary splits: nodes are allowed to have no more than two branches.
  - Collapse tree: this parameter collapses a subtree to a node starting from the parents of the leaves if the training error does not increase after collapsing. This process is applied before pruning.

- Pruning changes:

  - No pruning: training without a pruning phase.
  - Confidence threshold for pruning: if pruning is applied, it is necessary to calculate whether the replacement of a subtree with a leaf node will affect performance. This confidence threshold regulates how pessimistic the error estimation is, and, consequently, whether pruning is more conservative or aggressive. The value range for this threshold is $[0, 0.5]$. A smaller threshold value indicates a more pessimistic error estimation, leading to more pruning.
  - Reduced error pruning: see Section 2.4.4.

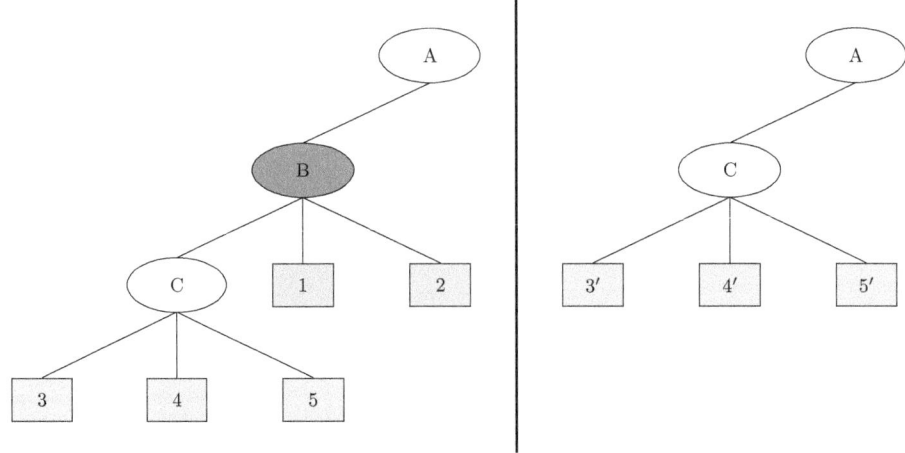

FIGURE 7.5
Subtree raising applied to node B (in red). The largest branch (C) replaces B, and the instances in leaves 1 and 2 (in orange) are moved to the children of node C.

– **Subtree raising**: this parameter decides whether replacing a subtree with its largest branch (branch with a higher number of instances) improves error estimation. If the subtree is substituted by its largest branch, all the subtree instances not belonging to the largest branch are relocated in the largest branch. Fig. 7.5 shows an example of the subtree raising transformation.

7.3.3 Rule Induction

Rule induction methods try to induce a set of rules of the form:

$$\text{IF } X_i = x_i \text{ AND } X_j = x_j \text{ AND } \ldots \text{ THEN } C = c$$

where $x_i \in \Omega_{X_i}, x_j \in \Omega_{X_j}, c \in \Omega_C$. Rules can be analyzed by humans to extract useful knowledge. We use the RIPPER algorithm (Cohen, 1995) to induce rules. RIPPER evolved out of another algorithm called IREP.

The IREP algorithm induces a set of rules by creating one rule at a time using greedy search. The rule induction procedure is composed of a greedy growing rule phase, followed by a greedy pruning rule phase for each rule. In each step of the growing or pruning phase, the rules should cover as many positive instances as possible while trying to maximize a custom criterion. Section 2.4.5 provides further details on the IREP and RIPPER algorithms.

The parameters used by RIPPER are

• Minimal required weight: the minimum total weight of the instances covered by each rule. Commonly, the weight of each instance is the same and equal to 1. Nevertheless, more important instances may be weighted higher.

- Number of optimization runs: the number of times that the optimization step is executed.

- Pruning: training with rule pruning.

- Error rate: this parameter checks whether or not there is an error rate of at least 0.5 in the stopping criterion.

7.3.4 Artificial Neural Networks

Artificial neural networks (McCulloch and Pitts, 1943) are biologically-inspired methods that aim to mimic the behavior of animal brains. A neural network is usually represented as a graph, where the nodes represent neurons. The neurons are connected with each other by edges that contain a weight and imitate a synaptic signaling process within an animal brain. The weight of each edge indicates the strength of the connection between two neurons and can be negative. The artificial neural network that we use is called multilayer perceptron. Further details about artificial neural networks are given in Section 2.4.6.

The multilayer perceptron in WEKA is trained using the backpropagation algorithm. The backpropagation algorithm has some parameters that modify the training phase:

- Learning rate (η): a value in the range $[0, 1]$ that changes the speed at which the weights of each connection between neurons is updated. A lower value makes slight changes to the weights, as a result of which it can take longer to get a (usually local) optimal value. A greater value makes bigger changes to the weights, possibly leading to a faster convergence to local optima. However, a higher value can easily overshoot the optimal point, again possibly failing to reach an optimum. This behavior is illustrated in Fig. 7.6, where the low learning rate in (a) makes slight changes to the weight values, usually leading to small changes in the objective function. The last update comes very close to the optimum point. However, it makes many more weight updates than the high learning rate example in (b).

- **Momentum**: a value in the range $[0, 1]$ that uses the direction of previous weight updates to adjust the weight change speed. Thus, if weights were previously updated in the same direction, the weight change speed can be increased because we are definitely moving in the right direction towards the optimization of the objective function. However, if weights were updated in opposite directions, the speed of weight change should be decreased. Fig. 7.6(c) illustrates high momentum weight updates. If the changes are too large when the weights are near the optimum, the optimum is overshot. Thus, the momentum causes a reduction in the weight change speed. Low

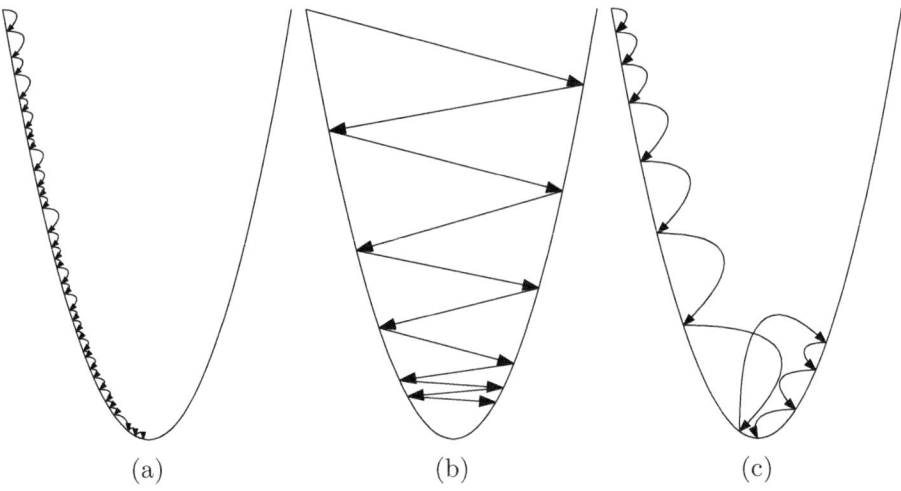

FIGURE 7.6
Example of weight optimization with different parameters. (a) Low learning rate, (b) high learning rate and (c) high momentum.

momentum weight changes are almost equal, regardless of the direction of the weight update.

- **Number of epochs**: number of epochs (iterations) of the training process.

- Percentage size of validation set: ratio of the size of the validation set to the whole dataset, used to prevent overfitting in the training phase.

- Network topology: Number of neurons in each hidden layer.

- **Learning rate decay**: the learning rate is decreased as the training progresses. This aims to reduce large weights in the network.

- Transfer function (f): the function that defines the output of each neuron given its inputs. The sigmoid function is a common option.

7.3.5   Support Vector Machines

A support vector machine (SVM) model aims to maximize the margin in the classification decision boundary. The assumption is that margin maximization can produce better generalization capabilities than other decision boundaries.

   In linearly separable problems, this is equivalent to finding the hyperplane that has the widest margin (or distance) between the hyperplane and the nearest instances of both classes to the hyperplane. The nearest instances to the hyperplane are called support vectors, hence, the method's name. In non-linearly separable problems, the kernel trick is used to, hopefully, yield a linearly separable problem in an often higher-dimensional space without having to explicitly translate the feature space to the higher-dimensional space in question.

Finding the best hyperplane is usually stated as an optimization problem solved using the Lagrange multiplier method. The sequential minimal optimization (SMO) algorithm by Platt (1999) is a method that quickly computes the Lagrange multipliers to solve the optimization problem. We use SMO to train our SVM models. Section 2.4.7 provides further details.

The SMO algorithm uses the following parameters:

- Complexity constant or cost (M): see Section 2.4.7. It can take any value in the domain of positive real numbers, but values in the range $[0, 1]$ are common.

- Tolerance: the tolerance parameter controls the amount of permissible SVM optimization problem-solving error. This value is usually equal to 10^{-3}. More accurate results will have a slower convergence.

- Kernel function (K): see Section 2.4.7.

7.3.6 Logistic Regression

The logistic regression model (Hosmer and Lemeshow, 2000) is a discriminative model designed to estimate $p(C|\mathbf{x})$ by fitting a parameter vector $\boldsymbol{\beta}$ for each class. The parameter vectors are used within a logistic function to predict the probability of each class label. The parameter vectors $\boldsymbol{\beta}$ are usually computed using the Newton-Raphson numerical algorithm. Section 2.4.8 provides further details.

Logistic regression has the following parameter:

- **Ridge**: a regularization scheme that penalizes oversized $\boldsymbol{\beta}$ vector parameters. Training with ridge regularization returns parameters that are closer to 0, thus reducing the classifier variance. This reduces the minimum square error. See Section 2.4.8.

7.3.7 Bayesian Network Classifiers

We apply three different kinds of Bayesian network classifiers: naive Bayes, tree augmented naive Bayes (TAN) and unrestricted Bayesian network classifiers learned with the K2 algorithm. The naive Bayes classifier assumes the independence of all variables given the class, and its structure is fixed unless there is feature subset selection. In order to relax this assumption, the TAN classifier (Friedman et al., 1997) builds a tree structure over the variables. Therefore, each variable has the class and at most one other variable as a parent. As discussed in Section 2.4.9, the tree learning procedure uses Kruskal's algorithm (Kruskal, 1956) on the variables with a score criterion (usually conditional mutual information between a variable and class variable) to assess an edge between two variables. Both of the above classifiers have a totally (naive) or partially (TAN) fixed structure in order to reduce the computational complexity of the training. This is why we also use an unrestricted Bayesian network classifier learned using the K2 algorithm (Cooper and Herskovits, 1992) for classification. The K2 algorithm can learn any network structure, although some constraints, such as the maximum number of parents per node, may be imposed on the algorithm. The WEKA implementation of the K2 algorithm only works with discrete variables, and, therefore, continuous variables should be discretized.

Naive Bayes has a fixed structure, so there is no structure learning. The only possible changes concern how it deals with continuous variables. There are two common options:

- Use a kernel density estimation model (Parzen, 1962) to non-parametrically estimate the probabilities of the continuous variables, that is, $p(X_i|C)$.

- Discretize continuous variables.

The K2 algorithm can be tuned using the following parameter:

- Maximum number of parents per node.

Moreover, the K2 and TAN algorithms have two parameters in common:

- Scoring metric: although BDe and conditional mutual information criteria were used in the seminal K2 and TAN algorithms, respectively, some other criteria could be selected. Examples of scoring criteria are AIC, BIC, or MDL (Section 2.5.3).

- Prior count to estimate Bayesian network parameters: this number defines the a priori count of examples. See the Lindstone rule in Section 2.4.9.

7.3.8 Metaclassifiers

As discussed in Section 2.4.10, metaclassifiers (Kuncheva, 2004) combine the results of multiple base classifiers to classify an instance. We use four different types of metaclassifiers: stacking, bagging, random forest and AdaBoost.M1.

The stacking method stores multiple layers of classifiers. Each layer uses the results from the previous layer, and the last layer makes the final decision. Typically, different types of classifiers are used to complement each other. The stacking generalization has to learn how to combine the classifiers in the previous layer to achieve the best results. The parameterization required by the stacking classifier is the definition of the base classifier hierarchy.

The bagging method trains several classifiers using slightly different training sets. Thus, each classifier is trained with a bootstrap sample of the training set. These bootstrap samples are usually called bags. The bagging method is commonly used with unstable classifiers, where a slight change in the training data can cause large changes in the trained models. A new instance is classified by majority vote of all classifiers. The bagging method has the following parameters:

- Size of each bootstrap bag: this parameter controls the number of instances of each bag used to train each classifier.

- Number of trained classifiers.

The random forest method trains several decision trees with different datasets, all of which are sampled from the training set. Unlike the bagging method, not only does it sample instances from the training set, but it also selects a random set of variables from the training set. As in the bagging algorithm, majority voting is usually performed to classify a new instance. The random forest method has the following parameters:

- Size of each bootstrap bag: this parameter controls the number of instances of each bag used to train each classifier.

- Number of variables to be selected in each bag.

- Number of trees to be trained.

- Parameters controlling the behavior of each tree:

  - Minimum number of instances per leaf.
  - Maximum depth.

The AdaBoost.M1 method trains several models sequentially, where each model aims to correctly classify instances that were misclassified by previous classifiers. To do this, a weight is assigned to each instance. Any instances that have been misclassified by the previous classifiers will have larger weights and will be more likely to be selected in the training phase of the new classifier. In the classification phase, a voting procedure is used to predict the class, where each classifier has a different weight based upon its classification accuracy. AdaBoost.M1 has the following parameters:

- Weight sum of each bag: this parameter controls the weight sum of each training bag. The weight sum of a bag is the sum of the weights in a training bag. As opposed to the bagging and random forest methods, the weight sum is used instead of the number of instances. Using the weight sum, the new training bags tend to contain instances misclassified by previous classifiers because the instances that are harder to classify tend to have larger weights. This alleviates the computational burden of classifying easy instances too often.

- Number of trained classifiers.

The stacking, bagging and AdaBoost.M1 methods have to pick which base classifiers to use. In the case of random forests, we know that the base classifiers are trees. The base classifiers can have parameters of their own that can affect performance. Furthermore, the combination of multiple types of classifiers can generate a large number of parameters for each metaclassifier.

7.3.9 Implementation Details of Classification Algorithms

Some issues regarding the parameters of the WEKA implementation of each classifier are worthy of note:

- WEKA classifiers usually have more parameters than are mentioned above. The remaining parameters are usually devoted to computational concerns (e.g., whether an algorithm should be parallelized) or possible previous data preprocessing (e.g., the SMO algorithm has a parameter to normalize or standardize the data before they are processed by the algorithm).

- Parameters can be configured using WEKA's graphical user interface ("Explorer") or, if WEKA is run from the command line, by entering the name of each parameter.

- The documentation on WEKA parameters is available at `http://weka.sourceforge.net/doc.stable/`.

7.4   Results and Discussion

This section shows how to compare multiple classifiers. In Section 7.4.1, we describe the selected parametrization for each classifier. We use stratified k-fold cross-validation for honest classification performance assessment. Once the honest performance measures have been estimated for each classifier, we look at which classifiers perform better on our dataset. However, it does not suffice to find the classifier with the highest accuracy or area under the ROC curve (AUC) or whichever measure is selected. Bear in mind that our dataset is just a sample of the total population that we want to analyze. Some of the differences among classifiers could be caused by sample representativeness. Instead, we need to find statistically significant differences between classifier performance. To check for statistical differences, we apply a hypothesis testing procedure. However, as discussed in Section 7.4.2, it is necessary to control for family-wise error to output scientific results.

We should underscore that this section does not focus on classifier performance improvement through optimal tuning, although we spent some time hand-tuning their parameters. Instead, the main goal of this section is to report a sound and fair procedure to compare multiple classifiers. Remember that the results for this dataset are not in any way representative of the overall performance of each classifier type (no free lunch theorem).

7.4.1 Compared Classifiers

Table 7.3 shows the parameters used for each classifier in this case study. These values were gathered by trial-and-error from the final Cargo 2000 dataset. We use the following labels for the classifier, shortening multilayer perceptron to MLP, support vector machine to SVM, logistic regression to logistic, naive Bayes to NB, stacking to stack, bagging to bag, random forest to RF and AdaBoost.M1 to boost.

TABLE 7.3
Parameters selected for the compared classifiers

k-NN	
k value	4
Search algorithm	Linear search
Distance function	Minkowski distance with $p = 6.5$
Weighting scheme	Inverse of distance

C4.5	
Minimum number of instances per leaf	2
Binary splits	No
Collapse tree	Yes
No pruning	No
Confidence threshold for pruning	0.32
Reduced error pruning	No
Subtree raising	Yes

RIPPER	
Minimal required weight	4
Number of optimization runs	9
Pruning	Yes
Error rate	Do not check

Multilayer perceptron	
Learning rate	0.1
Momentum	0.9
Number of epochs	500
Percentage size of validation set	30
Network topology	1 hidden layer with 42 neurons
Learning rate decay	Yes

Transfer function	Sigmoid

Support vector machine	
Complexity constant	1
Tolerance	0.001
Kernel function	Polynomial kernel, $(\mathbf{x}^T \cdot \mathbf{x} + 1)$
Standardize data before training (Section 7.3.9)	

Logistic regression	
Ridge	0.09766

Bayesian classifiers	NB	TAN	K2
Discretize continuous variables[1]	Yes	Yes	Yes
Scoring metric	NA	MDL	AIC
Maximum number of parents per node	1	2	100,000
Prior count to estimate Bayesian network parameters	NA	0.7	0.5

Stacking		
2 layers of classifiers: a base classifier layer and a metaclassifier layer		
Base classifier	SVM	Complexity constant	1
		Tolerance	0.001
		Kernel function	$(\mathbf{x}^T \cdot \mathbf{x})$
		Standardize data before training (Section 7.3.9)	
Metaclassifier	MLP	Learning rate	0.1
		Momentum	0.9
		Number of epochs	500
		Percentage size of validation set	30
		Network topology	1 hidden layer with 44 neurons
		Learning rate decay	Yes
		Transfer function	Sigmoid

---

[1]WEKA Bayesian classifiers, except naive Bayes, only work with discrete variables. Therefore, they are automatically discretized using the discretization procedure introduced by Fayyad and Irani (1993).

Bagging		
Size of each bootstrap bag		100%
Number of trained classifiers		10
Base classifier	MLP	
		Learning rate	0.2
		Momentum	0.9
		Number of epochs	500
		Percentage size of validation set	30
		Network topology	1 hidden layer with 2 neurons
		Learning rate decay	No
		Transfer function	Sigmoid

Random forest	
Size of each bootstrap bag	100%
Number of variables to be selected in each bag	15
Number of trees to be trained	100
Minimum number of instances per leaf	5
Maximum depth	11

AdaBoost.M1		
Weight sum of each bag		100%
Number of trained classifiers		10
Base classifier	C4.5	
		Minimum number of instances per leaf	5
		Binary splits	No
		Collapse tree	Yes
		No pruning	No
		Confidence threshold for pruning	0.5
		Reduced error pruning	No
		Subtree raising	Yes

7.4.2   Quantitative Comparison of Classifiers

In this section, we perform hypothesis testing to select the best classifier or the best set of classifiers to solve the air freight delay forecasting problem. The basic concepts of hypothesis testing are discussed in Section 2.2.2. We then formulate the multiple hypothesis problem to find pairwise performance differences and propose some solutions. Finally, we apply multiple hypothesis testing to solve our problem.

7.4.2.1 Multiple Hypothesis Testing

The Friedman test was introduced in Section 2.2.2. In the Friedman test there are b blocks (datasets) and $k \geq 2$ treatments (classifiers) are applied to each block. The aim of the test is to detect differences among the k treatments. For example, suppose we had to compare three different classifiers: naive Bayes, C4.5 and SVM. The H_0 for the Friedman test would be:

$$H_0 : \mu_{NB} = \mu_{C4.5} = \mu_{SVM} \tag{7.2}$$

Here, μ_X denotes the mean performance (or any other figure of merit) of classifier X. If there is any statistical difference between any pair of classifiers, Eq. 7.2 will be rejected. However, this test only checks whether there is a statistical difference in treatments. If we want to find pairwise statistical differences between the treatments, we should apply a post-hoc test. The post-hoc test can only be applied if the null hypothesis of Eq. 7.2 was rejected previously. In that case, our example of three classifiers, we would now have three different H_0 to reject:

$$
\begin{aligned}
H_0^1 &: \mu_{NB} = \mu_{C4.5} \\
H_0^2 &: \mu_{NB} = \mu_{SVM} \\
H_0^3 &: \mu_{C4.5} = \mu_{SVM}
\end{aligned}
\tag{7.3}
$$

If, for example, we reject H_0^1 and H_0^2, we could say that naive Bayes performs better/worse than C4.5 and SVM. The problem with the hypotheses in Eq. 7.3 is how to control the **family-wise error** (FWER), i.e., the probability of making at least one type I error. Performing multiple tests increases the probability of a type I error. Suppose that we want to conduct a post-hoc test as in Eq. 7.3, making individual tests with $\alpha' = 0.05$ for each H_0. The probability of not making any type I errors in all three tests is equal to $(1 - 0.05)^3$. Thus, there is a probability of $1 - (1 - 0.05)^3 \approx 0.14$ of making at least one type I error. This value is the true α for all three tests in Eq. 7.3. The expected α for m comparisons with α' (probability of type I error in each comparison) is equal to $1 - (1 - \alpha')^m$. Of course, there is a higher probability of making a type I error when α' and the number of classifiers increase because the number of pairwise comparisons is equal to $m = k(k-1)/2$. If $k = 13$, as in this case study, and $\alpha' = 0.05$ for each test, $\alpha \approx 0.98$, which is usually an unacceptable value for drawing any conclusion.

The **Bonferroni correction** or Bonferroni-Dunn test (Dunn, 1961) can be used to adjust α' in order to control the FWER, i.e., the α of the experiment. The Bonferroni correction divides α by the number of comparisons being tested to compute α'. In our example, there are three hypotheses in Eq. 7.3, hence $\alpha' = 0.05/3 \approx 0.0166$. With this α', α is guaranteed to be below 0.05, and, in fact, $\alpha \approx 0.49$. The Bonferroni correction is a very simple post-hoc test with very low power, especially when the number of comparisons increases.

Related to this idea, the **Nemenyi test** makes pairwise comparisons by rejecting any hypotheses whose p-value is lower than α/m, with m being the number of comparisons (García and Herrera, 2008). Another way of looking at the Nemenyi test is that the performance of two classifiers is significantly different if the corresponding ranks differ by at least the critical difference (Demšar, 2006):

$$CD = q_\alpha \sqrt{\frac{k(k+1)}{6b}}, \qquad (7.4)$$

where q_α are critical values based on the Studentized range statistic divided by $\sqrt{2}$. A table of values can be found in Demšar (2006). More advanced methods are discussed in further detail in Demšar (2006); García and Herrera (2008).

7.4.2.2 Online Classification of Business Processes

This section shows classifier behavior during online classification on the Cargo 2000 dataset. As the business process progresses, new actual times become available for each service execution, and we analyze how classifier performance improves with the new information. Fig. 7.2 shows the resulting UML 2.0 diagram for the business process after preprocessing the data. This diagram includes up to eight service executions for each transport leg: 1 RCS + 3 DEP + 3 RCF + 1 DLV. As there are two transport legs, there are up to 16 service executions in the business process. These 16 services, on top of the case with no completed services, are the checkpoints that will be used to test the online performance of the classifiers. Therefore, if each service corresponds to a checkpoint, we can create a dataset for each checkpoint including the actual service times up to the current checkpoint only. All the planned times should be available in every checkpoint dataset because this information is known in advance, as are the airports and the number of legs and trips for each leg. If there is more than one inbound transport leg, a checkpoint is considered to have been reached if the respective service for every inbound transport leg has been completed. Bearing in mind that, even though the preprocessing, described in Section 7.2.1, selects only one transport leg (the bottleneck transport leg), we have to consider all three inbound transport legs for each checkpoint dataset to decide which one will be the bottleneck transport leg.

Fig. 7.7 shows the results of the online classification process for all classifiers. Classifiers of the same family are highlighted in the same color, albeit using different line styles and marker shapes to distinguish each one. The black line in the middle of the figure marks the end of the inbound transport legs and the start of the outbound transport leg. The representation of each class label is somewhat unbalanced in the Cargo 2000 dataset, as shown in Table 7.1 (around 26% of the business processes are delayed). For this reason, the selected performance measure is the area under the ROC curve (AUC), as it is considered to be a better performance measure when there are unbalanced data (He and Garcia, 2009). There are no actual times available at the starting checkpoint, whereas all information is available in the end checkpoint. We find that performance increases substantially for all classifiers the more information is available. However, not all services contribute to improving performance. In fact, there is a sizable performance increase for DLV services. When the information on other services is received, however, there is no major performance increase, and, in some cases, there is even a slight drop in performance. This phenomenon will be explored in more detail later.

Random forest appears to be the best classifier for this problem, and stacking and SVM are the worst classifiers. However, we conduct a statistical test to detect statistically significant differences ($\alpha = 0.05$). Table 7.4 tabulates the results shown in Fig. 7.7. These were the average results for stratified 10-fold cross-validation run 30 times with different seeds as recommended by Pizarro et al. (2002). The rank of each algorithm on each dataset is shown in parentheses. The sum of ranks, R_j in Eq. 2.1, and the average rank for each classifier, are shown at the bottom of the table. Before executing the post-hoc tests, we first need to reject the null hypothesis that the performance of all classifiers is equal. In our case, $k = 13$ and $b = 17$. Therefore, the Friedman statistic in Eq. 2.1 for our dataset is equal to:

$$S = \left[\frac{12}{17 \cdot 13 \cdot 14} (161^2 + \cdots + 109^2) \right] - 3 \cdot 17 \cdot 14 = 184.297,$$

a value of a random variable distributed according to χ^2 with 12 degrees of freedom if the null hypothesis is true. The corresponding p-value is equal to 9.76E-11. As the p-value of the statistic is well below $\alpha = 0.05$, we can reject the null hypothesis of equality between classifiers. The next step is to run a Nemenyi test. First of all, we compute the critical difference (Eq. 7.4):

$$CD = 3.3127 \sqrt{\frac{13 \cdot 14}{6 \cdot 17}} = 4.425.$$

Any classifiers with a rank difference above 4.425 can be considered to have a statistically significant difference in performance. These differences are commonly plotted using the **critical difference diagram**. Fig. 7.8 illustrates the differences found between the classifiers in our case study. The diagram plots an axis representing the classifier ranks. In our case, the ranks range from 1 to 13. The vertical lines connecting the rank axis are labeled with the classifier name. The critical distance specified at the top of the figure visualizes the minimum distance between classifiers required for differences to be statistically significant. The horizontal lines below the axis indicate groups of classifiers that are not significantly different. Therefore, we can say that there is no significant difference between random forest, logistic regression, multilayer perceptron, TAN and bagging classifiers. This is because they are linked by the first horizontal line below the rank axis. However, there is a difference between the classifiers in the best group: for example, random forest is significantly better than AdaBoost.M1, but logistic regression is not significantly better than AdaBoost.M1 and naive Bayes. In the worst classifiers group, the performance is clearly poorer for stacking and SVM than for the other classifiers until the inbound transport leg finishes (Fig. 7.7). Then, there is a slight increase in performance up to the point that they outperform RIPPER. One possible cause of the performance of the worst classifiers is that it is not easy to generalize well using the same parameter configuration for multiple datasets.

7.4.3 Qualitative Comparison of Classifiers

This section provides a qualitative analysis of the information yielded by each classifier taking advantage of its intrinsic characteristics, e.g., the tree structure of a C4.5 algorithm. Not all algorithms are easy to analyze. These algorithms, usually referred to in the literature as blackbox classifiers, will be omitted from this qualitative comparison. The following are blackbox classifiers:

- k-NN: this algorithm merely saves the data and matches instances to the training set for classification. It does not provide any additional qualitative information.

- MLP: the usual representation of an artificial neural network is a matrix/vector containing the neuron weights. This model is especially difficult to interpret because of the large number of weights involved. Neither are the hidden neurons meaningful in the context of the interpretation.

- SVM: it could be difficult to show the max-margin boundary hyperplane when the dimensionality of the data projection is above three.

- Metaclassifiers: these classifiers are composed of multiple base classifiers. Interpretability depends on the number and type of base classifiers. If, for example, we use a multilayer perceptron as a base classifier, the algorithm is at least as difficult to interpret as a multilayer perceptron. In the case of the random forest, the classifier is composed of trees. However, it is rather difficult to interpret random forests due to the large number of trees.

We report the key findings for the other classifiers, and we reason about the relations between the dataset and the trained models.

7.4.3.1 C4.5

The simplest way to interpret a C4.5 model is to look at the structure of the tree. Trees have two important facets: the variables selected as tree nodes and the branching values used for each node. In the case of discrete values, the branching usually covers all possible values. However, a cut point is selected in the case of continuous variables to discretize the range values.

Fig. 7.9 shows the representation of a partial C4.5 classifier learned in Section 7.4.1. The complete tree is quite large (95 leaves and 189 respective

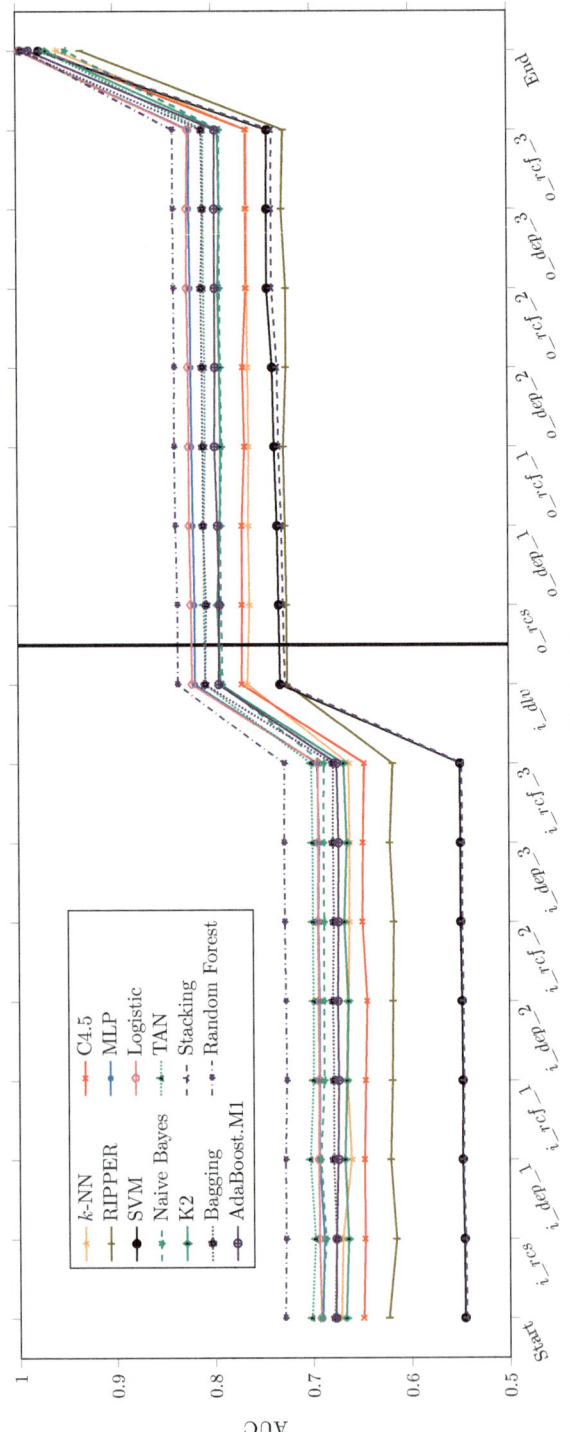

FIGURE 7.7
Classifier performance at different times of the business process.

TABLE 7.4

AUC values rounded to three decimal places for each classifier on each checkpoint dataset. The rank of each algorithm for the given datasets is shown in parentheses. The best algorithm for each dataset is marked in bold. Sum and average of the computed ranks are shown at the bottom of the table

Dataset	k-NN	C4.5	RIPPER	MLP	SVM	Logistic	NB	TAN	K2	Stack.	Bag.	RF	Boost.
Start	0.671 (8)	0.649 (10)	0.623 (11)	0.690 (5)	0.546 (12)	0.692 (3)	0.692 (4)	0.701 (2)	0.666 (9)	0.544 (13)	0.678 (6)	**0.728 (1)**	0.677 (7)
i_rcs	0.670 (8)	0.647 (10)	0.616 (11)	0.688 (4)	0.546 (12)	0.693 (3)	0.687 (5)	0.697 (2)	0.664 (9)	0.545 (13)	0.676 (7)	**0.727 (1)**	0.676 (6)
i_dep_1	0.661 (9)	0.647 (10)	0.621 (11)	0.693 (4)	0.548 (12)	0.694 (3)	0.692 (5)	0.702 (2)	0.667 (8)	0.547 (13)	0.679 (6)	**0.728 (1)**	0.674 (7)
i_rcf_1	0.665 (9)	0.646 (10)	0.619 (11)	0.693 (4)	0.548 (12)	0.693 (3)	0.688 (5)	0.699 (2)	0.665 (8)	0.546 (13)	0.678 (6)	**0.726 (1)**	0.673 (7)
i_dep_2	0.663 (9)	0.645 (10)	0.618 (11)	0.693 (4)	0.548 (12)	0.693 (3)	0.688 (5)	0.699 (2)	0.664 (8)	0.547 (13)	0.679 (6)	**0.727 (1)**	0.674 (7)
i_rcf_2	0.662 (9)	0.649 (10)	0.618 (11)	0.693 (4)	0.550 (12)	0.694 (3)	0.688 (5)	0.699 (2)	0.668 (8)	0.548 (13)	0.678 (6)	**0.728 (1)**	0.674 (7)
i_dep_3	0.662 (9)	0.649 (10)	0.621 (11)	0.694 (3)	0.550 (12)	0.694 (4)	0.688 (5)	0.699 (2)	0.665 (8)	0.548 (13)	0.679 (6)	**0.728 (1)**	0.673 (7)
i_rcf_3	0.663 (9)	0.647 (10)	0.618 (11)	0.694 (3)	0.550 (12)	0.694 (4)	0.688 (5)	0.700 (2)	0.668 (8)	0.548 (13)	0.679 (6)	**0.728 (1)**	0.675 (7)
i_dlv	0.765 (10)	0.770 (9)	0.725 (13)	0.819 (3)	0.732 (11)	0.822 (2)	0.790 (8)	0.808 (5)	0.792 (7)	0.727 (12)	0.808 (4)	**0.836 (1)**	0.794 (6)
o_rcs	0.762 (10)	0.770 (9)	0.725 (13)	0.819 (3)	0.733 (11)	0.822 (2)	0.791 (8)	0.809 (4)	0.795 (6)	0.728 (12)	0.807 (5)	**0.836 (1)**	0.793 (7)
o_dep_1	0.763 (10)	0.770 (9)	0.726 (13)	0.820 (3)	0.734 (11)	0.824 (2)	0.792 (8)	0.809 (5)	0.792 (7)	0.730 (12)	0.810 (4)	**0.838 (1)**	0.795 (6)
o_rcf_1	0.763 (10)	0.767 (9)	0.727 (13)	0.821 (3)	0.737 (11)	0.824 (2)	0.790 (8)	0.807 (5)	0.792 (7)	0.732 (12)	0.810 (4)	**0.839 (1)**	0.797 (6)
o_dep_2	0.763 (10)	0.768 (9)	0.725 (13)	0.822 (3)	0.739 (11)	0.824 (2)	0.791 (8)	0.807 (5)	0.792 (7)	0.734 (12)	0.810 (4)	**0.839 (1)**	0.797 (6)
o_rcf_2	0.764 (10)	0.765 (9)	0.724 (13)	0.822 (3)	0.744 (11)	0.826 (2)	0.792 (8)	0.808 (5)	0.793 (7)	0.739 (12)	0.811 (4)	**0.839 (1)**	0.797 (6)
o_dep_3	0.764 (10)	0.765 (9)	0.729 (13)	0.823 (3)	0.744 (11)	0.825 (2)	0.792 (8)	0.808 (5)	0.792 (7)	0.739 (12)	0.809 (4)	**0.839 (1)**	0.797 (6)
o_rcf_3	0.764 (10)	0.765 (9)	0.727 (13)	0.823 (3)	0.743 (11)	0.824 (2)	0.792 (8)	0.808 (5)	0.793 (7)	0.739 (12)	0.810 (4)	**0.840 (1)**	0.796 (6)
End	0.957 (11)	0.970 (8)	0.933 (13)	0.996 (2)	0.976 (6)	**0.997 (1)**	0.949 (12)	0.970 (9)	0.969 (10)	0.976 (7)	0.995 (3)	**0.990 (4)**	0.987 (5)
R_j	161	160	205	58	190	42	115	64	131	207	85	**20**	109
Avg. Rank	9.471	9.412	12.059	3.412	11.176	2.471	6.765	3.765	7.706	12.176	5.0	**1.176**	6.412

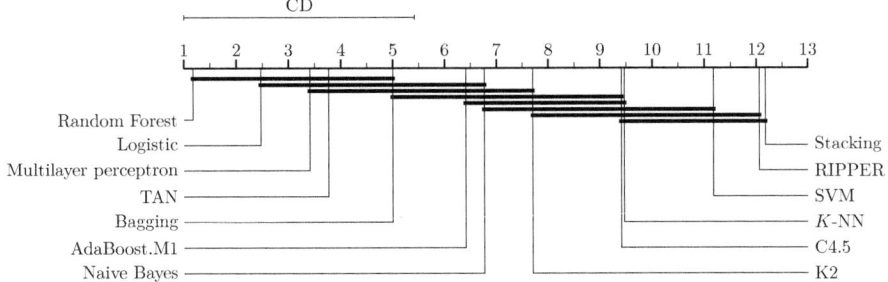

FIGURE 7.8
Critical difference diagram of the results in Table 7.4.

rules). Only a small portion of the tree is shown here. The subtrees that are not shown in this figure are represented by the nodes labeled with . . .. The leaves show the expected class label and the distribution of TRUE/FALSE instances in parentheses.

First of all, we find that the majority of the variables selected near the root node are of the DLV type. This suggests that DLV variables play an important role in detecting delays. The complete tree does not contain any *_place* variable. Therefore, we could say that the airport does not have much bearing on delivery performance. We check if $i1\_dlv\_e$ is greater than 0.47 in the root of the tree and again greater than 0.70 in the right branch. If the bottleneck leg of the DLV service accounted for more than 70% of the time taken by the business process, the process will be classified as delayed. If $0.47 \leq i1\_dlv\_e \leq 0.70$, then the $o\_rcf\_1\_e$ and the o_dlv_e variables are checked. When the actual times are lower than a computed threshold, the tree should classify the Delay as FALSE. Similarly, when actual times are higher, the tree should classify the Delay as TRUE.

The branch on the left of the root contains instances in which the DLV service in the bottleneck leg does not take too long. For such instances, the tree then checks whether the DLV service in the outbound transport leg took too much time. If this is the case ($o\_dlv\_e \geq 0.65$), the tree classifies the business process as delayed. Let us look at what happens when $0.40 \leq o\_dlv\_e \leq 0.65$, that is, when the actual DLV times are rather long, albeit not long enough to confirm a delay. In this case, the tree also checks the planned DLV service times, which tend to behave contrary to the actual times. When the planned times are lower than a computed threshold, the tree should classify the Delay as TRUE. Accordingly, when planned times are higher, the tree should classify the Delay as FALSE. This behavior makes perfect sense: if the tree is not sure because the actual times are borderline, then the planned times should be compared against the actual times. However, the last $i1\_dlv\_p$ check, where two leaf nodes are created with two and six instances, respectively, does not

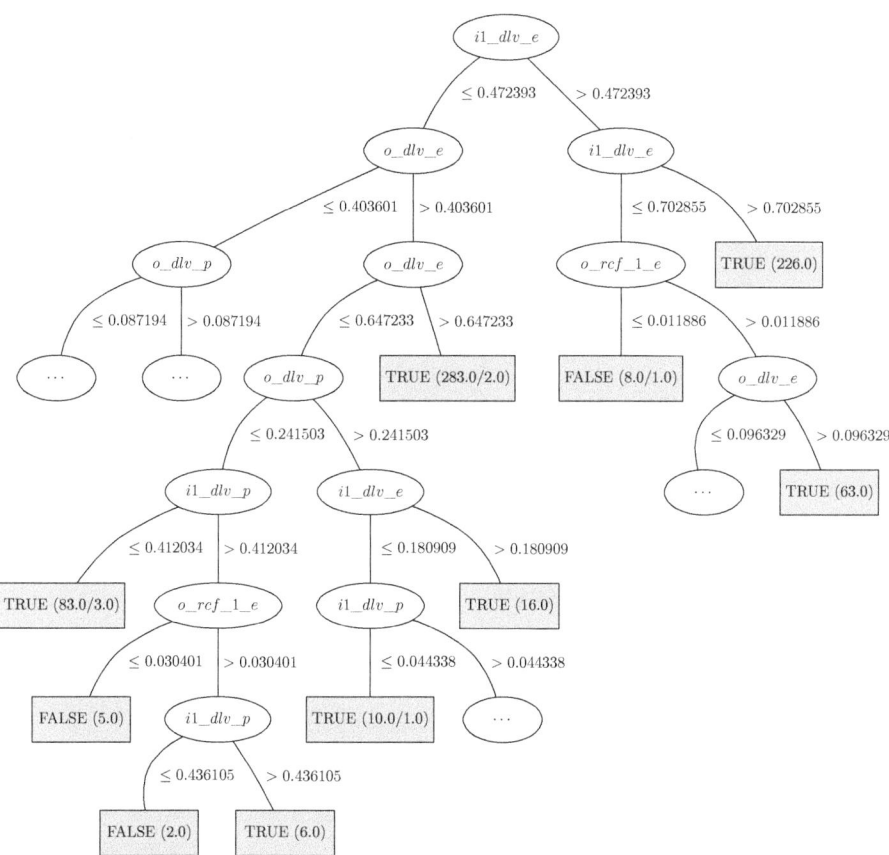

FIGURE 7.9
Partial representation of the C4.5 structure. The nodes representing omitted
subtrees are labeled with ....

obey this rule. A possible ground is overfitting, which causes the tree to make the above comparison to correctly classify the above eight instances.

Now, one may wonder why the decision tree attached so much importance to the DLV variables. The DLV variables also produced a sizable performance increase in Fig. 7.7. We analyzed the behavior of the different types of services using descriptive statistics of the data for business processes with Delay=TRUE. We analyzed two different issues: the rate or frequency and the severity of service violations when there is a business process violation. We say that a service has been violated when it takes longer than planned. Table 7.5 summarizes the information regarding the rate of service violations. At the top of the table, we find that DEP and DLV are the most often violated services. Thus, 84% of DEP services are violated in a business process where there is a delay. This information suggests that DEP variables are likely to be more informative than DLV variables. However, the bottom row of the table shows how many business processes are affected by at least one service violation. Thus, we find that 99.61% of the delayed business processes have at least one DLV service violation (in the bottleneck or the outbound transport legs). This value is close to 99.14% for DEP times. Thus, the rate of DEP and DLV service violations can be considered to be more or less the same.

However, the rate of service violations does not provide the whole picture. We should analyze the severity of each violation to understand its effects on business process delays. To measure the severity of each service violation, we have to check whether the delay in the service violations accounted for a significant amount of time with respect to the business process delay. Table 7.6 summarizes this information. We say that a service satisfies condition V_X if the delay in the service execution is at least $X\%$ of the total business process delay, that is,

$$sd > pd \cdot \frac{X}{100}, \quad \text{with } sd, pd > 0,$$

where sd denotes the service delay as the difference between the actual and planned times of the service, and pd denotes the business process delay as the difference between the actual and planned total business process times. From Table 7.6, top, we find that more than 50% of DLV services accounted for at least 50% of the total business process delay. In fact, 37.93% of DLV services suffered a delay equal to or greater than the business process delay. The service could be delayed longer than the business process if the other services were faster than planned. This analysis leads us to conclude that the violations of the DLV services are much more severe than for other services. The bottom row of the table shows the number of business processes in which there is at least one service satisfying condition V_{50} and V_{100}. We find that at least one DLV satisfied condition V_{50} in a remarkable 98.47% of the violated business processes. This statistic shows that the delays in the DLV services provide a pretty good explanation of a business process delay. For this reason, the C4.5 tree tends to use its values.

TABLE 7.5
Descriptive statistic of the rate of service violations when Delay=TRUE.
Percentages are shown in parentheses

	RCS	DEP	RCF	DLV
Sum of services	2,096	3,044	3,044	2,096
Sum of violated services	144 (6.87)	2,565 (84.26)	696 (22.86)	1,404 (66.99)
Business processes with Delay=TRUE		1048		
Business processes with at least one service violation	144 (13.74)	1,039 (99.14)	526 (50.19)	1,044 (99.61)

TABLE 7.6
Descriptive statistics of process violations severity when Delay=TRUE.
Percentages are shown in parentheses

	RCS	DEP	RCF	DLV
Services satisfying restriction V_{50}	4 (0.19)	396 (13)	47 (1.54)	1,093 (52.15)
Services satisfying restriction V_{100}	1 (0.04)	224 (7.36)	26 (0.85)	795 (37.93)
Business processes where $\exists V_{50}$	4 (0.38)	270 (25.76)	44 (4.2)	1,032 (98.47)
Business processes where $\exists V_{100}$	1 (0.1)	155 (14.79)	24 (2.29)	783 (74.71)

7.4.3.2   RIPPER

The RIPPER algorithm learned the set of rules shown in Table 7.7. The values used by the rules were rounded to two decimal places for ease of representation. RIPPER generated 17 rules to try to recognize a delay. If the business process does not satisfy any of the above rules, the 18th rule is applied, where the business process is classified as not delayed. There are many similarities between the results of RIPPER and C4.5. First of all, this set of rules again denotes the importance of DLV services. The DLV service values are used exclusively in the first rules and extensively in the rest of the rules. Also, longer actual times and shorter planned times tend to be classified as delayed in both models. For this reason, most actual times are compared using a "greater than" sign, while planned times are compared using a "less than" sign.

The set of rules is more compact than the tree learned using C4.5. This is a desirable property because, with so few rules, a human can review all rules one by one to picture the problem.

7.4.3.3   Bayesian Network Classifiers

For the Bayesian network classifiers, the easiest way to draw conclusions is usually to observe their structure. The set of conditional independences revealed by the structure can be useful for understanding what is happening in the dataset under study. However, it can also be helpful to observe the CPTs of some interesting nodes, as the example in this section illustrates.

Note that WEKA uses minimum description length principle-based discretization (Section 2.2.1.5) introduced by Fayyad and Irani (1993) to discretize the continuous variables prior to the learning process. In the discretization step, some variables were discretized into a single range $(-\infty, +\infty)$. In practice, then, the variable values are omitted because, for a single-range variable X_d, $p(X_d|\mathbf{Pa}(X_d)) = 1$ for every possible value of X_d. Therefore, a change in the value of X_d makes no contribution to the classification process. The irrelevant variables are:

$i1\_dep\_2\_e$, $i1\_dep\_3\_p$, $i1\_dep\_3\_e$, $o\_dep\_3\_p$, $o\_dep\_3\_e$,
$i1\_rcf\_2\_p$, $i1\_rcf\_2\_e$, $o\_rcf\_2\_p$, $i1\_rcf\_3\_p$, $i1\_rcf\_3\_e$,
$o\_rcf\_3\_p$, $o\_rcf\_3\_e$, $i1\_hops$, o_hops.

As shown in the above list of variables, the DEP and RCF variables of the first trip were unaffected by this issue. This suggests that the discretizer attaches more importance to the first trip of each transport leg because it is more likely to take place than the second and third trips.

There are some interesting connections between variables in the TAN classifier. The planned and actual times of a service are, predictably, frequently connected. One such case refers to the o_dlv variables, as illustrated in Fig. 7.10. Table 7.8 shows the corresponding CPT for variable o_dlv_e. The values for the ranges in both o_dlv_p and o_dlv_e have been rounded to two decimal places. If Delay=FALSE, then the values of o_dlv_e are more likely to be

TABLE 7.7

Set of rules learned by RIPPER

Nr.	Rule
1	IF ($o\_dlv\_e \geq 0.54$) THEN Delay=TRUE (375.0/17.0)
2	IF ($i1\_dlv\_e \geq 0.56$) THEN Delay=TRUE (285.0/6.0)
3	IF ($o\_dlv\_p \leq 0.19$ AND $o\_dlv\_e \geq 0.33$ AND $i1\_dlv\_p \leq 0.38$) THEN Delay=TRUE (56.0/3.0)
4	IF ($o\_dlv\_p \leq 0.19$ AND $o\_dlv\_e \geq 0.12$ AND $i1\_dlv\_e \geq 0.18$) THEN Delay=TRUE (77.0/2.0)
5	IF ($i1\_dlv\_p \leq 0.23$ AND $o\_dlv\_e \geq 0.47$) THEN Delay=TRUE (18.0/2.0)
6	IF ($i1\_dlv\_p \leq 0.10$ AND $o\_dlv\_p \leq 0.07$ AND $i1\_dlv\_e \geq 0.10$ AND $i1\_rcs\_p \geq 0.17$) THEN Delay=TRUE (42.0/3.0)
7	IF ($i1\_dlv\_p \leq 0.10$ AND $o\_dlv\_p \leq 0.07$ AND $o\_dlv\_e \geq 0.1$) THEN Delay=TRUE (33.0/6.0)
8	IF ($i1\_dlv\_e \geq 0.14$ AND $o\_dlv\_e \geq 0.28$ AND $i1\_dep\_1\_e \geq 0.03$ AND $i1\_dlv\_p \leq 0.41$) THEN Delay=TRUE (42.0/5.0)
9	IF ($i1\_dlv\_e \geq 0.31$ AND $i1\_rcs\_e \geq 0.13$) THEN Delay=TRUE (44.0/12.0)
10	IF ($i1\_dlv\_p \leq 0.09$ AND $o\_dlv\_e \geq 0.17$ AND $o\_dlv\_p \leq 0.21$) THEN Delay=TRUE (22.0/6.0)
11	IF ($i1\_dlv\_e \geq 0.14$ AND $o\_dlv\_p \leq 0.08$ AND $i1\_dlv\_p \leq 0.12$ AND $o\_dlv\_p \geq 0.06$) THEN Delay=TRUE (15.0/1.0)
12	IF ($o\_rcs\_e \geq 0.08$ AND $i1\_dlv\_e \geq 0.42$) THEN Delay=TRUE (27.0/8.0)
13	IF ($o\_dlv\_p \leq 0.05$ AND $o\_rcs\_p \geq 0.53$ AND $o\_dep\_1\_e \geq 0.02$) THEN Delay=TRUE (14.0/0.0)
14	IF ($o\_dlv\_e \geq 0.18$ AND $i1\_rcs\_p \geq 0.31$ AND $o\_dep\_1\_p \geq 0.02$) THEN Delay=TRUE (8.0/1.0)
15	IF ($i1\_dlv\_p \leq 0.07$ AND $o\_dlv\_e \geq 0.24$ AND $i1\_dep\_1\_e \leq 0.03$) THEN Delay=TRUE (8.0/1.0)
16	IF ($i1\_rcf\_1\_e \geq 0.11$ AND $i1\_dlv\_p \leq 0.11$ AND $o\_dlv\_p \leq 0.20$ AND $i1\_dlv\_e \geq 0.02$) THEN Delay=TRUE (10.0/1.0)
17	IF ($o\_dlv\_e \geq 0.31$ AND $i1\_dlv\_e \geq 0.27$) THEN Delay=TRUE (8.0/2.0)
18	IF $\emptyset$ THEN Delay=FALSE (2,858.0/40.0)

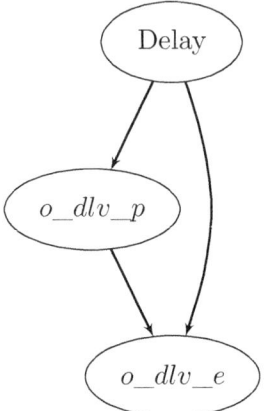

FIGURE 7.10
Partial representation of the TAN structure, showing how the *o_dlv* variables are related.

TABLE 7.8
Conditional probability table of *o_dlv_e* for the TAN classifier

Delay	o_dlv_p	o_dlv_e				
		[0, 0.08]	(0.08, 0.23]	(0.23, 0.4]	(0.4, 0.65]	(0.65, 1]
FALSE	[0, 0.07]	0.669	0.259	0.059	0.01	0.003
FALSE	(0.07, 0.21]	0.705	0.232	0.057	0.005	0.001
FALSE	(0.21, 1]	0.565	0.313	0.085	0.035	0.001
TRUE	[0, 0.07]	0.312	0.309	0.206	0.082	0.092
TRUE	(0.07, 0.21]	0.233	0.211	0.165	0.174	0.217
TRUE	(0.21, 1]	0.155	0.103	0.119	0.153	0.469

lower. Therefore, if we know that the business process has not been delayed, the actual times of *o_dlv* usually account for less than the 23% of the total business process time. Note that this applies even when the planned time for *o_dlv* is in the range (0.21, 1], where there is only a slight increase in the probability of higher actual times. We would expect there to be a greater probability of the range of *o_dlv_e* being [0, 0.08] if *o_dlv_p* is in the range [0, 0.07]. Correspondingly, if *o_dlv_p* is in the range (0.07, 0.21], the most probable range for *o_dlv_e* would be (0.08, 0.23]. However, this is not the case because the greatest probability is for [0, 0.08], suggesting that *o_dlv* tends to take shorter when the business process is not delayed.

If Delay=TRUE, there is a greater probability of the values of *o_dlv_e* being higher, as expected. There is again a dependence between *o_dlv_p* and *o_dlv_e* because when *o_dlv_p* increases then *o_dlv_e* tends to increase. The pairwise comparison of the rows with equal *o_dlv_p* with Delay=FALSE

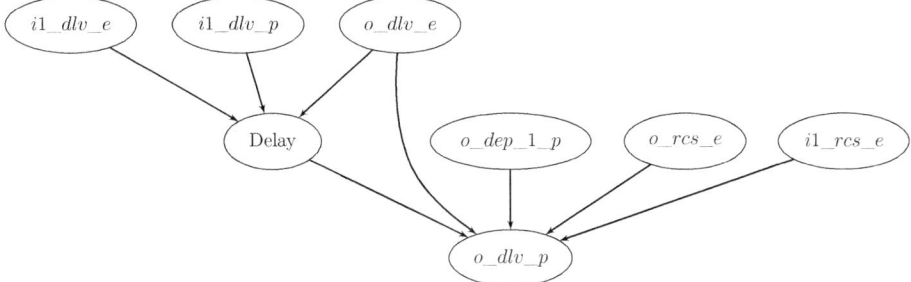

FIGURE 7.11
Markov blanket structure of the Delay variable in the K2 algorithm.

and Delay=TRUE indicates that the behavior of the *o_dlv_e* variable is completely different when the business process is delayed.

We conduct the structure analysis using the result of the K2 algorithm because it has more freedom to select the relevant arcs. K2 is a random algorithm because it depends on the selected node ordering. Therefore, the results can vary across different algorithm runs. The K2 algorithm can be used to build unrestricted Bayesian network classifiers. As we are using the K2 algorithm to construct a classifier, we do not need the entire structure. Instead, we can use the Markov blanket (Section 2.4.9) of the Delay variable, which would yield the exact same classification results. For this reason, Fig. 7.11 just shows the Markov blanket of the Delay variable, resulting in a simpler and interpretable network. To select one K2 classifier out of multiple random K2 algorithm outcomes, we opted for the classifier with the smallest Markov blanket (in terms of nodes and edges). First of all, we found that DLV variables are both the parents and children of the Delay variable. This finding is consistent with the discussion in previous sections. However, the DLV variables behave slightly differently in the inbound and the outbound transport legs. In the outbound transport leg, the planned time is a child of the actual time, whereas there is no such relation between actual and planned times in the inbound transport leg. Also, the parents of the *o_dlv_p* variable are *o_dep_1_p*, *o_rcs_e*, *i1_rcs_e*. Some of these conditional dependences are inscrutable as regards the behavior of the business process. For example, if we take the CPT $p(o\_dlv\_p|\text{Delay}, o\_dlv\_e, o\_dep\_1\_p, o\_rcs\_e, i1\_rcs\_e)$ and marginalize out to yield $p(o\_dlv\_p|o\_dep\_1\_p)$, we get the CPT in Table 7.9. This CPT tells us that when *o_dep_1_p* tends to take really low values, the *o_dlv_p* variable takes high values. As each variable represents a percentage of time with respect to the total planned business process time, the variable value affects the value of other variables (even if the original dataset was totally independent). Therefore, if one variable has an unusually high value, other variables are less likely to take a large percentage of time. This is an undesirable effect of the preprocessing performed in Section 7.2.1.4. Variables *o_rcs_e*, and *i1_rcs_e* are expected to behave similarly.

TABLE 7.9

Conditional probability table of $p(\text{o\_dlv\_p}|\text{o\_dep\_1\_p})$ for the K2 classifier

o_dep_1_p	o_dlv_p		
	$[0, 0.068]$	$(0.068, 0.214]$	$(0.214, 1]$
$[0, 0.026]$	0.155	0.264	0.581
$(0.026, 1]$	0.435	0.34	0.225

7.4.4   Feature Subset Selection

Section 7.4.3 provided some insights into the most important parts of the Cargo 2000 business processes. In fact, we found that some interpretable classifiers (Section 7.4.3) used the DLV variables to classify the business process delays. From the classifier interpretation, we concluded that some variables are considered irrelevant by all the interpretable classifiers. It is harder to gather a set of irrelevant variables for the non-interpretable classifiers, because their analysis is more complex. Section 2.4.2 presents some feature subset selection procedures. Applying these methods, we can select a set of relevant and non-redundant features, thus reducing data dimensionality. This usually produces simpler classifiers. In this section, some filter feature subset selection methods are applied to the Cargo 2000 dataset to illustrate how they work.

The information gain (Section 2.4.4) criterion can be used to select variable subsets. As the information gain evaluates the merit of each variable rather than of a whole subset, it can be used to construct a variable ranking. The rank of the best 10 variables is shown in Table 7.10. As expected, all the DLV variables rank among the best five variables. Note that there is a sizable difference between the information gain of the second- and third-best variables. This suggests that the actual times of the DLV services are more important than the planned times.

Correlation-based feature selection (CFS) (Hall, 1999) can also be applied on the entire Cargo 2000 dataset. The CFS method (Section 2.4.2) aims to select high relevance and low redundancy feature subsets. Hence, we consider a multivariate filter. The CFS algorithm is also implemented in the WEKA framework. It uses a greedy hillclimbing search procedure, which, provided that the CFS score of the entire selected subset does not decrease, includes the variable with the best CFS score at each step. The WEKA implementation of the search procedure includes the option of performing some backtracking (i.e., unselecting some features) to avoid trapping in local optima.

Applied to the Cargo 2000 dataset (with 43 predictive variables), CFS method selects the following nine variables:

o_rcs_p, i1_dep_1_e, i1_dep_2_p, o_dep_1_p, o_rcf_2_e,
o_rcf_3_place, i1_dlv_p, i1_dlv_e, o_dlv_e.

Again, the CFS method selected three out of four DLV variables. Also,

TABLE 7.10
Ranking of information gain for the 10 best variables

Rank	Variable	Information gain
1	*o_dlv_e*	0.236425
2	*i1_dlv_e*	0.192751
3	*o_dlv_p*	0.041598
4	*o_dep_1_p*	0.031145
5	*i1_dlv_p*	0.025441
6	*o_dep_1_e*	0.022247
7	*o_dep_1_place*	0.019748
8	*o_rcf_1_e*	0.019397
9	*i1_dep_1_p*	0.019228
10	*i1_rcf_1_e*	0.015636

the selected subset included some DEP variables. This could be due to the high impact that they have on business process delays, as shown in Table 7.5. However, the selection of the variable *o_rcf_3_place* is noteworthy, because this variable was not used by the interpretable models in Section 7.4.3.

As an illustrative example, Table 7.11 shows the AUC values for the classifiers in Section 7.4.1 after applying the above feature subset selection procedures. The column labeled Full includes the results with the entire dataset for comparison. The performance of the unfiltered dataset was better for seven out of 13 classifiers, whereas the information gain and CFS methods performed better for five and one classifiers, respectively. Note that classifier parametrization was driven by the unfiltered dataset. Therefore, it is expected to have an impact on the performance of the filtered datasets. However, the application of feature subset selection improved classifier performance for almost half of the classifiers. Therefore, this example shows that feature subset selection procedures are useful.

7.5 Conclusions and Future Research

7.5.1 Conclusions

This case study shows how supervised classification methods can be applied to a real distribution-level dataset to forecast air freight delays. Supervised classification algorithms can, in most cases, successfully predict shipment delays, especially when part of the business process has been completed. Delay prediction can be used in the decision-making process to provide a better quality service, increasing the robustness of a company's entire logistics process.

TABLE 7.11
AUC values rounded to three decimal places for each classifier using the full
dataset or feature subset selection based on the information gain or CFS
criteria. The accuracy of the best option for feature selection is shown in bold

Classifier	Full	Information gain	CFS
k-NN	0.957	**0.985**	0.968
C4.5	0.970	**0.973**	0.965
RIPPER	0.933	**0.933**	0.906
Multilayer perceptron	**0.996**	0.991	0.976
Support vector machine	**0.976**	0.940	0.908
Logistic regression	**0.997**	0.991	0.979
Naive Bayes	0.949	0.960	**0.964**
TAN	0.970	**0.972**	0.962
K2	0.969	**0.973**	0.965
Stacking	**0.976**	0.938	0.905
Bagging	**0.995**	0.992	0.980
Random forest	**0.990**	0.990	0.982
AdaBoost.M1	**0.987**	0.985	0.974

Also, during the exploration of some classifiers, we identified the transport
services that account for the largest part of business process instability. Both
the forecasting process and the discovery of the business process dynamics
add value to the company: decision makers detected the weak spots in the
company's shipment process and could then implement appropriate measures
to improve the most risky transport services.

First, we showed the preprocessing necessary to test multiple classifiers on
the Cargo 2000 dataset. Thanks to this preprocessing step, any supervised
classifier can be applied and dataset comprehensibility improved as a special
meaning is attached to each transport leg. The preprocessing step shows that
the application of machine learning techniques requires human expertise and
supervision because the algorithms must be fed with the adequate data. Of
course, the user can be shielded from machine learning algorithm complexities
by hiding the algorithm implementation details: all the system user needs is a
dashboard highlighting the business processes that are expected to be delayed.
The user can use this information to filter out most of the business processes
that will be on time and will only have to make decisions on the most suspect
shipments, thereby increasing productivity.

After a thorough review of classifier parameter meanings, we selected an
instantiation of each classifier type. The selected classifiers were compared
both quantitatively and qualitatively. For quantitative comparison, we applied
multiple hypothesis testing. Multiple hypothesis testing is an essential tool for
anyone trying to draw conclusions on classifier performance. For qualitative
comparison, we took advantage of human-interpretable classifiers to gain more

insights into how the business processes unfold. Not every supervised classifier is suitable for a qualitative analysis. Therefore, we compared only the most promising classifiers: classification trees, rules and Bayesian classifiers.

An online classification procedure was shown where each business process classification is updated when new information about service completion is received. The addition of actual times increased classifier performance as expected. However, performance only increased for the key service executions. The qualitative comparison of classifiers also found key service executions to be important. Thus, this case study proves that supervised machine learning classification algorithms are applicable in the distribution industry and play an important role in detecting weak points in business processes.

7.5.2   Future Research

Our approach is highly dependent on the selected preprocessing step. Each classifier uses the bottleneck transport leg instead of the three transport legs. Possible future research should investigate how classifiers can be set up to use multiple transport legs at the same time, taking into account that the number of transport legs may vary.

Also, in the online classification setup, a checkpoint is reached only when every inbound transport leg has executed the same service. This setup is not at all optimal, because if a transport leg executes services at a higher speed than other transport legs, it may take too long to consider the actual times of the faster transport leg. For example, if, in a business process with three inbound transport legs, each inbound transport leg has finished the following services:

- i1: $i1\_rcs$, $i1\_dep\_1$, $i1\_rcf\_1$,

- i2: $i2\_rcs$, $i2\_dep\_1$,

- i3: $i3\_rcs$,

we would consider that the business process is currently at the i_rcs checkpoint, even though we have more information for the i1 transport leg. This is especially relevant if the i1 transport leg is the bottleneck transport leg. This is not, fortunately, an overly common scenario because the bottleneck transport leg is usually the slowest throughout the entire business process. Even so, an expected bottleneck transport leg could happen to be faster than other inbound transport legs or faster for some services and then slower for others later on.

The algorithm tuning is another potential area for improvement. Some tools, such as AutoWeka (Kotthoff et al., 2017), could help to search for optimal classifier parameters. Such tools have some limitations (e.g., they cannot optimize all parameters). However, they can reduce the amount of time required to find a reasonably good solution.

The feature subset selection procedure could be improved by taking into account the relations between the planned and actual time variables. Information gain evaluates single variables by measuring the reduction of the class entropy when a variable is present, that is,

$$\mathbb{I}(\text{variable}, \text{Delay}) = \mathbb{H}(\text{Delay}) - \mathbb{H}(\text{Delay}|\text{variable}).$$

However, the comparison between the planned and actual times appears to be reasonable for delay detection and was confirmed by C4.5. The feature subset selection procedure could potentially be improved by evaluating pairs of features composed of the planned and actual times of each service execution. Therefore, the information gain for a service execution, say o_rcs, could be computed as

$$\mathbb{I}(\{o\_rcs\_p, o\_rcs\_e\}, \text{Delay}) = \mathbb{H}(\text{Delay}) - \mathbb{H}(\text{Delay}|o\_rcs\_p, o\_rcs\_e).$$

If $\mathbb{I}(\{o\_rcs\_p, o\_rcs\_e\}, \text{Delay})$ was a large value, the variables o_rcs_p, o_rcs_e would be added to the subset of selected variables.

Bibliography

Abraham, A., Pedregosa, F., Eickenberg, M., Gervias, P., Mueller, A., Kossaifi, J., Gramfort, A., Thirion, B., and Varoquaux, G. (2014). Machine learning for neuroimaging with scikit-learn. *Frontiers in Neuroinformatics*, 8:Article 14.

Acevedo, F., Jiménez, J., Maldonado, S., Domínguez, E., and A, N. (2007). Classification of wines produced in specific regions by UV-visible spectroscopy combined with support vector machines. *Journal of Agricultural and Food Chemistry*, 55:6842–6849.

Aggarwal, C., Han, J., Wang, J., and Yu, P. (2004). A framework for projected clustering evolving data streams. In *Proceedings of the 29th International Conference on Very Large Data Bases*, pages 81–92.

Aggarwal, C., Han, J., Wang, J., and Yu, P. (2006). A framework for on-demand classification of evolving data streams. *IEEE Transactions on Knowledge and Data Engeniering*, 18(5):577–589.

Agresti, A. (2013). *Categorical Data Analysis*. Wiley.

Aha, D., Kibler, D., and Albert, M. (1991). Instance-based learning algorithms. *Machine Learning*, 6(1):37–66.

Akaike, H. (1974). A new look at the statistical model identification. *IEEE Transactions on Automatic Control*, 19(6):716–723.

Akyildiz, I. F., Su, W., Sankarasubramaniam, Y., and Cayirci, E. (2002). Wireless sensor networks: A survey. *Computer Networks*, 38(4):393–422.

Ali, A., Shah, G. A., Farooq, M. O., and Ghani, U. (2017). Technologies and challenges in developing machine-to-machine applications: A survey. *Journal of Network and Computer Applications*, 83:124–139.

Alippi, C., Braione, P., Piuri, V., and Scotti, F. (2001). A methodological approach to multisensor classification for innovative laser material processing units. In *Proceedings of the 18th IEEE Instrumentation and Measurement Technology Conference*, volume 3, pages 1762–1767. IEEE Press.

Arias, M., Díez, F., M.A. Palacios-Alonso, M. Y., and Fernández, J. (2012).

POMDPs in OpenMarkov and ProbModelXML. In *The 7th Annual Workshop on Multiagent Sequential Decision-Making Under Uncertainty*, pages 1–8.

Armañanzas, R., Larrañaga, P., and Bielza, C. (2012). Ensemble transcript interaction networks: A case study on Alzheimer's disease. *Computer Methods and Programs in Biomedicine*, 108(1):442–450.

Arnborg, S., Corneil, D., and Proskurowski, A. (1987). Complexity of finding embeddings in a k-tree. *SIAM Journal on Algebraic Discrete Methods*, 8(2):277–284.

Arthur, D. and Vassilvitskii, S. (2007). K-means++: The advantages of careful seeding. In *Proceedings of 18th Symposium on Discrete Algorithms*, pages 1027–1035. Society for Industrial and Applied Mathematics.

Atienza, D., Bielza, C., and Larrañaga, P. (2016). Anomaly detection with a spatio-temporal tracking of the laser spot. In *Frontiers in Artificial Intelligence and Applications Series*, volume 284, pages 137–142. IOS Press.

Awoyemi, J., Adelunmbi, A., and Oluwadare, S. (2017). Credit card fraud detection using machine learning techniques: A comparative analysis. In *2017 International Conference on Computing Networking and Informatics*, pages 1–9. IEEE Press.

Ayer, T., Alagoz, O., Chhatwal, J., Shavlik, J., Kahn, C., and Burnside, E. (2010). Breast cancer risk estimation with artificial neural netwroks revisited. *Cancer*, 116:3310–3321.

Babu, D. K., Ramadevi, Y., and Ramana, K. (2017). RGNBC: Rough Gaussian naive Bayes classifier for data stream classification with recurring concept drift. *Arabian Journal for Science and Engineering*, 42:705–714.

Baheti, R. and Gill, H. (2011). Cyber-physical systems. *The Impact of Control Technology*, 12:161–166.

Bakhshipour, A., Sanaeifar, A., Payman, S., and de la Guardia, M. (2018). Evaluation of data mining strategies for classification of black tea based on image-based features. *Food Analytical Methods*, 11(4):1041–1050.

Ban, G.-Y., El Karoui, N., and Lim, A. E. B. (2016). Machine learning and portfolio optimization. *Management Science*, 64(3):1136–1154.

Bar-Yossef, Z. and Mashiach, L.-T. (2008). Local approximation of PageRank and Reverse PageRank. In *Proceedings of the 17th ACM Conference on Information and Knowledge Management*, pages 279–288. ACM.

Barber, D. and Cemgil, T. (2010). Graphical models for time series. *IEEE Signal Processing Magazine*, 27(6):18–28.

Baum, L., Petrie, T., Soules, G., and Weiss, N. (1970). A maximization technique occurring in the statistical analysis of probabilistic functions of Markov chains. *The Annals of Mathematical Statistics*, 41(1):164–171.

Bellman, R. E. (1957). *Dynamic Programming*. Princeton University Press.

Ben-Hur, A. and Weston, J. (2010). A user's guide to support vector machines. In *Data Mining Techniques for the Life Sciences*, volume 609, pages 223–239. Humana Press.

Bennett, R. G. (1985). Computer integrated manufacturing. *Plastic World*, 43(6):65–68.

Bernick, J. (2015). The role of machine learning in drug design and delivery. *Journal of Developing Drugs*, 4(3):1–2.

Bertelè, U. and Brioschi, F. (1972). *Nonserial Dynamic Programming*. Academic Press.

Berthold, M. R., Cebron, N., Dill, F., Gabriel, T. R., Kotter, T., Meinl, T., Ohl, P., Sieb, C., Thiel, K., and Wiswedel, B. (2008). Knime: The Konstanz information miner. In *Data Analysis, Machine Learning and Applications*, pages 319–326. Springer.

Bielza, C. and Larrañaga, P. (2014a). Bayesian networks in neuroscience: A survey. *Frontiers in Computational Neuroscience*, 8:Article 131.

Bielza, C. and Larrañaga, P. (2014b). Discrete Bayesian network classifiers: A survey. *ACM Computing Surveys*, 47(1):Article 5.

Bielza, C., Li, G., and Larrañaga, P. (2011). Multi-dimensional classification with Bayesian networks. *International Journal of Approximate Reasoning*, 52:705–727.

Biernacki, C., Celeux, G., and Govaert, G. (2000). Assessing a mixture model for clustering with the integrated completed likelihood. *IEEE Transactions on Pattern Analysis and Machine Intelligence*, 22(7):719–725.

Bifet, A., Holmes, G., and Kirkby, R. (2012). MOA: Massive online analysis. *Journal of Machine Learning Research*, 11:1601–1604.

Bind, S., Tiwari, A., and Sahani, A. (2015). A survey of machine learning based approaches for Parkinson disease prediction. *International Journal of Computer Science and Information Technologies*, 6(2):1648–1655.

Bishop, C. M. (1994). Novelty detection and neural network validation. *IEE Proceedings - Vision, Image and Signal Processing*, 141(4):217–222.

Blanco, R., Inza, I., Merino, M., Quiroga, J., and Larrañaga, P. (2005). Feature selection in Bayesian classifiers for the prognosis of survival of cirrhotic patients treated with TIPS. *Journal of Biomedical Informatics*, 38(5):376–388.

Böcker, A., Derksen, S., Schmidt, E., Teckentrup, A., and Schneider, G. (2005). A hierarchical clustering approach for large compound libraries. *Journal of Chemical Information and Modeling*, 45(4):807–815.

Bolton, R. and Hand, D. (2002). Statistical fraud detection: A review. *Statistical Science*, 17(3):235–255.

Borchani, H., Bielza, C., Martínez-Martín, P., and Larrañaga, P. (2014). Predicting the EQ-5D from the Parkinson's disease questionnaire (PDQ-8) using multi-dimensional Bayesian network classifiers. *Biomedical Engineering Applications, Basis and Communications*, 26(1):1450015–1.

Bose, I. and Mahapatra, R. K. (2001). Business data mining — a machine learning perspective. *Information & Management*, 39(3):211–225.

Bouckaert, R. R. (2003). Choosing between two learning algorithms based on calibrated tests. In *Proceedings of the 20th International Conference on Machine Learning*, pages 51–58. AAAI Press.

Bouejla, A., Chaze, X., Guarnieri, F., and Napoli, A. (2012). Bayesian networks in the management of oil field piracy risk. In *International Conference on Risk Analysis and Hazard Mitigation*, pages 31–42. WIT Press.

Breiman, L. (1996). Bagging predictors. *Machine Learning*, 24(2):123–140.

Breiman, L. (2001a). Random forests. *Machine Learning*, 45(1):5–32.

Breiman, L. (2001b). Statistical modeling: The two cultures. *Statistical Science*, 16(3):199–231.

Breiman, L., Friedman, J., Olshen, R., and Stone, C. (1984). *Classification and Regression Trees*. Wadsworth Press.

Breunig, M. M., Kriegel, H.-P., Ng, R. T., and Sander, J. (2000). LOF: identifying density-based local outliers. In *Proceedings of the 2000 ACM SIGMOD International Conference on Management of Data*, pages 93–104. ACM.

Brier, G. (1950). Verification of forecasts expressed in terms of probability. *Monthly Weather Review*, 78:1–3.

Buczak, A. L. and Guven, E. (2016). A survey of data mining and machine learning methods for cyber security intrusion detection. *IEEE Communications Surveys Tutorials*, 18(2):1153–1176.

Buntine, W. (1991). Theory refinement on Bayesian networks. In *Proceedings of the 7th Conference on Uncertainty in Artificial Intelligence*, pages 52–60. Morgan Kaufmann.

Bürger, F., Buck, C., Pauli, J., and Luther, W. (2014). Image-based object classification of defects in steel using data-driven machine learning optimization. In *2014 International Conference on Computer Vision Theory and Applications*, volume 2, pages 143–152.

Caesarenda, W. and Tjahjowidodo, T. (2017). A review of feature extraction methods in vibration-based condition monitoring and its application for degradation trend estimation of low-speed slew bearing. *Machines*, 5(4):Article 21.

Carbonneau, R., Laframboise, K., and Vahidov, R. (2008). Application of machine learning techniques for supply chain demand forecasting. *European Journal of Operational Research*, 184(3):1140–1154.

Carey, C., Boucher, T., Mahadevan, S., Bartholomew, P., and Dyar, M. D. (2015). Machine learning tools for mineral recognition and classification from raman spectroscopy. *Journal of Raman Spectroscopy*, 46(10):894–903.

Cartella, F., Lemeire, J., Dimiccoli, L., and Sahli, H. (2015). Hidden semi-Markov models for predictive maintenance. *Mathematical Problems in Engineering*, 2015:1–23.

Catlett, J. (1991). On changing continuous attributes into ordered discrete attributes. In *Proceedings of the European Working Session on Learning*, pages 164–178.

Celtikci, E. (2017). A systematic review on machine learning in neurosurgery: The future of decision-making in patient care. *Turkish Neurosurgery*, 28(2):167–173.

Chandola, V., Banerjee, A., and Kumar, V. (2009). Anomaly detection: A survey. *ACM Computing Surveys*, 41(3):15.

Chen, K.-Y., Chen, L.-S., Chen, M.-C., and Lee, C.-L. (2011). Using SVM based method for equipment fault detection in a thermal power plant. *Computers in Industry*, 62(1):42–50.

Chen, N., Ribeiro, B., and Chen, A. (2016). Financial credit risk assessment: A recent review. *Artificial Intelligence Review*, 45(1):1–23.

Chen, Z., Li, Y., Xia, T., and Pan, E. (2018). Hidden Markov model with auto-correlated observations for remaining useful life prediction and optimal maintenance policy. *Reliability Engineering and System Safety*, In press.

Chernoff, H. (1973). The use of faces to represent points in k-dimensional space graphically. *Journal of the American Statistical Association*, 68(342):361–368.

Chickering, D. (1995). A transformational characterization of equivalent Bayesian network structures. In *Proceedings of the 11th Conference on Uncertainty in Artificial Intelligence*, pages 87–98. Morgan Kaufmann.

Chickering, D. (1996). Learning Bayesian networks is NP-complete. In *Learning from Data: Artificial Intelligence and Statistics V*, pages 121–130. Springer.

Chinnam, R. B. (2002). Support vector machines for recognizing shifts in correlated and other manufacturing processes. *International Journal of Production Research*, 40(17):4449–4466.

Chong, M., Abraham, A., and Paprzycki, M. (2005). Traffic accident analysis using machine learning paradigms. *Informatica*, 29:89–98.

Ciccio, C. D., van der Aa, H., Cabanillas, C., Mendling, J., and Prescher, J. (2016). Detecting flight trajectory anomalies and predicting diversions in freight transportation. *Decision Support Systems*, 88:1–17.

Clark, P. and Niblett, T. (1989). The CN2 induction algorithm. *Machine Learning*, 3:261–283.

Codetta-Raiteri, D. and Portinale, L. (2015). Dynamic Bayesian networks for fault detection, identification, and recovery in autonomous spacecraft. *IEEE Transactions on Systems, Man, and Cybernetics Systems*, 45(1):13–24.

Cohen, J. (1960). A coefficient of agreement for nominal scales. *Educational and Psychological Measurements*, 20:37–46.

Cohen, W. W. (1995). Fast effective rule induction. In *Machine Learning: Proceedings of the 12th Annual Conference*, pages 115–123. Morgan Kaufmann.

Cooper, G. (1990). The computational complexity of probabilistic inference using Bayesian belief networks. *Artificial Intelligence*, 42(2–3):393–405.

Cooper, G. and Herskovits, E. (1992). A Bayesian method for the induction of probabilistic networks from data. *Machine Learning*, 9:309–347.

Cortes, C. and Vapnik, V. (1995). Support-vector networks. *Machine Learning*, 20(3):273–297.

Cover, T. (1965). Geometrical and statistical properties of systems of linear inequalities with applications in pattern recognition. *IEEE Transactions on Electronic Computers*, EC-14(3):326–334.

Cover, T. M. and Hart, P. E. (1967). Nearest neighbor pattern classification. *IEEE Transactions on Information Theory*, 13(1):21–27.

Cruz-Ramírez, N., Acosta-Mesa, H., Carrillo-Calvet, H., Nava-Fernández, L., and Barrientos-Martínez, R. (2007). Diagnosis of breast cancer using Bayesian networks: A case study. *Computers in Biology and Medicine*, 37:1553–1564.

Dadoun, M. (2017). Predicting fashion using machine learning techniques. Master's thesis, KTH Royal Institute of Technology.

Dagum, P. and Luby, M. (1993). Approximating probabilistic inference in Bayesian belief networks is NP-hard. *Artificial Intelligence*, 60(1):141–153.

Dang, X., Lee, V., Ng, W., Ciptadi, A., and Ong, K. (2009). An EM-based algorithm for clustering data streams in sliding windows. In *Database Systems for Advanced Applications*, volume 5463 of *Lecture Notes in Computer Science*, pages 230–235. Springer.

Darcy, A., Louie, A., and Roberts, L. (2016). Machine learning and the profession of medicine. *Journal of the American Medical Association*, 315(6):551–552.

Day, N. (1969). Estimating the components of a mixture of normal distributions. *Biometrika*, 56(3):463–474.

de Souza, E. N., Boerder, K., Matwin, S., and Worm, B. (2016). Improving fishing pattern detection from satellite AIS using data mining and machine learning. *PLOS ONE*, 11(7):e0158248.

Dean, T. and Kanazawa, K. (1989). A model for reasoning about persistence and causation. *Computational Intelligence*, 5(3):142–150.

Dearden, J. and Rowe, P. (2015). Use of artificial neural networks in the QSAR prediction of physicochemical properties and toxicities for REACH legislation. In *Artificial Neural Networks*, pages 65–88. Springer.

DeFelipe, J., López-Cruz, P., Benavides-Piccione, R., Bielza, C., Larrañaga, P., Anderson, S., Burkhalter, A., Cauli, B., Fairén, A., Feldmeyer, D., Fishell, G., Fitzpatrick, D., Freund, T. F., González-Burgos, G., Hestrin, S., Hill, S., Hof, P., Huang, J., Jones, E., Kawaguchi, Y., Kisvárday, Z., Kubota, Y., Lewis, D., Marín, O., Markram, H., McBain, C., Meyer, H., Monyer, H., Nelson, S., Rockland, K., Rossier, J., Rubenstein, J., Rudy, B., Scanziani, M., Shepherd, G., Sherwood, C., Staiger, J., Tamás, G., Thomson, A., Wang, Y., Yuste, R., and Ascoli, G. (2013). New insights into the classification and nomenclature of cortical GABAergic interneurons. *Nature Reviews Neuroscience*, 14(3):202–216.

DeGregory, K., Kuiper, P., DeSilvio, T., Pleuss, J., Miller, R., Roginski, J., Fisher, C., Harness, D., Viswanath, S., Heymsfield, S., Dungan, I., and Thomas, D. (2006). A review of machine learning in obesity. *Obesity Reviews*, 17(1):86–112.

Dempster, A., Laird, N., and Rubin, D. (1977). Maximum likelihood from incomplete data via the EM algorithm. *Journal of the Royal Statistical Society, Series B*, 39(1):1–38.

Demšar, J. (2006). Statistical comparisons of classifiers over multiple data sets. *Journal of Machine Learning Research*, 7:1–30.

Diaz, J., Bielza, C., Ocaña, J. L., and Larrañaga, P. (2016). Development of a cyber-physical system based on selective Gaussian naïve Bayes model for a self-predict laser surface heat treatment process control. In *Machine Learning for Cyber Physical Systems*, pages 1–8. Springer.

Diaz-Rozo, J., Bielza, C., and Larrañaga, P. (2017). Machine learning-based CPS for clustering high throughput machining cycle conditions. *Procedia Manufacturing*, 10:997–1008.

Diehl, C. P. and Hampshire, J. B. (2002). Real-time object classification and novelty detection for collaborative video surveillance. In *Proceedings of the 2002 International Joint Conference on Neural Networks*, volume 3, pages 2620–2625. IEEE Press.

d'Ocagne, M. (1885). *Coordonnées Parallèles et Axiales: Méthode de Transformation Géométrique et Procédé Nouveau de Calcul Graphique Déduits de la Considération des Coordonnées Parallèles*. Gauthier-Villars.

Doksum, K. and Hbyland, A. (1992). Models for variable-stress accelerated life testing experiments based on Wiener processes and the inverse Gaussian distribution. *Technometrics*, 34:74–82.

Domingos, P. and Hulten, G. (2000). Mining high-speed data streams. In *Proceedings of the 6th ACM SIGKDD International Conference on Knowledge Discovery and Data Mining*, pages 71–80.

Dong, S. and Luo, T. (2013). Bearing degradation process prediction based on the PCA and optimized LS-SVM model. *Measurement*, 46:3143–3152.

Dorronsoro, J. R., Ginel, F., Sánchez, C., and Cruz, C. S. (1997). Neural fraud detection in credit card operations. *IEEE Transactions on Neural Networks*, 8(4):827–834.

Druzdzel, M. (1999). SMILE: Structural modeling, inference, and learning engine and GeNIe: A development enviroment for graphical decision-theoretic models. In *Proceedings of the 16th American Association for Artificial Intelligence*, pages 902–903. Morgan Kaufmann.

Dua, S., Acharva, U., and Dua, P. (2013). *Machine Learning in Healthare Informatics*. Springer.

Dunn, O. J. (1961). Multiple comparisons among means. *Journal of the American Statistical Association*, 56(293):52–64.

Efron, B. (1979). Bootstrap methods: Another look at the jackknife. *Annals of Statistics*, 7:1–26.

Exarchos, K., Goletsis, Y., and Fotiadis, D. (2012). Multiparametric decision support system for the prediction of oral cancer reocurrence. *IEEE Transaction on Information Technology in Biomedicine*, 16:1127–1134.

Ezawa, K. and Norton, S. (1996). Constructing Bayesian networks to predict uncollectible telecommunications accounts. *IEEE Expert*, 11(5):45–51.

Fan, D., Yang, H., Li, F., Sun, L., Di, P., Li, W., Tang, Y., and Liu, G. (2018). In silico prediction of chemical genotoxicity using machine learning methods and structural alerts. *Toxicology Research*, 7(2):211–220.

Faria, E. R., Gonçalves, I. J., de Carvalho, A. C., and Gama, J. (2016). Novelty detection in data streams. *Artificial Intelligence Review*, 45(2):235–269.

Fawcett, T. (2006). An introduction to ROC analysis. *Pattern Recognition Letters*, 27(8):861–874.

Fayyad, U. and Irani, K. (1993). Multi-interval discretization of continuous-valued attributes for classification learning. In *Proceedings of the 13th International Joint Conference on Artificial Intelligence*, pages 1022–1029.

Fefilatyev, S., Smarodzinava, V., Hall, L. O., and Goldgof, D. B. (2006). Horizon detection using machine learning techniques. In *5th International Conference on Machine Learning and Applications*, pages 17–21.

Fei-Fei, L., Fergus, R., and Perona, P. (2006). One-shot learning of object categories. *IEEE Transactions on Pattern Analysis and Machine Intelligence*, 28(4):594–611.

Figueiredo, M. and Jain, A. K. (2002). Unsupervised learning of finite mixture models. *IEEE Transactions on Pattern Analysis and Machine Intelligence*, 24(3):381–396.

Fix, E. and Hodges, J. (1951). Discriminatory analysis, nonparametric discrimination: Consistency properties. Technical Report 4, USAF School of Aviation Medicine, Randolph Field, Texas.

Fletcher, R. (2000). *Practical Methods of Optimization*. Wiley.

Florek, K., Lukaszewicz, J., Perkal, H., Steinhaus, H., and Zubrzycki, S. (1951). Sur la liaison et la division des points d'un ensemble fini. *Colloquium Mathematicum*, 2:282–285.

Flores, M. and Gámez, J. (2007). A review on distinct methods and approaches to perform triangulation for Bayesian networks. In *Advances in Probabilistic Graphical Models*, pages 127–152. Springer.

Flores, M. J., Gámez, J., Martínez, A., and Salmerón, A. (2011). Mixture of truncated exponentials in supervised classification: Case study for the naive Bayes and averaged one-dependence estimators classifiers. In *11th International Conference on Intelligent Systems Design and Applications*, pages 593–598. IEEE Press.

Foley, A. M., Leahy, P. G., Marvuglia, A., and McKeogh, E. J. (2012). Current methods and advances in forecasting of wind power generation. *Renewable Energy*, 37(1):1–8.

Forgy, E. (1965). Cluster analysis of multivariate data: Efficiency versus interpretability of classifications. *Biometrics*, 21:768–769.

Fournier, F. A., McCall, J., Petrovski, A., and Barclay, P. J. (2010). Evolved Bayesian network models of rig operations in the Gulf of Mexico. In *IEEE Congress on Evolutionary Computation*, pages 1–7. IEEE Press.

Freeman, L. C. (1977). A set of measures of centrality based on betweenness. *Sociometry*, pages 35–41.

Freund, Y. and Schapire, R. (1997). A decision-theoretic generalization of on-line learning and an application to boosting. *Journal of Computer and System Sciences*, 55(1):119–139.

Frey, B. J. and Dueck, D. (2007). Clustering by passing messages between data points. *Science*, 315:972–976.

Friedman, M. (1937). The use of ranks to avoid the assumption of normality implicit in the analysis of variance. *Journal of the American Statistical Association*, 32(200):675–701.

Friedman, N. (1998). The Bayesian structural EM algorithm. In *Proceedings of the 14th Conference on Uncertainty in Artificial Intelligence*, pages 129–138. Morgan Kaufmann.

Friedman, N., Geiger, D., and Goldszmidt, M. (1997). Bayesian network classifiers. *Machine Learning*, 29:131–163.

Friedman, N., Goldszmidt, M., and Lee, T. (1998a). Bayesian network classification with continuous attibutes: Getting the best of both discretization and parametric fitting. In *Proceedings of the 15th National Conference on Machine Learning*, pages 179–187.

Friedman, N., Linial, M., Nachman, I., and Pe'er, D. (2000). Using Bayesian networks to analyze expression data. *Journal of Computational Biology*, 7(3-4):601–620.

Friedman, N., Murphy, K., and Russell, S. (1998b). Learning the structure of dynamic probabilistic networks. In *Proceedings of the 14th Conference on Uncertainty in Artificial Intelligence*, pages 139–147. Morgan Kaufmann.

Frigyik, B. A., Kapila, A., and Gupta, M. (2010). Introduction to the Dirichlet distribution and related processes. Technical Report, University of Washington.

Frutos-Pascual, M. and García-Zapirain, B. (2017). Review of the use of AI techniques in serious games: Decision making and machine learning. *IEEE Transactions on Computational Intelligence and AI in Games*, 9(2):133–152.

Fung, R. and Chang, K.-C. (1990). Weighing and integrating evidence for stochastic simulation in Bayesian networks. In *Proceedings of the 6th Conference on Uncertainty in Artificial Intelligence*, pages 209–220. Elsevier.

Fürnkranz, J. and Widmer, G. (1994). Incremental reduced error pruning. In *Machine Learning: Proceedings of the 11th Annual Conference*, pages 70–77. Morgan Kaufmann.

Gabilondo, A., Domínguez, J., Soriano, C., and Ocaña, J. (2015). Method and system for laser hardening of a surface of a workpiece. US20150211083A1 patent.

Galán, S., Arroyo-Figueroa, G., Díez, F., and Sucar, L. (2007). Comparison of two types of event Bayesian networks: A case study. *Applied Artificial Intelligence*, 21(3):185–209.

Gama, J. (2010). *Knowledge Discovery from Data Streams*. CRC Press.

Gama, J., Sebastião, R., and Rodrigues, P. (2013). On evaluating stream learning algorithms. *Machine Learning*, 90(3):317–346.

Gao, S. and Lei, Y. (2017). A new approach for crude oil price prediction based on stream learning. *Geoscience Frontiers*, 8:183–187.

García, S., Derrac, J., Cano, J., and Herrera, F. (2012). Prototype selection for nearest neighbor classification: Taxonomy and empirical study. *IEEE Transactions on Pattern Analysis and Machine Intelligence*, 34(3):417–435.

García, S. and Herrera, F. (2008). An extension on "Statistical Comparisons of Classifiers over Multiple Data Sets" for all pairwise comparisons. *Journal of Machine Learning Research*, 9:2677–2694.

Geiger, D. and Heckerman, D. (1996). Knowledge representation and inference in similarity networks and Bayesian multinets. *Artificial Intelligence*, 82:45–74.

Geng, X., Liang, H., Yu, B., Zhao, P., He, L., and Huang, R. (2017). A scenario-adaptive driving behavior prediction approach to urban autonomous driving. *Applied Sciences*, 7:Article 426.

Gevaert, O., De Smet, F., Timmerman, D., Moreau, Y., and De Moor, B. (2006). Predicting the prognosis of breast cancer by integrating clinical and microarray data with Bayesian networks. *Bioinformatics*, 22(14):184–190.

Gill, H. (2006). NSF perspective and status on cyber-physical systems. In *National Workshop on Cyber-physical Systems*. National Science Foundation.

Gillispie, S. and Perlman, M. (2002). The size distribution for Markov equivalence classes of acyclic digraph models. *Artificial Intelligence*, 141(1/2):137–155.

Gleich, D. F. (2015). PageRank beyond the Web. *SIAM Review*, 57(3):321–363.

Golnabi, H. and Asadpour, A. (2007). Design and application of industrial machine vision systems. *Robotics and Computer-Integrated Manufacturing*, 23(6):630–637.

Gonzalez-Viejo, C., Fuentes, S., Torrico, D., Howell, K., and Dunshea, F. (2018). Assessment of beer quality based on foamability and chemical composition using computer vision algorithms, near infrared spectroscopy and machine learning algorithms. *Journal of the Science and Food and Agriculture*, 98(2):618–627.

Goodwin, R., Maria, J., Das, P., Horesh, R., Segal, R., Fu, J., and Harris, C. (2017). AI for fragrance design. In *Machine Learning for Creativity and Design. Workshop of NIPS2017*.

Gordon, A. D. (1987). A review of hierarchical classification. *Journal of the Royal Statistical Society. Series A*, 150(2):119–137.

Gosangi, R. and Gutierrez-Osuna, R. (2011). Data-driven modeling of metal-oxide sensors with dynamic Bayesian networks. *American Institute of Physics Conference Series*, 1362:135–136.

Gupta, Y. (2018). Selection of important features and predicting wine quality using machine learning techniques. *Procedia Computer Science*, 125:305–312.

Halawani, S. M. (2014). A study of decision tree ensembles and feature selection for steel plates faults detection. *International Journal of Technical Research and Applications*, 2(4):127–131.

Hall, M. (1999). *Correlation-Based Feature Selection for Machine Learning*. PhD thesis, Department of Computer Science, University of Waikato.

Hall, M., Frank, E., Holmes, G., Pfahringer, B., Reutemann, P., and Witten, I. (2009). The WEKA data mining software: An update. *SIGKDD Explorations*, 11(1):10–18.

Hansson, K., Yella, S., Dougherty, M., and Fleyeh, H. (2016). Machine learning algorithms in heavy process manufacturing. *American Journal of Intelligent Systems*, 6(1):1–13.

Hart, P. E. (1968). The condensed nearest neighbor rule. *IEEE Transactions on Information Theory*, 14(3):515–516.

Harvey, A. and Fotopoulos, G. (2016). Geological mapping using machine learning algorithms. *ISPRS - International Archives of the Photogrammetry, Remote Sensing and Spatial Information Sciences*, XLI-B8:423–430.

He, H. and Garcia, E. A. (2009). Learning from imbalanced data. *IEEE Transactions on Knowledge and Data Engineering*, 21(9):1263–1284.

Heckerman, D., Geiger, D., and Chickering, D. (1995). Learning Bayesian networks: The combination of knowledge and statistical data. *Machine Learning*, 20:197–243.

Henrion, M. (1988). Propagating uncertainty in Bayesian networks by probabilistic logic sampling. In *Uncertainty in Artificial Intelligence 2*, pages 149–163. Elsevier Science.

Hernández-Leal, P., González, J., Morales, E., and Sucar, L. (2013). Learning temporal nodes Bayesian networks. *International Journal of Approximate Reasoning*, 54(8):956–977.

Herrera, M., Torgo, L., Izquierdo, J., and Pérez-García, R. (2010). Predictive models for forecasting hourly urban water demand. *Journal of Hydrology*, 387(1):141–150.

Herterich, M. M., Uebernickel, F., and Brenner, W. (2016). Stepwise evolution of capabilities for harnessing digital data streams in data-driven industrial services. *MIS Quarterly Executive*, 15(4):297–318.

Hofmann, M. and Klinkenberg, R. (2013). *RapidMiner: Data Mining Use Cases and Business Applications*. CRC Press.

Højsgaard, S. (2012). Graphical independence networks with the `gRain` package for `R`. *Journal of Statistical Software*, 46(10):1–26.

Hosmer, D. and Lemeshow, S. (2000). *Applied Logistic Regression*. Wiley Interscience.

Hsu, C.-I., Shih, M.-L., Huang, B.-W., Lin, B.-Y., and Lin, C.-N. (2009). Predicting tourism loyalty using an integrated Bayesian network mechanism. *Expert Systems with Applications*, 36:11760–11763.

Hsu, C.-W. and Lin, C.-J. (2002). A comparison of methods for multiclass support vector machines. *IEEE Transactions on Neural Networks*, 13(2):415–425.

Hsu, S.-C. and Chien, C.-F. (2007). Hybrid data mining approach for pattern extraction from wafer bin map to improve yield in semiconductor manufacturing. *International Journal of Production Economics*, 107(1):88–103.

Huang, S.-H. and Pan, Y.-C. (2015). Automated visual inspection in the semiconductor industry: A survey. *Computers in Industry*, 66:1–10.

Huang, Y. and Bian, L. (2009). A Bayesian network and analytic hierarchy process based personalized recommendations for tourist attractions over the Internet. *Expert Systems with Applications*, 36:933–943.

Hulst, J. (2006). *Modeling Physiological Processes with Dynamic Bayesian Networks*. PhD thesis, Delft University of Technology.

Husmeier, D. (2003). Sensitivity and specificity of inferring genetic regulatory interactions from microarray experiments with dynamic Bayesian networks. *Bioinformatics*, 19(17):2271–2282.

Iglesias, C., Alves-Santos, A., Martínez, J., Pereira, H., and Anjos, O. (2017). Influence of heartwood on wood density and pulp properties explained by machine learning techniques. *Forests*, 8(20).

Inman, R. H., Pedro, H. T., and Coimbra, C. F. (2013). Solar forecasting methods for renewable energy integration. *Progress in Energy and Combustion Science*, 39(6):535–576.

Inza, I., Larrañaga, P., Blanco, R., and Cerrolaza, A. (2004). Filter versus wrapper gene selection approaches in DNA microarray domains. *Artificial Intelligence in Medicine*, 31(2):91–103.

Jäger, M., Knoll, C., and Hamprecht, F. A. (2008). Weakly supervised learning of a classifier for unusual event detection. *IEEE Transactions on Image Processing*, 17(9):1700–1708.

Jain, A. K. (2010). Data clustering: 50 years beyond K-means. *Pattern Recognition Letters*, 31(8):651–666.

Japkowicz, N. and Mohak, S. (2011). *Evaluating Learning Algorithms. A Classification Perspective*. Cambridge University Press.

Jiang, F., Jiang, Y., Zhi, H., Dong, Y., Li, H., Ma, S., Wang, Y., Dong, Q., Shen, H., and Wang, Y. (2017). Artificial intelligence in healthcare: Past, present and future. *Stroke and Vascular Neurology*, e000101.

John, G. H., Kohavi, R., and Pfleger, P. (1994). Irrelevant features and the subset selection problem. In *Proceedings of the 11th International Conference in Machine Learning*, pages 121–129. Morgan Kaufmann.

Jolliffe, J. (1986). *Principal Component Analysis*. Springer.

Jordan, M. and Mitchell, T. (2015). Machine learning: Trends, perspectives, and prospects. *Science*, 349(6245):255–260.

Jothi, N., Rashid, N., and Husain, W. (2015). Data mining in healthcare. A review. *Procedia Computer Science*, 72:306–313.

Judson, R., Elloumi, F., Setzer, R. W., Li, Z., and Shah, I. (2008). A comparison of machine learning algorithms for chemical toxicity classification using a simulated multi-scale data model. *BMC Bioinformatics*, 9:241.

Kagermann, H., Wahlster, W., and Helbig, J. (2013). Securing the future of German manufacturing industry. Recommendations for Implementing the Strategic Initiative INDUSTRIE 4.0. Technical report, National Academy of Science and Engineering (ACATECH).

Kamp, B., Ochoa, A., and Diaz, J. (2017). Smart servitization within the context of industrial user–supplier relationships: contingencies according to a machine tool manufacturer. *International Journal on Interactive Design and Manufacturing*, 11(3):651–663.

Kavakiotis, I., Tsave, O., Salifoglou, A., Maglaveras, N., Vlahavas, I., and Chouvarda, I. (2017). Machine learning and data mining methods in diabetes research. *Computational and Structural Biotechnology Journal*, 15:104–116.

Kaynak, C. and Alpaydin, E. (2000). Multistage cascading of multiple classifiers: One man's noise is another man's data. In *Proceedings of the 17th International Conference on Machine Learning*, pages 455–462. Morgan Kaufmann.

Kearns, M. and Nevmyvaka, Y. (2013). Machine learning for market microstructure and high frequency trading. In *High Frequency Trading. New Realities for Traders, Markets and Regulators*, pages 1–21. Risk Books.

Keogh, E. and Pazzani, M. (2002). Learning the structure of augmented Bayesian classifiers. *International Journal on Artificial Intelligence Tools*, 11(4):587–601.

Kezunovic, M., Obradovic, Z., Dokic, T., Zhang, B., Stojanovic, J., Dehghanian, P., and Chen, P.-C. (2017). Predicting spatiotemporal impacts of weather on power systems using big data science. In *Data Science and Big Data: An Environment of Computational Intelligence*, pages 265–299. Springer.

Khare, A., Jeon, M., Sethi, I., and Xu, B. (2017). Machine learning theory and applications for healtcare. *Journal of Healtcare Engineering*, ID 5263570.

Kim, D., Kang, P., Cho, S., Lee, H., and Doh, S. (2012). Machine learning-based novelty detection for faulty wafer detection in semiconductor manufacturing. *Expert Systems with Applications*, 39(4):4075–4083.

Kim, J. and Pearl, J. (1983). A computational model for combined causal and diagnostic reasoning in inference systems. In *Proceedings of the 87th International Joint Conference on Artificial Intelligence*, volume 1, pages 190–193.

Klaine, P. V., Imran, M. A., Onireti, O., and Souza, R. D. (2017). A survey of machine learning techniques applied to self-organizing cellular networks. *IEEE Communications Surveys and Tutorials*, 19(4):2392–2431.

Kleinrock, L. (1961). *Information Flow in Large Communication Nets.* PhD thesis, MIT.

Kohavi, R. (1996). Scaling up the accuracy of naive-Bayes classifiers: A decision-tree hybrid. In *Proceedings of the 2nd International Conference on Knowledge Discovery and Data Mining*, pages 202–207.

Koller, D. and Friedman, N. (2009). *Probabilistic Graphical Models: Principles and Techniques.* The MIT Press.

Koller, D. and Sahami, M. (1996). Toward optimal feature selection. In *Proceedings of the 13th International Conference on Machine Learning*, pages 284–292.

Kotthoff, L., Thornton, C., Hoos, H. H., Hutter, F., and Leyton-Brown, K. (2017). Auto-WEKA 2.0: Automatic model selection and hyperparameter optimization in WEKA. *Journal of Machine Learning Research*, 18(25):1–5.

Kourou, K., Exarchos, T., Exarchos, K. P., Karamouzis, M., and Fotiadis, D. (2015). Machine learning applications in cancer prognosis and prediction. *Computational and Structural Biotechnology Journal*, 13:8–17.

Kowalski, J., Krawczyk, B., and Woźniak, M. (2017). Fault diagnosis of marine 4-stroke diesel engines using a one-vs-one extreme learning ensemble. *Engineering Applications of Artificial Intelligence*, 57:134–141.

Kraska, T., Beutel, A., Chi, E. H., Dean, J., and Polyzotis, N. (2017). The case for learned index structures. *ArXiv 1712.01208*.

Kruskal, J. B. (1956). On the shortest spanning subtree of a graph and the traveling salesman problem. *Proceedings of the American Mathematical Society*, 7(1):48–50.

Kuncheva, L. (2004). *Combining Pattern Classifiers: Methods and Algorithms.* Wiley-Interscience.

Kurtz, A. (1948). A research test of Rorschach test. *Personnel Psychology*, 1:41–53.

Lafaye de Micheaux, P., Drouihet, R., and Liquet, B. (2013). *The R Software. Fundamentals of Programming and Statistical Analysis.* Springer.

Landhuis, E. (2017). Big brain, big data. *Nature*, 541:559–561.

Landwehr, N., Hall, M., and Frank, E. (2003). Logistic model trees. *Machine Learning*, 59(1-2):161–205.

Lane, T. and Brodley, C. E. (1997). An application of machine learning to anomaly detection. In *Proceedings of the 20th National Information Systems Security Conference*, volume 377, pages 366–380.

Lang, T., Flachsenberg, F., von Luxburg, U., and Rarey, M. (2016). Feasibility of active machine learning for multiclass compound classification. *Journal of Chemical Information and Modeling*, 56(1):12–20.

Langley, P. and Sage, S. (1994). Induction of selective Bayesian classifiers. In *Proceedings of the 10th Conference on Uncertainty in Artificial Intelligence*, pages 399–406. Morgan Kaufmann.

Larrañaga, P., Calvo, B., Santana, R., Bielza, C., Galdiano, J., Inza, I., Lozano, J. A., Armañanzas, R., Santafé, G., and Pérez, A. (2006). Machine learning in bioinformatics. *Briefings in Bioinformatics*, 17(1):86–112.

Lauritzen, S. (1995). The EM algorithm for graphical association models with missing data. *Computational Statistics and Data Analysis*, 19:191–201.

Lauritzen, S. and Jensen, F. (2001). Stable local computation with conditional Gaussian distributions. *Statistics and Computing*, 11(2):191–203.

Lauritzen, S. and Spiegelhalter, D. (1988). Local computations with probabilities on graphical structures and their application to expert systems. *Journal of the Royal Statistical Society, Series B (Methodological)*, 50(2):157–224.

Lauritzen, S. and Wermuth, N. (1989). Graphical models for associations between variables, some of which are qualitative and some quantitative. *The Annals of Statistics*, 17(1):31–57.

Lauritzen, S. L., Dawid, A. P., Larsen, B. N., and Leimer, H.-G. (1990). Independence properties of directed Markov fields. *Networks*, 20(5):491–505.

Lavecchia, A. (2015). Machine-learning approaches in drug discovery: Methods and applications. *Drug Discovery Today*, 20(3):318–331.

Law, A. and Kelton, D. (1999). *Simulation Modeling and Analysis.* McGraw-Hill Higher Education.

Le, T., Berenguer, C., and Chatelain, F. (2015). Prognosis based on multi-branch hidden semi-Markov models: A case study. *IFAC-PapersOnLine*, 48-21:91–96.

Lee, H., Kim, Y., and Kim, C. O. (2017). A deep learning model for robust wafer fault monitoring with sensor measurement noise. *IEEE Transactions on Semiconductor Manufacturing*, 30(1):23–31.

Lee, J., Bagheri, B., and Kao, H.-A. (2015). A cyber-physical systems architecture for industry 4.0-based manufacturing systems. *Manufacturing Letters*, 3:18–23.

Lee, J., Kao, H.-A., and Yang, S. (2014). Service innovation and smart analytics for industry 4.0 and big data environment. *Procedia CIRP*, 16:3–8.

Leite, D., Costa, P., and Gomide, F. (2010). Evolving granular neural network for semi-supervised data stream classification. In *The 2010 International Joint Conference on Neural Networks*, pages 1–8.

Lessmann, S., Baesens, B., Seow, H.-V., and Thomas, L. C. (2015). Benchmarking state-of-the-art classification algorithms for credit scoring: An update of research. *European Journal of Operational Research*, 247:124–136.

Lewis, P. (1962). The characteristic selection problem in recognition systems. *IRE Transactions on Information Theory*, 8:171–178.

Li, H., Liang, Y., and Xu, Q. (2009). Support vector machines and its applications in chemistry. *Chemometrics and Intelligent Laboratory Systems*, 95(2):188–198.

Li, H. and Zhu, X. (2004). Application of support vector machine method in prediction of Kappa number of kraft pulping process. In *Proceedings of the Fifth World Congress on Intelligent Control and Automation*, volume 4, pages 3325–3330.

Li, K., Zhang, X., Leung, J. Y.-T., and Yang, S.-L. (2016). Parallel machine scheduling problems in green manufacturing industry. *Journal of Manufacturing Systems*, 38:98–106.

Li, S., Xu, L. D., and Wang, X. (2013). Compressed sensing signal and data acquisition in wireless sensor networks and Internet of Things. *IEEE Transactions on Industrial Informatics*, 9(4):2177–2186.

Li, Y. (2017). Backorder prediction using machine learning for Danish craft beer breweries. Master's thesis, Aalborg University.

Lima, A., Philot, E., Trossini, G., Scott, L., Maltarollo, V., and Honorio, K. (2016). Use of machine learning approaches for novel drug discovery. *Expert Opinion on Drug Discovery*, 11(3):225–239.

Lin, S.-C. and Chen, K.-C. (2016). Statistical QoS control of network coded multipath routing in large cognitive machine-to-machine networks. *IEEE Internet of Things Journal*, 3(4):619–627.

Lin, S.-W., Crawford, M., and Mellor, S. (2017). The Industrial Internet of Things Reference Architecture. Technical Report Volume G1, Industrial Internet Consortium.

Lipton, Z. C. (2016). The mythos of model interpretability. In *ICML Workshop on Human Interpretability in Machine Learning*, pages 96–100.

Liu, H., Hussain, F., Tan, C., and Dash, M. (2002). Discretization: An enabling technique. *Data Mining and Knowledge Discovery*, 6(4):393–423.

Liu, J., Seraoui, R., Vitelli, V., and Zio, E. (2013). Nuclear power plant components condition monitoring by probabilistic support vector machine. *Annals of Nuclear Energy*, 56:23–33.

Liu, Y., Li, S., Li, F., Song, L., and Rehg, J. (2015). Efficient learning of continuous-time hidden Markov models for disease progression. *Advances in Neural Information Processing Systems*, 28:3600–3608.

Lu, C. and Meeker, W. (1993). Using degradation measures to estimate a time-to-failure distribution. *Technometrics*, pages 161–174.

Lusted, L. (1960). Logical analysis in roentgen diagnosis. *Radiology*, 74:178–193.

Luxburg, U. (2007). A tutorial on spectral clustering. *Statistics and Computing*, 17:395–416.

MacQueen, J. (1967). Some methods for classification and analysis of multivariate observations. In *Proceedings of 5th Berkeley Symposium on Mathematical Statistics and Probability*, pages 281–297.

Madsen, A., Jensen, F., Kjærulff, U., and Lang, M. (2005). The HUGIN tool for probabilistic graphical models. *International Journal of Artificial Intelligence Tools*, 14(3):507–543.

Malamas, E. N., Petrakis, E. G., Zervakis, M., Petit, L., and Legat, J.-D. (2003). A survey on industrial vision systems, applications and tools. *Image and Vision Computing*, 21(2):171–188.

Maltarollo, V., Gertrudes, J., Oliveira, P., and Honorio, K. (2015). Applying machine learning techniques for ADME-Tox prediction: A review. *Expert Opinion on Drug Metabolism & Toxicology*, 11(2):259–271.

Markou, M. and Singh, S. (2003). Novelty detection: A review. Part 2: Neural network based approaches. *Signal Processing*, 83(12):2499–2521.

Markou, M. and Singh, S. (2006). A neural network-based novelty detector for image sequence analysis. *IEEE Transactions on Pattern Analysis and Machine Intelligence*, 28(10):1664–1677.

Markowitz, H. (1952). Portfolio selection. *The Journal of Finance*, 7(1):77–91.

Marvuglia, A. and Messineo, A. (2012). Monitoring of wind farms' power curves using machine learning techniques. *Applied Energy*, 98:574–583.

McCulloch, W. and Pitts, W. (1943). A logical calculus of the ideas immanent in nervous activity. *Bulletin of Mathematical Biophysics*, 5:115–133.

McEliece, R. J., MacKay, D. J. C., and Cheng, J.-F. (1998). Turbo decoding as an instance of Pearl's "belief propagation" algorithm. *IEEE Journal on Selected Areas in Communications*, 16(2):140–152.

McLachlan, G. and Krishnan, T. (1997). *The EM Algorithm and Extensions*. Wiley.

McLachlan, G. and Peel, D. (2004). *Finite Mixture Models*. John Wiley & Sons.

Mengistu, A. D., Alemayehu, D., and Mengistu, S. (2016). Ethiopian coffee plant diseases recognition based on imaging and machine learning techniques. *International Journal of Database Theory and Application*, 9(4):79–88.

Metzger, A., Leitner, P., Ivanović, D., Schmieders, E., Franklin, R., Carro, M., Dustdar, S., and Pohl, K. (2015). Comparing and combining predictive business process monitoring techniques. *IEEE Transactions on Systems, Man, and Cybernetics: Systems*, 45(2):276–290.

Michalski, R. S. and Chilausky, R. (1980). Learning by being told and learning from examples: An experimental comparison of the two methods of knowledge acquisition in the context of developing an expert system for soybean disease diagnosis. *International Journal of Policy Analysis and Information Systems*, 4:125–160.

Minsky, M. (1961). Steps toward artificial intelligence. *Transactions on Institute of Radio Engineers*, 49:8–30.

Minsky, M. L. and Papert, S. (1969). *Perceptrons*. The MIT Press.

Mirowski, P. and LeCun, Y. (2018). Statistical machine learning and dissolved gas analysis: A review. *IEEE Transactions on Power Delivery*, 27(4):1791–1799.

Mohamed, A., Hamdi, M. S., and Tahar, S. (2015). A machine learning approach for big data in oil and gas pipelines. In *International Conference on Future Internet of Things and Cloud*, pages 585–590. IEEE Press.

Mu, J., Chaudhuri, K., Bielza, C., De Pedro, J., Larrañaga, P., and Martínez-Martín, P. (2017). Parkinson's disease subtypes identified from cluster analysis of motor and non-motor symptoms. *Frontiers in Aging Neuroscience*, 9:Article 301.

Murray, J. F., Hughes, G. F., and Kreutz-Delgado, K. (2005). Machine learning methods for predicting failures in hard drives: A multiple-instance application. *Journal of Machine Learning Research*, 6:783–816.

Natarajan, P., Frenzel, J., and Smaltz, D. (2017). *Demystifying Big Data and Machine Learning for Healthcare*. CRC Press.

National Academy of Sciences and The Royal Society (2017). *The Frontiers of Machine Learning*. The National Academies Press.

Navarro, P., Fernández, C., Borraz, R., and Alonso, D. (2017). A machine learning approach to pedestrian detection for autonomous vehicles using high-definition 3D range data. *Sensors*, 17:Article 18.

Nectoux, P., Gouriveau, R., Medjaher, K., Ramasso, E., Morello, B., Zerhouni, N., and Varnier, C. (2012). PRONOSTIA: An experimental platform for bearings accelerated life test. *IEEE International Conference on Prognostics and Health Management*, pages 1–8.

Newman, T. S. and Jain, A. K. (1995). A survey of automated visual inspection. *Computer Vision and Image Understanding*, 61(2):231–262.

Nguyen, H.-L., Woon, Y.-K., and Ng, W.-K. (2015). A survey on data stream clustering and classification. *Knowledge Information Systems*, 45:535–569.

Niu, D., Wang, Y., and Wu, D. D. (2010). Power load forecasting using support vector machine and ant colony optimization. *Expert Systems with Applications*, 37(3):2531–2539.

Nodelman, U., Shelton, C., and Koller, D. (2002). Continuous time Bayesian networks. In *Proceedings of the 18th Conference on Uncertainty in Artificial Intelligence*, pages 378–387.

Nwiabu, N. and Amadi, M. (2017). Building a decision support system for crude oil price prediction using Bayesian networks. *American Scientific Research Journal for Engineering, Technology, and Sciences*, 38(2):1–17.

O'Callaghan, L., Mishra, N., Meyerson, A., Guha, S., and Motwani, R. (2002). Streaming-data algorithms for high-quality clustering. In *Proceedings of the 18th International Conference on Data Engineering*, pages 685–694.

Ogbechie, A., Díaz-Rozo, J., Larrañaga, P., and Bielza, C. (2017). Dynamic Bayesian network-based anomaly detection for in-process visual inspection of laser surface heat treatment. In *Machine Learning for Cyber Physical Systems*, pages 17–24. Springer.

Olesen, J., Gustavsson, Q., Svensson, M., Wittchen, H., and Jonson, B. (2012). The economic cost of brain disorders in Europe. *European Journal of Neurology*, 19(1):155–162.

Onisko, A. and Austin, R. (2015). Dynamic Bayesian network for cervical cancer screening. In *Biomedical Knowledge Representation*, pages 207–218. Springer.

Oza, N. and Russell, S. (2005). Online bagging and boosting. In *2005 IEEE International Conference on Systems, Man and Cybernetics*, pages 2340–2345.

Page, L., Brin, S., Motwani, R., and Winograd, T. (1999). The PageRank citation ranking: Bringing order to the web. Technical report, Stanford InfoLab.

Pardakhti, M., Moharreri, E., Wanik, D., Suib, S., and Srivastava, R. (2017). Machine learning using combined structural and chemical descriptors for prediction of methane adsorption performance of metal organic frameworks (MOFs). *ACS Combinatorial Science*, 19(10):640–645.

Park, K., Ali, A., Kim, D., An, Y., Kim, M., and Shin, H. (2013). Robust predictive model for evaluating breast cancer survivability. *English Applied Artificial Intelligence*, 26:2194–2205.

Park, S., Jaewook, L., and Youngdoo, S. (2016). Predicting market impact costs using nonparametric machine learning models. *PLOS ONE*, 11(2):e0150243.

Parzen, E. (1962). On estimation of a probability density function and mode. *The Annals of Mathematical Statistics*, 33(3):1065–1076.

Pazzani, M. (1996). Constructive induction of Cartesian product attributes. In *Proceedings of the Information, Statistics and Induction in Science Conference*, pages 66–77.

Pazzani, M. and Billsus, D. (1997). Learning and revising user profiles: The identification of interesting web sites. *Machine Learning*, 27:313–331.

Pearl, J. (1982). Reverend Bayes on inference engines: A distributed hierarchical approach. In *Proceedings of the 2nd National Conference on Artificial Intelligence*, pages 133–136. AAAI Press.

Pearl, J. (1987). Evidential reasoning using stochastic simulation of causal models. *Artificial Intelligence*, 32(2):245–257.

Pearl, J. (1988). *Probabilistic Reasoning in Intelligent Systems*. Morgan Kaufmann.

Pedregosa, F., Varoquaux, G., Gramfort, A., Michel, V., Thirion, B., Grisel, O., Blondel, M., Prettenhofer, P., Weiss, R., Dubourg, V., Vanderplas, J., Passos, A., Cournapeau, D., Brucher, M., Perrot, M., and Duchesnay, E. (2011). Scikit-learn: Machine learning in Python. *Journal of Machine Learning Research*, 12:2825–2830.

Peng, H., Long, F., and Ding, C. (2005). Feature selection based on mutual information: Criteria of max-dependency, max-relevance, and min-redundancy. *IEEE Transactions on Pattern Analysis and Machine Intelligence*, 27(8):1226–1238.

Pérez, A., Larrañaga, P., and Inza, I. (2006). Supervised classification with conditional Gaussian networks: Increasing the structure complexity from naive Bayes. *International Journal of Approximate Reasoning*, 43:1–25.

Pérez, A., Larrañaga, P., and Inza, I. (2009). Bayesian classifiers based on kernel density estimation: Flexible classifiers. *International Journal of Approximate Reasoning*, 50:341–362.

Petropoulos, A., Chatzis, S., and Xanthopoulos, S. (2017). A hidden Markov model with dependence jumps for predictive modeling of multidimensional time-series. *Information Sciences*, 412-413:50–66.

Pimentel, M. A., Clifton, D. A., Clifton, L., and Tarassenko, L. (2014). A review of novelty detection. *Signal Processing*, 99:215–249.

Pizarro, J., Guerrero, E., and Galindo, P. L. (2002). Multiple comparison procedures applied to model selection. *Neurocomputing*, 48(1):155–173.

Platt, J. (1999). Fast training of support vector machines using sequential minimal optimization. In *Advances in Kernel Methods - Support Vector Learning*, pages 185–208. The MIT Press.

Pokrajac, D., Lazarevic, A., and Latecki, L. J. (2007). Incremental local outlier detection for data streams. In *IEEE Symposium on Computational Intelligence and Data Mining, 2007*, pages 504–515. IEEE Press.

PricewaterhouseCoopers (2017). Innovation for the earth. Technical Report 161222-113251-LA-OS, World Economic Forum, Davos.

Qian, Y., Yan, R., and Hu, S. (2014). Bearing degradation evaluation using recurrence quantification analysis and Kalman filter. *IEEE Transactions on Instrumentation and Measurement Society*, 63:2599–2610.

Quinlan, J. (1986). Induction of decision trees. *Machine Learning*, 1(1):81–106.

Quinlan, J. (1987). Simplifying decision trees. *International Journal of Man-Machine Studies*, 27(3):221–234.

Quinlan, J. (1993). *C4.5: Programs for Machine Learning*. Morgan Kaufmann.

Rabiner, L. (1989). A tutorial on hidden Markov models and selected applications in speech recognition. *Proceedings of the IEEE*, 77(2).

Rabiner, L. and Juang, B. (1986). An introduction to hidden Markov models. *IEEE Acoustics, Speech and Signal Processing Magazine*, 3:4–16.

Rajapakse, J. C. and Zhou, J. (2007). Learning effective brain connectivity with dynamic Bayesian networks. *Neuroimage*, 37(3):749–760.

Ribeiro, B. (2005). Support vector machines for quality monitoring in a plastic injection molding process. *IEEE Transactions on Systems, Man, and Cybernetics, Part C (Applications and Reviews)*, 35(3):401–410.

Robinson, J. W. and Hartemink, A. J. (2010). Learning non-stationary dynamic Bayesian networks. *Journal of Machine Learning Research*, 11:3647–3680.

Robinson, R. (1977). Counting unlabeled acyclic digraphs. In *Combinatorial Mathematics V*, volume 622 of *Lecture Notes in Mathematics*, pages 28–43. Springer.

Rosenbrock, C., Homer, E., Csányi, G., and Hart, G. (2017). Discovering the building blocks of atomic systems using machine learning: Application to grain boundaries. *Computational Materials*, 3(29).

Rudin, W. (1976). *Principles of Mathematical Analysis*. McGraw-Hill.

Rumí, R., Salmerón, A., and Moral, S. (2006). Estimating mixtures of truncated exponentials in hybrid Bayesian networks. *TEST*, 15:397–421.

Sabidussi, G. (1966). The centrality index of a graph. *Psychometrika*, 31(4):581–603.

Saha, S., Saha, B., Saxena, A., and Goebel, K. (2010). Distributed prognostic health management with Gaussian process regression. *IEEE Aerospace Conference*, pages 1–8.

Sahami, M. (1996). Learning limited dependence Bayesian classifiers. In *Proceedings of the 2nd International Conference on Knowledge Discovery and Data Mining*, pages 335–338.

Samuel, A. L. (1959). Some studies in machine learning using the game of checkers. *IBM Journal of Research and Development*, 3(3):210–229.

Sarigul, E., Abbott, A., Schmoldt, D., and Araman, P. (2005). An interactive machine-learning approach for defect detection in computed tomography (CT) images of hardwood logs. In *Proceedings of Scan Tech 2005 International Conference*, pages 15–26.

Sbarufatti, C., Corbetta, M., Manes, A., and Giglio, M. (2016). Sequential Monte-Carlo sampling based on a committee of artificial neural networks for posterior state estimation and residual lifetime prediction. *International Journal of Fatigue*, 83:10–23.

Schmidhuber, J. (2015). Deep learning in neural networks: An overview. *Neural Networks*, 61:85–117.

Schölkopf, B., Williamson, R., Smola, A., Shawe-Taylor, J., Platt, J., Solla, S., Leen, T., and Müller, K.-R. (2000). Support vector method for novelty detection. In *13th Annual Neural Information Processing Systems Conference*, pages 582–588. The MIT Press.

Schwarting, W., Alonso-Mora, J., and Rus, D. (2018). Planning and decision-making for autonomous vehicles. *Annual Review of Control, Robotics and Autonomous Systems*, 1:8.1–8.24.

Schwarz, G. (1978). Estimating the dimension of a model. *The Annals of Statistics*, 6(2):461–464.

Scutari, M. (2010). Learning Bayesian network with the `bnlearn` R package. *Journal of Statistical Software*, 35(3):1–22.

Sesen, M. B., Nicholson, A., Banares-Alcantar, R., Kidor, T., and Brady, M. (2013). Bayesian networks for clinical decision support in lung cancer care. *PLOS ONE*, 8(12):e82349.

Shachter, R. and Kenley, C. (1989). Gaussian influence diagrams. *Management Science*, 35(5):527–550.

Shachter, R. and Peot, M. (1989). Simulation approaches to general probabilistic inference on belief networks. In *Proceedings of the 5th Annual Conference on Uncertainty in Artificial Intelligence*, pages 221–234. Elsevier.

Shafer, G. and Shenoy, P. (1990). Probability propagation. *Annals of Mathematics and Artificial Intelligence*, 2:327–352.

Shakoor, M. T., Rahman, K., Rayta, S. N., and Chakrabarty, A. (2017). Agricultural production output prediction using supervised machine learning techniques. In *International Conference on Next Generation Computing Applications*, pages 182–187. IEEE Press.

Shameer, K., Johson, K., Glicksberg, B., Dudley, J., and Sengupta, P. (2018). Machine learning in cardiovascular medicine: Are we there yet? *Heart*, 104:1156–1164.

Shannon, C. E. (1948). A mathematical theory of communication. *The Bell System Technical Journal*, 27(3):379–423.

Shannon, C. E. (1949). Communication in the presence of noise. *Proceedings of the IRE*, 37(1):10–21.

Sharp, H. (1968). Cardinality of finite topologies. *Journal of Combinatorial Theory*, 5:82–86.

Shearer, C. (2000). The CRISP-DM model: The new blueprint for data mining. *Journal of Data Warehousing*, 5:13–22.

Shelton, C., Fan, Y., Lam, W., Lee, J., and Xu, J. (2010). Continuous time Bayesian network reasoning and learning engine. *Journal of Machine Learning Research*, 11:1137–1140.

Shenoy, P. and West, J. (2011). Inference in hybrid Bayesian networks using mixtures of polynomials. *International Journal of Approximate Reasoning*, 52(5):641–657.

Shi, J. and Malik, J. (2000). Normalized cuts and image segmentation. *IEEE Transactions on Pattern Analysis and Machine Intelligence*, 22(8):888–905.

Shi, J., Yin, W., Osher, S., and Sajda, P. (2010). A fast hybrid algorithm for large-scale l_1-regularized logistic regression. *Journal of Machine Learning Research*, 11(1):713–741.

Shigley, J. E., Budynas, R. G., and Mischke, C. R. (2004). *Mechanical Engineering Design*. McGraw-Hill.

Shigley, J. E. and Mischke, C. R. (1956). *Standard Handbook of Machine Design*. McGraw-Hill.

Shukla, D. and Desai, A. (2016). Recognition of fruits using hybrid features and machine learning. In *International Conference on Computing, Analytics and Security Trends*, pages 572–577. IEEE Press.

Siddique, A., Yadava, G., and Singh, B. (2005). A review of stator fault monitoring techniques of induction motors. *IEEE Transactions on Energy Conversion*, 20(1):106–114.

Silva, J. A., Faria, E. R., Barros, R. C., Hruschka, E. R., de Carvalho, A. C., and Gama, J. (2013). Data stream clustering: A survey. *ACM Computing Surveys*, 46(1):13.

Silverman, B. (1986). *Density Estimation for Statistics and Data Analysis*. Chapman and Hall.

Simsir, U., Amasyalı, M. F., Bal, M., Çelebi, U. B., and Ertugrul, S. (2014). Decision support system for collision avoidance of vessels. *Applied Soft Computing*, 25:369–378.

Sing, T., Sander, O., Beerenwinkel, N., and Lengauer, T. (2005). ROCR: Visualizing classifier performance in R. *Bioinformatics*, 21:3940–3941.

Sjöberg, J., Zhang, Q., Ljung, L., Benveniste, A., Delyon, B., Glorennec, P.-Y., Hjalmarsson, H., and Juditsky, A. (1995). Nonlinear black-box modeling in system identification: A unified overview. *Automatica*, 31(12):1691–1724.

Smusz, S., Kurczab, R., and Bojarski, A. (2013). A multidimensional analysis of machine learning methods performance in the classification of bioactive compounds. *Chemometrics and Intelligent Laboratory Systems*, 128:89–100.

Smyth, P. (1994). Markov monitoring with unknown states. *IEEE Journal on Selected Areas in Communications*, 12(9):1600–1612.

Sokal, R. and Michener, C. (1958). A statistical method for evaluating systematic relationships. *University of Kansas Scientific Bulletin*, 38:1409–1438.

Sorensen, T. (1948). A method for establishing groups of equal amplitude in plant sociology based on similarity of species contents and its application to analyzes of the vegetation on Danish commons. *Biologiske Skrifter*, 5:1–34.

Spiegelhalter, D. and Lauritzen, S. (1990). Sequential updating of conditional probabilities on directed graphical structures. *Networks*, 20:579–605.

Spirtes, P. and Glymour, C. (1991). An algorithm for fast recovery of sparse causal graphs. *Social Science Computer Review*, 90(1):62–72.

Srivastava, A., Kundu, A., Sural, S., and Majumdar, A. K. (2008). Credit card fraud detection using hidden Markov model. *IEEE Transactions on Dependable and Secure Computing*, 5(1):37–48.

Sterne, J. (2017). *Artificial Intelligence for Marketing: Practical Applications*. Wiley.

Stirling, D. and Buntine, W. (1988). Process routings in a steel mill: A challenging induction problem. In *Artificial Intelligence Developments and Applications*, pages 301–313. Elsevier Science.

Strohbach, M., Daubert, J., Ravkin, H., and Lischka, M. (2016). Big data storage. In *New Horizons for a Data-Driven Economy*, pages 119–141. Springer.

Sun, T.-H., Tien, F.-C., Tien, F.-C., and Kuo, R.-J. (2016). Automated thermal fuse inspection using machine vision and artificial neural networks. *Journal of Intelligent Manufacturing*, 27(3):639–651.

Surace, C. and Worden, K. (2010). Novelty detection in a changing environment: A negative selection approach. *Mechanical Systems and Signal Processing*, 24(4):1114–1128.

Sztipanovits, J., Ying, S., Cohen, I., Corman, D., Davis, J., Khurana, H., Mosterman, P., Prasad, V., and Stormo, L. (2012). Strategic R&D opportunities for 21st century cyber-physical systems. Technical report, Steering Committee for Foundation in Innovation for Cyber-Physical Systems.

Talbi, E.-G. (2009). *Metaheuristics: From Design to Implementation*. Wiley.

Tax, D. M. and Duin, R. P. (1999). Support vector domain description. *Pattern Recognition Letters*, 20(11):1191–1199.

Taylor, B., Fingal, D., and Aberdeen, D. (2007). The war against spam: A report from the front line. In *NIPS 2007 Workshop on Machine Learning in Adversarial Environments for Computer Security*.

Tejeswinee, K., Jacob, S., and Athilakshmi, R. (2017). Feature selection techniques for prediction of neuro-degenerative disorders: A case-study with Alzheimer's and Parkinson's disease. *Procedia Computer Science*, 115:188–194.

Tibshirani, R. (1996). Regression shrinkage and selection via the lasso. *Journal of the Royal Statistical Society, Series B*, 58(1):267–288.

Tibshirani, R., Walther, G., and Hastie, T. (2001). Estimating the number of clusters in a data set via the gap statistic. *Journal of the Royal Statistical Society: Series B (Statistical Methodology)*, 63(2):411–423.

Tikhonov, A. (1943). On the stability of inverse problems. *Doklady Akademii Nauk SSSR*, 39(5):176–179.

Timusk, M., Lipsett, M., and Mechefske, C. K. (2008). Fault detection using transient machine signals. *Mechanical Systems and Signal Processing*, 22(7):1724–1749.

Tippannavar, S. and Soma, S. (2017). A machine learning system for recognition of vegetable plant and classification of abnormality using leaf texture analysis. *International Journal of Scientific and Engineering Research*, 8(6):1558–1563.

Tiwari, M. K. and Adamowski, J. F. (2015). Medium-term urban water demand forecasting with limited data using an ensemble wavelet-bootstrap machine-learning approach. *Journal of Water Resources Planning and Management*, 141(2):1–12.

Tobon-Mejia, D. A., Medjaher, K., Zerhouni, N., and Tripot, G. (2012). A data-driven failure prognostics method based on mixture of Gaussians hidden Markov models. *IEEE Transactions on Reliability*, 61(2):491–503.

Torgerson, W. (1952). Multidimensional scaling: I. Theory and method. *Psychometrika*, 17(4):401–419.

Trabelsi, G. (2013). *New Structure Learning Algorithms and Evaluation Methods for Large Dynamic Bayesian Networks*. PhD thesis, Université de Nantes.

Tsamardinos, I., Brown, L. E., and Aliferis, C. F. (2006). The max-min hill-climbing Bayesian network structure learning algorithm. *Machine Learning*, 65(1):31–78.

Tsang, I., Kocsor, A., and Kwok, J. T. (2007). Simpler core vector machines with enclosing balls. In *Proceedings of the 9th ACM SIGKDD International Conference on Knowledge Discovery and Data Mining*, pages 226–235.

Tüfekci, P. (2014). Prediction of full load electrical power output of a base load operated combined cycle power plant using machine learning methods. *International Journal of Electrical Power and Energy Systems*, 60:126–140.

Tukey, J. (1977). *Exploratory Data Analysis*. Addison-Wesley.

Tuna, G., Kogias, D. G., Gungor, V. C., Gezer, C., Taşkın, E., and Ayday, E. (2017). A survey on information security threats and solutions for machine to machine (M2M) communications. *Journal of Parallel and Distributed Computing*, 109:142–154.

Turing, A. M. (1950). Computing machinery and intelligence. *Mind*, 59(236):433–460.

Tylman, W., Waszyrowski, T., Napieralski, A., Kaminski, M., Trafidlo, T., Kulesza, Z., Kotas, R., Marciniak, P., Tomala, R., and Wenerski, M. (2016). Real-time prediction of acute cardiovascular events using hardware-implemented Bayesian networks. *Computers in Biology and Medicine*, 69:245–253.

van der Maaten, L. and Hinton, G. (2008). Visualizing high-dimensional data using t-SNE. *Journal of Machine Learning Research*, 9:2579–2605.

van Noortwijk, J. (2009). A survey of the application of gamma processes in maintenance. *Reliability Engineering and System Safety*, 94:2–21.

Vapnik, V. (1998). *Statistical Learning Theory*. Wiley.

Verma, T. and Pearl, J. (1990a). Causal networks: Semantics and expressiveness. In *Proceedings of the 4th Annual Conference on Uncertainty in Artificial Intelligence*, pages 69–78. North-Holland.

Verma, T. and Pearl, J. (1990b). Equivalence and synthesis of causal models. In *Proceedings of the 6th Conference on Uncertainty in Artificial Intelligence*, pages 255–270. Elsevier.

Viterbi, A. (1967). Error bounds for convolutional codes and an asymptotically optimum decoding algorithm. *IEEE Transactions on Information Theory*, 13(2):260–269.

von Luxburg, U. (2007). A tutorial on spectral clustering. *Statistics and Computing*, 17(4):395–416.

Voyant, C., Notton, G., Kalogirou, S., Nivet, M.-L., Paoli, C., Motte, F., and Fouilloy, A. (2017). Machine learning methods for solar radiation forecasting: A review. *Renewable Energy*, 105:569–582.

Wang, K.-J., Chen, J. C., and Lin, Y.-S. (2005). A hybrid knowledge discovery model using decision tree and neural network for selecting dispatching rules of a semiconductor final testing factory. *Production Planning and Control*, 16(7):665–680.

Wang, W. (2007). Application of Bayesian network to tendency prediction of blast furnace silicon content in hot metal. In *Bio-Inspired Computational Intelligence and Applications*, pages 590–597. Springer.

Wang, W., Golnaraghi, M., and Ismail, F. (2004). Prognosis of machine health condition using neuro-fuzzy systems. *Mechanical Systems and Signal Processing*, 18:813–831.

Wang, X. and Xu, D. (2010). An inverse Gaussian process model for degradation data. *Technometrics*, 52:188–197.

Ward, J. (1963). Hierarchical grouping to optimize an objective function. *Journal of the American Statistical Association*, 58:236–244.

Webb, G. I., Boughton, J., and Wang, Z. (2005). Not so naive Bayes: Aggregating one-dependence estimators. *Machine Learning*, 58:5–24.

Wiens, J. and Wallace, B. (2016). Editorial: Special issue on machine learning for learning and medicine. *Machine Learning*, 102:305–307.

Williams, G. (2009). Rattle: A data mining GUI for R. *The R Journal*, 1(2):45–55.

Wilson, D. (1972). Asympotic properties of nearest neighbor rules using edited data. *IEEE Transactions on Systems, Man, and Cybernetics*, 2(3):408–421.

Wishart, J. (1928). The generalised product moment distribution in samples from a normal multivariate population. *Biometrika*, 20(1-2):32–52.

Wolfert, S., Ge, L., Verdouw, C., and Bogaardt, M. (2017). Big data in smart farming. A review. *Agricultural Systems*, 153:69–80.

Wolpert, D. (1992). Stacked generalization. *Neural Networks*, 5:241–259.

Wolpert, D. and Macready, W. (1997). No free lunch theorems for optimization. *IEEE Transactions on Evolutionary Computation*, 1(1):67–82.

Wong, J.-Y. and Chung, P.-H. (2008). Retaining passenger loyalty through data mining: A case study of Taiwanese airlines. *Transportation Journal*, 47:17–29.

Wuest, T., Weimer, D., Irgens, C., and Thoben, K.-D. (2016). Machine learning in manufacturing: Advantages, challenges, and applications. *Production and Manufacturing Research*, 4(1):23–45.

Xie, L., Huang, R., Gu, N., and Cao, Z. (2014). A novel defect detection and identification method in optical inspection. *Neural Computing and Applications*, 24(7-8):1953–1962.

Xie, W., Yu, L., Xu, S., and Wang, S. (2006). A new method for crude oil price forecasting based on support vector machines. In *Lectures Notes in Coputer Sciences 2994*, pages 444–451. Springer.

Xu, D. and Tian, Y. (2015). A comprehensive survey of clustering algorithms. *Annals of Data Science*, 2(2):165–193.

Xu, S., Tan, H., Jiao, X., Lau, F., and Pan, Y. (2007). A generic pigment model for digital painting. *Computer Graphics Forum*, 26(3):609–618.

Yang, Y. and Webb, G. (2009). Discretization for naive-Bayes learning: Managing discretization bias and variance. *Machine Learning*, 74(1):39–74.

Ye, Q., Zhang, Z., and Law, R. (2009). Sentiment classification of online reviews to travel destinations by supervised machine learning approaches. *Expert Systems with Applications*, 36:6527–6535.

Yeo, M., Fletcher, T., and Shawe-Taylor, J. (2015). Machine learning in fine wine price prediction. *Journal of Wine Economics*, 10(2):151–172.

Yeung, D.-Y. and Ding, Y. (2003). Host-based intrusion detection using dynamic and static behavioral models. *Pattern Recognition*, 36(1):229–243.

Yu, L., Wang, S., and Lai, K. (2008). Forecasting crude oil price with an EMD-based neural network ensemble learning paradigm. *Energy Economics*, 30:2623–2635.

Zaman, T. R. (2011). *Information Extraction with Network Centralities: Finding Rumor Sources, Measuring Influence, and Learning Community Structure*. PhD thesis, Massachusetts Institute of Technology.

Zarei, E., Azadeh, A., Khakzad, N., and Aliabadi, M. M. (2017). Dynamic safety assessment of natural gas stations using Bayesian network. *Journal of Hazardous Materials*, 321:830–840.

Zeng, X., Hu, W., Li, W., Zhang, X., and Xu, B. (2008). Key-frame extraction using dominant-set clustering. In *IEEE International Conference on Multimedia and Expo*, pages 1285–1288. IEEE Press.

Zhang, D. and Tsai, J. J. (2003). Machine learning and software engineering. *Software Quality Journal*, 11(2):87–119.

Zhang, J. and Wang, H. (2006). Detecting outlying subspaces for high-dimensional data: The new task, algorithms, and performance. *Knowledge and Information Systems*, 10(3):333–355.

Zhang, N. and Poole, D. (1994). A simple approach to Bayesian network computations. In *Proceedings of the 10th Biennial Canadian Conference on Artificial Intelligence*, pages 171–178.

Zhang, Y., Wang, J., and Wang, X. (2014). Review on probabilistic forecasting of wind power generation. *Renewable and Sustainable Energy Reviews*, 32:255–270.

Zheng, Z. and Webb, G. (2000). Lazy learning of Bayesian rules. *Machine Learning*, 41(1):53–84.

Zonglei, L., Jiandong, W., and Guansheng, Z. (2008). A new method to alarm large scale of flights delay based on machine learning. In *2008 International Symposium on Knowledge Acquisition and Modeling*, pages 589–592.

Zorriassatine, F., Al-Habaibeh, A., Parkin, R., Jackson, M., and Coy, J. (2005). Novelty detection for practical pattern recognition in condition monitoring of multivariate processes: A case study. *The International Journal of Advanced Manufacturing Technology*, 25(9-10):954–963.

Index